REFRAMING AMERICA'S INFRASTRUCTURE

A **Ruins** to **Renaissance** Playbook

MARC GRAVELY

Reframing America's Infrastructure: A Ruins to Renaissance Playbook
is published by Sutton Hart Press, llc
Vancouver, Washington

Inquiries: inquiries@suttonhart.com
Website: www.suttonhart.com
Author Website: www.gravelylaw.com
First Printing: January 2, 2022

ISBN
Hardcover: 9781947779310
Digital: 9781947779327

Printed in the United States of America
Media and Reviewer Contact: maggie@platformstrategy.com
Layout Design: Enterline Design Services

TABLE OF CONTENTS

DEDICATION

To my precious wife Janelle

...for your love

To my children Sumner, Dave, Andrew & Abby

...for your grace

To my parents Lawrence Edmond Gravely & Nancy Ann Necessary Gravely

and grandparents

Robert Henry Necessary, Polly Biddle Necessary, Paul Quaintance Gravely

& Ethel Mae Shuck Gravely

...love without end

FOREWORD BY NORM PATTIS

If you think infrastructure doesn't matter, try walking to your next doctor's appointment, or to work, or to the grocery store. Swim across the next river you need to cross. And, by all means, grow your own food, weave your own clothing, and manufacture all the goods you require to live as you do.

My point is simple: we live as dependents on a vast, interconnected web of roads, bridges and other connective devices. Infrastructure is the connective tissue of civilization.

And Marc Gravely has plenty worth hearing to say about it all.

Gravely is a man for all seasons. His resume is impressive: An undergraduate degree in biology, a master's degree in biotechnology, and then law degrees, first, the ordinary juris doctorate that is required of all who practice law, but then something more, an L.L.M. in insurance law. Gravely has an insatiable curiosity about how the world works. As a result, he knows what to do when things don't work.

Hence, this book, apparently his first.

I wasn't sure what to expect when I picked it up. My focus is civil rights and criminal defense. You call me when someone is arrested or is otherwise discomfited by government. I take for granted the fact that there will be roads on which to travel, and buildings safe to enter. I read without questioning court opinions online, and order books that arrive, as if by magic, at the press of a key. I take much for granted.

Not so, Gravely. His law firm, Gravely Attorneys and Counselors, specializes in construction defect and insurance claims. While the rest of us are bitching and moaning about the line at the ice cream stand, Gravely and company are making sure the facility is safe, and that there is a place worth lining up for at all. Reading this book was a wake-up call: the work of civilization is infinitely complex, and the foundations on which we stand support all we cherish. I kept thinking of the Roman roads, built millennia ago, but still crisscrossing modern Europe.

But lest you think of Gravely as a mere technician, read on. He is a visionary. He takes seriously the dialectic of desire and creation: we create what we want and need only to become in some sense trapped within those very webs. Our wishes become our jailers, and we free ourselves only with the courage to outgrow comfortable dreams. He quotes Brian Larkin: "[Infrastructures exist] as forms separate from their purely technical functioning. . . they emerge out of and store within them forms of desire and fantasy and can take on fetish-like aspects that sometimes can be wholly autonomous from their technical function."

The interstate highway system transformed American life in the era following the Second World War. Spawned as a means of uniting a vast nation and enabling it to respond to security threats, it yielded unheard-of mobility, replete with suburbs, and now exurbs, and the easy movement of material by means of trucking. People and things moved easily, and quickly took us to an age of unheard-of affluence for the common man.

Ideas were soon untethered and sent spinning from place to place at unheard-of speed. The Internet, too, is infrastructure, and we are entirely dependent on it. I write this introduction in Connecticut, to send to an editor in Oregon, for a book I received from a man in Texas. I will press a key soon and instantaneously, these words will move more quickly than flight across a continent. I don't know how it happens. I merely know that it does. Infrastructure. It's everywhere. I am trapped happily within its web.

And what about the development of green technology as we struggle to adapt to a changing climate, or the pressure of a global economy? I hear populists decry globalism and I chafe against being the keeper of brothers I've never met on continents I will most likely never visit. But the pressure to evolve as a member of a species increasingly united by—yes, infrastructure—is undeniable.

The pace of change makes my head spin. Thankfully, folks like Gravely aren't dizzied by it all.

Gravely is a big-picture kind of guy. You can trust him in a courtroom.

But he is much more. He has stubbed his toe more than a few times against the limits of this Brave New World we are creating, which, in turn, is creating us. He is a humanist in the best sense of the word. What does it all mean? What is the best version of ourselves and of our society possible? How can we build, and then live well, in the world we are creating?

Gravely doesn't have all the answers. But he has the integrity, training, and experience to ask the right questions. I am listening, Marc. You should listen, too. This book is a good place to start. I had the sense while reading it of being in the room with an adult, a wise, caring man who knew what I needed; the challenge was to listen.

INTRODUCTION

"Infrastructure is the foundation of economic development."
—Craig Lesser

America will hit its 250th-year mark in 2026, reaching what some scholars list as the average lifespan of leading civilizations throughout history. A look into trends preceding the passing of the torch reveals the staggering impact infrastructure has on the success and demise of nations.

Robust investments in infrastructure foreshadow a powerful economy, national security, and world leadership. Post-World War II expansion took America to the top in business, employment, mobility, opportunities, and ideas. Solid structures, reliable transport, and efficient use of resources bolster the American machine.

Beyond our position as a nation—and just as important—American infrastructure connects our people and businesses. We rely on it for safety, productivity, social interaction, education, and entertainment. Infrastructure is community. It's how we experience life. Infrastructure defines us from the Hoover Dam to the Golden Gate Bridge, the Empire State Building, and the Erie Canal.

Aside from community, investment in infrastructure is an intergenerational duty. Past generations built the foundation for the nation we enjoy today. We strive to do the same.

However, we get comfortable. Decades of affluence and exciting technological shifts detracted from maintenance and investment in even the basics. A quick-fix, patchwork approach replaced thoughtful planning and financing. Now, capacity is failing to meet demands. Life expectancies of the very systems that allow us to operate are running out, and investment is scant.

American bridges, dams, and waterway locks are deteriorating from erosion, overload, geotechnical changes, and extreme weather. We drive roads of disintegrating concrete and supply water from decayed pipes and wells, threatening safety and accelerating erosion.

Overwhelmed drains and wastewater systems are clogging and flooding. Freezing temperatures and extreme heat are stressing power distribution lines to breaking point, power outages are becoming a common and dangerous occurrence. Outdated port facilities and shallow, narrow harbors are causing costly delays, affecting trade, and stunting manufacturing, agriculture, and extraction—all vital economic drivers.

Space systems are becoming critical infrastructure. We rely on thousands of high-functioning space stations and satellites for communications, navigation, information processing, and national security. Yet, we still struggle to coordinate the resources, programs, and security standards supporting this infrastructure.

Developments in green infrastructure like wetlands, green roofs, permeable pavements, and rain gardens promise to restore many of the natural mechanics necessary to sound water management and durable urban environments. But more experimentation is needed. Architects, engineers, and administrators are only beginning to refine techniques and installation.

Our national parks, important to environmental protection and tourism, need improved energy efficiency, better ecosystem resilience, decarbonization, pollutant management, and revised habitat connectivity. They've fallen to the bottom of the priority list.

The future of America depends on the decisions we make today. Innovative ideas in engineering, design, and financing are poised to take us into a productive and profitable next century. Today's visionaries are already delivering the goods, devising revolutionary tactics to balance infrastructure and conservation, and looking to examples from other nations to upgrade American performance.

But reversing course after decades of a "cheap and fast" approach to infrastructure calls for reformative action on every level. Congress, states, investors, industry owners, and innovators play a critical role in the big picture.

At this moment, our nation's billionaires are investing in space infrastructure and technology, creating new modes of transport, expanding communications, and giving rise to alternative energy sources. But the impact of a broader group of visionaries will be even greater—offering AI solutions, fresh approaches to recycling, and creative strategies for resource efficiency.

Those town council members and school board members electing more efficient energy sources or new recycling angles are as critical to the mosaic as Bezos and Musk. Everybody contributes, entrepreneurs, thought leaders, decision-makers, voters, and those who spread the word.

It is the incremental progress and aggregate effect that moves us forward. Future generations are depending on the social conscience of current decision-makers and the cumulative effect of every choice.

We are mere custodians of our planet—just passing through. Perspective is fundamental as we define priorities and develop plans, strengthening the U.S. economy and our quality of life moving forward. We can leave it better than we found it.

PART I:
BRIEF HISTORY OF INFRASTRUCTURE

CHAPTER 1:

Ancient Infrastructure

"Cities are more than the sum of their infrastructure.
They transcend brick and mortar, concrete and steel.
They're the vessels into which human knowledge is poured."
—Rick Yancey

Unlike many types of human innovation, infrastructure has remained largely unchanged since its conception. Much of modern American infrastructure still reflects that of ancient civilizations in both purpose and design. Dense populations dot the map where resources and opportunity abound. Highway systems and ports transport goods and people between cities. Dams provide water and power, bridges and tunnels bypass geographical obstacles. Throughout recorded history, the success of each city and its country has been heavily contingent on the strength and adaptability of its infrastructure.

Ancient forms of infrastructure were certainly adaptable. While technology continues to evolve and transform how we plan, design, and operate our cities, the general blueprint used for thousands of years remains. Today, operators control waterways from their smartphones, computers take our roadway tolls, and we can mount solar panels to make energy from the sun—but the waterways, roads, and power grids haven't changed much in centuries. Many of the original infrastructure approaches are able to adapt to new technology while fulfilling modern objectives.

Irrigation Cities

In examining the birth of infrastructure as we know it today, most historians home in on the empires of Mesopotamia, Egypt, China, and India. Rivers were key. The bigger, the better. The close proximity of the great Tigris, Euphrates, Nile, Yellow, and Ganges rivers expedited the development of these pioneer civilizations. Here, humans were able to make the titanic shift from hunters and gatherers to farmers and merchants.

Prior to agricultural knowledge, infrastructure was somewhat redundant. Artifacts suggest that busy nomadic hunters and gatherers had only enough time to construct temporary dwellings, religious monuments, and tombs—mostly with the aid of natural structures like stones, plant material, and caves. But as early as 11000-8000 B.C., people near the great rivers began domesticating animals and plants. Farming allowed people to obtain all necessary resources from a central location, increasing the immediate populations, encouraging trade between nearby groups, and freeing up time for innovation. An eventual surplus in resources supported the development of craftsmen, non-farming residents specializing in other beneficial trades.

Some of the earliest cities arose in Southwest Asia. Around 5500 B.C., several small agricultural groups located between the Tigris and Euphrates rivers increased to as many as 50,000 members, forming the Mesopotamian Sumerian civilization. These ancient Sumerians are one of the first civilizations to construct protective walls and villages. Some historians credit them with inventing the plow; the spoked wheel; and the first complex irrigation, canal, and water reservoir systems. [1]

Meanwhile, ancient India, Egypt, and China were also constructing dikes

1 Kramer, S. N. (1963). *The Sumerians: Their History, Culture, and Character*. Chicago: University of Chicago Press.

and irrigation channels to direct water over their crops and transport goods. Controlling these great rivers brought agricultural profits and flourishing trade centers. But it also brought annual flooding. Eventually, waterway construction and the need to control and utilize flood waters became major engineering feats, compelling state organization. Mesopotamia became several city-states, each with its own irrigation board competing for water rights. Social and political systems evolved to initiate preventative measures and damage relief for the intricate canals, dikes, irrigation channels, sewage systems, and domestic water supplies. Social roles, government systems, and a new understanding of knowledge application and systematic organization were born from these ancient irrigation cities.[2]

In addition to agricultural success, controlled water resources offered a new source of energy. Prior to water control, power sources were limited to the muscle power of animals and people. Once these civilizations discovered how to use water as a power source, productivity increased exponentially. For example, while ancient Egypt obtained most of its wealth from agriculture, it also mined limestone, transporting massive blocks down the Nile on wooden barges to construct pyramids.

By 2500 B.C., the Egyptians had completed the iconic, 482-foot-tall Great Pyramid from an estimated 2.5 million blocks of stone weighing 2.5 tons each.[3,4] While a packhorse on land could carry a mere fraction of a ton, placing goods on a barge in a transport canal allowed one horse to pull a 30-ton load. The importance of water supply infrastructure within these ancient empires is demonstrated by the numerous enemy attacks specifically targeting irrigation structures.

---

2 Drucker, P. (1970). *Technology, Management and Society*. London: William Heinemann Ltd.
3 Klemm F. (1964). *A History of Western Technology*. Cambridge: The M.I.T. Press. Cambridge. 1964.
4 Kranzberg, M., Pursell, C. W., & American Council of Learned Societies. (1967). *Technology in Western civilization*.

Trade and Transportation

As successful agricultural enterprises cultivated trade between cities, the demand for more efficient means of transportation grew. Evidence suggests that the earliest civilizations used well-worn animal paths to travel between settlements. However, frequent use and harsh weather quickly eroded dirt trails. Rivers and mountains also presented obstacles limiting trade opportunities.

Artifacts show that during the late Neolithic period (around 4500-3000 B.C.), civilizations began constructing paths and bridges from wood planks, pegs, and rails. Without saws or iron tools, these structures were built with stone axes and wood wedges. An interesting example can be seen at England's Shapwick Heath National Nature Reserve, where artifacts of a wooden trackway bridge called "Sweet Track" were found running through a reed swamp.

Built around 3806 B.C., this early bridge was constructed by hammering two sharpened wood poles into the peat under the water in a "V" shape. Wooden walking planks rested in this "V" and were fixed in place with long wooden pegs driven through the planks and peat into the deep clay underneath (Fig. 1). Similar paths were made across the land, pegging wood planks into smaller wooden cross beams to create a path more resistant to erosion and weathering.

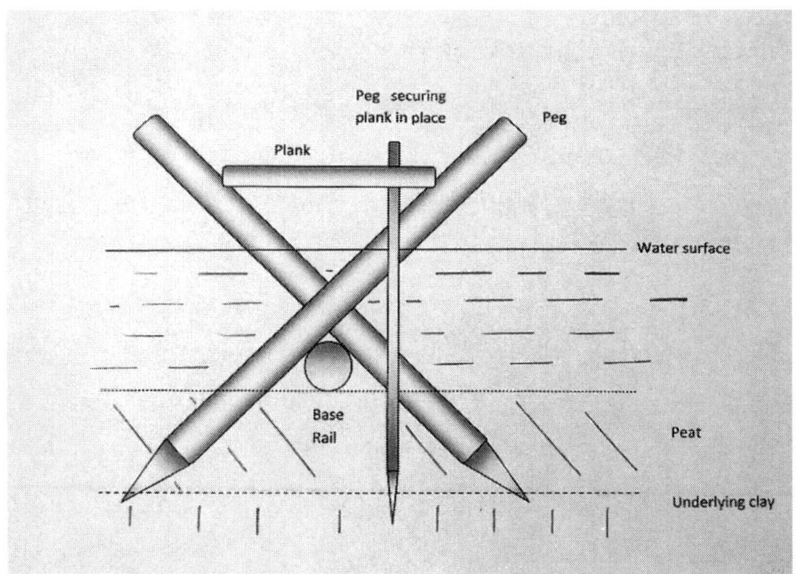

Figure 1. Wooden Trackway Bridge, 3800 B.C.[5]

During the 3500 years from 4500 to 1000 B.C., advances in mining allowed many civilizations to transition from the Stone Age to the Iron Age, upgrading mining tools, farm equipment, and weapons to more durable iron implements. Farming, mining, land clearing, and construction all would benefit.[6] With the Iron Age came improvements in wheeled transport, namely, the transition from spoked to disk wheels beginning around 3500 B.C. Knowledge of this new, hard-wearing wheel design spread from Hungary, Romania, and the Ukraine to the Netherlands and Denmark by as early as 2000 B.C.[7]

Still, even as late as 1000 B.C., much of the civilized world was using rivers and canals for long-distance travel.[8] Wheeled wagons and chariots were

5 Richerman. (2010). *Sweet Track* [Image]. Retrieved 28 August 2021, from https://commons.wikimedia.org/wiki/File:Sweet_track_cross_section2.jpg.

6 Singer, C. (1954). *A History of Technology*. Clarendon.

7 Fagan, B. M. (1979). *Civilization: Readings from Scientific American*. San Francisco: W.H. Freeman and Company.

8 Hodges, H. (1970) Technology in The Ancient World. New York: Alfred A. Knopf Publishers.

available but required extensive infrastructure to function. Well-paved roads, weight-bearing bridges, and organized maintenance of these structures were a necessity.

To support the weight of loaded wagons, bridges were constructed from wide arches of stone. The oldest surviving example may be the Arkadiko Bridge in Greece. Still in use today, this bridge was constructed in 1300-1190 B.C. to extend the road from Tiryns to Epidaurus. Ancient civilizations also began designing purposeful, highly planned road systems. Around 750 B.C., pre-Columbian Mesoamerican Mayans began building complex trade networks connected by "sacbe," raised roads paved with limestone.

Just as irrigation channels and waterways urged the formation of social roles and government systems within civilizations, the wheeled wagon prompted the earliest forms of infrastructure investment. No matter how wealthy the city or the number of chariots, a chariot is no good without a road. And the chariot owner alone cannot construct and maintain it. Naturally, infrastructure investment was followed by the need for institution building to assist development—organizational building to "improve the functioning of society by creating, strengthening or changing the way people relate to one another in the context of public action and public activities."[9]

Rise of Innovation

During the period from 1000 B.C. to 500 A.D., Greek civilization arose from the Crete Minoan and the Mycenaean civilizations (which had grown up in the Aegean region since 1600 B.C). Spanning from the Black Sea to

9 *Institution Building as A Development Assistance Method: A Review of Literature and Ideas.* The Swedish International Development Cooperation Agency.(1995). Retrieved 28 August 2021, from https://cdn.sida.se/publications/files/-institution-building-as-a-development-assistance-method---a-review-of-literature-and-ideas.pdf.

Spain, early Greece found itself surrounded by the sea and mountainous regions. The geography of the area produced smaller independent districts instead of the large uniform empires formed in places like ancient Egypt and Mesopotamia. As a result, the Greeks bypassed specialization to master a plethora of trades.

During its prime, Greece influenced civilization in numerous ways: politically, culturally, and technologically. As early as 300 B.C., Greek engineers developed a means of regulating canal water flow in the Suez Canal using canal locks.[10] Furthering the application of waterpower, the Greeks invented the water mill—a structure that used aqueduct water to turn millstones for grinding grain or saws for cutting slabs of marble.

The Greek mathematician Archimedes developed novel screw, fulcrum, and lever systems for transporting mining equipment and ore. Alexandrian mathematician Euclid defined the geometric properties and interrelations of angles, lines, and surfaces. Greece advanced the use of geometry in what many regard as among the greatest of architectural engineering accomplishments, the Parthenon (constructed 447-438 B.C.).[11]

Historically, the Roman Empire soon dominated the Greeks. Quality infrastructure played a large role in this domination. Unlike the Greeks, the Romans were not innovators. However, they knew how to apply and adapt the technologies of other civilizations, improving upon ideas for drainage, architecture, and transportation. While the Greeks struggled with the necessary expansion and maintenance of water and road infrastructure, the Roman Empire met these problems with quick and novel solutions.

Covering much of Europe and extending around the Mediterranean

---

10 Moore, F. (1950). Three Canal Projects, Roman and Byzantine. *American Journal of Archaeology, 54*(2), 97-111. doi:10.2307/500198

11 Bowra, C. (1990). *Classical Greece.* New York: Time-Life.

Basin, the Roman Empire treated infrastructure with strategic military importance—paved roads being the priority. In total, the early Romans constructed or upgraded more than 50,000 miles of paved roads and highways extending from the Danube to northern Africa and Spain, and from Britain to the Tigris-Euphrates river system. Roman engineers believed in building through geographic obstacles rather than around them, tunneling through mountains, draining bodies of water, and diverting rivers.

The Romans paved their roads with dense concrete made from a mixture of lime and ash. Roads were built wide enough to allow travel in both directions simultaneously and were laid with a slight slope to promote water runoff. From 312 B.C. to 264 B.C., the Romans built the greatest of its roads, the Appian Way—extending over 310 miles from Rome to the Adriatic Sea. The impressive roadway consisted of four layers of materials, reached a depth of 4 to 10 feet, and included drains and culverts to prevent flooding.[12]

The Roman Empire also improved on existing aqueduct designs, constructing 485 miles of aqueducts made of concrete arches and channels to direct as much as 11 billion gallons of freshwater per year to towns and cities from surrounding mountains.[13] The Romans applied extensive aqueducts to a water and drainage system for elaborate public baths and toilets along with irrigation and drinking water.

During this time, the Greeks and Romans employed a central city to conduct legal, business, and religious affairs, consisting of public buildings, markets, and temples surrounded by large stone walls. Wealthy citizens devoted income and activities to public improvements and commissioned immense works of art. Much of ancient Rome circulated around the

12 Landels, J. G. (2000). *Engineering in The Ancient World.* Berkeley: University of California Press.

13 Blakemore, E. (2015). *How Much Water Did Rome's Aqueducts Really Carry?*. Smithsonian Magazine. Retrieved 28 August 2021, from https://www.smithsonianmag.com/smart-news/how-much-water-did-romes-aqueducts-really-carry-180955568/.

Forum, where they conducted commercial, judicial, religious, and economic activities.

The Romans constructed impressive buildings in and around the Forum, each serving a specific public function, including basilicas, the Colosseum, shops, temples, and meeting places. Romans were able to erect arches without the use of supporting buttresses by combining concrete with brick.

Eventually, this period of advancement in infrastructure dwindled with political, economic, and social dissolution. Wars, famine, and epidemics took the Roman Empire from its peak of over one million citizens in 100 A.D. to less than 50,000 by 350 A.D. A testament to the incredible workmanship of the time, portions of many of the grand buildings of the Empire are still standing 2,000 years later, including portions of the Colosseum, the Roman Forum, and Castel Sant'Angelo.

The Renaissance

In Western Europe, political disorder had prompted a feudal system and a very different type of civilization. Land ownership laws and the need for protection resulted in the construction of medieval castles across Europe between 800 and 1400 A.D. As opposed to palaces, castles controlled large surrounding territories and had a major impact on the growth of new towns acting as satellites to the castle.[14] Indestructible stone walls connected the towns to the castles, providing security for the towns in exchange for land use.

The crusades soon brought Western Europe in contact with the East, stimulating trade and cultural exchange. Commerce increased, navigation

14 Thompson, M. W. (2008). *The Rise of The Castle*. Cambridge: Cambridge University Press.

technology improved, and currency and credit evolved. Castles lost their rights to labor and taxes, land was partitioned, and surrounding towns were free to join a new government. Capital accumulation generated demand for the formation of three national governments: England, Spain, and France.

Significant political, economic, cultural, and artistic achievements followed. From the 14th to the 17th century, the Renaissance period provided progress in global exploration, individual accomplishment in the arts and sciences, and reformation. France, England, and Spain became nations, and powerful cities in Italy, namely Venice and Florence, broke ground in philosophy and cultural values.

Venice, surrounded by waterways and the sea, grew into a highly populated city with an extensive network of canals forming the major transportation for trade and commerce. Bridge design became an art in itself. The Rialto Bridge and Ponte dell'Accademia arched out over the Grand Canal to connect the two halves of Venice. A network of 45 smaller canals branched out from the Grand Canal, decorated by up to 350 bridges. Until 1,480, most of these bridges were constructed of wood, soon to be replaced by stone arches.[15]

Renaissance inventors advanced interior heating, burning coal as fuel instead of wood, and creating clay tile and cast-iron stoves. Much of the architecture during the Renaissance revived the Romans' styles, materials, and techniques, including vaults, round arches, domes, brick masonry techniques, timber trusses, and transparent glass. During the 16th century, Venetians took the Roman method of making dinner plates—spinning molten glass into flat pieces—and applied it to windows. Crown glass windows were installed in a London Banqueting House designed by English

15 Cenni, N., & Pauli, E. (2004). *Art and history of Venice.* Florence, Italy: Bonechi.

architect Indigo Jones in 1685 and became common in window installations in the 1700s.[16]

As trade expanded, so did global exploration, particularly in sub-Saharan Africa, Southeast Asia, and the Americas. During the 13th and 14th centuries, much of this exploration was done by land. But by the 15th century, the use of wind power had transformed water transport. Massive multi-masted sea vessels combined with the magnetic compass and night-sky navigation allowed Europeans to explore oceanic routes for global trade.[17]

In a search for a new trade route to India, China, and Japan during the 15th century, Spain sponsored Italian navigator Christopher Columbus to cross the Atlantic Ocean in four voyages, adding Cuba, Hispaniola, the West Indies, and Central America to the map.

Perhaps the most trademark characteristic of the Renaissance was a significant shift in thinking. Like other great creators of the era, freedom of expression and an open mind allowed the naval and military engineer Leonardo da Vinci to spend his time creating, recording his experiments and findings on flying machines, self-propelled tanks, alarm clocks, two-tier cities, and diving equipment in private journals. Da Vinci's concepts on canal locks and flood control are still used today.[18]

The printed book allowed new concepts in technology, philosophy, medicine, and astronomy to spread from Italian thought leaders like da Vinci and Niccolo Machiavelli to northern countries. The exchange of ideas expanded interests, promoted experimentation and critical analysis, and redefined authority.

From ancient history through the 17th century, more efficient means

---

16 *Construction — The Renaissance*. Encyclopedia Britannica. Retrieved 28 August 2021, from https://www.britannica.com/technology/construction/The-Renaissance.

17 Singer, C. (1954). *A History of Technology*. Clarendon.

18 Cronin, V. (2001). *The Flowering of The Renaissance*. London: Folio Society.

of transporting goods, resources, people, and information allowed for the evolution of more complex and organized societies. In examining history, certain interacting and determining factors prompted significant achievements in infrastructure: the experience, skill, and materials available, along with the economic, social, and philosophical conditions of the era.

Advances in infrastructure dramatically influenced socioeconomic development. Controlled water resources permitted a surplus of supplies, hastening the development of cities and organized craftsmanship. Transportation improvements aided the spread of knowledge, generating a mindset of creative thought and invention. As technology improved, the economy improved. Science, philosophy, and religion divided, preparing scientists and engineers to enter the Industrial Revolution.

CHAPTER 2:

Early American Infrastructure

"This is our history—from the Transcontinental Railroad to the Hoover Dam, to the dredging of our ports and building of our most historic bridges—our American ancestors prioritized growth and investment in our nation's infrastructure."
—Cory Booker

Infrastructure was instrumental to the building of our nation. Canals, roads, railroads, and advances in communications technology helped the U.S. colonies survive and expand. An immediate emphasis on fostering infrastructure for the new nation prompted the drafting of the United States Constitution, and infrastructure affairs continue to sculpt the legal landscape we know today, ingrained in debates over local politics, employment rates, and environmental issues.

In post-colonial America, infrastructure projects became a beacon of national identity, a material demonstration of the new sovereign nation's potential. Today, they still dominate the political debate and sometimes define elections.

As our country fought wars abroad over the last 20 years, nation-building at home was often neglected.

The question of internal improvements has been a controversial one since the founding of our nation. Before the Civil War, John C. Calhoun urged Congress to "bind the Republic together with a perfect system of roads and canals."[19] Roosevelt devised his public works program "to put more men back to work, both directly on the public works themselves, and indirectly in the industries supplying the materials for these public works."[20] Later on, Eisenhower would dream of "a modern, efficient highway system. . . to meet the needs of our growing population, our expanding economy, and our national security."[21]

Many years earlier, as he envisioned the future of our nation, George Washington wrote about binding "all parts of the Union together by indissoluble bonds,"[22] stating, "The Western settlers. . . stand as it were upon a pivot; the touch of a feather, would turn them any way. . . they have no other means of coming to us but by a long Land transportation and unimproved roads. . . But smooth the road once, and make easy the way for them, and then see what an influx of articles will be poured upon us; how amazingly our exports will be encreased by them, and how amply we shall be compensated for any trouble and expence we may encounter to effect it."[23] In the 18th century and in the 21st, there has never been any promising road to progress other than infrastructure.

The American Revolution

During the Age of Exploration between 1500 and 1800, a trend of colonizing the Americas took place. Voyagers from Spain, Britain, France, and Portugal

---

19 Larson, J. (1987). "Bind the Republic Together": The National Union and The Struggle for A System of Internal Improvements. *The Journal Of American History*, *74*(2), 363. doi: 10.2307/1900027

20 White, A. (2012). Infrastructure Policy: Lessons from American History. Retrieved 23 June 2021, from https://www.thenewatlantis.com/publications/infrastructure-policy-lessons-from-american-history

21 Gold, J. (2009). A Modern Electric Grid: The New Highway System? Retrieved 23 June 2021, from https://www.npr.org/templates/story/story.php?storyId=103349614

22 Washington, G. (1784). Letter to Benjamin Harrison — Teaching American History. Retrieved 23 June 2021, from https://teachingamericanhistory.org/library/document/letter-to-benjamin-harrison-3/

23 Washington, G. (1784). Letter to Benjamin Harrison - Teaching American History. Retrieved 23 June 2021, from https://teachingamericanhistory.org/library/document/letter-to-benjamin-harrison-3/

began establishing settlements and colony-states in the northeast. High wages, abundant resources, and cheap land meant that by 1774, colonial Americans had achieved the highest standard of living of any nation. At the time, these early settlers earned an average of £13.85 per year, compared to an average £11.00 in Britain and less than £10.00 in France.[24]

As the population expanded, colonists gained momentum, fighting indigenous nations for territory and seeking independence from Europe. Starting in 1765, Britain imposed a deluge of taxes on American colonists to help pay off their French and Indian war debt. A newfound feeling of autonomy, mixed with outrage regarding the new taxes, sparked 13 North American colonies to fight for independence from British rule.

In 1770, a British army troop in Boston opened fire on a mob of colonists. Three years later, a group of Boston colonists disguised themselves as Mohawk Indians, boarded a British East India Company ship, and dumped thousands of dollars worth of tea into the harbor in protest of unfair tea taxes. Britain retaliated by imposing the Intolerable Acts of 1774. Colonists called on Britain to revoke the Acts. In response, Britain sent more army troops to America. Though the American colonists lost the 1775 Battle of Bunker Hill, more than 40 percent of British troops were killed.[25]

On July 4, 1776, the Continental Congress adopted the Declaration of Independence. Britain formally recognized U.S. independence in 1783 and withdrew troops, and in 1789 the U.S. Constitution became the national framework of government for the 13 American colonies.

General George Washington believed that the survival and strength of the new nation hinged on its infrastructure. In his famous letter to Virginia

---

24 Jones, A. (1980). Wealth of a Nation to Be. New York: Columbia University Press.

25 Battle of Bunker Hill. (2019). Retrieved 23 June 2021, from https://www.history.com/topics/american-revolution/battle-of-bunker-hill

Governor Benjamin Harrison, Washington explains that they must conquer those lands to establish lines of trade and communication with settlers and foreigners. In reference to difficult terrain and geographical obstacles, Washington comments, "A people however, who are possessed of the spirit of commerce, who see, and who will pursue their advantages, may achieve almost anything. In the meantime, under the uncertainty of these undertakings, they are smoothing the roads and paving the ways for the trade of that western World." [26]

Having grown up on the English colony of Virginia on the Potomac River, Washington wrote of "the immense advantages which Virginia and Maryland might derive (and at a very small comparative expense) by making Potomac the channel of commerce between Great Britain and that immense tract of country which is unfolding to our view the advantages of which are too great, and too obvious I should think to become the subject of serious debate."[27]

Moving forward, the Founding Fathers regarded infrastructure as a means of fulfilling both private and public interests. Connecting river and canal developments of the inland regions with eastern trading populations would both expedite growth and assure a loyal assimilation of the West with the Union.

When local segments protested the idea of paying taxes to support these grand plans, leaders formed corporations. Washington formed his Patowmack Company to improve navigation on the Potomac and collect ongoing tolls.

By 1786, the Mount Vernon Compact and Annapolis Convention had

---

26 Jones, A. (1980). Wealth of a Nation to Be. New York: Columbia University Press.

27 Bacon-Foster, C. (1912). Early Chapters in The Development of The Potomac Route to The West. *Records of the Columbia Historical Society, Washington, D.C., 15*, 96-322. Retrieved June 23, 2021, from http://www.jstor.org/stable/40067035

established a set of values for interstate cooperation in navigation and commerce on the Potomac and Chesapeake Rivers. Representatives soon determined that navigation and commerce issues were exposing deficiencies in the Articles of Confederation, leading to the 1787 Constitutional Convention.

Though trade and navigation were not the focus of the convention, the final draft of the U.S. Constitution gave Congress the power "to regulate commerce with foreign nations, and among the several States," and "to make all laws that shall be necessary and proper for carrying into execution the foregoing powers, and all other powers vested, by this Constitution, in the government of the United States."

Later, in The Federalist, Alexander Hamilton wrote, "There are rights of great moment to the trade of America which are rights of the Union—I allude to the fisheries, to the navigation of the Western lakes, and to that of the Mississippi."[28]

James Madison added, "the intercourse throughout the Union will be facilitated by new improvements. Roads will everywhere be shortened, and kept in better order; accommodations for travelers will be multiplied and ameliorated; an interior navigation on our eastern side will be opened throughout, or nearly throughout, the whole extent of the thirteen States. The communication between the Western and Atlantic districts, and between different parts of each, will be rendered more and more easy by those numerous canals with which the beneficence of nature has intersected our country, and which art finds it so little difficult to connect and complete."[29]

In 1794, Congress passed a comprehensive blueprint for roads and post

---

28 Hamilton, A. (1787). The Utility of The Union in Respect to Commercial Relations and a Navy for The Independent Journal. Retrieved 23 June 2021, from https://constitution.org/1-Constitution/fed/federa11.htm

29 Madison, J. (1787). Objections to The Proposed Constitution from Extent of Territory Answered. Retrieved 23 June 2021, from https://constitution.com/the-federalist-papers-no-14/

offices—"post-roads." In the 1791 Report on Manufactures. Hamilton noted that "good roads, canals, and navigable rivers" diminished transportation costs, putting remote regions "more nearly upon a level" with the main administrative centers. "They are, upon that account, the greatest of all improvements," he concluded.[30]

Despite federal support, U.S. infrastructure development got off to a slow start. The Federalists knew they had to earn the trust of the states before jumping into internal improvements. In 1796, Thomas Jefferson wrote that he was concerned the Federalists would fall into "boundless patronage to the executive, jobbing to members of Congress and their friends, and a bottomless abyss of public money" for infrastructure programs.[31]

The Steam Engine

The arrival of the steam engine completely changed the landscape of early American infrastructure. For the first time in history, the chemical energy of wood and coal could be used efficiently to drive technologically advanced machinery. Though it was based on scientific principles that had been known for hundreds of years, James Watt's steam engine was patented in 1769. An improvement on Newcomen's steam engine from 1712, the Scottish inventor's creation was vital for the changes brought about by the Industrial Revolution.

The basic design of a steam engine features a boiler that produces hot steam, which expands under pressure, producing energy. In 1781, Watts patented the more advanced rotative steam engine, which expanded the invention's industrial applications. By the early 1800s, the technology had

30 Hamilton, A., Syrett, H., & Cooke, J. (1966). *The Papers of Alexander Hamilton vol. 10, December 1791—January 1792* (pp. 230—340). New York: Columbia University Press.

31 Kurland, P., & Lerner, R. (2000). *The Founders' Constitution.* Thomas Jefferson to James Madison, 1796 (Volume 3, Article 1, Section 8, Clause 7, Document 4). Indianapolis: Liberty Fund.

been successfully applied to trains and boats, connecting the world like never before and giving tremendous impulse to commerce.

Approximately 2,000 steam engines were produced in the 18th century, and nearly 500 were used to power the textile industry.[32] By the mid-1800s, the engines were also being used to remove water from mines and build canals.

1799 Waterworks

The city of Philadelphia installed one of the first advanced water systems in the U.S. in response to several yellow fever epidemics that wreaked havoc in the region during the 1790s. The city hired British-American engineer Benjamin Latrobe to design the new waterworks and supervise construction.

In 1799, Latrobe proposed to supply Philadelphia with "wholesome water for culinary purposes." As Philadelphia endured freezing winter temperatures, the canals would freeze, and rapid spring thaws would repeatedly destroy valuable water mills. Latrobe argued that, with the help of steam engines, the city could pump its water into large reservoirs, then actively pump it into the city, providing cool water in the summer for public bathing, allowing the construction of fountains to cool the air and prevent freezing during the winter.

Latrobe's proposal was ambitious: to install two steam engines and two 20,862 gallon tanks.[33] Wood and iron pipes would be used, which cost less than cast iron pipes. Latrobe also presented a unique form of funding, suggesting the water system's construction be funded and controlled municipally

---

32 Kanefsky, J., & Robey, J. (1980). Steam Engines in 18th-Century Britain: A Quantitative Assessment. *Technology And Culture, 21*(2), 161. doi: 10.2307/3103337

33 Documentary History of American Water-works. (2015). Retrieved 23 June 2021, from http://www.waterworkshistory.us/PA/Philadelphia/

by taxing property owners, promising access to quality drinking water in return. This concept was more efficient than the British pattern of private distribution. By charging property owners for water access, everyone on the property would have access to the water, including low-income renters. For non-renters, water would be available for free at public pumps.

While the property tax idea didn't come to fruition, the waterworks did. Philadelphia adopted the plan and funded it by selling shares in the waterworks, and the city ensured the water would be available "at the conduits emptying into the streets," and "be for the free use of all persons."[34] By 1822, the city had replaced the expensive steam-powered pumps with water-powered pumps by damming the Schuylkill River.

1802 National Road

The Founding Fathers knew the importance of infrastructure in creating bonds between the Union and those areas of the U.S. that held different interests. By the time he became President in 1801, Jefferson had gained confidence in the incipient U.S. government. Just one year into office, he signed the Ohio Enabling Act, putting five percent of Ohio public land sales toward the construction of a National Road that would reach 130 miles between Virginia and Maryland. By his second inaugural address, Jefferson asked Congress to contribute all budget surpluses to "rivers, canals, roads, arts, manufactures, education, and other great objects within each state."[35]

---

34 *An Ordinance Providing for The Raising of A Sum Of Money for Supplying The City of Philadelphia with Wholesome Water. [electronic resource] : Printed by Order of the Corporation of Philadelphia.* (1799). Printed by Zachariah Poulson, Junior, no. 106, Chesnut-Street.

35 Jefferson, T. (1805). Second Inaugural Address, Washington D.C., March 4, 1805. *Presidential Addresses and Messages* (Lit2Go Edition). Retrieved June 23, 2021, from https://etc.usf.edu/lit2go/132/presidential-addresses-and-messages/5165/second-inaugural-address-washington-dc-march-4-1805/

Completed in 1837, the National Road project marked the birth of large-scale U.S. infrastructure. Still, the constitutionality of infrastructure programs was up for decades of debate, hindering any major internal improvements for the next 15 years. At this point, canals, roads, and bridges were typically privately owned but required government charters, meaning the government could set hours and rates. But the government would soon relinquish control over public works and transportation infrastructure as demand would incite novel forms of funding.

The American System Plan

After the war of 1812, a new nationalism was born in the United States. One of the strongest nationalists at the time was Kentucky Senator Henry Clay. A firm believer in national sovereignty, he thought our country should depend on no other nation for any of its basic needs. Clay promoted a plan known as the "American System," which was presented to Congress in 1815.

The American System was based on three principles, which translated into three actions[36]:

- Protective tariffs to shield products produced in America by taxing foreign goods.
- The creation of a national bank.
- Upgrading transportation infrastructure.

Following the War of 1812, Clay's program to "harmonize and balance the nation's agriculture, commerce, and industry" had the goal of eliminating

36 Baxter, M. (1995). *Henry Clay and The American System*. Lexington, Kentucky: University Press of Kentucky. Retrieved June 23, 2021, from http://www.jstor.org/stable/j.ctt130j8jq

the chance of "renewed subservience to the free-trade, laissez-faire 'British System.'"[37]

The American System was an early nationalist effort to make America economically independent from British colonial power. Though some of its programs didn't receive enough funding to come to fruition, some of its reforms, especially in the case of tariffs, were implemented. Many of Senator Clay's ideals would be realized much later as the United States developed into a powerful independent nation.

Expanding American Infrastructure

The most ambitious state-led infrastructure project of the early 19th century was the Erie Canal. Construction began in 1817. The man-made waterway spanned 364 miles between the Hudson River in Albany, NY, and Lake Erie in Buffalo, connecting the Atlantic Ocean with the Great Lakes region. Impulse from the canal project, combined with steamboat technology developments, created a comprehensive water transportation network over the following decades.

A few years after the canal was completed, similar projects followed in affluent agricultural, lumbering, and coal mining areas in other parts of the country.

The industrial revolution spread rapidly through the textile mills of New England and other manufacturing endeavors. These industries required a solid credit system, thus fostering the development of banking.

With banks ready to loan money to entrepreneurs to purchase raw

37 Byrd, R. (1994). *The Senate, 1789-1989: Classic Speeches, 1830-1993.* (p. 81). Washington, D.C.: U.S. Government Printing Office.

materials and build manufacturing facilities, and waterways to help them transport their goods, industries blossomed, and the Market Revolution ensued.

States invested heavily on transportation infrastructure that helped grow the nation's economy. The system of finance evolved to support business endeavors that created wealth. Modeled on British banking institutions, American banks became increasingly stable and profitable.

The Industrial Revolution

As the Industrial Revolution unfolded, the young nation would add the postal system, banking structures, railroads, electricity, natural gas, the telegraph, the telephone, and radio broadcasting to the canals, railroads, and roads.

In the early 19th century, most Americans earned money by farming. Communities were widespread and rural. But between 1820 and 1870, agriculture and textile manufacturing underwent great technological advances. The advent of the steam engine, combustible engine, sewing machine, lightbulb, and calculator increased production dramatically.

With the growth in factories came a growth in employment opportunities, and operating a factory paid more than operating a farm. People moved from rural to urban communities nearer to the cities, creating demand for city planning improvements. The increase in production efficiency lowered labor costs, resulting in reduced prices for supplies and bringing in new customer populations. The American Industrial Revolution also instigated improvements in education and science, fostering medical advances like the X-ray machine and modern anesthetics.

Such rapid technological advancement did not come without its problems. For the first time in centuries, the move from farm to factory resulted in U.S. food shortages. While fewer people worked in food production, consumer demand grew. Technology came to the rescue, modernizing the production and distribution of food. Thanks to mechanization and artificial fertilizers, farms were able to produce more food faster. At the same time, the emergence of food preserving technologies and improved transportation systems facilitated bringing food from farm to consumer faster and better.

On the flip side, the sudden, high concentration of people living in cities led to depleted resources and poor living conditions. Factories dumped waste into rivers, and water supplies became contaminated with sewage. With skyrocketing profits came high demands for production, leading to unfair wages, unsafe working conditions, and overworked factory employees.

In spite of these problems, some of which still plague us today, the industrial revolution spurred economic growth and spectacular achievements in infrastructure. As urban living expanded, investments in water systems, streetcars, and power grids improved living standards across U.S. cities.

The United States' infrastructure overhaul would soon pay off. By the late 1800s, mail, telephone, and railroads had enabled companies like Sears and Roebuck to expand their business through mail-order catalog and delivery endeavors. In 1900, the United States became the largest economy in the world, surpassing Great Britain, the very nation where the industrial revolution was born.

The revolution's impact owes much to the courage of American industrialists such as Andrew Carnegie, who first established modern steel mills on U.S. soil. Having imported the innovative "Bessemer process" from Britain, Carnegie was able to mass produce steel, accumulating enough wealth to acquire an interest in steel mines, railroads, and shipping lines. In this way, the pioneering businessman controlled every aspect of steel production and commercialization.

Formed in 1901, Carnegie's United States Steel Corporation was the first company in the world with a market capitalization surpassing $1 billion.[38] Thanks to the technology imported by Carnegie, steel quickly replaced iron in railroad projects.

Meanwhile, John D. Rockefeller, formed a trust that monopolized 90 percent of the oil industry: Standard Oil Trust. [39]As powerful men like Carnegie and Rockefeller demanded favorable policies, the government provided them, facilitating the building of railroads and keeping tariffs high to protect U.S. industry.

America did not only adopt technologies made in Britain. Local-born inventors like Alexander Graham Bell and Thomas Alva Edison contributed many valuable inventions that improved manufacturing, communication, and transportation. Bell is recognized as the inventor of the telephone, while Edison created the light bulb and the phonograph, among many other influential innovations. These new technologies were instrumental in the development of America's communications infrastructure.

Railroads

With the steam engine's success came a new type of transportation infrastructure—the railroad. The first trains carried passengers to and from large cities like Boston and New York. It was not until the second half of the 19th century that freight trains began to carry industrial products.

Rather than providing financial support, the federal government could offer up land to support this type of project. Federal backing for small railroad projects came in the form of Land Grant Acts for several states. Once the idea

38 What Was The First Company with A $1 Billion Market Cap? (2021). Retrieved 23 June 2021, from https://www.investopedia.com/ask/answers/09/1-billion-market-cap.asp

39 Chernow, R. (1998). *Titan: The Life of John D. Rockefeller, Sr.* New York: Random House.

of a transcontinental railroad took hold, the federal government created the Union Pacific Railroad via the 1862 Pacific Railway Act.

The granting of land and the availability of cheap U.S.-made steel facilitated railroad projects. Primarily developed between the 1820s and the turn of the century, U.S. railroads went on to dominate the nation's transportation system for many decades.

Before the 1850s, the majority of railroads were local, but the network soon expanded across state lines. By the Civil War, plans for a transcontinental railroad were already in place. Railroad projects were public/private endeavors, mostly funded by the private sector but relying on public intervention to guarantee project completion. The impact of these infrastructure developments played a major role in America's breakneck-pace industrial revolution.

The Civil War

The fact that America became a leading industrial power at the turn of the century owes much to the technologies refined during the Civil War. As the largely urban North faced the rural South, it became evident that the Confederacy was at a disadvantage. Lacking the Union's railroads and factories, and the resulting economic capacity, the South struggled to mobilize the necessary resources to win the war.

Meanwhile, the North increased production, mechanizing farms as farmers enlisted in the army. The railroad industry boomed during the conflict, and the Union was naturally in the lead. By the end of the Civil War, America boasted the world's largest railroad network.

In 1862, Abraham Lincoln signed the Homestead Act into law, offering free title to parcels of undeveloped federal land to any individual willing to cultivate it and live on it. The Morrill Act allotted land to states for the creation of Agricultural and Mechanical colleges. This legislation was instrumental in the modernization of farming and manufacturing.

In terms of infrastructure, one of Lincoln's greatest contributions was the Pacific Railway Act, also approved in 1862. Linking East and West, the transcontinental railroad project would create thousands of jobs in both manufacturing and the laying of tracks. New towns popped up along the new train lines, farm products began to move easily between the Atlantic and the Pacific, and the landscape of America was changed forever. As the first federal currency was created and the first income tax was imposed, the federal government became more powerful, impacting industry, agriculture, and finance.

Post-War Reconstruction

Following the Civil War, modernizing the South and its production matrix became imperative. Railroads needed to be expanded, and with the abolition of slavery, depending on cotton production was no longer sustainable. The era of reconstruction was also a time of reconciliation. As Robert Selph Henry once wrote, "The hardest part of war is not the fighting, but the cleaning up after."[40] America was no exception. The Reconstruction was a lengthy effort with many failures along the way.

In spite of these difficulties, by May 1869, the transcontinental railroad was complete. Around the same time, oil pipelines became a convenient alternative to the transportation of oil by rail. With the Rockefeller company controlling railway oil transport, Standard Oil's competitors were forced to

40 Chido, D. (2018). Everything Old Is New Again: Stabilization Lessons from Reconstruction. Retrieved 23 June 2021, from https://warroom.armywarcollege.edu/articles/everything-old-is-new-again-stabilization-lessons-from-reconstruction/

lay the first long-distance pipeline, a development that had a massive impact on the U.S. economy.

The Tidewater Pipeline was 110 miles long. A spectacular achievement at the time, the project caused Rockefeller's corporation to become even more aggressive. Soon enough Standard Oil would acquire a stake in Tidewater and build new pipelines of its own.

Through its pipelines, Standard Oil controlled oil transportation across America's oil-producing regions. With captive customers who had no alternative for moving their product to market, the conglomerate was able to develop large infrastructure projects without public support.

Standard Oil's power was so vast that Henry Demarest Lloyd once wrote, "The Standard has done everything with the Pennsylvania legislature, except refine it."[41] Legislators would eventually break up the trust, asserting the government's power to regulate interstate oil pipelines, in 1906. While the monopoly lasted, however, it certainly contributed to the advance of U.S. infrastructure.

In the last decades of the 19th century, the model of privately led and federally regulated infrastructure projects became the norm. This is how the interstate power grid and gas pipelines were developed. After the turn of the century, the federal government slowly withdrew from national infrastructure development.

Efforts by Congress to build roads and highways to support the automobile era were timid. Under the 1921 Highway Act, the federal government committed to cover only half of the costs of building roads and none of the costs of maintaining them, which was left to individual states. Salient exceptions to this government restraint policy included the Hoover Dam.

---

41 Lloyd, H. (1881). The Story of A Great Monopoly. Retrieved 23 June 2021, from https://www.theatlantic.com/magazine/archive/1881/03/the-story-of-a-great-monopoly/306019/

Roosevelt's New Deal

National infrastructure took center stage once more when Franklin Roosevelt became president. In line with what is now known as Keynesian policy, Roosevelt sought to reactivate the economy through large infrastructure projects. The idea was not centered on building needed infrastructure, but on creating jobs and putting money on the street. Wage workers employed in the building of roads and bridges, economists believed, would buy consumer goods and reactivate commerce.

Through the National Industrial Recovery Act, Roosevelt vowed to create a million jobs without putting money into financially unsound projects. The economist John Maynard Keynes theorized that if the government injected money into society through infrastructure projects, it would eventually come back in the shape of taxes and other indirect returns.

In one of his fireside chats, Roosevelt explained, "Two points should be made clear in the allotting and administration of these projects—first, we are using the utmost care to choose labor-creating, quick-acting, useful projects, avoiding the smell of the pork barrel; and secondly, we are hoping that at least half of the money will come back to the government from projects which will pay for themselves over a period of years."[42]

Roosevelt's New Deal transformed the nation. Two agencies, the Public Works Administration (PWA) and the Civil Works Administration (CWA), administered a multi-billion-dollar infrastructure budget. The WPA would eventually focus on smaller projects where the main aim was to create jobs, while the PWA managed large-scale construction.

Prominent New Deal projects include many landmarks that became a

---

42 Roosevelt, F., Buhite, R., & Levy, D. (1992). *FDR's Fireside Chats* (p. 31). New York: Penguin Books.

part of our national identity, such as LaGuardia Airport, the Hoover Dam, Lincoln Tunnel, the San Francisco-Oakland Bay Bridge, New Orleans City Park, the first freeway (now known as Pasadena freeway), Queens Boulevard, the Triborough Bridge, and FDR Drive, among many others. The WPA launched projects that employed 8.5 million people and built or improved over 120,000 public buildings, including nearly 2,500 hospitals. Over 75,000 bridges, 800 airports, and 650,000 miles of roads were built. Eight thousand parks were created or renovated, and billions of trees were planted.[43]

As the Great Depression catalyzed Roosevelt's infrastructure program, the Second World War also prompted new national infrastructure developments. During the post-war years, Eisenhower signed the Federal-Aid Highway Act, which initiated the construction of more than 40,000 miles of interstate highway, funded through a gasoline tax.

Between the end of the Second World War and the turn of the century, America was the most prosperous it had ever been. "American infrastructure was state-of-the-art. . . in the 1950s,"[44] global infrastructure analyst Dylan Ratigan explains. "Our highway system, our power generation system, our Water Management and sewage systems, our communication systems" were the best in the world during the second half of the 20th century, Ratigan argues. What happened between then and now? And "why is the cell phone service in Kenya superior to the cell phone service in America?"

According to Ratigan, the new paradigm of infrastructure is "super high-performance decentralized waterpower and communication systems as opposed to simply trying to transfer the legacy system from operation inside

43 Works Progress Administration (WPA) (1935) - Living New Deal. (2021). Retrieved 23 June 2021, from https://livingnewdeal.org/glossary/works-progress-administration-wpa-1935/

44 *American Infrastructure Was State of The Art! ...In 1950.* (2017). [Video]. Retrieved from https://www.youtube.com/watch?v=GQzLXzpxhU8

of the government to operation outside of the government."[45]

After having been a world leader in infrastructure projects in those early days, America now faces the challenge of rebuilding its infrastructure, not with the tools of the past, but with those of the future.

45 *American Infrastructure Was State of The Art! ...In 1950.* (2017). [Video]. Retrieved from https://www.youtube.com/watch?v=GQzLXzpxhU8

CHAPTER 3:

The Modern Era

"[Infrastructures exist] as forms separate from their purely technical functioning. . . they emerge out of and store within them forms of desire and fantasy and can take on fetish-like aspects that sometimes can be wholly autonomous from their technical function."

—Brian Larkin

After the Second World War, America was heavily invested in the reconstruction of Europe, which created great demand for U.S. products in the Old World. In the 1950s, President Eisenhower focused on U.S. infrastructure again. In his view, developing the interstate highway system was crucial to the nation's competitiveness. His vision of modern America involved "a mighty network of highways" that would spread across the country.[46] As his dream started to become a reality, the highway network contributed 30 percent to our country's annual productivity rate.

The Highway Network

President Eisenhower's 1956 Federal Aid Highway Act permanently changed the way Americans travel. The president was impressed by the highway systems he saw in Germany during the war, and he vowed to emulate them. The federal government would pay for 90 percent of Eisenhower's 41,000

46 50th Anniversary Interstate Highway System. Retrieved 13 July 2021, from https://www.fhwa.dot.gov/interstate/audiogallery.cfm

miles of highway, with states footing only 10 percent of the bill.[47]

The new highways reduced transportation costs and revitalized the economy by creating jobs in the construction industry. New businesses thrived along the interstates, and others that were circumvented by it died.

In spite of temporary funding issues, Kennedy would move forward with Eisenhower's plans. In 1963, when the new President attended the opening of the Maryland Northeastern Expressway-Delaware Turnpike, he said:

> "[This highway symbolizes], first of all, the partnership between the Federal Government and the States, which is essential to the progress of all of our people; and secondly, it symbolizes the effort we have made to achieve the most modern Interstate highway system in the world, a system which, when completed, will save over 8000 lives a year and $9 billion in cost. And third, it symbolizes the effort which we are giving and must be giving to organizing an effective communication system here in the United States of America."[48]

The highway system took time to build; it demanded great resources, but it was a triumph. With more and better roads, the automobile industry boomed. The government spent much more on highways than on mass transit projects. Railways suffered as Americans opted for cars and buses, and cargo was increasingly transported by truck.

Thanks to new corrosion protection technology, piping infrastructure was greatly improved. Bridges benefited from technological advances like prestressed concrete beams and weathering steel. America's transportation

47 Weingroff, R. The Greatest Decade 1956-1966. Retrieved 13 July 2021, from https://www.fhwa.dot.gov/infrastructure/50interstate.cfm

48 Remarks at The Dedication of The Delaware-Maryland Turnpike. Retrieved 13 July 2021, from https://www.presidency.ucsb.edu/documents/remarks-the-dedication-the-delaware-maryland-turnpike

and energy infrastructure were changing and expanding rapidly, in part, thanks to 'big government.'

The Era of Affluence

The period between the end of the Second World War and the 1970s came to be known as the Era of Affluence and Big Government.[49] The war effort led to a 10-fold increase in the national budget, from $10 billion in 1941 to nearly $100 billion in 1945.[50] Income tax legislation passed in 1942 made large amounts of money available to the government. This strengthened the Federal Reserve System and catalyzed educational programs for veterans and massive investments in both physical infrastructure and human capital.

The Baby Boom that lasted until the mid-1960s created a surge in population and rising demand for water systems, homes, schools, energy infrastructure, and highways.

The Cold War years prompted many scientific advances, as the U.S. invested in research to try to stay ahead of communist bloc countries. Advances in telecommunications technology and computing were abundant, and the Space Race led to spectacular developments in the fields of weather forecasting and satellite communication.[51]

Federal investment in non-defense projects had a great impact. But when spending focused on waging war in Vietnam, the national debt skyrocketed,[52] and infrastructure investments dwindled.

---

49 Judt, T. (2007). The Age of Affluence. *Advertising & Society Review* 8(4), doi:10.1353/asr.2007.0050.

50 Tassava, C. American Economy in World War II. Retrieved 13 July 2021, from https://eh.net/?s=American+economy+in+World+War+II

51 Cold War Technology. Retrieved 13 July 2021, from https://publish.uwo.ca/~acopp2/historyofwar/coldwar/technology.html

52 Riddell, T. (1989). Inflationary Impact of The Vietnam War. Vol. 1 : No. 1 , Article 4.Retrieved 13 July 2021, from https://digitalcommons.lasalle.edu/cgi/viewcontent.cgi?article=1003&context=vietnamgeneration

In spite of the war effort, infrastructure continued to improve in the homeland. In 1968, the new Federal Highway Act implemented mandatory periodic bridge inspections.[53] In the 1970s, the introduction of prefabricated deck forms facilitated shorter construction times, safer sites, and more affordable building projects. Significant advances in the industry included corrugated metal, fiberboard, and precast concrete.[54]

In the 1970s, the energy crisis highlighted the shortcomings of our country's energy infrastructure. With Middle East producers in control of pricing,[55] it became apparent that America needed to become energy independent, something we wouldn't glimpse until the shale revolution.

The Shift to Lighter Infrastructure

In the 1980s and 1990s, prefabricated construction technology continued to develop rapidly. With new materials and groundbreaking manufacturing techniques, large pipes, retaining wall systems, and bridge decks could now be delivered directly to construction sites, boosting both building speed and safety.[56]

Government funding of traditional infrastructures decreased steadily after the 1980s, but the advent of the Internet and the deregulation of railways, airlines, trucks, energy, and finance fostered great infrastructure investments.

AT&T monopolized communication devices for decades, but in the 1980s,

53 Timeline - Contributions and Crossroads: Our National Road System's Impact on The U.S. Economy and Way of Life (1916- 2016) | Federal Highway Administration. Retrieved 13 July 2021, from https://www.fhwa.dot.gov/candc/timeline.cfm

54 The History of Infrastructure Innovation. Retrieved 13 July 2021, from https://truetechbridge.com/about-us/history/

55 Energy Crisis (1970s). Retrieved 13 July 2021, from https://www.history.com/topics/1970s/energy-crisis

56 The History of Infrastructure Innovation. Retrieved 13 July 2021, from https://truetechbridge.com/about-us/history/

it was unable to keep up with demand, and the market was deregulated.[57] Companies like Microsoft, IBM, and Apple were soon developing innovative products based on government-sponsored research.

In the energy sector, deregulation came in the late 1970s, expanding exploration, often with the help of government subsidies. Technological advances like horizontal drilling, and later fracking, would foster massive infrastructure developments.

In the 2000s, the shale boom unleashed massive amounts of fossil fuels, leading to the construction of LNG plants and pipelines.[58] At the same time, renewable energy projects cropped up all over the country, complete with large-scale wind and solar infrastructure developments.

No other infrastructure development had the scale and importance of the Internet during the last years of the 20th century and the beginning of the 21st.

The Internet Era

Originally a system designed to enable scientists, research institutions, and government agencies to exchange memos, the Internet would evolve to dominate global communications. By 1993, there were approximately 40,000 linked networks and 90,000[59] users across America. In 2015, that number would escalate to 3.2 billion users globally.[60]

The Internet infrastructure enabled companies like Amazon to transform

---

57 We Can Learn from The History of Deregulation: U.S. Telecommunications. Retrieved 13 July 2021, from https://www.directenergy.com/learning-center/history-of-deregulation-telecommunication

58 The Shale Gas and Tight Oil Boom. Retrieved 13 July 2021, from https://www.cfr.org/report/shale-gas-and-tight-oil-boom

59 Web History Timeline. Retrieved 13 July 2021, from https://www.pewresearch.org/internet/2014/03/11/world-wide-web-timeline/

60 Internet Used by 3.2 Billion People in 2015. Retrieved 13 July 2021, from https://www.bbc.com/news/technology-32884867

the world of retail and consumer goods forever. And by 2009, the number of systems and devices connected to the Internet surpassed the number of people using it. The Internet of Things soon became a household term,[61] and cyber infrastructure became a necessity for virtually every business and human activity.

As cyber infrastructure boomed, new technology also favored transportation infrastructure. In the early 2000s, highway construction picked up thanks to the implementation of accelerated construction methods and economic incentives to build infrastructure faster.[62]

The Networked Economy

The introduction of personal computers in the 1980s, accompanied by the breakup of the Bell System, triggered a technological revolution.[63]

During the first decade, computer use was restricted to businesses. In the 1990s, they entered American homes. As the 20th century drew to a close, computer chips were doubling in power every 18 months. By 2010, Intel had built a chip 100 times more advanced than the ones designed around the end of the 1990s.[64]

The breakup of Bell triggered massive fiber-optic infrastructure developments led by companies like Sprint and MCI. With the advent of the Internet, these companies switched from voice communications to moving

---

61 Why The Internet of Things is Called Internet of Things: Definition, History, Disambiguation. Retrieved 13 July 2021, from https://iot-analytics.com/internet-of-things-definition/

62 The History of Infrastructure Innovation. Retrieved 13 July 2021, from https://truetechbridge.com/about-us/history/

63 Bell System Breakup Opens Era of Great Expectations and Great Concern. (1984). Retrieved 13 July 2021, from https://www.nytimes.com/1984/01/01/us/bell-system-breakup-opens-era-of-great-expectations-and-great-concern.html

64 We're Not Prepared for The End of Moore's Law. Retrieved 13 July 2021, from https://www.technologyreview.com/2020/02/24/905789/were-not-prepared-for-the-end-of-moores-law/

data. Mobile phones prompted satellite infrastructure developments. The Teledesic Internet network followed the Iridium phone network.[65] By the early 2000s, the information infrastructure reached planetary scale, pioneered by America's infrastructure.

Chronicling the breakup of Bell, a New York Times reporter wrote in 1984, "The telephone system is, in effect, the highway system of the Information Age, and its health affects the competitiveness of all American industry. If the telephone breakup spurs innovation, it could help all industries."[66] Around the same time, an MIT spokesperson predicted, "We'll get new technologies rushing forward."[67] He could hardly imagine the scope of the innovations to come.

In the late 1990s and early 2000s, building information infrastructure became one of the most lucrative business opportunities. After big media companies got into the business of the Internet, online commerce exploded, and sales hit $10 billion by 2000.[68]

As the networked economy developed, organizations became more productive and efficient. By 2000, the economy was growing at a rate of 4 percent.

The 21st century brought a new wave of groundbreaking technologies. Biotechnology took center stage after the Human Genome Project was completed in 2003.[69] Gene therapies for cancer were already in advanced

65 Bell System Breakup Opens Era of Great Expectations and Great Concern. (1984). Retrieved 13 July 2021, from https://www.nytimes.com/1984/01/01/us/bell-system-breakup-opens-era-of-great-expectations-and-great-concern.html

66 Bell System Breakup Opens Era of Great Expectations and Great Concern. (1984). Retrieved 13 July 2021, from https://www.nytimes.com/1984/01/01/us/bell-system-breakup-opens-era-of-great-expectations-and-great-concern.html

67 Bell System Breakup Opens Era of Great Expectations and Great Concern. (1984). Retrieved 13 July 2021, from https://www.nytimes.com/1984/01/01/us/bell-system-breakup-opens-era-of-great-expectations-and-great-concern.html

68 Greenspan, S. (2021). The 2010s eCommerce and Online Shopping Decade in Review. Retrieved 13 July 2021, from https://jilt.com/blog/decade-ecommerce-2010s/

69 The Human Genome Project. Retrieved 13 July 2021, from https://www.genome.gov/human-genome-project

development by 2012.[70] Healthcare industry and biotechnology infrastructure developed rapidly.

Meanwhile, biotechnology research also influenced the agriculture and livestock sectors. With genetically engineered, super productive animals and plants, food production became cheaper and faster. Eventually, nanotechnology and quantum computing took digital technology infrastructure to the next level.

The Renewable Energy Revolution

Around the turn of the century, traditional automakers rolled out the first hybrid cars, which featured both gasoline-fueled and electric motors. Hydrogen-powered hybrids were once the market's biggest hope. With hydrogen powering electric motors, the new hybrids could finally realize the dream of zero emissions.[71]

As environmental legislation was developed, the market was ripe for the new hybrids, and carmakers started developing many new models. In the end, the plug-in electric vehicle would come to dominate the zero-emission market, while hydrogen remained on the fringes of the industry. Though fossil fuels have continued to dominate the market over the first decades of the 21st century, the majority of new cars will be electric sooner than later. This will require a massive infrastructure project to develop servicing and charging networks for the new vehicles.

---

70 Ortiz, R., Melguizo, C., Prados, J., J. Alvarez, P., Caba, O., & Rodriguez-Serrano, F. et al. (2012). New Gene Therapy Strategies for Cancer Treatment: A Review of Recent Patents. *Recent Patents on Anti-Cancer Drug Discovery*, *7*(3), 297-312. doi: 10.2174/157489212801820093

71 A Brief History of Hybrid Cars. (2020). Retrieved 13 July 2021, from https://www.carsdirect.com/green-cars/a-brief-history-of-hybrid-cars

The Globalized World

The end of the Cold War and the fall of Europe's communist regimes marked the beginning of globalization. As the U.S.S.R. was dismembered and China embraced many elements of a capitalist economy, the world was transformed. While Japan had been on the cutting edge of technology in the 1980s, by the late 1990s, the United States became the networked economy's global leader.[72]

The development of cyber infrastructure played a key role in this power shift. Over the next decades, China would become a world leader on par with the U.S. in terms of technology and groundbreaking infrastructure developments, albeit with a much less affluent population to enjoy them.

As the Internet abolished the borders of knowledge and creativity, the new telecommunications infrastructure flourished. Cyber infrastructure sparked growth in the U.S. and abroad.

Growth Driving Infrastructure

The Internet boom, the blockchain revolution, and the new decentralization in all its forms created new opportunities, fueling a new brand of optimism comparable to that of the postwar years. Leaving the occasional crisis aside, our country has experienced a level of growth that filled the tax coffers and catalyzed investments in infrastructure.

With new jobs and more upward mobility in American society, more infrastructure was needed. The new technology-driven culture needed a new education infrastructure, and the 2000s saw a complete overhaul of many aspects of education and learning. In the new era, talented innovators are a

72 The Information Age: Economy, Society and Culture. Retrieved 13 July 2021, from https://en.wikipedia.org/wiki/The_Information_Age:_Economy,_Society_and_Culture

key competitive advantage. Both the public and the private sector understand just how crucial it is to invest in the kind of infrastructure that can foster the development of original thinking minds and innovative technologies.

Between 1960 and 2010, physical capital was the focus of most non-defense federal investments. During the 2010s, however, the government's investment in education far exceeded spending on traditional infrastructure.[73] In the wake of the 2008 crisis, the American Recovery and Reinvestment Act of 2009,[74] in particular, poured significant resources into postsecondary education grants for underprivileged students.

The Internet has democratized learning and entertainment, allowing kids with cell phones and an Internet connection to become overnight stars and young coders to raise billions of dollars in venture capital. The infrastructure that makes the world go round today is not always visible or palpable, and it is becoming increasingly complex.

As we glimpse the obsolescence of many human occupations, the eve of space tourism, and the potential of gene therapies, it is easy to understand that we haven't seen the last infrastructure revolution of our lifetime.

The 2020-2021 pandemic has shown us that the world's problems can no longer be solved unilaterally. In a globalized world and a space age, we must look at infrastructure from a planetary perspective. It is pointless to reduce carbon emissions to zero in the U.S. if other countries are still polluting the only planet we all have. We live in an era of tremendous opportunity, but if our infrastructure lags, we'll miss the train. The time to invest in American infrastructure and collaborate with our allies on international infrastructure projects is now.

---

73 Investing in Roads Versus Schools. Retrieved 13 July 2021, from https://voxeu.org/article/investing-roads-versus-schools

74 American Recovery and Reinvestment Act (ARRA). Retrieved 13 July 2021, from https://www.investopedia.com/terms/a/american-recovery-and-reinvestment-act.asp

Private vs. Public Infrastructure

Historically, a private-public partnership has been quite successful for large-scale infrastructure projects. While some advocate privatization, privatized road, water, and prison infrastructure developments have had mixed results.

A public-private partnership combines the best of both worlds, enhancing transparency and helping cut down costs. While this approach has been successful, insufficient spending on maintenance has caused American infrastructure to crumble over the last decades.

Investing in infrastructure brings great benefits to the economy. If the government had increased infrastructure investments in the aftermath of the 2008 crisis, the rebound from the recession might have been much faster.

Infrastructure Spending

Measured as a percentage of the national GDP, infrastructure Investment in the U.S. went from more than 4 percent in the 1960s to 2.5 percent in 2016. Over the same period, investment in structures, in particular, went down from 2.9 percent to 1.5 percent of GDP.[75]

These meager percentages put the U.S. way behind other top economies, especially in the case of transportation infrastructure, including construction and maintenance of railways, ports, airports, and roads. When compared to G7 countries, our nation invests 0.6 percent of GDP in transportation infrastructure, surpassing only Germany's and Italy's spending, and lagging behind the G7 average of 0.8 percent.[76]

75 Stupak, J. (2018). Economic Impact of Infrastructure Investment. Retrieved 13 July 2021, from https://fas.org/sgp/crs/misc/R44896.pdf

76 IN BRIEF: Why The G7 Summit Matters, in Seven Charts. (2021). Retrieved 13 July 2021, from https://www.atlanticcouncil.org/blogs/new-atlanticist/in-brief-why-the-g7-summit-matters-in-seven-charts/

Infrastructure investments have a positive impact on economic output. They allow both companies and individuals to be more efficient and more productive. Better transportation infrastructure frees up valuable time and resources by reducing commute times and allowing goods to be delivered faster.

Statistics have shown that a 1 percent increase in public capital stock, in the shape of infrastructure, results in a 0.083 percent rise in the public sector's economic output in the short term and 0.122 percent in the long term.[77]

The Future

Writing in WIRED, in 1997, Peter Schwartz and Peter Leyden imagined what the world would be like in 2020: "In many ways, it's a civilization of civilizations. . . We're building a framework where all the world's civilizations can exist side by side and thrive. Where the best attributes of each can stand out and make their unique contributions. Where the peculiarities are cherished and allowed to live on. We're entering an age where diversity is truly valued—the more options, the better. Our ecosystem works best that way. Our market economy works best that way. Our civilization, the realm of our ideas, works best that way, too."[78] We haven't gotten there yet, but one can only hope.

As boomers fade from leadership positions and millennials rise to power, this techno-savvy generation will deliver us to the new world. American millennials are a generation of endless optimism. They have solved massive

---

77 Stupak, J. (2018). Economic Impact of Infrastructure Investment. Retrieved 13 July 2021, from https://fas.org/sgp/crs/misc/R44896.pdf

78 Schwartz, P., & Leyden, P. (1997). The Long Boom: A History of The Future, 1980—2020. Retrieved 13 July 2021, from https://www.wired.com/1997/07/longboom/

infrastructure problems with apps that weigh only a few megabytes. They believe they can reverse aging, colonize Mars, solve the problems of poverty, climate change, and multicultural integration, all with innovative technologies and disruptive creativity. Let us not be the ones to tell them it can't be done. Because, in many ways, they are already doing it. The infrastructure we need today is simply a platform where new ideas can thrive.

PART II:

CHEAP, FAST, AND BROKEN

CHAPTER 4:

Bridges | Busted & Rusted

"It is both a sad and a happy fact of engineering history that disasters have been powerful instruments of change. Designers learn from failure."

—Edward Tenner

August 1, 2007 in downtown Minneapolis was a calm summer evening. At just after 6 p.m., the peak rush-hour traffic was moving slowly across the Interstate 35 West bridge over the Mississippi River. Opened in 1967, the eight-lane, steel truss arch bridge was Minnesota's third largest, serving more than 140,000 vehicles a day. Suddenly, a resounding clank was heard, and the bridge trembled. Seconds later, about 1,000 feet of the bridge collapsed, and more than 450 feet of the main span plunged 100 feet into the river and onto its banks.

Dozens of cars plunged into the water, where motorists, injured from the 10-story drop, struggled against the water filling their vehicles. Emergency crews scrambled to free them and bring them to safety. Still, other vehicles were trapped atop the fragmented bridge, including a packed school bus, as fires sparked by leaked fuel threatened immolation. When it was all over, 13 people had died, and 145 had been injured.

The I-35W collapse sent shockwaves across the country. Governor Tim Pawlenty stated, "Obviously this is a catastrophe of historic proportions for Minnesota," but the disaster had nationwide implications. To an anxious public eager to learn the cause of the tragedy, this was not like the Cypress

Freeway collapse of 1989, inflicted by a powerful earthquake. Nor was it like the I-40 bridge collapse of 2002 in Webbers Falls, Oklahoma, where a river barge had struck a support. No outside force had affected I-35W. The structure had simply failed under normal use.

According to *The New York Times*, annual inspections had noted "assorted cracks, corrosion and fatigue."[79] Journalist Anderson Cooper reported, "It's obvious there were troubling safety questions about this bridge years before the collapse." Governor Pawlenty conceded, "there were problems with the bridge, but not a recommendation to immediately close it." He stressed that "Just because it falls into this category doesn't mean it is necessarily unsafe." He asked the public to be patient until investigations were complete.

Ultimately, the National Transportation Safety Board (NTSB) determined a design flaw had produced a defect in the truss structure, which made its collapse inevitable. The flaw, steel support plates of only half the thickness necessary, had been overlooked forty years earlier during the bridge's construction.

The conclusion raised a series of questions that shook the nation's confidence in our bridge infrastructure. Was this flaw unique to I-35W, or was it common to bridges built during the 1960s? Did the age of the structure and negligent maintenance factor into the collapse? How many other bridges across the United States were compromised by defects or decrepitude, and when would the next fatal collapse occur? But though these questions were raised, they were never satisfactorily answered as the story faded from the headlines.

Fourteen years later, how are our country's bridges faring? If you think the tragedy of I-35W led to a renaissance in bridge construction and maintenance

---

79 *When A Bridge Falls... | The New York Times.* (2014). [Video]. Retrieved from https://www.youtube.com/watch?v=74JNl5n-YdI

as municipalities everywhere vowed, "Never again!", you are an optimist. Certainly, infrastructure funding has been increased in recent years, and bridges have been prioritized. Notable projects have been completed, such as a new Bay Bridge between San Francisco and Oakland, California, and a new Tappan Zee Bridge spanning the Hudson River. But numerous sources report that our nation's bridges remain in dangerous disrepair, suggesting the question of another commuter bridge collapse is not "if" but "when."

Take Minnesota, for example, where we would expect a visceral response to bridge infrastructure questions. In 2017, the American Road and Transportation Builders Association reported that of Minnesota's 13,355 bridges, 800, or 6 percent, were structurally deficient. The state itself has identified 2,020 bridges in need of repair, which will cost about $780 million[80]. The state's most traveled structurally deficient bridge is TH 36 over Lexington Avenue in Ramsey County, where 85,000 vehicles cross per day. If Minnesota isn't more determined to prevent another tragedy, what does that say for the rest of the country?

ASCE's Verdict

Infrastructure Report Card is an assessment issued by the American Society of Civil Engineers every four years. In the 2017 Report Card, ASCE assigned a grade of C+ for our nation's bridges. But before we get too ecstatic about a "passing grade," let's examine some of the facts behind the letter.

"You're not getting older, you're getting better," was a popular advertising slogan in the 1970s, but it hardly applies to bridges built in that era or even

80 Simpson, I. (2017). Almost 56,000 U.S. Bridges Structurally Deficient, Report Says | INFORUM. Retrieved 4 June 2021, from https://www.inforum.com/News/4218609-Almost-56000-Us-Bridges-Structurally-Deficient-Report-Says

earlier. ASCE found that nearly 40 percent of America's 614,387 bridges were 50 years of age and older, with the average age being 43 years. Of the total, 56,007 were rated structurally deficient, yet in 2016 Americans made 188 million trips across those structurally deficient bridges every day.

ASCE cautions that structurally deficient bridges are not necessarily unsafe but could quickly become so and would need to be quickly shut down to prevent a tragedy. Bridges are not designed to last forever, and too many of our bridges are reaching the end of their design lifespan without a viable plan for replacement. ASCE estimates the price tag for national bridge rehabilitation at $123 billion, no small sum for a country whose national debt is $27.75 trillion and growing.

But the news is not all bad. Progress has been made over the last decade, as the percentage of structurally deficient bridges declined from 12.3 percent to 9.1 percent. Certain states are doing a better job than others in maintaining their bridges. Nevada rates best with only 1.6 percent of its bridges deficient, while Rhode Island is the worst state in the nation with 24.9 percent deficiency.

There's also the issue of obsolescence. A bridge may be structurally sound, but if the community it serves has experienced growth since it was built, the bridge might not meet the current demands for traffic flow, especially when it comes to larger vehicles. ASCE estimates that 13.6 percent of bridges are functionally obsolete. These bridges act as traffic chokepoints, causing congestion and delays. This means economic and quality-of-life losses to the community, as well as wasted fuel harming the environment.

The State of Bridges Across The Nation

Let's take a closer look at how a few states are attempting to manage their bridge infrastructure issues.

New York

Shortly after the I-35W collapse, *The New York Times* reported that a 2007 inspection had rated the Brooklyn Bridge approach ramps "poor."[81] Echoing MN Gov. Pawlenty, a spokesman for the New York City Department of Transportation, said the bridge was not in a dangerous state but did require renovation. This assessment surprised no one. After all, the bridge had been opened in 1883, and after more than a century of continuous operation was serving 120,000 vehicles a day.

Repair work on the approaches and deck began in 2010 as part of a plan that included widening two approach ramps, raising the clearance above surface streets, seismic retrofitting, replacement of rusted railings and safety barriers, and resurfacing. Originally, the project was scheduled for completion in 2014, but work lasted until 2017. Cost also soared, from an initial budget of $508 million to $811 million.

Yet, the bridge still required additional work. Plans were made to expand the bicycle and pedestrian paths, reinforce the foundations, repair masonry arches on the approach ramps damaged by Hurricane Sandy in 2012, and renovate the suspension towers and approach ramps. This price tag exceeds $330 million, and work is expected to be completed in 2023.

During this time, the Empire State also took a major step forward with the construction of the Governor Mario M. Cuomo Bridge, a twin-span, cable-stayed overpass of the Hudson River from Tarrytown to Nyack, to replace the aging Tappan Zee Bridge. The cost was steep: initially budgeted at $3.98 billion for construction and administrative costs, the project finished under a cloud of

81 Chan, S. (2007). Brooklyn Bridge Is One of 3 With Poor Rating. Retrieved 4 June 2021, from https://cityroom.blogs.nytimes.com/2007/08/02/brooklyn-bridge-is-one-of-3-with-poor-rating/

litigation, as contractors claimed an additional $900 million was owed.[82]

Another major concern was the Verrazzano-Narrows Bridge, connecting Brooklyn and Staten Island. At the time of its completion in 1964, the Verrazzano was the longest suspension bridge in the world. As of 2015, its 13 lanes were servicing around 200,000 vehicles every day. Saving the Verrazzano was a major priority, and so $1.5 billion was allocated for restoration. The first stage consisted of replacing the existing upper deck sections, removing the divider, and adding an HOV lane, and was finished in 2017.[83] Then, in August 2020, the Metropolitan Transportation Authority announced it had completed a project restoring the Verrazzano's tower foundation pedestals early and under budget.[84]

Clearly, the Empire State took the I-35W collapse to heart. All told, the state has built almost 1,300 bridges and rehabilitated more than 600 over the last decade. Yet after all this work, ASCE still scores 11 percent of New York's bridges structurally deficient and 25 percent functionally obsolete. That means extensive spending to fix about 6,500 structures. Current estimates place the cost of repairing New York's remaining bridges at $75 billion, no small sum for a state with a $14 billion budget deficit that has lost 37 percent of its tax revenue over the last year.[85]

---

82 Rubinstein, D. (2019). More Evidence Emerges That Mario M. Cuomo Bridge Faces Budgetary Risks. Retrieved 4 June 2021, from https://www.politico.com/states/new-york/city-hall/story/2019/11/22/more-evidence-emerges-that-mario-m-cuomo-bridge-faces-budgetary-risks-1229054

83 Katinas, P. (2015). Verrazano Bridge Repair Work Brings Lane Closure Until 2017. Retrieved 4 June 2021, from http://www.brooklyneagle.com/articles/2015/3/10/verrazano-bridge-repair-work-brings-lane-closure-until-2017

84 Bascome, E. (2020). Verrazzano-Narrows Bridge Tower Pedestals Restored ahead of Schedule. Retrieved 4 June 2021, from https://www.silive.com/news/2020/08/verrazzano-narrows-bridge-tower-pedestals-restored-ahead-of-schedule.html

85 Dewitt, K. (2020). New York Has Lost A Greater Share of Revenue Than Most States Due to COVID-19. Retrieved 4 June 2021, from https://www.npr.org/2020/08/03/895384547/new-york-has-lost-a-greater-share-of-revenue-than-most-states-due-to-covid-19

Oklahoma

Perhaps because the disastrous I-40 collapse of 2002 appeared to be a freak accident, Oklahoma has not acted with the urgency citizens have a right to expect from a state with 15 percent structurally deficient bridges. On the morning of May 23 of the year, a towboat pulling a barge on the Arkansas River caused the barge to collide with the pier supporting the bridge structure. The incident occurred when the captain of the towboat experienced a "syncopal episode," which caused him to lose consciousness. A 550-foot span of the bridge plummeted into the river. Delays in stopping traffic prolonged the tragedy, as several more passenger vehicles and semi-trucks drove off the edge. When it was over, 14 people were dead, and 11 more had been injured.

Today, Oklahoma has more than 23,000 bridges, and almost 3,500 are considered structurally unsound. Ironically, the most traveled span is another stretch of I-40 over Crooked Oak Creek in Oklahoma City, where more than 87,000 vehicles cross each day. In its defense, Oklahoma has made great strides over the past five years, decreasing its number of structurally deficient bridges by 753, according to the American Road and Transportation Builders Association.[86]

Rhode Island

The smallest state in the Union has the highest percentage of structurally deficient bridges in the country. Thus, The Ocean State earned a D- for bridge infrastructure from ASCE in 2020. ASCE estimates that 4 million residents and nonresidents pass over those bridges each day. Rhode Island

86 230,000 U.S. Bridges Need Repair, New Analysis of Federal Data Finds. (2020). Retrieved 4 June 2021, from https://www.artba.org/2020/04/12/230000-u-s-bridges-need-repair-new-analysis-of-federal-data-finds/

is seeking to reverse decades of neglect with a program called *RhodeWorks*[87], encompassing the repair of 150 structurally deficient bridges, as well as preventative maintenance on 500 more. The state hopes to generate sufficient funding from tolls on large commercial trucks and grants from the 2015 FAST Act. *RhodeWorks* is part of a larger plan to jumpstart the state's faltering economy and ease the pain of an $800 million, COVID-induced shortfall.

California

On October 17, 1989, the San Francisco Bay Area was poised for the third game of the World Series between the San Francisco Giants and the Oakland Athletics. The latter had taken the first two games of what had been dubbed the Bay Bridge Series after the structure connecting the rival cities. But now the series had shifted to Candlestick Park and Giants fans were hoping that home-field advantage would bring a change of luck. They couldn't have been more wrong.

On a crisp, clear afternoon, at 5:04 pm, the earth trembled as an intense seismic shock hit the Santa Cruz Mountains in the vicinity of Loma Prieta Peak and rolled out in all directions. The earthquake measuring 6.9 on the Richter scale hit San Francisco hard, interrupting the pregame television broadcast and canceling the evening's game when chunks of Candlestick Park rained down on the ground. The Bay Bridge was also hit hard when a 76-by-50-foot section of the upper deck fell onto the deck below, killing one person.

Across the bay, the damage was even worse, as the double decks of Cypress Street Viaduct of Interstate 880 crumbled for a mile and a quarter,

87 RhodeWorks — Rhode Island Rhode Island Department of Transportation. Retrieved 4 June 2021, from http://www.dot.ri.gov/rhodeworks/

crushing dozens of vehicles. Fuel fires started in the wreckage. According to *ABCNews7.com*[88], "a witness at the time said, 'You could hear voices. You could hear voices screaming, 'help me, help me, help me,' until the fires just start, poof, and then you don't hear them no more.'" The collapse killed 42 commuters and injured many more.

Eighty-nine hours after the collapse, rescue and recovery workers were rewarded. Within a car crushed to three feet in height, a 57-year-old Longshoreman, Buck Helms, responded to a passing flashlight with a gesture that said he was still alive. Helms was freed from his vehicle and placed in an ambulance amidst cheering and clapping. To Bay Area residents, his survival seemed emblematic of their losses and their hopes. For a month and a day, Helms struggled to recover but finally succumbed to his injuries.

Reconstruction of the Cypress freeway would not be completed until 2001. The Bay Bridge was closed for a month for repairs. That process also revealed serious problems that had to be addressed sooner rather than later. Yet, the saga of the Bay Bridge would last for decades. and the costs would be staggering.

The ASCE 2019 Infrastructure Report Card for California notes that the Golden State has made progress "over the past decade to increase the percentage of California bridges in good condition and to reduce the number that are classified as structurally deficient (SD)."[89] As a result, "California has fewer SD bridges than the national average," and there is optimism that "passage of the Road and Repair Accountability Act (SB 1)" will allow that good work to continue. However, about half of the state's bridges have

88 Miguel, K., & Brinkley, L. (2019). 1989 Loma Prieta Earthquake: Cypress Freeway Collapse Survivor Buck Helms Remembered. Retrieved 4 June 2021, from https://abc7news.com/loma-prieta-quake-earthquake-when-was-magnitude/5605965/

89 2019 Report Card for California's Infrastructure. (2019). Retrieved 4 June 2021, from https://www.infrastructurereportcard.org/state-item/california/

exceeded their design life and suffer from backlogged maintenance. Given the fault lines zigzagging throughout the state, a great deal of urgent work remains, especially as it relates to seismic retrofitting to improve safety in the event of an earthquake.

California is home to the nation's top 14 most-traveled, structurally deficient bridges, the foremost of which is the Interstate 110 bridge over Los Angeles County's Dominguez Channel, serving 274,000 vehicles a day.[90] California also ranks second nationally in the percentage of "functionally obsolete" (FO) bridges, and is among the worst states for bridges whose deck area is in poor condition. This means that some of the state's largest bridges—along I-5 in San Diego, Highway 101 in Los Angeles, and I-80 in Sacramento—need major rehabilitation. How capable is California—reeling under a two-year deficit of $54.3 billion[91], and a projected revenue decline of 22.3 percent for 2020-21[92]—of martialing the resources necessary to face this crisis?

That question brings us back to the Bay Bridge saga.[93] In the years after Loma Prieta, officials developed an economic plan to retrofit the bridge, but that planning came to a screeching halt with the Northridge quake of 1994. Suddenly, 6.9 shakers were twice-a-decade events, so entirely replacing the eastern span of the Bay Bridge seemed a more prudent course. It would take three more years before the California legislature finally allocated $1.3 billion for that project, but the debate raged on.

---

90 Simpson, I. (2017). Almost 56,000 U.S. Bridges Structurally Deficient, Report Says | INFORUM. Retrieved 4 June 2021, from https://www.inforum.com/news/4218609-almost-56000-us-bridges-structurally-deficient-report-says

91 Varguese, R. (2020). California 'Wall of Debt' Returns as State Bets on Federal Aid. Retrieved 4 June 2021, from https://www.bloomberg.com/news/articles/2020-06-30/california-wall-of-debt-returns-as-state-bets-on-federal-aid

92 Hinkley, S. (2020). Fiscal Impacts of COVID-19 and California's Economy - UC Berkeley Labor Center. Retrieved 4 June 2021, from https://laborcenter.berkeley.edu/fiscal-impacts-of-covid-19-and-californias-economy/

93 Angell, I. (2013). Why The New Bay Bridge Cost $6.4 Billion | WNYC | New York Public Radio. Retrieved 4 June 2021, from https://www.wnyc.org/story/316201-brief-history-64-billion-bay-bridge/

Critics decried the "vanilla structure," calling the viaduct design a "freeway on stilts." How could such a blandly functional trestle exist in the very shadow of the picturesque Golden Gate Bridge? Perish the thought! In 1997, the Metropolitan Transportation Commission (MTC) decided it would be acceptable to raise tolls to build a more aesthetically pleasing bridge, so the call went out for more artistic designs. The process dragged on, as every politician had an opinion and some square of turf to defend. It wasn't until 1998 that the MTC chose a design featuring a 525-foot tower and the longest self-anchored suspension span in the world. The cost of the bridge was then estimated at $1.5 billion to be completed by 2004, a full 15 years since Loma Prieta had revealed urgent structural problems.

Yet, for myriad reasons, each pettier than the last, construction had not even begun by 2001. Meanwhile, the cost had nearly doubled to $2.6 billion, and the deadline had been extended to 2007. Then the terrorist attacks on New York City on September 11, 2001 impacted the cost, as insurance premiums for landmark structures soared.

Delays continued, and by 2004 steel prices rose 50 percent. The bridge cost rose to $5.6 billion and Caltrans had to return to the Legislature to beg for more funding. By that time, Arnold Schwarzenegger had become governor by virtue of star power and a vague promise to manage resources responsibly. He demanded that Caltrans simplify the project, perhaps reconsidering the "freeway on stilts." By 2005, the functionalists and the aesthetics reached a compromise that kept the "signature span" design, at a new estimated price tag of $6.3 billion. So much for reining in costs.

Over the next seven years, the cost went up another $100 million, but the bridge finally opened in September 2013. Almost 24 years had elapsed since the Loma Prieta quake had revealed the need for immediate action. Clearly, if California is to address its infrastructure needs responsibly, its officials must learn from this debacle.

Washington and Oregon

Bridge repair is hard enough when the structure resides within a single state, but interstate bridges pose greater challenges because two state bureaucracies must come to an agreement. Such is the case of the Columbia River Interstate Bridge on I-5 connecting Portland, Oregon, with Vancouver, Washington. The I-5 Bridge is actually two structures, one opened in 1917, which now carries northbound traffic, and a twin opened in 1958, which carries southbound vehicles.[94] Together, these bridges handle more than 130,000 vehicles a day. In 2019, ASCE graded Oregon an overall C- with a C for bridges[95]; Washington's latest grade as a C overall and a C+ for bridges[96]. The I-5 Bridge is emblematic of each state's infrastructure struggles, and its saga shows the difficulty of negotiating reconstruction across state lines.

The I-5 Bridge is functionally obsolete, with the sufficiency ratings of 18.3 percent for the original span and 49.4 percent for the second span, and is regarded as the worst bottleneck for traffic on the I-5 corridor, which stretches from Mexico to Canada. The two states have been kicking around proposals for a replacement bridge, dubbed the Columbia River Crossing (CRC) project, since 2005.

Costs were originally estimated at $2 billion, but climbed steadily to $3.4 billion in 2012, though an independent assessment in 2010 set the cost closer to $10 billion. The project was canceled in June 2013, when Washington's legislature refused to authorize funding. The Interstate Bridge Replacement Program was relaunched in 2019 with assistance from the federal government.

---

94 Wortman, S., Wortman, E., & Norman, J. (2006). *The Portland Bridge Book* (pp. 107—112). Portland, OR: Urban Adventure Press.

95 Jamestaun Kraupp, E. (2019). 2019 Oregon Infrastructure Report Card. Retrieved 4 June 2021, from https://www.asceor.org/news/category/2019-oregon-infrastructure-report-card

96 2019 Infrastructure Report Card Washington. (2019). Retrieved 4 June 2021, from https://www.infrastructurereportcard.org/wp-content/uploads/2016/10/ASCE_Brochure—WA2019.pdf

As of this writing, 16 years have elapsed since the 2005 decision to replace the spans with still no ground breaking. The two states seem determined to prove that California is no outlier.

But while we're discussing motor vehicle crossings, we must also bear in mind the potential danger of pedestrian walkway collapses. Technically, the deadliest bridge collapse in U.S. history was the failure of the Hyatt-Regency walkways in Kansas City, Missouri on July 17, 1981.[97] Guests had gathered on the walkways, about 40 on the second and 20 or so on the fourth floor, overlooking the lobby, where some 1,600 guests were enjoying a Tea Dance. At 7:00 pm, the structures gave way in an avalanche of concrete, steel, glass and bodies. A damaged sprinkler system gushed water onto the scene. Rescue crews responded to the atrium, which was described as a war zone, and worked for 14 hours to free injured parties from the rubble. When it was over, 114 guests had perished and 200 more were injured.

Construction of the hotel had only begun three years earlier. How could such a disaster have happened? An investigation by structural engineers discovered shocking negligence: design changes made on the fly, over the phone without due consideration, had rendered the walkways dangerously unsafe.

A similar, though less deadly, incident occurred just three years ago, when a pedestrian bridge, still under construction, collapsed in Miami, crushing eight vehicles, killing six people and injuring 10 more. The bridge was designed to connect Florida International University with the town of Sweetwater.[98] An investigation by the National Transportation Safety Board found that

97 McFadden, C. (2021). Countdown to Disaster: The Hyatt Regency Walkway Collapse. Retrieved 4 June 2021, from https://interestingengineering.com/understanding-hyatt-regency-walkway-collapse

98 Design Errors Draw Blame in Collapse of FIU Pedestrian Bridge That Killed 6. (2019). Retrieved 4 June 2021, from https://www.usatoday.com/story/news/nation/2019/10/22/design-error-blamed-florida-international-university-pedestrian-bridge-collapse/2449316001/

calculation errors, as well as an engineer's failure to grasp the implications of cracks in the structure, had caused the tragedy. NTSB Chairman Robert Sumwalt also blamed the lack of "public safety oversight" that allowed the university to manage the project without a state Transportation Department inspector on-site.

Urban planners view pedestrian walkways as important tools to protect pedestrians from the dangers of fast-moving traffic. As municipalities build additional walkways, design and construction flaws must be addressed to prevent similar tragedies from occurring.

How to Fix America´s Bridges

But returning to our main topic of discussion, what is the remedy for our substandard bridge infrastructure? The ASCE 2017 Report Card lists several recommendations on how to raise the grade:

- Increase funding for bridge rehabilitation and repair from all levels of government.
- Adopt smart designs based on maintenance and rehabilitation costs across the bridge's entire lifecycle.
- Raise the federal gas tax and tie future increases to inflation to replenish the federal Highway Trust Fund.
- Re-evaluate state funding mechanisms to ensure sufficient investment in bridges.
- States and the federal government should find long-term funding solutions outside of taxes, including perhaps mileage-based user fees.

By now, it should be evident that bridge maintenance costs are inevitable and predictable, and that failure to maintain bridges in good working order is not an option. Government agencies must budget for bridge maintenance, and the fairest way to get dedicated funds is through bridge tolls. Funding maintenance through tolls ensures that bridge users are the ones paying for repairs.

Unfortunately, too many states use bridge tolls to raise revenue for unrelated expenditures, in essence stiffing the bridges, and forcing bridge agencies to lobby state legislators for funding whenever a structural problem rears its ugly head. In New York, for example, bridge and tunnel tolls provide 12 percent of the revenue for the operation of the Metropolitan Transit Authority, but the MTA only allots four percent of its budget for bridges and tunnels.[99] This system allowed decades of maintenance to be deferred until New York faced a crisis of decrepitude with several of its structures. As long as bridges are shorted on their toll revenue, there will be maintenance shortfalls that endanger the public. Immediate reforms are sorely needed.

99 Guse, C. (2021). *NEW YORK NY Lawmakers Call for Feds to Permanently Subsidize MTA's Operating Costs*. Retrieved 29 August 2021, from https://www.nydailynews.com/new-york/ny-mta-operating-costs-federal-subsidies-legislature-20210607-ulfsjobvkradvipegd7325xoy4-story.html.

CHAPTER 5:

Aging Dams & Climate Change | A Disastrous Combo

"Climate change is killing Americans. Wildfires, heat waves, mudslides, hurricanes, and floods lead to hundreds if not thousands of deaths every year. But those are only the direct fatalities."

—Annie Lowrey

At the foot of the San Gabriel Mountains lie the sprawling suburbs of Los Angeles, where millions of people live, work, and play. The best of all worlds in some respects, these "Gateway Cities" to the east of the country's second-largest metropolitan center offer warm weather,[100] beautiful scenery, and bustling commercial districts. Crime is relatively low in most of these areas, and schools are generally good.

Residents of these idyllic communities, such as Glendora, Monrovia, and Whittier, may not realize how much their safety depends on a network of aging dams. Starting in the 1920s, state and federal agencies began work on a series of dams along the San Gabriel River and its tributaries to keep flooding in check.[101] Today, the oldest of these dams are more than 90 years old, and

100 Gateway Cities. Retrieved 5 June 2021, from https://www.metro.net/about/local-service-councils/gwc

101 The Morris San Gabriel Dam, San Gabriel River Canyon, California - Postcard - Department of Archives and Special Collections, William H. Hannon Library, Loyola Marymount University. (1938). [Image]. Retrieved from https://digitalcollections.lmu.edu/Documents/Detail/the-morris-san-gabriel-dam-san-gabriel-river-canyon-california/25089

the decades of wear and tear are starting to show. If one were to suddenly buckle or burst during events such as a torrential storm or an earthquake, the result would be catastrophic. Whole towns would be wiped out, and people would die.

All of the Los Angeles-area dams along the San Gabriel River are deemed "high hazard dams" by federal and local safety officials. The "high hazard" classification is used for dams whose failure could likely cause loss of life and massive property destruction.[102] This is not an unusual designation to have. In the U.S., one in six of roughly 91,000 dams are considered "high hazard" according to the American Society of Civil Engineers. That fact, combined with the age of these dams—by 2025, 70 percent will be at least 50 years old—means that the probability of disaster grows with each passing day.

It happened just this past year in Midland, Michigan. The town of roughly 42,000 sits in the central portion of the state, about 18 miles away from the Edenville Dam. An earthen embankment dam built in 1925, Edenville was used for hydroelectric power and flood control. After decades, it was also in desperate need of repairs.

In May 2020, days of record rainfall inundated the Upper Midwest, causing rivers and lakes to overflow.[103] Positioned at the confluence of the Tittabawassee River and the Tobacco River, Edenville Dam was overwhelmed by the swell of water and burst.[104] Gushing water caused a chain reaction and the breach of another dam a little farther downstream.

Soon a wave 20 feet high engulfed Midland. The flooding caused as much as $250 million in destruction and more than 11,000 people had to be

102 2017 Infrastructure Report Card - Dams. (2017). Retrieved 5 June 2021, from https://www.infrastructurereportcard.org/wp-content/uploads/2017/01/Dams-Final.pdf

103 USA — Floods in Illinois and Michigan After Days of Heavy Rain. (2020). Retrieved 5 June 2021, from http://floodlist.com/america/usa/floods-illinois-michigan-may-2020

104 Whitmer, G. (2020). Edenville Dam Preliminary Report. Retrieved 5 June 2021, from https://www.michigan.gov/documents/egle/egle-EdenvilleDamPreliminaryReport_700997_7.pdf

evacuated. The event was especially devastating given the timing. Residents were already struggling with widespread business shutdowns during the coronavirus pandemic.

Dam operators and state officials faced criticism and a lawsuit in the aftermath of the breach for failing to ensure the structure was sound. For at least five years before the event, the Federal Energy Regulatory Commission had demanded operator Boyce Hydro make needed repairs and expand the dam's spillway capacity, to no avail. Litigation over the company's license and violations assessed against it over maintenance lapses had been ongoing when the flooding occurred.[105]

"This entirely preventable disaster has upended the lives and businesses of thousands, forcing residents into crowded shelters amid a pandemic and shutting down already-suffering businesses during a recession," lawyers for Midland residents said in their class action against Boyce Hydro and state environmental, energy, and natural resources officials.[106]

"Despite knowing the threat posed by these unsafe dams, the defendants allegedly refused to pay for much-needed repairs and upgrades," the lawyers said in May 2020. "Instead, we alleged they chose to try to conceal the deteriorating conditions of the dam."[107]

Luckily, no deaths or major injuries resulted from the deluge. Had the sudden breach of a dam occurred in a more populated area, it would likely have been a much more harrowing story.

---

105 Roth, C. (2020). Timeline: The Edenville Dam Saga, Before, During and After The Break. Retrieved 5 June 2021, from https://www.mlive.com/news/2020/09/timeline-the-edenville-dam-saga-before-during-and-after-the-break.html

106 Fonger, R. (2020). After Edenville Dam Failure, Lawsuits Pour In Against Owners, State Regulators. Retrieved 5 June 2021, from https://www.mlive.com/news/saginaw-bay-city/2020/05/after-edenville-dam-failure-lawsuits-pour-in-against-owners-state-regulators.html

107 Fedschun, T. (2020). Michigan Residents Sue State, Operators Over Dam Failures That Led to Flooding; Whitmer Orders Probe. Retrieved 5 June 2021, from https://www.foxnews.com/us/michigan-residents-lawsuit-whitmer-tittabawassee-river-dam-failure-500-year-event

Of all the crumbling, aging infrastructure in America, dams pose perhaps the biggest physical threat to public safety. A collapsing bridge could hurt or kill dozens or hundreds of people; a blowout of a major dam near a population center could easily impact thousands.

Meanwhile, ordinary people don't spend much time interacting with dams and thinking about their potential hazards. Unlike bridges, which area residents may see or travel over regularly, dams are usually built in out-of-the-way places. Most were also built many decades ago, before modern safety standards and concerns about climate change, along with more intense storms and flooding, came into the picture.[108]

When most Americans do think of dams, it's probably the Hoover Dam that comes to mind. The towering concrete arch-gravity dam along the mighty Colorado River on the border of Nevada and Arizona was constructed during the Great Depression. Operated by the U.S. Bureau of Reclamation, it ranks among the best-maintained dams in the U.S., despite its age. Creating the 247 square-mile Lake Mead, the 726-foot-tall dam is also a major tourist attraction. Roughly one million people tour the dam in a typical year.[109]

Many other dams in the U.S. are just as old but far less carefully managed, overseen by a patchwork of operators and regulators. This makes them unlike most other infrastructure in the country in that they are mostly owned by corporations rather than government agencies, and therefore harder to regulate. In its most recent infrastructure report card, the American Society of Civil Engineers gave the nation's dams a "D," slightly below the rating of "D+" for infrastructure overall.[110] The grade considers factors such as

108 Wei-Haas, M. (2020). The Problem America Has Neglected for Too Long: Deteriorating Dams. Retrieved 5 June 2021, from https://www.nationalgeographic.com/science/article/problem-america-neglected-too-long-deteriorating-dams#close

109 Hoover Dam Tour Information. Retrieved 5 June 2021, from https://web.archive.org/web/20100528053724/http://www.usbr.gov/lc/hooverdam/service/index.html

110 2021 Infrastructure Report Card |Overview of Dams. (2021). Retrieved 5 June 2021, from https://

capacity, condition, levels of funding, operation and maintenance, public safety issues, resilience, and innovation.

Getting U.S. dams up to a high grade would take tens of billions of dollars in funding, and well in excess of what is currently allocated in many budgets. Making needed repairs to all the dams in the country would cost $64 billion, according to the Association of State Dam officials.[111]

Dams handled by private operators pose added risks if they were not built up to appropriate safety standards. As development moves farther out to the fringes of communities, more and more dams built as "low hazard" dams have since become "high hazard"—meaning they should be subject to more rigorous standards because of the potential loss of life. Of all the "high hazard" dams in the U.S., as many as 1,688 are rated in "poor" or "unsatisfactory" condition by safety officials, according to a 2019 analysis by the Associated Press.[112]

"Most people have no clue about the vulnerabilities when they live downstream from these private dams," Craig Fugate, a former administrator at the Federal Emergency Management Agency, told the *AP*.[113] "When they fail, they don't fail with warning. They just fail, and suddenly you can find yourself in a situation where you have a wall of water and debris racing toward your house with very little time, if any, to get out."

---

infrastructurereportcard.org/cat-item/dams/

111 Dam Facts and Stats for the Media and Public. (2020). Retrieved 5 June 2021, from https://damsafety.org/media/statistics

112 Casey, M., Lieb, D., & Minkoff, M. (2019). Thousands at Risk Because of Aging U.S. Dams, Including Some in Colorado, AP Finds. Retrieved 5 June 2021, from https://www.denverpost.com/2019/11/10/aging-u-s-dams-risky-colorado-water/

113 Aging Dams in U.S. Expose Thousands to Risk. (2019). Retrieved 5 June 2021, from https://weather.com/news/news/2019-11-10-associated-press-aging-dams-risk-united-states

The History of Dam Construction

Humans have been building dams since the dawn of recorded history. Simple on a conceptual level, they can be constructed out of a variety of materials across rivers and streams to hold back water for a number of purposes. Using sticks and mud, beavers build dams to create ponds where they can raise young and hide from predators.[114] Humans build dams to control flooding, to store water for irrigating crops, to harness flowing water for power generation, and to develop man-made lakes for recreation.

The oldest known dams were built by Mesopotamians in the ancient city of Jawa, located in present-day Jordan, sometime around 3000 B.C.[115] The basalt desert of the region was subject to long dry periods and bouts of heavy rain and flooding. Developers installed stone gravity dams to control the flow and provide a consistent source of freshwater, enabling the city to flourish in an unlikely environment for 1,500 years.

Ancient Egyptians also built dams for similar reasons. A masonry-covered earthen dam, Sadd-el-Kafara, was constructed around 2700 or 2600 BCE in an area 19 miles south of present-day Cairo.[116] Missing a spillway to help resist erosion, the dam did not last long, however. Before it was even fully completed, a heavy flood breached the dam and washed it away, according to an analysis by contemporary engineers.

Similarly, remains of flood-control dams have been unearthed in China, dating from approximately the same period. Archeologists discovered the evidence of the ancient Chinese dams in 2016 in Hangzhou, a wealthy city

---

114 Build a Beaver Dam. Retrieved 5 June 2021, from https://www.nps.gov/articles/buildabeaverdam.htm

115 Key Developments in The History of Gravity Dams. Retrieved 5 June 2021, from http://www.lassp.cornell.edu/sethna/SimScience/cracks/advanced/grav_hist1.html

116 Brown, J. Guthrie and Jackson, Donald C. (2020, March 24). Dam. Encyclopedia Britannica. https://www.britannica.com/technology/dam-engineering

near the end of a major waterway that leads out to the ocean.[117] The scenic area was favored by emperors for millennia and remains popular for Chinese vacationers.[118] Ancient rulers may have taken a special interest in protecting it.

Romans excelled at building dams, along with their other impressive public works projects of the day, such as sewers and aqueducts.[119] In the first century A.D., the emperor Nero had a dam constructed to make a lake near his villa in Italy. Over the next couple of hundred years, Romans built many, many dams throughout modern-day Spain and Portugal, North Africa, and the Middle East. Heavy and substantial, these dams endured for many centuries.

One of those, the Cornalvo Dam near Merida, Spain, still stands.[120] Built on the Albarregas River, the earth and brick gravity dam is roughly 80 feet high, 650 feet long, and highly impregnable at 26 feet thick.[121] It fell into disrepair in the Middle Ages but was patched up in the 1700s and remains in use.

During the Medieval period in Europe, small dams became a popular means to harness waterpower for grinding grain into flour, sawing wood, and other localized purposes.[122] Millers, who operated water and windmills, served a vital function in that society and existed in every town and village.[123]

Mills became bigger and more powerful during the Industrial Revolution, when they were used to run machines in factories.[124] This was made possible

117 Kaihao, W. (2016). Early Civilization Sophisticated, Dam Dig Reveals. Retrieved 5 June 2021, from https://www.chinadaily.com.cn/china/2016-03/18/content_23936224.htm

118 Hangzhou Travel. Retrieved 5 June 2021, from https://www.lonelyplanet.com/china/zhejiang/hangzhou

119 Key Developments in The History of Gravity Dams. Retrieved 5 June 2021, from http://www.lassp.cornell.edu/sethna/SimScience/cracks/advanced/grav_hist1.html

120 Witmer, S. (2016). Cornalvo Dam and Natural Park | EPOD | A Service of USRA. Retrieved 5 June 2021, from https://epod.usra.edu/blog/2016/05/cornalvo-dam-and-natural-park.html

121 Roman Aqueducts: Cornalvo dam / Merida (Spain). Retrieved 5 June 2021, from http://www.romanaqueducts.info/aquasite/cornalvo/index.html

122 Encyclopedic Entry - Dams. Retrieved 5 June 2021, from https://www.nationalgeographic.org/encyclopedia/dams/

123 Medieval Miller. Retrieved 5 June 2021, from https://www.medievalchronicles.com/medieval-people/medieval-tradesmen-and-merchants/medieval-miller/

124 Encyclopedic Entry | Dams. Retrieved 5 June 2021, from https://www.nationalgeographic.org/encyclopedia/dams/

by the construction of larger and more sophisticated dams, which could hold back and direct the flow of a greater volume of water.

In America, demand for hydroelectric power in the 1900s fueled a boom in dam building. A large number of major dam projects came during the Great Depression as part of President Franklin Roosevelt's New Deal programs, aimed at putting people back to work.[125] The Tennessee Valley Authority, for instance, was chartered in 1933 as a federally owned corporation that built dozens of dams as part of a mission to improve navigation, flood control, and electricity generation in the Tennessee river valley. Other large dams were built as part of Roosevelt's Public Works Administration and Works Progress Administration initiatives.

Massive undertakings, big dam projects required years of toil by thousands of laborers, who often worked in unpleasant or dangerous conditions. About 80 workers died over nine years of building the Grand Coulee Dam on the Columbia River in Washington state.[126] The largest number of deaths resulted from falling from the dam, while others died as a result of vehicle accidents, being crushed by heavy objects, electrocution, burns, and drowning.[127]

More than 100 workers died in the process of constructing the Hoover Dam from causes such as explosions, rockslides, heatstroke, and carbon monoxide poisoning from using gas-powered equipment in poorly ventilated areas. Rumors abound that some workers are entombed within the massive amount of concrete poured for the dam.[128] Historians and other investigators

---

125 New Deal Projects | Dams. Retrieved 5 June 2021, from https://livingnewdeal.org/new-deal-categories/infrastructure/dams/

126 McFadden, C. (2021). Some of the Deadliest Construction Projects in History. Retrieved 5 June 2021, from https://interestingengineering.com/some-of-the-deadliest-construction-projects-in-history

127 Wagner, J. (2018). Finally Telling The Stories of Those Who Died on The Dam. Retrieved 5 June 2021, from https://www.grandcoulee.com/story/2018/01/03/news/finally-telling-the-stories-of-those-who-died-on-the-dam/9817.html

128 Veronese, K. (2012). Who Is Buried in The Hoover Dam?. Retrieved 5 June 2021, from https://io9.gizmodo.com/who-is-buried-in-the-hoover-dam-5893183

have been unable to confirm those tales, although one worker did die after falling into wet concrete. His body was removed.

Around the same time, however, a structural failure at the Fort Peck Dam in Montana caused the death of eight workers in a collapse. Recovery personnel were only able to remove two of the bodies, leaving the remains of six workers still inside the dam.

In addition to the massive New Deal dams, thousands of smaller dam projects were also built across the country between the 1930s and the 1970s. The U.S. Army Corps of Engineers tracks an inventory of about 90,000 dams in the U.S. that are at least 6-feet tall. Including smaller, privately-owned structures, the total number of dams in the U.S. could be over 2.5 million, according to the National Research Council.[129]

Globally, about half of all major river systems are controlled through the use of dams, and only 23 percent of rivers flow to the ocean without human-made obstructions.[130]

Types of Dams

Although the idea of a dam is not complex, Mother Nature does not make it easy to permanently alter her forces. Building dams that can stand up to years of pressure from flowing water, including floods, takes substantial engineering prowess. To that end, humans have developed a number of different types of dams to take physics into account.

The earliest and simplest types of dams were earthen embankment dams,

129 Macy, C. (2010). Dams Across America. Retrieved 5 June 2021, from https://placesjournal.org/article/dams-across-america/?cn-reloaded=1&cn-reloaded=1

130 Boulange, J., Hanasaki, N., Yamazaki, D. *et al.* Role of Dams in Reducing Global Flood Exposure Under Climate Change. *Nat Commun* 12, 417 (2021). https://doi.org/10.1038/s41467-020-20704-0

basic walls of soil, clay, and rock.[131] They are relatively cheap to build and still dot the landscape of the U.S. A spillway is still usually required, however, to reduce pressure on the dam. Because the materials are not particularly durable, these dams require constant maintenance. A poorly maintained embankment dam might be subject to a sudden blow-out with little warning.

A more sophisticated type of dam is a gravity dam, typically built out of concrete or masonry, which are used to counteract the pressure of the water.[132] They are more intensive to build than earthen dams, more suitable for gorges and steep sloping areas, but less resistant to earthquakes. Gravity dams have a triangular structure, proportioned to maximize resistance. Highly durable, they do not require constant maintenance. Indeed, the longest-surviving ancient dams were gravity dams.

A more technically complex dam still is an arch dam, built using a curvature, which employs the strength of the arch to resist water pressure.[133] Some modern dams which must withstand particularly powerful forces, such as the Hoover Dam, have characteristics of both an arch dam and a gravity dam.

Dams can also be designed using buttresses,[134] multiple arches or curves,[135] or with the intent to overflow, creating a waterfall. A roller dam, built on some rivers, uses a series of large cylinders to limit water flow.[136]

131 What Is The Major Difference Between An Earthen Dam and A Gravity Dam? - Quora. (2018). Retrieved 14 June 2021, from https://www.quora.com/What-is-the-major-difference-between-an-earthen-dam-and-a-gravity-dam

132 Gravity Dam; Its Construction, Advantages and Disadvantages. Retrieved 14 June 2021, from https://www.civilknowledges.com/gravity-dam/

133 Arch Dam. Retrieved 14 June 2021, from https://www.britannica.com/technology/arch-dam

134 Types of Dams | USSD | United States Society on Dams. Retrieved 14 June 2021, from https://www.ussdams.org/dam-levee-education/overview/types-of-dams/

135 National Management Measures to Control Nonpoint Source Pollution from Hydromodification. (2007). Retrieved 14 June 2021, from https://www.epa.gov/sites/production/files/2015-09/documents/chapter_4_dams_web.pdf

136 Roller Dam & Locks. (2013). Retrieved 14 June 2021, from http://www.rockislandpreservation.org/postcards-from-home/roller-dam-locks/

While sudden blowouts are more common for earthen embankment dams, arch dams and gravity dams are not immune to failure. In the 1920s, amid a population boom in Los Angeles, city planners oversaw the construction of a series of dams to expand the community's sources of freshwater. The most ambitious, an arch-gravity dam called the St. Francis Dam, blew a river in the nearby San Francisquito Canyon. In 1928, less than two years after it was completed, it collapsed.[137]

Around midnight one night, hours after an inspector took note of a possible leak in the dam, the wall suddenly burst, sending 12 billion gallons of water roaring through the canyon to communities below. Considered one of the worst civil engineering disasters of the 20th century, the dam's failure took 450 lives and wreaked Biblical destruction. Investigators later determined the dam had been erroneously built on the site of a former landslide, and the loose ground shifted under its weight, destabilizing its foundation.

Recognizing the perils that come with possible dam failures, the state's governor at the time, C.C. Young noted that the growth of Los Angeles would nonetheless have to rely on continued dam building.

"While fully cognizant of the appalling loss of life and great destruction of property caused by this frightful disaster, it is at the same time self-evident that the full development of this great commonwealth requires that her water resources be fully conserved," he said in a state report on the accident.[138] "This can be done only by containing the constructions of great dams, such as those which are now doing their work without signs of weakness."

---

137 Blitz, M. (2015). On Occasions Like This, I Envy The Dead: The St. Francis Dam Disaster. Retrieved 14 June 2021, from https://www.smithsonianmag.com/history/occasions-i-envy-dead-st-francis-dam-disaster-180954543/?page=2

138 Blitz, M. (2015). On Occasions Like This, I Envy The Dead: The St. Francis Dam Disaster. Retrieved 14 June 2021, from https://www.smithsonianmag.com/history/occasions-i-envy-dead-st-francis-dam-disaster-180954543/?page=2

The Downsides of Dams

Like a modern-day equivalent of Egyptian pyramids, big dams can inspire awe. Bestriding great rivers such as the Colorado, the Columbia, and the Missouri, large-scale dams convey a majesty in their ability to reshape waterways and the surrounding landscape. But it is this very quality that also makes dams highly unpopular with environmental advocates.

The ecology of rivers and streams depends on a delicate balance that is easily thrown off by altering the flow of water. By blocking rivers, dams can halt or greatly impede the migration of some fish species. Slowing down the flow of water can lead to pollution, algae blooms, and a decrease in dissolved oxygen levels. Managed releases of water for hydroelectric power generation can disrupt species' natural reproduction cycles.

Environmental group American Rivers lobbies for the safe removal of dams to protect threatened habitats.[139] The organization contends that older dams create safety hazards for human populations as well as constant stress for plant and animal species. The decades' old dams that dot America's waterways were mostly installed long before the enactment of environmental laws such as the Clean Water Act, the National Environmental Policy Act, and the Endangered Species Act, and were not designed with regard for protecting plant and animal species.

"Examples include decline in salmon fisheries in the Columbia River basin and extinction of snails and mussel species in the Coosa River basin," the group says on its website.[140] "By building dams, we choked the life out

139 How Dams Are Removed. Retrieved 14 June 2021, from https://www.americanrivers.org/threats-solutions/restoring-damaged-rivers/how-dams-are-removed/

140 Dams Are Problem Creators, Not Problem Solvers. Retrieved 14 June 2021, from https://www.americanrivers.org/threats-solutions/energy-development/dams-problem-creators-not-problem-solvers/

of rivers, thereby causing much damage to people, local economies, and the species that needed healthy rivers to survive."

In addition to posing environmental threats, dams create direct safety hazards for humans who try to swim, boat, or engage in other recreation in their immediate vicinity. Jumping off a dam or sliding over a spillway in a kayak can seem like a fun activity—until someone drowns. Hidden currents around dams can often be deadly and unexpected.[141] One common type of currents formed by dams is called a "hydraulic roller." Even while wearing a life jacket, a swimmer caught in this circular, backward-flowing "washing machine" current may not be able to break free and resurface before it's too late.

Global Warming Raising the Stakes

The controversy surrounding dams and concern over their disrepair are both amplified by the impacts of climate change. A warming Earth means more rapid snowmelt, stronger storms, and heavier rainfall, all of which increase the likelihood of flooding. Heavy storms in the Northeast and Midwest brought up to 45 percent more rainfall in 2016 than they did in 1958, according to the Union of Concerned Scientists.[142] Within the past decade, areas including Denver, Colorado, Brenham, Texas, and West Virginia have been inundated with flooding after being hit with as much as 10 or 20 inches of rain in a single storm.

Dams continue to play a helpful role in controlling some of the heightened flood risks from global warming, a group of Japanese and U.S. researchers found in a study published in January 2021.[143] However, the researchers

141 Public Safety Hazards. Retrieved 14 June 2021, from https://damsafety.org/public-safety-hazards

142 Climate Change, Extreme Precipitation and Flooding: The Latest Science. (2018). Retrieved 14 June 2021, from https://www.ucsusa.org/sites/default/files/attach/2018/07/gw-fact-sheet-epif.pdf

143 Boulange, J., Hanasaki, N., Yamazaki, D. *et al.* Role of Dams in Reducing Global Flood Exposure Under Climate Change. *Nat Commun* 12, 417 (2021). https://doi.org/10.1038/s41467-020-20704-0

noted that their work did not take into account the possible impact of dam failures during extreme weather events. They suggested that improvements to dams such as enhanced spillway mechanisms will likely be necessary, however, to maintain flood protection as climate change results in heavier water flows.

The higher the water pressure is on a dam, the more it will be susceptible to erosion and a possible blowout. Key problems that can develop include loss of clay soils in earthen dams, seepage and leaks along pipes, damage to spillways, as well as cracking earth movement, according to the U.S. Environmental Protection Agency.[144] If these issues aren't caught early by dam operators and repaired, the structure can quickly be overwhelmed by a swell of rushing water.

Engineers today tend to design dams with a greater focus on increasing forces associated with global warming, and some states such as California specifically require designers to take climate change into account for infrastructure projects.[145] That doesn't do much good, though, for the thousands of older dams across the country.

---

144 National Management Measures to Control Nonpoint Source Pollution from Hydromodification. (2007). Retrieved 14 June 2021, from https://www.epa.gov/sites/production/files/2015-09/documents/chapter_4_dams_web.pdf

145 Fountain, H. (2020). 'Expect More': Climate Change Raises Risk of Dam Failures (Published 2020). Retrieved 14 June 2021, from https://www.nytimes.com/2020/05/21/climate/dam-failure-michigan-climate-change.html

Disasters Waiting to Happen

Since 1848, the U.S. has seen nearly 1,700 instances of recorded dam failures, according to civil engineering researchers at Stanford University.[146] The pace of those catastrophes has picked up after 1980, following the mid-century boom in dam-building as the structures start to show signs of age. Of all U.S. states, Georgia has had the most dam failures, at 238. Other states with significant numbers of dam failures include Colorado with 88 at California with 85.

How many more are we in for as climate change worsens and weather patterns become more intense? It's really anyone's guess. Any of the roughly 1,600 "high hazard" dams tracked by the U.S. Army Corps of Engineers, which are also in poor condition, could be susceptible.

One of those is Reservoir No. 1 in Atlanta, which has had leaks and other issues over the last few decades. A catastrophic failure of the dam would swamp more than 1,000 homes, businesses, and parts of a railroad and a federal highway, according to local emergency management officials.[147]

Another problem dam identified by the *Associated Press* was the 107-year-old Willett Pond Dam in Norwood, a suburban town outside of Boston.[148] In drastic need of spillway improvements, the dam is equipped to handle only 13 percent of the current expected flow from a major rainstorm. Anything heavier, and water would rise over the top of the dam, or worse, the dam would burst.

---

146 Dam Failures in The U.S. (2018). Retrieved 14 June 2021, from https://npdp.stanford.edu/sites/default/files/reports/npdp_dam_failure_summary_compilation_v1_2018.pdf

147 At Least 1,680 Dams Across The U.S. Pose Potential Risk. (2019). Retrieved 14 June 2021, from https://nypost.com/2019/11/11/at-least-1680-dams-across-the-us-pose-potential-risk/

148 Mercado, S. (2019). Willett Pond Dam: One of 39 in MA In Poor Condition: Report. Retrieved 14 June 2021, from https://patch.com/massachusetts/norwood/willett-pond-dam-one-39-ma-poor-condition-report

If that happened, much of the town of 30,000 people, including homes, businesses, and schools, would be inundated with floodwaters. A nonprofit corporation that owns the dam has been unable to raise the estimated $1 million to $5 million it would take to properly fix the dam.

Inspections also may fall short in identifying potential dam failures. In 2013, a 92-year-old dam in Nebraska that had been rated in "fair" condition by safety officials failed after intense snow and rain, killing a man who lived nearby when water washed over his home.[149] In some states, such as Missouri and Texas, regulations allow thousands of smaller dams to go without inspection at all. Only about half of dams in Texas are regularly inspected by state officials, and only about 650 of more than 5,000 dams get the same treatment in Missouri, according to the *Associated Press.*

Meanwhile, in 2017, California got a chilling reminder of the precarious state of its dams. The nation's tallest dam, the 770-foot-tall Oroville Dam, suffered a crack and rapid erosion at its spillway during a major winter storm. The incident, north of Sacramento, prompted the evacuation of about 200,000 people in the surrounding area, and emergency maneuvers to stabilize the area, such as dropping sandbags onto the spillway area with helicopters.[150] Fixing the spillway necessitated $1 billion in repairs. State officials knew, however, that they had narrowly avoided catastrophe.

149 At Least 1,680 Dams Across The U.S. Pose Potential Risk. (2019). Retrieved 14 June 2021, from https://nypost.com/2019/11/11/at-least-1680-dams-across-the-us-pose-potential-risk/

150 Vartabedian, R. (2017). Clues to Oroville Dam Spillway Failure "Were All There in The Files," Top Investigator Says. Retrieved 14 June 2021, from https://www.latimes.com/local/california/la-me-ln-oroville-spillway-failure-20170905-story.html

The Future of Dams

After taking office in January 2021, the Biden administration has promised a $2 trillion infrastructure investment plan. Echoing the promises of Roosevelt in the 1930s, President Joe Biden has pledged to "launch a national effort aimed at creating the jobs we need to build a modern, sustainable infrastructure now and deliver an equitable clean energy future."[151] The ambitious to-do list includes roads, bridges, green spaces, electricity systems, water systems, and broadband, as well as upgrading public transit, weatherizing buildings, improving agriculture, and spurring home construction.

If the big spending bill can pass Congress, how much of the amount will go to dam improvements remains to be seen. Controversy remains heated over dam construction. Environmental advocates such as American Rivers have lobbied the Biden administration to prioritize dam removal, especially in areas where fish species such as salmon are threatened.[152] Dam removals are often just as complex, difficult, and expensive as dam construction or major repair efforts.

Some states, such as Michigan, have convened task forces to improve the safety of dams.[153] But experts generally agree that a more concerted national effort is likely required to dramatically enhance dam oversight. Globally, structurally unsound dams continue to pose increasing risks. In February 2021, researchers with the United Nations found that the world has seen a steep increase in dam failures since just the 2000s.[154] Prior to 2005, major

---

151 The Biden Plan to Build A Modern, Sustainable Infrastructure and An Equitable Clean Energy Future | Joe Biden for President: Official Campaign Website. (2020). Retrieved 27 May 2021, from https://joebiden.com/clean-energy/

152 Irving, W. (2020). What The Biden Victory Means for Our Rivers and Clean Water. Retrieved 14 June 2021, from https://www.americanrivers.org/2020/11/what-the-biden-victory-means-for-our-rivers-and-clean-water/

153 EGLE — Michigan Dam Safety Task Force. Retrieved 27 May 2021, from https://www.michigan.gov/egle/0,9429,7-135-3306_88771_102319---,00.html

154 Water Warning: The Looming Threat of The World's Aging Dams. Retrieved 27 May 2021, from https://e360.yale.edu/features/water-warning-the-looming-threat-of-the-worlds-aging-dams

dam failures averaged below four per year worldwide. But between 2015 and 2019, there were more than 170 dam blowouts.

Without immediate action and sufficient funds for repairs, the probability of death or destruction from crumbling dams will only continue to rise. "By 2050, most of humanity will live downstream of large dams built in the 20th century" that are "at increasing risk of failure," the researchers said.

CHAPTER 6:

Drinking Water | Our H20 Problem

"Clean water is not an expenditure of Federal funds; clean water is an investment in the future of our country."

—Bud Shuster[155]

On a Sunday in January, volunteers combed the *barrio*, handing out flyers and explaining that the water coming from the faucets was not safe to drink.[156] The lead content was dangerously elevated, and other disease-causing contaminants were also present. Boiling before use would not help. The water needed to be filtered, or better yet, the people could get bottled water from aid stations.

A pregnant woman, hearing the news, burst into tears. "¿Qué le hará esto a mi bebé?" (What will this do to my baby?) she demanded. She had been drinking the water and bathing in it, and she desperately wanted to know if the child she was carrying would be harmed. Children in the neighborhood were already suffering, as some parents complained their skin was distressed and their hair was falling out. What could they do?

If this scene had played out in Mexico or Central America, our hearts

155 Former Representative for Pennsylvania's 9th District

156 Hellerstein, E. (2016). The Forgotten Victims of The Flint Water Crisis. Retrieved 8 June 2021, from https://archive.thinkprogress.org/the-forgotten-victims-of-the-flint-water-crisis-c57395f2983e/

might be troubled, but we wouldn't be shocked. Failed-state corruption and third-world infrastructure are never kind to the poor. But this scene played out on the streets of a once-great American small town: Flint, Michigan.

Once the epitome of middle-class living in the United States, Flint had been a thriving borough of 200,000 at the end of the 1970s. Flint was a company town, and that company was General Motors. But when GM decided it needed to outsource to survive, Flint entered a death spiral, dwindling over the succeeding decades to 100,000 residents, 45 percent of whom lived in abject poverty. It was this poverty, and a far worse type of leadership, that led to catastrophe.

In 2011, Flint was strapped for cash and burdened with a $25 million deficit. Michigan Governor Rick Snyder appointed an emergency manager to help the city out of its financial crisis. In 2013, this manager made the tragic decision to "end the city's five-decade practice of piping treated water for its residents from Detroit in favor of a cheaper alternative."

The town would temporarily pump water from the Flint River, coursing through the center of town, "until a new water pipeline from Lake Huron was built." Thus, the Flint River, a conduit for treated and untreated industrial waste for more than a century, became the town's source of drinking water. The water was so highly corrosive that it leached lead from the aging pipes poisoning thousands of homes.

Toxic Water

The health effects of lead exposure can be devastating. The Centers for Disease Control and Prevention warn that the consequences of short-term lead exposure for adult workers can include abdominal pain, constipation, fatigue and weakness, headaches, irritability, loss of appetite, and memory loss, as well as pain or tingling in the hands and feet.[157] These symptoms may come on slowly and might be overlooked until the exposure has reached dangerously high levels, which can cause anemia, kidney damage, brain damage, and death.

But lead is especially dangerous for children, starting in the womb. The CDC notes that "lead can cross the placental barrier," so that pregnant women who are exposed can, in turn, expose their unborn children. "Lead exposure can cause miscarriage, stillbirths, and infertility (in both men and women)."

Lead is toxic at lower levels for young children than it is for adults. Children can suffer neurological damage, leading to lowered IQ, slowed growth and development, decreased attention span, learning and behavior problems, and hearing and speech problems.[158] Sadly, this harm is generally permanent.

Health concerns surrounding lead have been documented from antiquity forward. Lead plumbing, housewares, and even makeup have been blamed for the cruel insanity of several Roman emperors. In our time, crusades against lead-based paint began in the 1960s to protect children from toxicity. And perhaps the greatest step forward for universal health in the United States came with the phasing out of lead from gasoline.

A 1985 study by the U.S. Environmental Protection Agency "estimated that as many as 5,000 Americans died annually from lead-related heart disease prior to the country's lead phaseout."[159] Moreover, a 1988 report to Congress from the Agency for Toxic Substances and Disease Registry estimated that "the blood-lead levels of up to 2 million children were reduced

---

157 Health Problems Caused by Lead | NIOSH | CDC. (2018). Retrieved 8 June 2021, from https://www.cdc.gov/niosh/topics/lead/health.html

158 Health Effects of Lead Exposure | Lead | CDC. (2020). Retrieved 8 June 2021, from https://www.cdc.gov/nceh/lead/prevention/health-effects.htm

159 The Secret History of Lead. (2000). Retrieved 8 June 2021, from https://www.thenation.com/article/archive/secret-history-lead/

every year to below toxic levels between 1970 and 1987 as leaded gasoline use was reduced."

Prior to the phaseout of lead in gasoline, perhaps "68 million young children had toxic exposures." Since the mandate for unleaded gasoline in 1986, the average blood-lead content for people in this country has dropped 75 percent. Yet, the Flint officials who planned the fatal switch to Flint River water failed to anticipate the lead danger and failed to react when that danger was discovered.

Nor was lead the only problem. Introduction of Flight River water "coincided with an outbreak of Legionnaires' disease (a severe form of pneumonia) that killed 12 and sickened at least 87 people between June 2014 and October 2015." Additionally, testing of water in 2014 revealed fecal coliform, a bacterium known to cause diarrhea, nausea, vomiting, cramps, and other gastro-intestinal distress, and which in extreme cases can infect the lungs, kidneys, nervous system, liver, skin, and eyes.[160] Effects can be severe and even fatal. This contamination was likely due to "the city's failure to maintain sufficient chlorine [levels]. . . to disinfect the water."[161] Flint officials promptly overcorrected, adding so much chlorine that they raised "levels of total trihalomethanes (TTHM), cancer-causing chemicals that are by-products of the chlorination of water."

To err, as we all know, is human. To persist in the most egregious error, to deny that an error has been made, and to tell the victims of that error to be silent and obey, well, that requires bureaucracy. Soon after Flint River water started flowing into households in April 2014, "residents started complaining

160 Coliform Bacteria and E. Coli — Coliform Bacteria Health Risks. (2009). Retrieved 8 June 2021, from http://coliformbacteria.net/health-risks-coliform-bacteria.html

161 Denchak, M. (2018). Flint Water Crisis: Everything You Need to Know. Retrieved 8 June 2021, from https://www.nrdc.org/stories/flint-water-crisis-everything-you-need-know#sec-timeline

that the water from their taps looked, smelled, and tasted foul."[162] On October 13, 2014, the General Motors plant announced it would stop using the local water in production because it was too corrosive of engine parts. Still, "officials maintained that the water was safe."

The first crack in the government's façade came on January 2, 2015, when officials notified residents their water was in violation of the Safe Drinking Water Act, not from lead, but from excess levels of TTHM, a fact that officials had learned months before. Ten days later, Detroit offered to reconnect Flint to its system, even waiving the $4 million reconnection fee. But Flint leaders declined, citing costs that "would not be in the best interests of the city or its water users."

In March, the Flint City Council would think better of the offer, voting 7-1 in favor of reconnection. But Jerry Ambrose, the emergency manager, overruled the Council, calling the decision "incomprehensible" and asserting that "water from Detroit is not safer than water from Flint."

As for the lead, researchers at Virginia Tech pinpointed the problem in September 2015. Water samples from 252 homes revealed that "lead levels had spiked." Although no level of lead is safe, more than 40 percent measured above 5 parts per billion of lead, indicative of a "very serious" problem, and nearly 17 percent came in above 15 ppb, the level at which federal regulations mandate corrective action.

Flint pediatrician Mona Hanna-Attisha recorded elevated blood-lead levels in children citywide. In fact, levels had "nearly doubled since 2014—and nearly tripled in certain neighborhoods." Finally, on September 25, 2015, the city issued its first lead advisory. By then, because officials had refused to recognize the problem they had created, "nearly 9,000 children [had been] supplied lead-contaminated water for 18 months."

162 Hellerstein, E. (2016). The Forgotten Victims of The Flint Water Crisis. Retrieved 8 June 2021, from https://archive.thinkprogress.org/the-forgotten-victims-of-the-flint-water-crisis-c57395f2983e/

Eventually, the citizens of Flint sued their state in federal court to demand clean water. In 2016, a judge ordered "door-to-door delivery of bottled water to every home without a properly installed and maintained faucet filter." Months later, officials entered a settlement whereby the state would pay to replace thousands of lead pipes and implement other mitigation and remediation measures. Yet, court battles continue as residents fight to force officials to keep their commitments under the settlement.

The tragedy of Flint, Michigan is one that should never be repeated, especially not in the wealthiest country on Earth. But that's exactly what seems to be happening just 215 miles south in the city of Chicago, where two-thirds of homes tested in 2018 had lead present in the drinking water and one-third had more than the level legally permitted in bottled water.

The problem has to do with "approximately 400,000 lead service lines [that] bring water into about 80 percent of the city's homes."[163] Lead service lines were required under Chicago's building codes until 1986, "when they were banned by federal law." Though no new lead lines were installed, nothing was done to remediate the existing lines, which have aged over the decades and now present the "worst documented lead line problem in the nation." If the lead problem in Flint, a community of 100,000 was bad, imagine the magnitude of the health crisis for a population of 2.7 million in America's Second City.

Chicago officials were quick to explain that any lead found was below the "action level" established by the EPA of 15 parts per billion. Critics noted there is no safe level of lead in drinking water, and that EPA testing methods often miss high concentrations of lead that other methods detect.

163 Slowey, K. (2020). Disasters Waiting to Happen: 5 Major Infrastructure Projects in Need Of Repair. Retrieved 8 June 2021, from https://www.constructiondive.com/news/disasters-waiting-to-happen-5-major-infrastructure-projects-in-need-of-rep/

Lead Monitoring Failure

In May 2020, *APM Reports* released a scathing indictment of EPA lead monitoring, charging widespread failure to keep Americans safe.[164] Salient points of its exposé include:

- Since 2011 the EPA has known its testing methods were inadequate, and its own experts have proposed changes to the Lead and Copper Rule, that would have resulted in more rigorous testing.
- EPA turned a deaf ear to its own experts, instead forming an "ad hoc advisory board with heavy representation from water utilities," who would have borne the cost of the higher standards. Surprising no one, the board left testing methods "largely unchanged."
- Utilities in Chicago and the state of Michigan, applying "more rigorous testing methods in thousands of homes with lead service lines," found "lead levels two times higher on average than the results from EPA's standard procedure."

One issue that exposed the flaws with testing was how lead levels rose as more water was drawn from the tap. A home might test at 15 ppb for the first liter—right at the EPA action level—but by the seven and eighth liters, the level would be consistently over 25 ppb.[165] Of course, health experts also criticize the action level. Christopher Portier, the former director of environmental health at the CDC, told *ARM Reports* that the rule "makes no sense in terms of serious protection of public health." He explained, "A child

164 Rosenthal, L., & Craft, W. (2020). How The EPA Has Left Americans Exposed to Lead in Drinking Water. Retrieved 8 June 2021, from https://www.apmreports.org/story/2020/05/04/epa-lead-pipes-drinking-water

165 Rosenthal, L., & Craft, W. (2020). How The EPA Has Left Americans Exposed to Lead in Drinking Water. Retrieved 8 June 2021, from https://www.apmreports.org/story/2020/05/04/epa-lead-pipes-drinking-water

drinking 15 parts per billion of lead… on a regular basis was going to exceed our [CDC lead limit] of 5 micrograms per deciliter in the blood."

Portier favors lowering the action level to at least 7.5 parts per billion. Yet, he's hardly radical in his view. "The American Academy of Pediatrics goes further, recommending a cap of 1 part per billion for water that kids drink in schools." *APM's* recitation of pertinent facts leads to the damning conclusion that if the EPA had taken seriously its mission to protect the public, it would have adopted standards that are more closely linked to human health, along with accurate testing designed to detect threats. Instead, the agency's complacency has allowed a crisis to go unchecked.

In September 2020, Mayor Lori Lightfoot announced plans to remove roughly 400,000 lead service lines, at an estimated cost of $8.5 billion.[166] Details are still to be worked out, and only about 750 lines are to be removed in the first year, 2021. Chicago City Council floor leader Gilbert Villegas, described as "a staunch Lightfoot ally," was nevertheless critical, tweeting that "the project should be done by 2553." Where Chicago, facing a projected deficit of $2 billion through 2021, will get the money to finance removal has not been determined.

Dangerous Pipes Across The Nation

Numerous other cities throughout the country are also wrestling with the lead issue. Headlines of the last few years have come from:

- Milwaukee, Wisconsin — The city has more than 70,000 lead service

166 Eng, M. (2020). Here's Mayor Lori Lightfoot's Plan to Remove Chicago's Lead Pipes. Retrieved 8 June 2021, from https://www.wbez.org/stories/chicagos-mayor-launches-lead-pipe-replacement-plan/579ec191-1862-4933-b123-72468f164fd7

lines and an estimated 176,000 lead pipes providing drinking water to homes and businesses. *Wisconsin Watch* accused the Governor's remediation plan of being no more than a band-aid.[167]

- Pittsburgh, Pennsylvania — The *Pittsburgh Post-Gazette* reported in January 2017 that drinking water tested high in lead for some residents utilizing the Pittsburgh Water and Sewer Authority, due to lead service lines in need of replacement.[168]
- Baltimore, Maryland — *The Baltimore Sun* reported in April 2016 that nearly 4 percent of water samples collected in 2015 contained elevated lead levels, though only two of 52 samples were above the EPA action level.[169]
- Boston, Massachusetts — *The Boston Globe* reported in 2016 that tests at roughly 300 public school buildings revealed that more than half of the buildings had at least one sample with lead levels above regulatory limits.[170]
- Trenton, New Jersey — In January 2017, the *Associated Press* reported that 21 school districts in the Garden State have elevated levels of lead in drinking water.[171]

There is no reason why drinking water in the United States cannot be clean and plentiful. Yet, in virtually every jurisdiction, water infrastructure

167 Wisconsin Must Do More to Protect Residents from Lead in Drinking Water, DNR And Milwaukee Leaders Agree | WisconsinWatch.org. (2016). Retrieved 8 June 2021, from https://wisconsinwatch.org/2016/09/wisconsin-must-do-more-to-protect-residents-from-lead-in-drinking-water-dnr-and-milwaukee-leaders-agree/

168 Pittsburgh Water and Sewer Authority Tests Find Lead Again. (2017). Retrieved 8 June 2021, from https://www.post-gazette.com/local/city/2017/01/20/Water-tests-find-lead-again/stories/201701200101

169 Dance, S. (2016). Four Percent of City Water Samples Contain Elevated Lead Levels. Retrieved 8 June 2021, from https://www.baltimoresun.com/maryland/baltimore-city/bs-md-ci-water-quality-report-20160418-story.html

170 Andersen, T. (2016). High Lead Levels Found More Than 160 School Buildings in Mass. Retrieved 8 June 2021, from https://www.bostonglobe.com/metro/2016/11/15/high-lead-levels-found-more-than-school-buildings-mass/XOOX7JS309896EtX7JhAZO/story.html

171 Elevated Lead Detected in Drinking Water in 21 New Jersey School Districts. (2017). Retrieved 8 June 2021, from https://abc7ny.com/education/elevated-lead-detected-in-drinking-water-in-21-nj-school-districts/1723498/

problems are made worse by faulty planning, complacency, and the arrogance of unaccountable officials. These problems must be addressed while the cost, steep as it is, is still relatively manageable.

D Is for Drinking

In 2017, the American Society of Civil Engineers issued its Infrastructure Report Card[172] for the nation's drinking water system, awarding a great, round D. The root problem was age, since the "one million miles of pipes" providing delivery had been "laid in the early to mid-20th century with a lifespan of 75 to 100 years." Thus, although "The quality of drinking water in the United States remains high," the declining condition of the system results in "an estimated 240,000 water main breaks per year in the United States, wasting over two trillion gallons of treated drinking water." Moreover, leaking pipes cause the loss of "nearly six billion gallons of treated drinking water" every day. ASCE estimates that poor pipes waste 14 to 18 percent of each day's treated water, an amount that "could support 15 million households."

In its summary of the conditions and capacity of the U.S. drinking water system, ASCE notes that the U.S. population "uses 42 billion gallons of water a day" at home and in industry. The sources for roughly 80 percent of our drinking water lies on the surface, in "rivers, lakes, reservoirs, and oceans," and we get "the remaining 20 percent from groundwater aquifers." Across the country, "there are approximately 155,000 active public drinking water systems." Yet, usage is not evenly distributed, since "just under 300 million people "receive their drinking water from one of the nation's 51,356 community water systems," and 92 percent of the total U.S. population

172 ASCE's 2021 Infrastructure Report Card | Drinking Water. (2021). Retrieved 8 June 2021, from https://www.infrastructurereportcard.org/cat-item/drinking_water/

receives water from just 17 percent of the systems.

This means large systems are overburdened, while small systems, serving the remaining 8 percent of the population, "frequently lack both economies of scale and financial, managerial, and technical capacity, which can lead to problems of meeting Safe Drinking Water Act standards."

Rehabilitation of the nation's drinking water system will take significant investment. The American Water Works Association puts the price tag at about "$1 trillion. . . over the next 25 years." Where might that money come from? At present, most funding "comes from revenue generated by rate payers."

Charges for water usage vary greatly from city to city: "the lowest average monthly water bill is $14.74 in Memphis, while Seattle residents pay the most at $61.43."

The higher rates might more accurately reflect "the true cost of service" and can easily be justified on the principle that the user should be responsible. But charging the true cost could be ruinous to poorer communities. This makes a direct charge for service approach impracticable without significant public assistance.

ASCE also notes that as the need for rehabilitation has grown, spending on water infrastructure has gone down. "Between 2009 and 2014," the period known as the Great Recession, "state and local governments decreased capital spending for both drinking water and wastewater by 22 percent." The federal government did not pick up the slack.

Federal government participation has mostly been "in the form of loans through the Drinking Water State Revolving Fund, which provides low-interest loans to state and local water infrastructure projects."[173] The

173 What is WIFIA?. Retrieved 8 June 2021, from https://www.epa.gov/wifia/what-wifia

Environmental Protection Agency "provides an allotment of funding for each state," which ponies up a matching 20 percent. The program has allocated "$32.5 billion of low-interest loans," and Congress has come through with additional sources of funding.

In 2014, Congress passed the Water Infrastructure Finance and Innovation Act, creating "a federal credit program administered by EPA for eligible water and wastewater infrastructure projects." WIFIA's low interest, long-term loans are meant to stimulate lending for water projects, and proponents estimate "a single dollar injected into the program can create $50 dollars for project lending."[174]

To qualify, projects serving large communities must cost at least $20 million, while projects serving populations of 25,000 or less could only cost $5 million. WIFIA loans can be used to fund up to 49 percent of the total costs, and total federal assistance for the project cannot exceed 80 percent. Borrowers are allowed 35 years from the date of substantial completion to repay the loan. Projects must be deemed creditworthy, meaning they are expected to generate revenue.

Water Infrastructure Funding

The EPA estimates that its "current budget authority may provide more than $1 billion in credit assistance and may finance over $2 billion in water infrastructure investment."[175] That certainly sounds like a lot of money, but compared to the estimated need, it's a mere drop in the bucket.

A major factor in planning is the future need for water resources. On this

174 Spring Coming, Increased Need for Infrastructure Funding. (2016). Retrieved 8 June 2021, from https://www.infrastructurereportcard.org/drinking-water/funding/

175 Spring Coming, Increased Need for Infrastructure Funding . (2016). Retrieved 8 June 2021, from https://www.infrastructurereportcard.org/drinking-water/funding/

front, we get some good news, as "municipal drinking water consumption in the United States has declined by 5 percent this decade." Withdrawals of freshwater from various sources declined across "almost every sector including agriculture, industrial, domestic, and thermoelectric."[176] ASCE attributes this reduction to "increased efficiencies," as well as the retirement of "coal-fired power plants."

The fact that drinking water consumption from the public supply "has been relatively flat since 1985 even as the population has increased by approximately 70 million people" speaks to the success of water conservation efforts. But while demand has lessened, population trends could nevertheless place an additional burden on large municipalities attempting to rehabilitate their systems. ASCE notes that "the Government Accountability Office estimates a significant number of midsized cities are shrinking."

Utility managers, therefore, have "fewer rate payers and a declining tax base," situations that "make it difficult to raise funds for capital infrastructure plans." If utilities respond by raising rates on the residents who've stayed behind, they risk "putting a burden on those who can least afford rate increases." On the other hand, in those areas to which more Americans are moving, "water managers must respond to increased overall demand."[177]

ASCE Recommendations

So, how can struggling states and municipalities improve water infrastructure, and in turn, raise that dreadful D grade for the entire country? ASCE has several suggestions, many of which rely on increased federal funding. For

176 ASCE's 2021 Infrastructure Report Card | Drinking Water. (2021). Retrieved 8 June 2021, from https://www.infrastructurereportcard.org/cat-item/drinking_water/

177 Schweighofer, J. (2013). The Impact of Extreme Weather and Climate Change on Inland Waterway Transport. *Natural Hazards*, *72*(1), 23-40. doi: 10.1007/s11069-012-0541-6

example, ASCE would like Congress to triple its appropriations to the Drinking Water State Revolving Loan Fund, a program of the EPA made possible under the Safe Drinking Water Act of 1996.

Under DWSRF, "EPA awards capitalization grants to each state. . . based upon the results of the most recent Drinking Water Infrastructure Needs Survey and Assessment," for which "the state provides a 20 percent match."[178] The capitalization grant enables loans to water systems for infrastructure projects. "As water systems repay their loans, the repayments and interest flow back into the dedicated revolving fund. These funds may be used to make additional loans." Thus, infrastructure funding is recycled like the water itself.

ASCE would also like Congress to provide funding for the WIFIA at the level authorized by the statute. In the past, there has been a disconnect between authorization and allocation. Since low-cost capital is essential for infrastructure development, especially for economically strapped jurisdictions, ASCE wants to assure the tax-exempt status of municipal bond financing.

The federal government should also set up a "Water Infrastructure Trust Fund to finance the national shortfall in funding of infrastructure systems under the Clean Water Act." Finally, ACSE calls for increased funding for green infrastructure, watershed permitting, and the promotion of the "one water" concept that treats the water cycle holistically rather than separating issues surrounding the water supply, wastewater, and stormwater systems.

On the state level, ASCE suggests the elimination of the caps on private activity bonds for water infrastructure projects. These, ASCE believes, would "bring an estimated $6 to $7 billion annually in new private financing."

178 How the Drinking Water State Revolving Fund Works. Retrieved 8 June 2021, from https://www.epa.gov/dwsrf/how-drinking-water-state-revolving-fund-works

States can also put forth legislation, policies, and ballot measures that fund initiatives to "protect source water." ASCE also hints at a coming crisis in competence as "engineers, operators, and maintenance staff begin to retire in large numbers." They urge greater commitment from the federal to the local level to promote "vocational training in the drinking water sector."

ASCE also has an action plan for utilities:

- Take regional approaches for water delivery to benefit from economies of scale.
- Conduct revenue forecasting to set rates at the true cost of supplying safe drinking water.
- Undertake asset management programs.
- Ensure that science-based decisions control operations and facility functions.

As water is the source of life, it's no exaggeration to say that the future of the country depends on safe, abundant drinking water. With prudent planning and a proper dedication of resources, we can address this critical issue.

CHAPTER 7:

Energy | Empowering the Energy System

"In the twenty-first century United States, an aging transmission infrastructure supports complex power transactions among every possible type of generating facility, from a hydroelectric plant more than one hundred years old, to a nuclear plant licensed in the 1960s, to the newest solar panels atop a residence. . . Without having to know what electricity is, where it is generated, or how it gets from the power plant to the switch, Americans rely utterly on the everyday miracle of electrification."[179]

—Julie A. Cohn

The Climes, They are A-Changin'

In February of 2021, harsh winter weather descended over the United States, plunging normally balmy areas of the South into a deep freeze. According to a report on *CNN.com*, on Monday, February 15, "More than a third of the continental US record[ed] below-zero temperatures. Snow, icy roads and power outages [began] to paralyze cities across the country, sparking emergency declarations in several states."[180]

Among the hardest-hit states was Texas, where major cities experienced their lowest temperatures in 30 years: Dallas, Austin, and San Antonio all

179 Cohn, J. (2018). *The Grid: Biography of An American Technology*. The MIT Press.

180 Maxouris, C. (2021). Here's How A Week of Frigid Weather and Catastrophe Unfolded in Texas. Retrieved 27 May 2021, from https://www.cnn.com/2021/02/21/weather/texas-winter-storm-timeline/index.html

stood at single digits. On the first morning of the cold snap, Texas residents began to experience rolling blackouts as the Electric Reliability Council of Texas (ERCOT), which operates a grid controlling about 90 percent of the state's electricity, struggled to meet "record-breaking electric demand." That demand soon crushed the grid, leaving roughly 4.3 million residents without any power.

The collapse of the grid was fatal for at least 26 Texas residents between February 11 and February 21, including many who died of carbon monoxide poisoning as they attempted to run their cars for heat. Home fires increased 187 percent as residents burned wood and a variety of other materials to keep warm.[181] Across the nation, 69 people reportedly died from weather-related injuries. Water for Texas residents ran out as frozen pipes ruptured, disabling 159 of the 254 public water systems in the state. The state capital, Austin, "lost 325 million gallons due to burst pipes."[182]

At the height of the crisis, the Texas Department of Emergency Management distributed as many as three million bottles of water in a single day. The risk-modeling firm Karen Clark & Company offered an early estimate of total property damage at $18 billion.

But how could Texas, the Energy State renowned for its vast oil and gas production, have lost its capacity to generate and deliver electricity? According to the *Associated Press,* Texas "has a generating capacity of about 67,000 megawatts in the winter compared with a peak capacity of about 86,000 megawatts in the summer."[183] The difference reflects the seasonal drop

---

181 69 deaths, 44 Hours of Freezing, $18 Billion in Damage: This Week's Winter Storm, by The Numbers. (2021). Retrieved 27 May 2021, from https://abc13.com/2021-texas-winter-storm-weather-how-many-people-lost-power-boil-water-advisory/10356914/

182 Maxouris, C. (2021). Here's How A Week of Frigid Weather and Catastrophe Unfolded in Texas. Retrieved 27 May 2021, from https://www.cnn.com/2021/02/21/weather/texas-winter-storm-timeline/index.html

183 EXPLAINER: Why The Power Grid Failed in Texas and Beyond. (2021). Retrieved 27 May 2021, from https://apnews.com/article/why-texas-power-grid-failed-2eaa659d2ac29ff87eb9220875f23b34

in usage, which generally allows power plants to go offline for maintenance. However, ERCOT et al. apparently had no contingencies in place for an emergency that would cause a spike in usage during the winter months.

As the arctic blast swept across the Lone Star State, natural gas supply lines froze, and ice paralyzed wind turbines. By day three of the crisis, "46,000 megawatts of power were offline statewide—28,000 from natural gas, coal, and nuclear plants and 18,000 from wind and solar."

ERCOT would like customers to believe the brutal weather event was unforeseeable and therefore unpreventable, to which Ed Hirs, an energy fellow at the University of Houston, answers, "That's nonsense." Mr. Hirs told the *AP* that "Every eight to 10 years we have really bad winters. This is not a surprise."

Yet, nothing had been done to prepare for the inevitable. Daniel Cohan, an associate professor of civil and environmental engineering at Rice University in Houston tweeted that "Every one of [our sources of power supply] is vulnerable to extreme weather and climate events in different ways. None of them were adequately weatherized or prepared for a full realm of weather and conditions."[184]

Weatherizing power sources is common practice in northern climes where prolonged deep freezes are not rare. Minnesota is not immune to rolling blackouts in ultra-severe weather, but for the most part, the North Star State manages to keep the juice flowing.

Another issue facing Texas is that for energy distribution purposes, the state is an island that lacks interregional connections to power systems that could have provided energy during this emergency. Unfortunately, no one foresaw the need to reach beyond state lines for assistance. With adequate

184 Tweet by Daniel Cohan, @cohan_ds, February 2021. Retrieved 27 May 2021, from https://twitter.com/cohan_ds/status/1362055810746970118

planning, the Texas debacle was preventable, but those in charge chose to allocate resources elsewhere, creating a classic example of the old adage that failing to plan is planning to fail.

Out of the Ice and Into The Fire

News of rolling blackouts across Texas conjured up images of California, which has been plagued with power shortages since 2017. Starting that year and continuing into 2018, Pacific Electric & Gas, the state's largest utility, was implicated in a series of "devastating wildfires," culminating in "the Camp Fire—the deadliest and most destructive fire in California history."

As reported by *CNBC.com*, "The Camp Fire destroyed most of the town of Paradise, California, resulting in 85 civilian fatalities and the destruction of more than 18,800 structures."[185] The cause of the Camp Fire was traced to "a malfunction of equipment on a Pacific Gas & Electric Company transmission line." A "flood of lawsuits" forced PG&E into bankruptcy in January 2019.

PG&E then began to use rolling blackouts as a means of fire prevention, a strategy necessitated by errant planning, according to Michael Shellenberger, energy contributor for *Forbes.com*. Mr. Shellenberger, reporting on a California grid failure in August 2020, blamed "The utility and California's leaders" who "had over the previous decade diverted billions meant for grid maintenance to renewables."[186]

When a severe heatwave hit the state, "Millions of Californians were denied electrical power and thus air conditioning during a heatwave, raising

185 Daniels, J. (2019). Officials: Camp Fire, Deadliest in California History, Was Caused by PG&E Electrical Transmission Lines. Retrieved 27 May 2021, from https://www.cnbc.com/2019/05/15/officials-camp-fire-deadliest-in-california-history-was-caused-by-pge-electrical-transmission-lines.html

186 Shellenberger, M. (2020). Why California's Climate Policies Are Causing Electricity Blackouts. Retrieved 27 May 2021, from https://www.forbes.com/sites/michaelshellenberger/2020/08/15/why-californias-climate-policies-are-causing-electricity-black-outs/?sh=79d7a9951591

the risk of heatstroke and death, particularly among the elderly and sick." Shellenberger noted that Governor Newsom's COVID-19 restrictions had exacerbated the situation, since "The blackouts [came] at a time when people, particularly the elderly, [were] forced to remain indoors. . . " The bottom line for Shellenberger was that "California had to impose rolling blackouts because it had failed to maintain sufficient reliable power from natural gas and nuclear plants, or pay in advance for enough guaranteed electricity imports from other states."[187]

When the California Energy Commission, Independent System Operator and Public Utilities Commission issued a report in October 2020, it split the blame between leadership and the weather. *The Los Angeles Times* reported that the problem stemmed from "climate-driven extreme heat," along with inadequate planning as the state phases out fossil fuels.[188] The August "heat storm" had delivered "four of its five hottest August days in the last 35 years." Electricity demand had spiked, prompting rolling blackouts, but with little interruption in service.

"Just under half a million homes and businesses lost power for as little as 15 minutes and as long as 2½ hours on Aug. 14, with another 321,000 utility customers going dark for anywhere from eight to 90 minutes the following evening." But even *The LA Times* could not completely exonerate state agencies which had "failed to adequately plan for that type of heat event despite knowing how quickly the world is heating up." (NASA places the rate of global warming at roughly 0.15-0.20°C per decade.)[189]

---

187 Shellenberger, M. (2020). Why California's Climate Policies Are Causing Electricity Blackouts — OpEd. Retrieved 27 May 2021, from https://www.eurasiareview.com/16082020-why-californias-climate-policies-are-causing-electricity-blackouts-oped/

188 What Caused California's Rolling Blackouts? Climate Change and Poor Planning. (2020). Retrieved 27 May 2021, from https://www.latimes.com/environment/story/2020-10-06/california-rolling-blackouts-climate-change-poor-planning

189 World of Change: Global Temperatures. (2020). Retrieved 27 May 2021, from https://earthobservatory.nasa.gov/world-of-change/decadaltemp.php

As their progressive energy policies came under fire, California officials vigorously defended their commitment to renewable sources. As *The LA Times* reported, "Officials have consistently said that intermittent power sources such as solar panels and wind turbines didn't cause the rolling blackouts. But gas-burning power plants that can fire up when the sun isn't shining or the wind isn't blowing have been shutting down in recent years, and California has largely failed to replace them with cleaner alternatives such as lithium-ion batteries."

Nevertheless, California remains resolute. The state will continue to phase out fossil fuels with the goal of "60 percent renewable energy by 2030 and 100 percent climate-friendly energy by 2045, as required by state law."[190]

California is betting heavily on the future, which is laudable, but is no excuse to neglect the present. In its zeal to avert apocalyptic climate catastrophe, California has allowed real and present destruction. Assessing the damage in October 2020, *The New York Times* provided this estimate: "in three of the past four years, including this one, fires are on track to cause damages in excess of $10 billion."[191] As California struggles to keep its lights on, the state comes off as a parent who won't buy his sick child's medicine, because the money has to go into the college fund. As other states struggle to manage reliability while transitioning to renewable energy sources, California serves as a cautionary tale.

There is, however, good news out of California, where one Indian tribe has shown it's possible to go green and enhance the reliability of service. The Blue Lake Rancheria Tribe in Northern California, a federally recognized tribal government, implemented a strategic climate action plan in 2008.

---

190 Here's How Local Governments Are Replacing State's Biggest Utilities. (2019). Retrieved 27 May 2021, from https://www.techwire.net/news/heres-how-local-governments-are-replacing-states-biggest-utilities.html

191 How Much Will the Wildfires Cost?. (2020). Retrieved 27 May 2021, from https://www.nytimes.com/2020/09/16/us/california-fires-cost.html

In 2014, President Barack Obama praised the tribe as "a regional leader in strategically planning and implementing both climate resiliency and greenhouse gas reduction measures."[192] Noting how the tribe had "reduced energy consumption by 35 percent and. . . committed to reduce greenhouse gas emissions 40 percent by 2018," Mr. Obama recognized the tribe as one of 16 "Climate Action Champions" in the United States.

Among its many initiatives, the Tribe had launched its own low-carbon, community microgrid project in 2015. Thus, when wildfires were ravaging neighboring areas, Blue Lake Rancheria never lost power and, in fact, was able to export power to outside communities.

The California and Texas stories illustrate an undeniable fact about energy production and transmission: the infrastructure that supports these processes is vulnerable to extreme weather. It is also certain, even if one does not embrace the various tenets of man-made climate change, that severe weather events will continue to occur. Therefore, energy planning must include weatherizing infrastructure to survive severe conditions.

The Current State of America's Power Grid

When we refer to the electric power grid, we are talking about the entire system of production and transmission up to the point of delivery to the consumer. Major sources of energy production, according to the U.S. Energy Information Administration 2019, include:

- Natural gas — 38.4 percent
- Coal — 23.5 percent

192 FACT SHEET: 16 U.S. Communities Recognized as Climate Action Champions for Leadership on Climate Change. (2014). Retrieved 27 May 2021, from https://obamawhitehouse.archives.gov/the-press-office/2014/12/03/fact-sheet-16-us-communities-recognized-climate-action-champions-leaders

- Nuclear — 19.7 percent
- Renewables — 17.5 percent (hydroelectricity, wind power, solar power, geothermal, biofuel, and other biomass energy sources)
- Petroleum — 0.5 percent

According to the American Society of Civil Engineers, the transmission and delivery system (T&D) consists of "600,000 miles of backbone transmission lines (240,000 miles of which are considered high-voltage lines or ≥ 230 Kilovolts), and around 5.5 million miles of local distribution lines."[193]

Unfortunately, "the majority of the nation's grid is aging, with some components over a century old—far past their 50-year life expectancy—and others, including 70 percent of T&D lines, are well into the second half of their lifespans." As much as 92 percent of interruptions to electric service occur in the T&D system, due to "aging infrastructure, severe weather events, and vandalism."

The age of the system is one reason ASCE gave American energy infrastructure a grade of C- in the 2021 Infrastructure Report Card. Although the grade is low, ASCE notes that increased investment in energy infrastructure resulted in performance improvements which raised the grade from the disappointing D+ of 2017.

For example, "Annual spending on high voltage transmission lines grew from $15.6 billion in 2012 to $21.9 billion in 2017, while annual spending on distribution systems—the 'last mile' of the electricity network—grew 54 percent over the past two decades." Investment in renewables spurred production from that sector. ASCE points out that "For the first time, renewables. . . accounted for the largest portion of new generating capacity

193 ASCE's 2021 Infrastructure Report Card | Energy. Retrieved 27 May 2021, from https://infrastructurereportcard.org/cat-item/energy/

in 2020. Renewables' share of the generating capacity is on track to increase significantly between now and 2023."

ASCE breaks down areas of concern as follows:

- **Oil and gas** — These traditional fossil-fuel sectors "supply 65 percent of the energy we use" and will continue to be vitally important in the conceivable future. Yet, the nation's pipeline system, comprised of "190,000 miles of oil pipelines and 2.4 million miles of gas pipelines," is showing its age, "as witnessed by increasing failures and leakage events." The system requires "improved inspection techniques, preservation technologies, and sound decision-making for upgrades and replacements."

  ASCE notes that "critical infrastructure bottlenecks also exist, including the gas delivery constraints to New England and New York and challenges with urban infrastructure upgrades." Residents of New York City have been shaken, literally, in recent years by gas explosions that destroyed residential buildings. The latest event occurred on February 28, 2021, when according to *The New York Times*, "A manhole fire and explosion in Manhattan early on Sunday morning damaged cars and storefronts, caused power failures and injured at least three people."[194] That explosion came on the heels of a February 18, 2021 blast "that rocked a three-story Bronx apartment building. . . injuring six adults and three young children—including a critically injured 3-year-old."[195]

  These are eerie reminders that after a gas explosion destroyed an

194 3 Injured in Manhole Fire and Explosion in Manhattan. (2021). Retrieved 27 May 2021, from https://www.nytimes.com/2021/02/28/nyregion/new-york-city-manhole-fires.html

195 Gas Explosion Rocks NYC Building. (2021). Retrieved 27 May 2021, from https://nypost.com/2021/02/18/gas-explosion-rocks-nyc-building/

East Village restaurant in March 2015, Governor Cuomo called such incidents a "disturbing trend." Subsequent investigation determined that aging natural gas pipelines owned and managed by Consolidated Edison, many of which were more than 100 years old, were among the most dangerous in the nation.

- **Funding future needs** — There are two major priorities guiding energy policy: meeting increasing demand and transitioning to cleaner sources of fuel. Both of these goals require increased investment, but ASCE warns there is a significant "investment gap."

  While money has been dedicated to renewable production, funds have been lacking for "upgrades and replacements of aging transmission infrastructure, system hardening, and resilience measures that minimize impacts from catastrophic events, improvements to comply with evolving transmission reliability and security compliance standards, and expansion of the transmission system to integrate renewables and natural gas have contributed to the increase in transmission spending."

  A more balanced approach is necessary since it's useless to generate electricity you cannot deliver. ASCE also takes issue with the Biden administration's cancelation of the Keystone XL pipeline. The "precedent of rescinding already granted permits," ASCE argues, "could harm future investment in all energy infrastructure."

  An area of need that is expected to grow exponentially is the charging of electric vehicles. EV sales in the United States have lagged behind other regions, such as the European Union and China, largely because of abundant and relatively inexpensive gasoline here and the lack of charging infrastructure.

  In January, President Biden issued an executive order expressing the administration's goal of replacing federal government vehicles with EVs built in America. This would give a sizeable jolt to the EV industry, given that "As of 2019, the U.S. government had 645,000 vehicles that were driven 4.5 billion miles and consumed 375 million gallons of gasoline and diesel fuel, according to the General Services Administration (GSA). About 35 percent of those vehicles were operated by the U.S. Postal Service, according to GSA."[196]

However, that many additional EVs on the road would require a significant increase in electric capacity as well as transmission and distribution infrastructure in the form of strategically placed charging stations.

- **Resilience and innovation** — Power outages are costly. The U.S. Department of Energy estimates the cost to the U.S. economy at anywhere from $28 billion to $169 billion annually. Fortunately, utilities are not simply "repairing the grid after a major disaster." Rather, "more utilities are taking proactive steps. . . strengthening the grid through resilience measures."

  ASCE points to examples of how utilities learned from Hurricane Harvey, when "wind and catastrophic flooding knocked down or damaged more than 6,200 distribution poles." Moreover, since Superstorm Sandy caused catastrophic outages across New York and New Jersey, "electric companies have invested more than $285 billion in T&D. . . partially to harden the energy grid and make it more resilient to future storms."
- Public safety — In addition to economic damage, power outages present a serious threat to public health and safety. Impacted areas include communications, transportation, drinking water

196 Michael, W. (2021). Biden Plans to Replace Government Fleet with Electric Vehicles. Retrieved 27 May 2021, from https://www.cnbc.com/2021/01/25/biden-plans-to-replace-government-fleet-with-electric-vehicles.html

and wastewater, and the sales of essential goods, such as groceries. Residents who rely on electricity for medical devices are endangered, and hospitals and emergency medical services may be impaired. Loss of power means food spoilage, as well as the inability to prepare hot meals. It's no exaggeration to say that without electricity, the nation quickly devolves back to the Stone Age.

In addition, grid vulnerability is a serious national security issue. An enemy who could cripple the grid could bring the most powerful nation on Earth to its knees.

Electromagnetic Pulse: The Existential Nightmare for America's Power Grid

An electromagnetic pulse is a burst of energy that creates a disturbance potentially damaging to electronic infrastructure. During the Cold War, the United States and the Soviet Union discovered that nuclear bomb tests created waves of electromagnetic energy that could cause wide-scale destruction.

For decades, the threat of an EMP attack loomed as part of the "mutually assured destruction" guaranteed in a nuclear exchange between the two superpowers. Today, the most feared EMP scenario involves a rocket attack from a rogue state or terrorist organization. It has been hypothesized that a single missile launched from a barge off the coast of the United States could explode a nuclear device above a major American city causing cascading destruction to most of our electric grid.

In a 2020 article entitled, *EMP Ignorance Is Bliss*, Dr. Peter Vincent Pry describes a scenario reminiscent of the *Mad Max* films: "High-altitude electromagnetic pulse (HEMP) is generated by a nuclear weapon detonated exo-atmospherically, at an altitude of 30-400 kilometers. No blast or fire or radioactive fallout from a nuclear explosion in the vacuum of outer space reaches the surface of the Earth, only the HEMP. A single nuclear weapon can generate a HEMP field covering much of North America that would blackout electric grids and other life-sustaining critical infrastructures, paralyze unprotected military forces, and blind radar and satellite National Technical Means needed to identify the attacker."[197]

This July 2017 assessment from the Congressional EMP Commission is positively chilling: "A long-term outage owing to EMP could disable most critical supply chains, leaving the U.S. population living in conditions similar to centuries past, prior to the advent of electric power. In the 1800s, the U.S. population was less than 60 million, and those people had many skills and assets necessary for survival without today's infrastructure. An extended blackout today could result in the death of a large fraction of the American people through the effects of societal collapse, disease, and starvation."

For decades, national security experts have urged hardening the grid against an EMP attack, but little has been done. According to The Secure the Grid Coalition, an *ad hoc* group of policy, energy, and national security experts, legislators, and industry insiders under the aegis of The Center for Security Policy, inaction by Congress is inexcusable.[198]

The Congressional EMP Commission met from 2001-2008 to develop "a plan to protect all infrastructures from EMP—a plan that would also mitigate threats from cyber-attack, sabotage, and natural disasters that could be implemented in 3-5 years at a cost of $10-20 billion." In 2008, the cost "to harden the grid's critical nodes (i.e., roughly 2,000 large and medium-sized transformers and their associated SCADA systems, etc.)" was estimated at $2 billion. That sum was "modest when compared with the unimaginably high

---

197 Pry, P. (2021). EMP ignorance is bliss | Secure the Grid. Retrieved 27 May 2021, from https://securethegrid.com/2020/08/05/emp-ignorance-is-bliss/

198 EMP: Technology's Worst Nightmare | Secure the Grid. (2014). Retrieved 27 May 2021, from https://securethegrid.com/emp-technologys-worst-nightmare/

costs associated with trying to remediate after an EMP event," yet Congress took no action on its own Commission's plan.

The EMP Commission was revived in Congress between 2017 and 2018. On March 26, 2019, President Trump issued an Executive Order on Coordinating National Resilience to Electromagnetic Pulses, stating, "An electromagnetic pulse (EMP) has the potential to disrupt, degrade, and damage technology and critical infrastructure systems. Human-made or naturally occurring EMPs can affect large geographic areas, disrupting elements critical to the Nation's security and economic prosperity, and could adversely affect global commerce and stability. The Federal Government must foster sustainable, efficient, and cost-effective approaches to improving the Nation's resilience to the effects of EMPs."[199]

Yet, according to the Electric Power Research Institute, the problem is currently "manageable." In May 2019, EPRI released a study finding that "relatively simple mitigation measures ... could help utilities manage the threat."[200] Entitled *High-Altitude Electromagnetic Pulse and the Bulk Power System—Potential Impacts and Mitigation Strategies*, the study relied on "mathematical modeling and lab testing to examine the impact of an EMP on the transmission system and 'economic' mitigation measures."

Claiming to have produced "the most extensive study ever on EMP," which contains "a treasure trove of good technical insights," Mike Howard, EPRI's president and CEO, hoped to "parse the facts from 'science fiction' advanced by some doomsday theorists." Although facts are always welcome in scientific inquiries, one must wonder whether Mr. Howard would have

---

199 Executive Order 13865—Coordinating National Resilience to Electromagnetic Pulses. (2019). Retrieved 27 May 2021, from https://www.govinfo.gov/content/pkg/DCPD-201900176/html/DCPD-201900176.htm

200 Bhambhani, D. (2019). EMP Study: Threat to U.S. Grid Is Manageable, Electric Sector Says It Would Be Ready. Retrieved 27 May 2021, from https://www.forbes.com/sites/dipkabhambhani/2019/05/03/emp-study-threat-to-u-s-grid-is-manageable-electric-sector-says-it-would-be-ready/?sh=19802f907c27

dismissed the possibility of single-digit temperatures in Texas as a doomsday theory.

ASCE Outlines What We Can Do Better

Having given U.S. energy infrastructure a C-, ASCE has several recommendations for steps needed to raise that grade. These include:

- Adopting a federal energy policy with "clear direction for meeting current and future demands" while "factoring in technology change, carbon reduction, renewables and distributed generation, state and market-based factors, and rate affordability."
- Requiring standards for all overhead transmission and distribution lines, structures, and substations to ensure safety and increase reliability.
- Improving grid and pipeline reliability through more frequent and thorough inspections of "critical assets" with an eye towards "risk mitigation."
- Developing a "national hardening plan" that protects and enables "rapid restoration of energy systems after natural and/or man-made disasters."
- Consolidating federal, state, and local environmental reviews and permitting processes to modernize energy infrastructure, including transmission/distribution and pipelines, more quickly and cost-effectively, while still considering environmental and community impacts.
- Designing energy infrastructure "to efficiently deliver power from generation sources to regions with greatest demand requirements."

America's energy landscape is changing, and in many ways, for the better. But in this is high-risk, high-reward arena, sound planning, and resource allocation are necessary to ensure a reliable level of service that enables future prosperity.

CHAPTER 8:

Roads | Rome Built To Last. So Can We.

"Safe roads are the bones of civilization."[201]
—Patrick Rothfuss

Does this sound familiar? You're driving at a moderate speed down a dimly lit road when, all of a sudden, the front, right side of your car drops about six inches with a loud bang that shakes you to your bones. That first impact is followed quickly by a second drop and bang at the rear of the car. Immediately, your steering is off. You slow down looking for a well-lighted place to stop. You get out of your car and examine your passenger side front tire. It's flat as a pancake, your rim is dented, and your hubcap is cracked. Your rear tire has not held up any better. You call AAA to arrange a tow to a garage that's already closed for the night. You drop your keys into their drop-box with a note of explanation and your phone number, then you take a cab home. The next day, you get the estimate from the garage, and it's staggering: two hubs need replacing along with your front axle. You'll also need an alignment.

Growling that, "Somebody's going to pay for this!" you drive a rental car to the spot of the mishap and see the gaping pothole that ruined your last

201 Rothfuss, P. (2011). *The Wise Man's Fear*. DAW Books.

16 hours. You snap photos of the hole, thinking you'll send a claim to the city. Weeks go by and you hear nothing about your claim of several hundred dollars in damages. Following up, you're put in touch with a clerk deep in the bowels of City Hall, who says, "Yeah, we don't pay those claims. If you want, you can sue. But I wouldn't try to fight City Hall."

If something like this has happened to you or someone you know, you or they are not alone. Each year, neglected road maintenance causes an absurd amount of damage to vehicles through unnecessary wear and tear, as well as collisions.

According to a 2015 report by TRIP, a national transportation research nonprofit organization, the annual price tag for vehicle damage due to faulty road maintenance is $109 billion, approximately $516 for every urban motorist.[202]

The costliest locales were these:[203]

- Washington DC — Perennially ranked as one of the worst cities for driving, our nation's capital also claims the dubious distinction of having America's worst roads. It is estimated that D.C. drivers shell out an extra $1,042 for vehicle maintenance due to poor road conditions. But before we get too giddy over the prospect of detached, unaccountable bureaucrats getting a taste of their horrid fiscal mismanagement, let's recall that DC is a city with a 13.5 percent poverty rate in 2019, so much of the cost amounts to an unconscionable tax on the poor.[204]

---

202 Bad Roads Cost Car Owners Billions: Report. (2015). Retrieved 3 June 2021, from https://autos.yahoo.com/news/bad-roads-cost-car-owners-162300817.html

203 What Are Your State's Roads Costing You? (2015). Retrieved 3 June 2021, from https://www.uniquepavingmaterials.com/driver-repair-costs-what-are-your-states-roads-costing-you/

204 Washington, District of Columbia (DC) Poverty Rate Data. Retrieved 3 June 2021, from http://www.city-data.com/poverty/poverty-Washington-District-of-Columbia.html

- Oklahoma —Tulsa takes the state crown for potholes. Despite filling approximately 250 road craters a day, workers in the Oil Capital of the World keep falling behind. Thus, Oklahoma drivers spend an average of $763 a year on car maintenance.
- California — While California chases the dream of high-speed rail, which may never be completed, the state has let its roads disintegrate. Three California cities (San Francisco, Los Angeles, and Long Beach) topped the worst list in the 500,000 or greater population category, while Antioch and Santa Rosa made the worst list for smaller cities with 250,000 to 500,000 people. Californians, already paying some of the country's highest taxes and gas prices, also fork over $762 in vehicle maintenance per year.
- Michigan — TRIP noted that 40 percent of the roads in Michigan were in poor condition resulting in costs to drivers of $686 a year for auto repairs. In Detroit, 50 percent of the roads were in disrepair, at a cost of $866 a year per driver, while the price tag in Flint was $839 per year.[205]
- New Jersey — In the Garden State, only 24 percent of the roads were rated in "good condition." The cost to drivers was just one dollar shy of the Michigan level at $685.

Returning to our opening scenario, the driver who is out of pocket has a legitimate claim against the government entity charged with maintaining the roads. Unfortunately, those entities, whether they be federal, state, county or municipal, rarely pay off. In some cases, there are simply too many claims to

---

205 Jansen, B. (2015). Report: 1 in 4 Urban Roads Damaged, Costing Motorists up to $1,000 Per Year. Retrieved 3 June 2021, from https://www.usatoday.com/story/news/nation/2015/07/22/highway-funding-damaged-roads/30528901/

process and pay. Chicago is a prime example of damage claims overwhelming the system and going unaddressed.

In March of 2018, *The Chicago Sun-Times* reported that 11,706 pothole complaints had been filed in the first two months of the year, a rise of 14 percent over the same two months of the previous year and the highest level in three years. The report noted that "For the 12 months from March 1, 2017, through Feb. 28, 43,502 pothole complaints were filed with the city. . . The Chicago Department of Transportation filled 456,333 potholes as a result of those complaints."[206]

Not every complaint results in a claim against the city for property damage. The year 2014 was especially bad for potholes, after a particularly severe winter. Motorists filed 5,431 claims. By contrast, in 2017, motorists filed only 731 claims with the city, about one claim for every 60 complaints. "Pothole damage accounted for more than two-thirds of vehicle and property claims filed." Of those 731 claims, the City Council only approved 88 pothole payments totaling $18,800.19, an average of $213.64 per claim. Chicago's policy is to pay roughly 50 percent of the amount claimed; "the city's reasoning being that drivers might have tried harder to avoid them." The maximum possible payment of a claim is $1,500 and can take up to six months. Altogether, it's not a good deal for Chicagoans.

Still, Windy City residents do better than their counterparts in Colorado Springs, where, according to a 2014 investigation by a local TV station KOAA, city officials were turning down 98 percent of pothole claims.[207] Meanwhile, in Arlington, Virginia, county officials are bullish on their sovereign immunity,

206 Ali, T. (2018). Pothole Complaints up 14 Percent in Chicago—The Most in 3 Years. Retrieved 3 June 2021, from https://chicago.suntimes.com/2018/3/10/18355736/pothole-complaints-up-14-percent-in-chicago-the-most-in-3-years

207 TUTTLE, B. (2014). Your City Could Pay for Car Damage Caused by Potholes. But It Probably Won't. Retrieved 3 June 2021, from https://time.com/50101/your-city-could-pay-for-car-damage-caused-by-potholes-but-it-probably-wont/

the legal doctrine that protects a government entity from being sued unless it agrees to be sued.

TIME magazine quotes an unnamed official as saying, "Only in unusual circumstances would the county pay damages, because the county has sovereign immunity and, therefore, under the law, generally has no legal liability. It would be a very unusual circumstance that would lead us to accepting a claim."[208]

So, a motorist can have a clear-cut case of liability for very real, expensive damages, and still get no satisfaction on a claim, if a city or county decides to hide behind the notion of sovereign immunity.

Taking a Toll on America's Roads

Many factors lead to road deterioration. Poor engineering and construction will cause a road to fail before the end of its projected lifetime. Seasonal temperature changes and water seepage, cause the expansion and contraction of materials and cracks throughout the structure. This problem is often exacerbated by inadequate drainage. But the number one cause of road damage is usage, and the number one culprit may be the commercial truck.

The American Trucking Association asserts that since the trucking industry represents 11 percent of all vehicles on the road, while paying 35 percent of all highway taxes, as well as higher tolls for tunnels and bridges, they are being good citizens.[209] But, according to a U.S. government study, one semi-truck inflicts as much wear and tear on the road as 9,600 passenger

208 TUTTLE, B. (2014). Your City Could Pay for Car Damage Caused by Potholes. But It Probably Won't. Retrieved 3 June 2021, from https://time.com/50101/your-city-could-pay-for-car-damage-caused-by-potholes-but-it-probably-wont/

209 The Hidden Trucking Industry Subsidy. (2009). Retrieved 3 June 2021, from https://truecostblog.com/2009/06/02/the-hidden-trucking-industry-subsidy/

cars.[210] This factoid has led some to conclude that commercial trucks cause as much as 99 percent of the human damage to the nation's roads.[211]

Should the government raise user fees to force truckers to pay their fair share and take the burden off the general citizenry? Some vociferous advocates think so. But most authorities are more sanguine about the problem, realizing that truckers would only pass on higher fees to the merchants they serve, and ultimately the consumers would wind up footing the bills. Still, if the object were to actually repair roads, higher fees would generate some funds, and the motoring public would ultimately benefit from reduced bills for auto maintenance.

As Pedestrian Deaths Increase, Many Wonder if U.S. Roads Are Too Dangerous by Design

Worse than property damages, personal injuries and deaths occur all too often on American roads. Smart Growth America, a 501(c)(3) organization that advocates for intelligent urban renewal and development, notes that in the decade from 2010-2019, the number of pedestrians "struck and killed by drivers nationwide. . . increased by an astonishing 45 percent," and totaled 53,435. The four most recent years for which records exist, (2016-2019) were the four deadliest years for pedestrians since 1990. The year 2019 saw 6,237 pedestrian deaths, which equals "more than 17 people killed per day."[212] It is simply mind boggling that annual death

210 Vehicle Weight and Road Damage. (2009). Retrieved 3 June 2021, from https://www.vabike.org/vehicle-weight-and-road-damage/

211 Murphy, B. (2017). Murphy's Law: How Trucks Destroy Our Roads. Retrieved 3 June 2021, from https://urbanmilwaukee.com/2017/06/22/murphys-law-how-trucks-destroy-our-roads/

212 Davis, S. (2021). 45 Percent Increase in People Struck and Killed While Walking Because Streets Are Dangerous by Design | Smart Growth America. Retrieved 3 June 2021, from https://smartgrowthamerica.org/people-struck-and-killed-while-walking-up-45-percent-in-a-decade-because-streets-are-dangerous-by-design/

totals equivalent to the population of a small city don't garner more attention and more outrage.

SGA identifies these 10 American cities as the most dangerous for pedestrians:

- Bakersfield, CA
- Deltona-Daytona Beach-Ormond Beach, FL
- Jackson, MS
- Jacksonville, FL
- Lakeland-Winter Haven, FL
- Memphis, TN-MS-AR
- North Port-Sarasota-Bradenton, FL
- Orlando-Kissimmee-Sanford, FL
- Palm Bay-Melbourne-Titusville, FL
- Tampa-St. Petersburg-Clearwater, FL

What accounts for this spike in fatalities? Some analysts are quick to point to "distracted walking" as the root of the problem. This makes sense on a certain level because pedestrian deaths did start to rise in 2009 when smartphones came into wide use. However, Angie Schmitt, writing for *StreetsBlogUSA,* cautions against blaming "zombie pedestrians" or "petextrians" for their own demise.[213]

Ms. Schmitt examines a 2017 report from the National Highway Traffic Safety Administration and finds that most pedestrians are struck and killed in situations where no one would "feel comfortable glancing down at the

213 Schmitt, A. (2019). Don't Blame 'Distracted' Pedestrians for Rising Death Toll. Retrieved 3 June 2021, from https://usa.streetsblog.org/2019/06/21/soaring-pedestrian-deaths-cant-be-blamed-on-distracted-walking/

Twitter app."[214] Among her salient points, she stresses that:

- Most pedestrians are killed at mid-block — Only about one-quarter of U.S. pedestrian fatalities occur in intersections. Mid-block is not the place where distracted cell phone users wander off the curb. This point, however, does not fully absolve the pedestrian, who may very well have darted into traffic without properly gauging traffic.
- Most deaths occur on wide, high-speed roads — The chance that a pedestrian will be killed increases in direct proportion to vehicle speed. Ms. Schmitt cites Transportation for America as reporting that "60 percent of pedestrian fatalities occur on 'arterial' roads where the speed limit was 40 mph or higher."
- Pedestrian deaths tend to be clustered — This data point would seem to indicate issues with the place as much as the unfortunate participants. "For example, in Philadelphia, more than 10 percent of all the traffic fatalities occur on just one street."[215]
- Three-quarters of pedestrian deaths occur at night — Darkness and alcohol consumption are factors in many pedestrian deaths.
- Victims tend to be older and/or poor — Older pedestrians need more time to cross the street and cannot react as quickly to speeding vehicles. The poor tend to live in overcrowded, poorly maintained neighborhoods.

When we consider these factors in totality, an image of inadequate infrastructure starts to crystalize. Often, broad, high-speed streets do not

---

214 Traffic Safety Facts 2017 Data. (2019). Retrieved 3 June 2021, from https://crashstats.nhtsa.dot.gov/Api/Public/ViewPublication/812681

215 Schmitt, A. (2021). Don't Blame 'Distracted' Pedestrians for Rising Death Toll. Retrieved 3 June 2021, from https://usa.streetsblog.org/2019/06/21/soaring-pedestrian-deaths-cant-be-blamed-on-distracted-walking/

adequately accommodate pedestrians with overpasses above traffic, properly timed "walk" signals, or medians where pedestrians can wait. Bus stops on these arteries are often in the middle of the block, so pedestrians running to catch a bus must often risk crossing in the middle of the block.

As for more urban areas, congested streets have long been death traps. When the Brooklyn Robins baseball team wanted a more descriptive name, they chose *The Trolley Dodgers*, shortened to *Dodgers* to fit on the jersey, alluding to the deadly sport of crossing the street. For the sake of commerce, streetcars, buses, autos, and trucks had been permitted to overwhelm city streets designed for handsome cabs, milk wagons, and peddler carts. Pedestrians had to keep their head on a swivel or pay the ultimate price.

Over time, urban development led to straighter grids for improved traffic flow, but advances were made for the sake of motor vehicles. Pedestrians, as well as bicyclists, were left behind.

Vision Zero: An Infrastructure-Based Initiative for Safer Roads

Developed in Sweden in the 1990s, the Vision Zero initiative spread rapidly throughout Europe and has found a following in numerous American cities.[216] Vision Zero, so named because its proponents imagine a world with zero traffic deaths, challenges communities to think differently about traffic accidents. Whereas conventional wisdom says traffic deaths are inevitable, Vision Zero sees them as preventable. Instead of trying to perfect human behavior, which is fundamentally impossible, Vision Zero aims to integrate our knowledge of human failure into safety planning.

---

216 What Is Vision Zero?. Retrieved 3 June 2021, from https://visionzeronetwork.org/about/what-is-vision-zero/

Acknowledging that it is impossible to prevent collisions, Vision Zero focuses on preventing severe injuries and fatalities. Vision Zero notes that our exclusive focus on individual responsibility and liability has impeded us from looking at systems that continue to allow accidents to happen. Finally, Vision Zero pushes back on our traditional view that changes made to save lives will be too expensive.

Vision Zero Network lists these communities as actively participating in the initiative:[217]

217 Vision Zero Communities. Retrieved 3 June 2021, from https://visionzeronetwork.org/resources/vision-zero-communities/#page

- Albuquerque, NM
- Alexandria, VA
- Anchorage, AK
- Austin, TX
- Bellevue, WA
- Bethlehem, PA
- Boston, MA
- Boulder, CO
- Cambridge, MA
- Charlotte, VA
- Chicago, IL
- Columbia, MO
- Denver, CO
- Denver Regional Council of Governments, CO
- Durham, NC
- Eugene, OR
- Fremont, CA
- Ft. Lauderdale, FL
- Harrisburg, PA
- Hillsborough County, FL
- Houston, TX
- Jersey City, NJ
- La Mesa, CA
- Laredo, TX
- Los Angeles, CA
- Macon, GA
- Minneapolis, MN
- Monterey, CA
- Montgomery County, AL

- New York City, NY
- Oregon Metro
- Orlando, FL
- Philadelphia, PA
- Portland, OR
- Richmond, VA
- Sacramento, CA
- San Antonio, TX
- San Diego, CA
- San Francisco, CA
- San Jose, CA
- San Luis Obispo, CA
- Santa Barbara, CA
- Seattle, WA
- Somerville, MA
- Tampa, FL
- Tempe, AZ
- Washington DC
- Watsonville, CA
- West Palm Beach, FL

Vision Zero is a multidisciplinary approach that includes behavioral adjustments, such as lower speed limits on surface streets. But it also calls for modifications to infrastructure to improve safety. For example, one of the most dangerous circumstances for pedestrians occurs when a car makes a left turn at an intersection on a sharp diagonal.

In Washington, DC, officials found they could protect pedestrians with "centerline hardening."[218] By installing bollards and rubber curbs to block the diagonal path through the intersection, road designers force drivers to make left turns at slower speeds, so they have a greater chance of seeing pedestrians.

Other recommended changes include:[219]

- Elevated pedestrian walkways over busy traffic
- Hardened bike lanes
- Longer "Walk" signals to allow mobility-challenged pedestrians to cross
- Raised medians where pedestrians can wait if they don't get all the way across on the light
- Rotaries that eliminate intersections altogether and keep traffic moving for greater fuel economy
- Speed bumps
- Upgraded traffic lights that use advanced technologies, such as digital countdown, activate Accessible Pedestrian Signals for the visually impaired.

Most of these corrective measures are frugal, as infrastructure investment

218 Simple Infrastructure Changes Make Left Turns Safer for Pedestrians. (2020). Retrieved 3 June 2021, from https://www.iihs.org/news/detail/simple-infrastructure-changes-make-left-turns-safer-for-pedestrians

219 Wagner, L. Vision Zero: A Revolutionary Approach to Road Safety—Inclusive City Maker. Retrieved 3 June 2021, from https://www.inclusivecitymaker.com/vision-zero-road-pedestrian-safety/

goes. However, expenses are much easier to justify when they offer targeted solutions to identified problems. A cornerstone of the Vision Zero program is collecting and analyzing accident data to understand the specific causes in precise spots and tailor remedies to the situation.

What is the Future for Our Country's Roadways?

America's roads are often called arteries, and for good reason. They are critical for moving people and goods, so everyday life and commerce can go on unimpeded. Unfortunately, these vital lifelines are generally underfunded, and more than 40 percent of the system is presently in mediocre to poor condition. The backlog for repairs continues to grow, burdening motorists who must pay for wasted fuel, delays, and auto repairs. Fatalities from traffic accidents, involving motor vehicle passengers and pedestrians alike, are unnecessarily and unconscionably high.

As tech companies envision a future of autonomous vehicles and electric vehicles that make driving safer and more economical, federal, state, and local governments must prioritize expenditures to preserve and improve roadways to keep our arteries open and minimize the human toll of vehicle traffic.

Current Condition, Capacity, and Congestion

The 2021 Infrastructure Report Card from the American Association of Civil Engineers grades our roads a disappointing D.[220] ASCE notes that the United States contains more than four million miles of public roadways. Yet, the

220 Infrastructure Report Card |Roads. (2021). Retrieved 3 June 2021, from https://infrastructurereportcard.org/cat-item/roads/

volume of traffic increases each year, "with vehicle miles traveled reaching more than 3.2 trillion in 2019, an 18 percent increase from 2000." But growth in usage cannot possibly continue on a system where 43 percent of the roads are in substandard conditions. The dilapidated condition of our roads imposes upon the public vehicle repair costs of nearly $130 billion each year.

Congestion is another issue, with 30 percent of motorist trips "impacted by severe or extreme congestion." ASCE posits that if current trends continue, a 60-minute commute will take 106 minutes in 2039. Congestion imposes additional costs, especially on urban Americans who must spend an extra 8.8 billion hours and purchase an extra 3.3 billion gallons of fuel each year. The overall cost to the nation is estimated at $166 billion annually, "or approximately $1,080 annually in wasted time and fuel for the average auto commuter." ASCE reasons that even though repair costs are appreciable, failure to make repairs will drive urban flight leading to suburban sprawl, and ultimately "inefficient roadway expansion," as there will be more miles of heavily traveled roadway in need of annual maintenance.[221]

Finally, since "our nation's highways and roads move 72 percent, or nearly $17 trillion, of the nation's goods," there is no escaping our responsibility to maintain our roadways.

Funding Repairs and Maintenance into The Future

ASCE estimates that we currently have a "$786 billion backlog of road and bridge capital needs." Of that, $435 billion is needed to repair existing roads. Another $120 billion should go for "targeted system expansion," and ASCE would like to see an additional $105 billion "for system enhancement

221 Infrastructure Report Card |Roads. (2021). Retrieved 3 June 2021, from https://infrastructurereportcard.org/cat-item/roads/

(which includes safety enhancements, operational improvements, and environmental projects)." Given the relatively sparse appropriations from the federal, state, and local governments ($177 billion in 2017), annual needs will not be met unless spending levels increase by 29 percent.

Historically, the Highway Trust Fund has paid for the federal government's contributions to highways and roads. But since the federal motor fuels tax "of 18.4 cents per gallon for gasoline and 24.4 cents for diesel has not been raised since 1993, and inflation has cut its purchasing power by 40 percent," the tax is not adequate, and "the Highway Trust Fund is projected to have a $15 billion deficit" by 2022. Meanwhile, increased fuel efficiency and ownership of hybrid and electric vehicles have undercut the motor fuel tax's efficacy. States have been actively raising their taxes to maintain state roads and are exploring other options, such as tolls and mileage-based user fees.

Public safety must also be a consideration for future expenditures. As we've discussed above, traffic fatalities are unacceptably high, and the link with roadway design, construction, and maintenance are undeniable.

Can Innovation Reduce Costs and Increase Efficiency?

ASCE notes that "increased use of innovative materials to preserve and rebuild pavements that are better suited to today's vehicle loading and more resilient to environmental impacts has led to longer-lasting pavements and lower life cycle costs." One advance is "smart pavement," where "moisture and temperature sensors are embedded in the pavement ... to collect information about the condition of road pavements more quickly and with less impact on roadway users." Next-generation traffic lights can provide solutions to congestion and "efficiently integrate bicycle and pedestrian traffic." I discuss the potential of these and other innovations abundantly in Part III of this book.

Raising the Grade for America's Roadways

ASCE believes that to improve the quality of our nation's roads, we must first preserve what exists, then build our way out of the dilemma posed by congestion. Initiatives must focus on improving travel time by maximizing the capacity of the existing network. This would be best done as we accelerate the development and deployment of new technologies.

Specific steps should include:

- Increasing funding from all levels of government and the private sector to address the condition and operations of the roadway system to maintain a state of good repair and ensure safety for all users.
- Fixing the federal Highway Trust Fund by raising the federal motor fuels tax by five cents each year over five years. To ensure long-term, sustainable funding for the federal surface transportation program, the current user fee of 18.4 cents per gallon on gasoline and 24.4 cents per gallon on diesel should be tied to inflation to restore its purchasing power, fill the funding deficit, and ensure reliable funding for the future.
- Developing state and local level comprehensive transportation asset management plans that link asset management efforts to long-term transportation planning and incorporate the use of life-cycle cost analysis.
- Creating dedicated federal investments to build resilience into the nation's road and bridge infrastructure and integrate resilience planning into State Transportation Asset Management Plans.

As we contemplate the future, we have arrived at a fork, where we can choose the road to ruin or take the road to renewal.

CHAPTER 9:

Schools | Campus Catastrophes

"Without undervaluing any other human agency,
it may be safely affirmed that the Common School, improved and energized,
as it can easily be, may become the most
effective and benignant of all the forces of civilization."
—Horace Mann

In the spring of 1903, the labor activist Mary Harris "Mother" Jones[222] visited Kensington, Pennsylvania, where seventy-five thousand textile workers were on strike for higher pay and shorter hours. In her 1925 biography, Mother Jones recalled that "at least ten thousand" of the striking workers "were little children." She described the industrial injuries these children suffered: lost hands, thumbs, or fingers. The children were "stooped things, round shouldered and skinny," since most had been working in the mills since the age of 10. The state law that prohibited employing children younger than 12 was not seriously enforced; parents who desperately needed the additional income to keep their children from starving were willing to lie about their children's ages.

To raise attention about the scourge of child labor, Mother Jones borrowed the children from their parents. She led them on a march from Pennsylvania

222 The March of The Mill Children from The Autobiography of Mother Jones. (2012). Retrieved 17 June 2021, from https://www.whatsoproudlywehail.org/wp-content/uploads/2012/11/Mother-Jones_The-March-of-the-Mill-Children.pdf

to the Long Island summer home of President Theodore Roosevelt at Oyster Bay. On the way, Mother Jones brought the children to Coney Island, where she told a large crowd, "We want President Roosevelt to hear the wail of the children who never have a chance to go to school but work eleven and twelve hours a day in the textile mills of Pennsylvania; who weave the carpets that he and you walk upon and the lace curtains in your windows, and the clothes of the people."[223]

President Roosevelt was not home when the March of the Mill Children reached Oyster Bay. But he and everyone else in Washington, DC, heard Mother's message and the voices of the people supporting her cause. Today, it is universally accepted that children belong in school where they can be protected, nurtured, and educated. So, how's that working out?

Much can be said that is critical of the U.S. school system and the quality of education it delivers. Critics focus on insufficient funding, poor prioritization of spending, the quality of instruction, the questionable culture of learning, the curriculum content, the outsized influence of the teachers' unions, and on and on. Our focus is infrastructure, where likewise, there is plenty of fodder for criticism.

The Literally Toxic Learning Environments of America's Schools

In September 2020, the former superintendent of the Scranton, Pennsylvania school district and two other officials were charged with felony child endangerment, after a grand jury returned indictments stemming from the trio's cover-up of lead and asbestos contamination in schools that

223 Cullen-DuPont, K. (2002). *American Women Activists' Writings: An Anthology, 1637-2001*. Cooper Square Press.

exposed students and staff to serious health risks.[224] The case against former Superintendent Alexis Kirijan, former Director of Operations Jeffrey Brazil, and Maintenance Supervisor Joseph Slack alleged that beginning in 2016, inspectors repeatedly warned about dangerous lead levels in drinking water in at least 10 schools. Still, the officials failed to remediate the situation and actively misled the public. The grand jury also found probable cause to believe that Kirijan and Brazil knew that inspectors had found asbestos risks in numerous locations, such as classrooms, restrooms, and a cafeteria, and had failed to act.

Environmental engineer Joseph Guzek is on record saying that he "first notified district officials in 2016 that he had found elevated lead levels in drinking water." On subsequent inspections in December 2018 and December 2019, he still found lead in the water. The problem was not isolated to a few pipes; of the 303 sinks and water fountains Guzek tested, more than half showed lead, which is unsafe at any level. Asbestos contamination was also pervasive; Guzek's testing disclosed 74 locations in district buildings that were "near the highest levels of danger."

Asbestos had been widely used in construction materials throughout the country, until it was phased out starting in the 1970s, due to concerns over asbestosis and mesothelioma. Asbestos is still permitted in a limited number of construction products. Removing asbestos from existing buildings is generally unnecessary and cost-prohibitive. As long as the asbestos-containing materials are sealed within the structure, there's no threat to occupants. But when buildings fall into disrepair, asbestos fibers are stirred up in the air, where occupants can breathe them in. This creates a risk of fatal disease developing decades into the future.

---

224 Rubinkam, M. (2020). School Officials Charged With Hiding Lead, Asbestos Problems. Retrieved 17 June 2021, from https://abcnews.go.com/US/wireStory/school-officials-charged-lead-asbestos-contamination-73339396

For this reason, one incident reported by the *Associated Press* is particularly damning. A school in the district was in such serious disrepair that "ceilings in several classrooms had collapsed, sending plaster and dust onto students and their desks and books." The principal had reported the issues to Kirijan and Brazil, but Kirijan told the principal to "stop emailing her about the problem and to instead communicate by phone." The principal, naturally, wanted documentation of the communications, so refused to do business by phone. Kirijan did not want to create a paper trail. The grand jury concluded that Kirijan had gone "out of her way to hide the extent of the district's asbestos problem."[225]

Subsequent events confirm this assessment. Brazil retired in March 2019 and Kirijan resigned in August 2019, but neither alerted their successors or the school board about the contamination issues. Fortunately, after state police warned the new district administration about the contamination, the new leadership took immediate steps "to disconnect tainted water sources and close school buildings for asbestos removal."

Scranton is not the only school district of the Keystone State with a lead and asbestos problem. In West Philadelphia, Cassidy Elementary School is "considered one of the most toxic public schools in the city due to elevated lead and asbestos levels." *Philly Voice* recently reported that "the School District of Philadelphia is building a $30 million facility to replace the school."[226]

In the City of Brotherly Love, about 2,700 children test positive for elevated blood lead levels each year. Throughout the country, urban industrial areas, home to mostly poor people of color, have elevated pollution levels,

---

225 *School officials charged with hiding lead, asbestos problems*. AP NEWS. Retrieved 29 August 2021, from https://apnews.com/article/health-pa-state-wire-child-endangerment-us-news-scranton-6d35aca462db96d3f8da9ebca293c896

226 Kopp, J. (2019). CNN Docuseries Shines Light on Lead Poisoning, Pollution in Philly and Chester. Retrieved 17 June 2021, from https://www.phillyvoice.com/cnn-united-shades-america-lead-poisoning-pollution-philly-chester-kamau-bell/

creating greater health risks for children. Yet, too often, the schools reinforce these problems rather than alleviating them.

Another widespread issue is the proximity of schools to highways. A joint investigation by the Center for Public Integrity and The Center for Investigative Reporting discovered that almost "8,000 U.S. public schools lie within 500 feet of highways, truck routes, and other roads with significant traffic."[227] That's roughly nine percent of public schools, with enrollments totaling 4.4 million students. Several thousand private schools are similarly situated.

Air pollution is concentrated along busy roads, creating "a toxic mix that can stunt lung growth, trigger asthma attacks, contribute to heart disease, and raise the risk of cancer." Constant exposure to carcinogens like benzene and polycyclic aromatic hydrocarbons is bad for anyone, but it is especially harmful to children. Exposure to such toxicity has been shown "to stunt lung growth, trigger asthma attacks, contribute to heart disease, and raise the risk of cancer."

Students in such environments also have trouble concentrating and wind up with lower average test scores. As George Thurston, a population-health professor at the New York University School of Medicine, told *PublicIntegrity.org*, "The expectation of every parent is that they're sending their child to a safe environment. And with this kind of pollution, they're not."[228]

In 2003, California banned most new-school construction within 500 feet of freeways, while allowing some exceptions. Since 2011, the U.S. Environmental Protection Agency has warned school districts about traffic

---

227 Smith Hopkins, J. (2017). The Invisible Hazard Afflicting Thousands of Schools—Center for Public Integrity. Retrieved 17 June 2021, from https://publicintegrity.org/environment/the-invisible-hazard-afflicting-thousands-of-schools/

228 Smith Hopkins, J. (2017). The Invisible Hazard Afflicting Thousands of Schools—Center for Public Integrity. Retrieved 17 June 2021, from https://publicintegrity.org/environment/the-invisible-hazard-afflicting-thousands-of-schools/

pollution, and the need to build away from major roads or truck routes. These cries have gone mostly unheeded. In fact, of the schools that opened in the 2014-2015 school year, almost 20 percent were built near roads "with daily traffic of at least 30,000 vehicles or with a minimum of 10,000 vehicles but at least 500 trucks." That rate of construction is worse than the *status quo* and it is taking the country in the wrong direction.

As with the lead and asbestos problems cited above, traffic pollution in schools seems to disproportionately affect minority and poor populations. The joint investigation found that "15 percent of schools where more than three-quarters of the students are racial or ethnic minorities are located near a busy road, compared with just four percent of schools where the demographics are reversed."[229]

A Tragic Misstep: Repurposing Industrial Sites as School Campuses

In many locales throughout the country, changing demographics have demanded the construction of new schools in previously underserved areas. In urban settings, finding spacious and affordable sites to build on is especially challenging. For the Los Angeles Unified School District, the answer seemed to be to repurpose industrial sites that were no longer in use. In at least one instance, this turned out to be a costly mistake.

Jefferson New Middle School opened in July of 1998, the first new junior high school that the Los Angeles Unified School District had built in 30 years.[230] The opening had been delayed one year over concerns that toxic

229 Smith Hopkins, J. (2017). The Invisible Hazard Afflicting Thousands of Schools—Center for Public Integrity. Retrieved 17 June 2021, from https://publicintegrity.org/environment/the-invisible-hazard-afflicting-thousands-of-schools/

230 Timmons, S. (1998). The Saga of A Toxic School - LA Weekly. Retrieved 17 June 2021, from https://www.laweekly.

contamination posed a threat to students and staff, after the site was found to be sitting atop "a subterranean reservoir of hexavalent chromium." As a result, the soil and air were tainted with carcinogens, including trichlorethylene, methylene chloride, and chloroform. How the pollutants got there, and how LAUSD could possibly have purchased the land and built a school upon it without knowing of the toxicity, would be the subject of more than a decade's litigation.

The Occupational Health and Safety Administration lists the following adverse effects of contact with hexavalent chromium: "occupational asthma, eye irritation and damage, perforated eardrums, respiratory irritation, kidney damage, liver damage, pulmonary congestion and edema, upper abdominal pain, nose irritation and damage, respiratory cancer, skin irritation, and erosion and discoloration of the teeth. Some workers can also develop an allergic skin reaction, called allergic contact dermatitis."[231]

Moviegoers may recall Julia Roberts in her Oscar-winning role of *Erin Brockovich*, a whistleblower on a crusade to save a community from hex chrome contamination and hold a major polluter accountable. That film was still a couple of years away, but the 1996 case of the real-life Erin Brockovich was fresh in the public's mind, especially in California. Pacific Gas & Electric, the state's largest utility, had agreed to pay $333 million, which was then the largest settlement ever paid in a direct-action lawsuit.

Ms. Brockovich was no doubt on State Senator Tom Hayden's mind when he chaired the highly dramatic public hearings over Jefferson's safety in 1997. California Assemblyman Scott Wildman revealed, "that LAUSD has a policy of siting new schools on industrial, largely toxic properties." Witnesses brought forth evidence that the district had not complied with state law, had

---

com/the-saga-of-a-toxic-school/

231 Hexavalent Chromium. Retrieved 17 June 2021, from https://www.osha.gov/hexavalent-chromium/health-effects

racked up 113 separate violations of its air-quality operating permit, and that a Health Risk Assessment attesting to Jefferson's safety for occupancy was unreliable. LAUSD was able to submit a subsequent report attesting to safety; the school was permitted to open, even though critics were not convinced.

Concern over the proposed school site had begun in 1995, when an inspector from the California EPA was investigating the former site of a small electroplating company called Hard Chrome Products, which had been destroyed in the riots of 1992 and had recently been designated as a Superfund site. The inspector, Ken Chiang, "was looking for hexavalent chromium, or hex chrome, a carcinogenic byproduct of the plating process."

Monitoring wells that Chiang installed detected an abundance of hex chrome. When Chiang observed that an entire city block across the street was under construction, he learned to his chagrin that the project was a school. Chiang knew that even if that parcel was not contaminated, school children would be at risk from contamination as remediation of the Superfund site took place.

When Chiang contacted LAUSD, he learned officials "had done limited research on potential hazards at the school." Worried that toxins leaching from Hard Chrome might have contaminated school grounds, putting construction workers and future students at risk, Chiang ordered testing on the school site. But the results for the school site were worse than Hard Chrome's. In fact, "the groundwater at the Jefferson site proved to have the highest concentrations of hex chrome ever discovered in California."

Where did the hex chrome come from? LAUSD would insist in litigation that Hard Chrome had contaminated the Jefferson site. However, a cursory investigation would turn up "at least three businesses, Weber Showcase, which made chrome refrigerator cases, Ayers Chambers, and Gillespie Furniture, [that] all did chrome plating" on the Jefferson grounds.

Attorneys for Hard Chrome presented evidence that one business on the Jefferson site had been a World War II defense contractor, producing disposable auxiliary fuel tanks for fighter planes. The tanks had been electroplated to protect against rust. A picture began to emerge of the Jefferson site being the greatest contributor to groundwater hex chrome contamination. In fact, later tests would show that the hex chrome cloud flowed from Jefferson towards Hard Chrome, not the other way around.

Then in June of 1996, excavation on the school site "revealed two underground concrete storage tanks that had evaded metal detectors." From those tanks, "trichlorethylene (TCE), a carcinogenic solvent whose poison can rise in fumes during its chemical breakdown, had leaked to 152 feet below ground surface." A specialist in environmental science would later accuse LAUSD of "gross negligence" for failing to find those tanks.

But for the most damning evidence against LAUSD, we have to go back to October 1988, when the district performed its initial site surveys. A report stated, "There is a potential for hazardous liquids to have impacted the subsurface of the site. . . A thorough environmental site assessment of potential toxic hazards shall be prepared."[232] Yet LAUSD never performed such an assessment. Instead, eager to grab up a huge parcel of land at a price it could afford, the district opted for a policy of willful ignorance, lest it uncover facts that would kill the deal. After the land purchase, LAUSD went so far as to fire Hamid Arabzadeh, the head of its environmental division, for his attempts to enforce toxic policies.

Remediation of the Jefferson site proved costly. One measure required removal of 12 to 20 feet of topsoil and replacement with 'clean fill.' However, by that time, the school had already been built, so the quality of the soil below

232 Toxic School Sites in Los Angeles: Weaknesses in The Site Acquisition Process. Special Report of The Joint Legislative Audit Committee. (1998). Retrieved 17 June 2021, from https://files.eric.ed.gov/fulltext/ED433680.pdf

the structure remains debatable. Nevertheless, one fact remains certain: it was easier for LAUSD to rehabilitate the soil than it was to restore its image.

The specter of hex chrome returned to Los Angeles area schools in October 2016, when testing at an intersection in the industrial town of Paramount revealed traces of the carcinogen in the air.[233] The Paramount Unified School District began periodic testing for hex chrome in 2017. PUSD partnered with the Los Angeles County Department of Public Health in September 2018 and again in August 2019 to test air and dust inside the Gaines and Lincoln Elementary Schools. The September tests detected hex chrome in half the classrooms tested. The August 2019 tests failed to detect hex chrome, indicating an improvement in air quality and safety.

How widespread of a problem is industrial pollution for U.S. schools? Given the long gestation period of related diseases, such as cancer, we may not know for many years. What we do know is that our children deserve greater diligence in vetting future sites for new school construction.

U.S. School Infrastructure Grade: Round and Disappointing

Up until now, we've been talking about the bare minimum expectation for school infrastructure: facilities that are not so toxic they poison the students. There are, however, myriad other concerns, which the American Society of Civil Engineers studiously reviews in its 2021 Infrastructure Report Card. Do U.S. schools pass the test? Yes, but just barely, with a D+.[234] Like parents

233 Health, L. Hexavalent Chromium in City of Paramount | Los Angeles County Department of Public Health - Environmental Health. Retrieved 17 June 2021, from http://publichealth.lacounty.gov/eh/chromium6/paramount.htm

234 ASCE's 2021 Infrastructure Report Card | Schools. (2021). Retrieved 17 June 2021, from https://infrastructurereportcard.org/cat-item/schools/

of a young Einstein presenting such a deficient mark, taxpayers in the richest nation on Earth should be horrified.

ASCE admits limitations to its study, since there is no comprehensive database to reference for information on K-12 public school infrastructure. This lack of accounting is disconcerting, given that more tax dollars go to school facilities than any other type of public infrastructure except highways.

Within the United States, there are about "84,000 public schools with nearly 100,000 buildings," which are expected to serve some 56.8 million students by 2026. Poring over existing data, ASCE finds about 53 percent of public-school districts have identified "the need to update or replace multiple building systems, including HVAC systems."

HVAC systems have a significant impact on the health and comfort of the interior environment, and state-of-the-art systems can play a significant role in reducing health concerns related to particulate matter and even the spread of germs and viruses. Given that students spend around eight hours a day within facilities, the interior environment should be a paramount concern.

ASCE further observes that public schools are dealing with capacity issues, as more than one-third rely on portable buildings. Of these structures, 45 percent are in poor or fair condition. Outdoor features were also rated fair or poor at a high rate. These include "school parking lots and roadways; fencing; bus lanes and drop-off areas; outdoor athletic facilities; and outdoor play areas/playgrounds."

Finally, noting that "public schools often serve a secondary function as emergency shelters and community resource facilities during man-made or natural disasters," ASCE states that upgrades are necessary to continue such services.

Yet, in the face of these needs, state capital funding for public schools has decreased substantially as a share of the overall economy. ASCE estimates the drop from FY 2008 to FY 2017 to be "the equivalent of a $20 billion cut," creating an annual funding gap nationwide of $38 billion. Budgetary constraints impose challenges for facility maintenance and new construction, which is often necessary to implement "improved health and safety standards, stronger accessibility requirements, and new technology." As a result, many school districts have invested heavily in technology infrastructure, which has paid dividends, especially during the COVID-19 pandemic, which forced many districts to rely on remote learning.

Unfortunately, despite being forced to do more with less, many school districts have not developed adequate long-term facility plans. ASCE estimates that only 40 percent of public schools have long-term plans for operations and maintenance. ASCE advises that "better planning through life-cycle cost analysis will lead to a better allocation of resources."

Funding and Future Needs

Most public schools rely on local revenues, generally property taxes, as their primary source of funding. Only 36 percent of schools rely primarily on state funds. Additional local funding comes from "grants, bonding, other taxes, and public-private partnerships." As previously noted, state funding as a share of the economy is down precipitously in recent years. Nevertheless, in the two decades from 1994 to 2013, school systems spent $925 billion on maintenance and operations and $973 billion on "new school construction and capital projects to improve existing schools." That's a combined outlay of $99 billion per year.

Unfortunately, ASCE places the price tag for "healthy and safe 21st-century learning environments" at about $145 billion per year. Simply to maintain existing facilities in good working order, school districts would have to spend $58 billion annually. It would take another "$77 billion per year to regularly upgrade existing facilities' systems, components, fixtures, equipment, and finishes as they reach the end of their anticipated life expectancy; systematically reduce the backlog of deferred maintenance that has accumulated; and alter existing facilities to respond to changing educational requirements." ASCE concludes there is a $46 billion annual funding gap between what is needed and what is available.

Public Safety and Resilience

In addition to the risks to health we have already discussed, public schools must be in good condition to withstand whatever nature throws their way. Depending on where the school is located, this can mean designing and engineering structures to survive seismic events, high winds, and floods, as well as harsh winters of snow and ice. These features are especially important since distressed communities often use public schools as emergency shelters and community resource facilities when disasters strike. For this reason, upgrades to schools might include "windows that can withstand high winds, structures designed to survive earthquakes, and rooms specifically designed as shelters from tornadoes."

ASCE's Suggestions for Raising the Grade

Much of the failure associated with school infrastructure has to do with failing to plan and perform due diligence. Therefore, the onus falls on superintendents, school boards, and higher officials in state and federal government to understand and remediate the school infrastructure problems.

With that in mind, ASCE suggests the following steps[235]:

235 ASCE's 2021 Infrastructure Report Card | Schools. (2021). Retrieved 17 June 2021, from https://infrastructurereportcard.org/cat-item/schools/

- The U.S. Department of Education should coordinate with state agencies and local school districts to obtain and publish nationwide statistics on school infrastructure at regular intervals.
- School districts should focus on Life-Cycle Cost Analysis (LCCA) principles in the planning and design processes to evaluate the total cost of projects.
- Design new campuses for the lowest net present value cost that includes life-cycle operation and maintenance in addition to capital construction.
- Implement building condition assessment of existing school infrastructure.
- Budget for the total cost of ownership and train facilities' staff to implement these policies.
- Develop responsive capital planning frameworks that can adjust to changing technologies and demographics.
- Encourage school districts to adopt regular, comprehensive major maintenance, renewal, and construction programs, and implement preventive maintenance programs to extend the life of school facilities.
- Explore alternative financing for public school facilities, including lease financing, as well as ownership and use arrangements, to facilitate school construction projects.

The philosophical problems swirling around public schools are not going away. But infrastructure issues have the advantage of being tangible, demonstrable, and provable. This should make them easier to solve, as long as there is a will to do better for our children.

CHAPTER 10:

Transit | Best Intentions Derailed

"The reality about transportation is that it's future-oriented. If we're planning for what we have, we're behind the curve."
—Anthony Foxx

On October 27, 1904, subway service was initiated in New York City with the fanfare of a circus, giving rides to an estimated 150,000 eager passengers from City Hall to 145th Street and Broadway. As *TIME* magazine reported, "All the afternoon the crowds hung around the curious-looking little stations, waiting for heads and shoulders to appear at their feet and grow into bodies. Much as the Subway has been talked about, New York was not prepared for this scene and did not seem able to grow used to it."[236] But grow used to it, they did. Though cramped and humid, the service was convenient and economical.

In the early decades of subway service, an adventurous strap-hanger could ride "22.65 miles from the remote reaches of The Bronx to even remoter reaches of Brooklyn," all for a nickel. By 1948, ridership was up to 3.25 million people who, again according to *TIME*, would twice a day "descend into the maelstrom of the subways with the haunted resignation of lemmings, there to die the small death of the rush hour."[237] Only now, their existential voyage would cost a dime.

236 Latson, J. (2014). Riding the NYC Subway Used to Be Fun—Then It Became A 'Small Death'. Retrieved 13 June 2021, from https://time.com/3534565/new-york-city-subway-history/

237 NEW YORK: The Nickel's Last Ride. (1948). Retrieved 16 June 2021, from http://content.time.com/time/subscriber/article/0,33009,798518,00.html

Like New York, virtually every medium-to-large city in America has become dependent on a transit system, composed of rail, light rail, trolleys, ferries, and bus lines. These systems are the blood streams of the cities, inextricably tied to their economies, public safety, and quality of life. According to ASCE, there are about 6,800 transit organizations in the United States, of which 2,207 received federal grant money in 2018. Of those, 928 serve urbanized areas, and 1,279 serve rural areas. Over the past 50 years, the overall number of passenger trips has increased by 37 percent. Between 2017 and 2019, bus ridership was the leading form of public transit, averaging 4.7 billion passenger trips annually, next was heavy rail at 3.8 billion, followed by light rail at 524 million, commuter rail at 503 million, demand response at 207 million, and trolley bus at 81 million.[238]

In the Infrastructure Report Card for 2021, ASCE notes that public transit in America "is essential to everyday living. . . providing access to jobs, schools, shopping, healthcare, and other services while enabling equitable access and sustainable mobility options."[239] Unfortunately, transit is the province of larger urban areas, so 45 percent of the population has no access to it. Where transit is available, the systems are often old and lack safety features that have become standard for newly constructed systems.

Urban transit has also lost its key selling feature: affordability. That nickel train ride of 1904 would cost $1.50 today, and the dime ride of 1948 would go for $1.11. Yet New York's MTA presently charges $2.75 per ride. However, even with steep fares, the services do not pay for themselves, so agencies struggle to obtain funds to upgrade infrastructure and equipment, resulting

238 ASCE's 2021 Infrastructure Report Card | Transit. (2021). Retrieved 13 June 2021, from https://infrastructurereportcard.org/cat-item/transit/

239 ASCE's 2021 Infrastructure Report Card | Transit. (2021). Retrieved 13 June 2021, from https://infrastructurereportcard.org/cat-item/transit/

in "a $176 billion transit backlog, a deficit that is expected to grow to more than $270 billion through 2029."

ASCE warns that "failure to address the transit revenue shortfall will only exacerbate ridership declines," as passengers seek more reliable modes of travel. This will inevitably lead to increased traffic congestion and poorer air quality. For these reasons and more, ASCE grades American transit a dismal D-.

A Closer Look at the Condition and Capacity of U.S. Public Transit

Demand for transit solutions has spurred growth, especially in bourgeoning communities. ASCE notes that "52 new systems and 124 extensions have opened" over the past two decades, comprising 1,393 miles of service and giving the nation more than 240,000 route miles. Of this, bus routes account for more than 226,000 miles. Commuter and hybrid railroads have grown 12 percent over the last decade and now operate over 9,227 miles of track. Light rail and streetcars have experienced an even sharper increase of 30 percent, and now travel along 1,811 miles of track.

But system growth means more routine maintenance, as well as capital improvements, and investments have not kept pace. When maintenance is not performed, delays and interruption of service occur, which disincentivize transit use. ASCE points to a 2017 report from the Department of Transportation covering a 10-year period where "poor condition" ratings[240] were issued for:

240 2017 National Transit Summary and Trends. (2018). Retrieved 13 June 2021, from https://www.transit.dot.gov/sites/fta.dot.gov/files/docs/ntd/130636/2017-national-transit-summaries-and-trends.pdf

- 36.4 percent of maintenance and storage facilities
- 21.4 percent of operations systems
- 18.5 percent of vehicles
- 6.4 percent of fixed guideway elements, such as tracks, tunnels, and bus guideways
- 5.5 percent of stations

Such deficiencies can lead to disappointing rider experiences that cause a downward spiral of ridership decline, diminished revenue, and deferred maintenance. Increasingly, state and local governments have been forced to fund transit system operations and maintenance work.

Transit Safety: Luxury or Necessity?

It's clear that when transit service falters, cities suffer. But transit systems are also barometers, gauges of the fiscal and cultural health of the cities they serve. If you want to experience the essence of a city, ride its transit. But you might want to think twice about riding it alone.

On January 16, 2021, *The New York Post* reported that "A naked maniac shoved a man off of a Harlem subway platform Saturday, but then also jumped down and zapped himself to death on the third rail during a crazed, on-the-tracks scuffle with a good Samaritan."[241] The incident took place in the middle of the day, around 3:40 p.m. After the shove landed the victim on the tracks, a bystander jumped down to help him. The "nude attacker" took umbrage at the do-gooder tampering with his handiwork, so he jumped down onto the tracks himself "and began pummeling the would-be rescuer."

241 Celona, L., & Dorn, S. (2021). Naked Subway Shover Dies In Melee On NYC Tracks: Cops. Retrieved 13 June 2021, from https://nypost.com/2021/01/16/naked-subway-shover-dies-in-melee-on-nyc-tracks-cops/

In the struggle, the attacker made contact with the electrified third rail and electrocuted himself. The victim and the Samaritan escaped with minor injuries, despite a train bearing down on the station while they were still on the tracks.

A freak occurrence? A station employee working in a payment booth at the time disagrees. "It happens more than you think," the employee told a *Post* reporter. "I mean, you live in New York? You know what it's like on the subway these days."[242] In fact, the shove attack was the fifth in New York City since November 2020, including one on Christmas Eve. Fortunately, all the victims survived. In addition to the electrocuted attacker, declared dead at the scene, two attackers were apprehended, and two escaped.

Although Mayor DeBlasio promised the New York Police Department would increase its presence within the subway system, subsequent attacks have occurred. On May 25, an attacker pushed a 36-year-old Asian man onto the tracks of the 21st Street-Queensbridge F train station around 7:45 a.m.[243] The oncoming train was able to stop without injuring the victim. The attacker fled, while a bystander jumped down to help the victim up off the tracks.

Then in June, a "highly intoxicated" 22-year-old homeless man pushed a 63-year-old woman onto the tracks.[244] She sustained a wound to her leg that required 40 stitches to close. The victim believes she was targeted because of her age. "They are picking on the elderly," she told *The New York Post*. "That's what they do. They pick on people that cannot defend themselves."

By now, you might be wondering, "How is this an infrastructure

---

242 Cherkis, A. (2021). It's 'Showtime' Again on The New York Subway. Retrieved 16 June 2021, from https://www.nytimes.com/2021/05/21/nyregion/nyc-subway-life.html

243 Weili, H. (2021). Asian Man Survives NYC Subway Shove. Retrieved 13 June 2021, from http://global.chinadaily.com.cn/a/202105/25/WS60ac8c63a31024ad0bac1465.html

244 Roberts, G., Moore, T., & Woods, A. (2021). Latest Subway Shove Victim 'Traumatized,' Won't Ride Trains Alone Again. Retrieved 13 June 2021, from https://nypost.com/2021/06/03/subway-shove-victim-traumatized-wont-ride-alone-again/

problem?" Decades ago, such incidents would have been met with cries for increased policing and mental health services. No one would have blamed an inanimate object, the subway, for the conscious actions of individuals. But times change, and technology advances. Understanding that these incidents are likely to happen, it becomes a duty to employ all available means to prevent them. One of those means is a re-design of transit infrastructure.

Platform Screen Doors: A Transit Innovation Whose Time Has Come

Platform screen doors (PSD) and platform edge doors (PED) are a relatively new transit innovation.[245] The point is to erect a barrier between the passenger platform and the track bed that opens via sliding doors in front of the train doors. The difference between a PSD and a PED is that PSD barriers go all the way up to the ceiling, while PED barriers are only as tall as the train itself, or even half that height.

PSDs and PEDs are widely used in transit systems throughout Asia and Europe. In America, they are commonly used on light rail lines serving airports, including:

- AeroTrain serving Washington Dulles International Airport
- AirTrain JFK, serving John F. Kennedy International Airport
- AirTrain Newark, serving Newark Liberty International Airport
- AirTrain, serving San Francisco International Airport
- Chicago's O'Hare International Airport
- Denver International Airport

245 Platform Screen Doors (PSD). Retrieved 13 June 2021, from http://www.railsystem.net/platform-screen-doors-psd/

- Hartsfield—Jackson Atlanta International Airport

Another notable "people mover" system employing a platform barrier system is the United States Capitol subway system, serving the U.S. Senate and the U.S. House of Representatives.

PSD or PED barriers offer many advantages, which include:

- Improved climate control within the station. Physically isolating the platform from the tunnel improves the efficiency of heating, ventilation, and air conditioning.
- Improved security by denying trespassers access to the tracks and tunnels.
- Lower manpower costs when used in conjunction with Automatic Train Operation, which eliminates the need for motormen or conductors.
- Muting the noise from incoming and outgoing trains improves the sound quality of platform announcements and makes for a more comfortable rider experience.
- Prevention of accidental falls onto the lower track area, which are common when riders faint, or experience a seizure or other medical emergency. The barriers also deter suicide attempts and homicides by pushing.
- Prevention of litter on the track, which draws rodents and can create a fire risk.
- Recent research also indicates that PSDs installed in Korean transit stations have reduced particulate matter in the air, which would be a

positive health benefit for riders.[246]

- Reduced risk of accidents, especially from service trains passing through a station at high speed.
- Reduction or elimination of wind onto the platform caused by the piston effect of the train rushing through the tunnel. Under some circumstances, such wind can make people fall over.

However, the cost of PSD systems is exorbitant, typically costing a few million dollars per station. That's not a meager amount for New York's Metropolitan Transit Authority with more than 470 stations. PSD systems also have to be compatible with train equipment, so the doors align properly. This problem can trigger additional costs to change rolling stock and retrofit depots.

New York's MTA has been discussing PSDs since at least 2007, when MTA officials said, "platform doors would be installed on the 7-train extension, and that they were considering doing the same for the new Second Ave. subway."[247] Those plans were nixed as "cost prohibitive" while the projects were under construction, citing "an estimated $1.5 million to install sliding doors along two platform edges in a new station, and more to retrofit an existing station."[248]

In 2010, the Authority released a Request for Information for a pilot program. MTA then had a chance to launch a pilot program for free, when Crown Infrastructure, a New York-based company, responded with an offer

246 Kim, K., Ho, D., Jeon, J., & Kim, J. (2012). A Noticeable Shift In Particulate Matter Levels After Platform Screen Door Installation In A Korean Subway Station. *Atmospheric Environment*, *49*, 219-223. doi: 10.1016/j.atmosenv.2011.11.058

247 Kabak, B. (2012). 'A screen door on a submarine...' - Second Ave. Sagas. Retrieved 13 June 2021, from https://secondavenuesagas.com/2012/12/31/a-screen-door-on-a-submarine/

248 Donohue, P. (2012). MTA considers installing sliding doors to prevent deaths, injuries. Retrieved 13 June 2021, from https://www.nydailynews.com/new-york/mta-mulling-sliding-doors-article-1.1229283

to install the doors at no charge, in exchange for future revenue from LED video advertising on the barriers. No action was taken.

At the end of 2012, a year that saw 54 people die violently on transit tracks, more than one death per week and a five-year high, *The New York Daily News* reported that "The MTA will reconsider installing sliding doors on some subway platforms to prevent riders from getting killed or injured by trains."[249] Given there had been "139 incidents in which people got hit by trains," that's one person struck every 2.63 days, interim MTA Executive Director Thomas Prendergast conceded, "We have to revisit [the pilot project to install sliding doors on the tracks]." His comments came the day after "a crazed woman killed a 46-year-old immigrant by shoving him into an oncoming train in Queens." That harrowing incident came on the heels of another shoving murder, when "a homeless drifter hurl[ed] a man onto a Times Square subway track, where he was fatally crushed by a train."

Asked what had happened to the previously proposed program, Prendergast admitted, "We haven't made a conscious decision to table it and not do it at all, but we haven't made a decision to keep it going either. It's suspended animation."

By 2017, the MTA had planned to test sliding doors at one subway station, the Third Avenue L stop, and in 2018 had even allocated part of its $30 million capital improvement allotment for the project.[250] However, in 2018, officials decided the money would be better spent on new elevators to make subway service more accessible to handicapped riders.

In response, Ruth Lowenkron, Director of the Disability Justice program at New York Lawyers for the Public Interest, accused the MTA of pitting one issue

249 Donohue, P. (2012). MTA considers installing sliding doors to prevent deaths, injuries. Retrieved 13 June 2021, from https://www.nydailynews.com/new-york/mta-mulling-sliding-doors-article-1.1229283

250 Furfaro, D. (2018). MTA decides not to test barriers on tracks at downtown station. Retrieved 13 June 2021, from https://nypost.com/2018/06/26/mta-decides-not-to-test-barriers-on-tracks-at-downtown-station/

of accessibility against another. "These platform doors are also very important to some of the same population," she said. "There is a great risk if you don't have some sort of a border that the wheelchair will tip into the tracks."[251]

The recent spate of shoving attacks prompted the City Council to re-revisit the matter. But when asked about installing PSDs in the New York City subway, Interim Transit President Sarah Feinberg called the systems "unbelievably expensive."[252] Noting that "it was a $2 billion solution, to put these in just a portion of our stations," Feinberg added, "They would be possible in some stations, but would be an extremely expensive solution to something that is typically viewed as a problem that happens on occasion, and not very often."

MTA Chairman Pat Foye concurred on the price tag, saying, "The subways were built by different investor groups 180 years ago, and we don't have the uniformity of platform size, platform curves, etcetera. It would be an extraordinary amount of money."

The MTA's reluctance on PSDs is not mere penny-pinching. Nor is it because one track death a week is too occasional a problem. The MTA is in serious financial straits and has been resisting cuts in bus and subway service in the neighborhood of 40 percent to deal with an $8 billion budget deficit through the end of 2024. Despite those woes, MTA had formulated an ambitious $54 billion modernization plan, which was suspended during the pandemic. Logistically, it would have been the perfect time to perform such work, but the sharp decrease in ridership to 20 percent of normal tanked revenues. In desperation, the MTA borrowed almost $3 billion through a Federal Reserve emergency lending program, adding to a debt load that was

251 Meyer, D. (2021). MTA says subway shove-preventing platform doors are too expensive. Retrieved 13 June 2021, from https://nypost.com/2021/02/10/mta-says-subway-shove-preventing-platform-doors-are-too-expensive/

252 Meyer, D. (2021). MTA Says Subway Shove-Preventing Platform Doors Are Too Expensive. Retrieved 13 June 2021, from https://nypost.com/2021/02/10/mta-says-subway-shove-preventing-platform-doors-are-too-expensive/

already substantial, as MTA officials lobbied aggressively in Washington, DC, for bailout funds.

In February 2021, *The New York Times* reported that Senator Chuck Schumer promised $8 billion for the MTA as part of a "$1.9 trillion stimulus package that President Biden is urging Congress to approve [which] includes up to $30 billion for public transit."[253] The MTA plans to use the money to "buy 90 buses, including 45 electric models, and new trains for the commuter railroads, and to complete repairs to the tunnel that carries the F line under the East River and was damaged during Hurricane Sandy." However, even this mountain of cash is not enough to guarantee solvency, since there are "the looming questions about whether ridership will return entirely and about the prospects for more federal aid." Analysts at McKinsey & Company predict that ridership may only return to 80 to 92 percent of pre-pandemic levels by 2024.[254]

Officials in New York City know their town has a long road to recovery from the pandemic shutdowns, and that its revitalization depends on a safe, functioning transit system. Yet, as the federal Treasury sags under $21 trillion in debt, it's going to be increasingly hard to convince taxpayers elsewhere in the country that New York City deserves additional bailouts.

Additional Public Health and Safety Concerns Related to Transit

Strong public transportation networks contribute to significantly lower traffic fatality rates in the communities they serve. ASCE mentions recent

253 Goldbaum, C. (2021). N.Y.C. Staves Off Cuts to Public Transit, Despite Dire Warnings. Retrieved 13 June 2021, from https://www.nytimes.com/2021/02/18/nyregion/nyc-subway-bus-budget.html

254 Goldbaum, C. (2021). N.Y.C. Staves Off Cuts to Public Transit, Despite Dire Warnings. Retrieved 13 June 2021, from https://www.nytimes.com/2021/02/18/nyregion/nyc-subway-bus-budget.html

studies that show metro areas with greater than 40 transit trips per capita per annum have only about half the traffic fatality rate compared to metro areas with fewer than 20 transit trips per capita. Thus, there are life-saving benefits to well-maintained transit systems.

Transit also improves the quality of life for people who need cost-effective and reliable transportation to pursue employment and education. ASCE stresses that "improved transit access has the potential to increase employment opportunities and broaden overall economic activity." According to a recent study, when viewed over a 20-year period "for every $1 billion invested in public transportation, roughly 49,000 jobs are created."[255]

Transit systems have made a concerted effort in recent years to minimize the environmental impact of their services. Only 25 years ago, 95 percent of the nation's buses were diesel-powered. Today, the number is closer to 42 percent. Hybrid electric buses were only one percent of the nation's fleet in 2005, but had grown to 18 percent in 2019, while natural-gas-powered bus usage also increased from 18 percent in 2009 to 29 percent in 2019.

Transit Systems Across America Strapped for Cash

Financial woes for transit systems are not limited to New York City. In 2020, *The New York Times* reported on the "existential peril" facing transit systems in numerous major cities.[256] The article highlighted the toll the pandemic shutdown was having on ridership. Washington, DC's Metro eliminated weekend, and late-night service and Atlanta suspended 70 of the city's 110 bus routes. Boston suffered a $600 million budget shortfall, and Chicago

255 ASCE's 2021 Infrastructure Report Card | Transit. (2021). Retrieved 13 June 2021, from https://infrastructurereportcard.org/cat-item/transit/

256 'Existential Peril': Mass Transit Faces Huge Service Cuts Across U.S. (2020). Retrieved 13 June 2021, from https://www.nytimes.com/2020/12/06/nyregion/mass-transit-service-cuts-covid.html

weighed in at minus $500 million. Yet were any of these systems financially healthy before the pandemic?

For the year ending December 31, 2019, Chicago's Transit Authority reported its current liabilities had increased 11.82 percent to $847,915,000.[257] In a report on the fiscal year ending June 30, 2019, the Washington Metropolitan Transit Authority reported current liabilities of $5,167,470, up from $4,961,992 in 2018.[258] The Massachusetts Bay Transportation Authority authorized $490.9 million in its FY 2020 budget for debt service in Boston.[259] But none of these systems can touch New York City's MTA, whose reported total liabilities and deferred inflows of resources for 2019 topped $87.2 billion. Transit boosters often cite sustainability as a reason to "invest" in transit, but it's hard to see how such levels of debt are sustainable for even the largest cities.[260]

According to a 2019 report by the Federal Transit Administration, funding for transit operations broke down as follows:[261]

- Directly generated revenues — 35.7 percent
- State sources —23 percent
- Local resources — 34.2 percent
- Federal funding — 7.1 percent

257 Chicago Transit Authority, Financial Statements, Years Ended December 31, 2019 and 2018. (2020). Retrieved 13 June 2021, from https://www.transitchicago.com/assets/1/6/CTA_Financial_Statement_Final_FY19.pdf

258 Washington Metropolitan Area Transit Authority, Financial Report for the Fiscal Years Ended June 30, 2019 and 2018. (2019). Retrieved 13 June 2021, from http://www.novatransit.org/uploads/WMATA/FY19-Final_CAFR.pdf

259 Massachusetts Bay Transportation Authority FY20 Final Itemized Budget. (2021). Retrieved 13 June 2021, from https://cdn.mbta.com/sites/default/files/fmcb-meeting-docs/2019/04-april/2018-04-08-fmcb-K-fy20-final-itemized-operating-budget-support-accessible.pdf

260 Metropolitan Transportation Authority (A Component Unit of The State of New York). (2020). Retrieved 13 June 2021, from https://new.mta.info/document/17661

261 Metropolitan Transportation Authority (A Component Unit of The State of New York). (2020). Retrieved 13 June 2021, from https://new.mta.info/document/17661

This means users of transit pay for less than 36 percent of its expenses, while 64 percent of the funding comes from tax revenue. Asking riders to bear the full cost of transit would put the final nail in the affordability coffin; imagine an NYC subway ride costing $8.25! Though asking non-riders to pay almost two-thirds of the cost might raise eyebrows among Constitutionalists, the public generally favors transit investment. ASCE points out that voters approved 70 percent of all transit-related ballot initiatives in the United States. Yet, despite this redistribution of wealth, ASCE identifies "a backlog of $176 billion for transit investments. . . a deficit that is expected to grow to nearly $270 billion through 2029."

Federal funding has included a $60 billion allocation to the FTA through the Fixing America's Surface Transportation (FAST) Act, $48 billion of which comes from the Highway Trust Fund. In October 2020, Congress extended the FAST Act for a year, authorizing $12.5 billion for FTA and $2.3 billion for the Capital Investment Grant program, "the primary federal discretionary source of funds for transit expansion."

Congress also provided $25 billion in emergency relief funding for operating expenses in the CARES Act and provided an additional $14 billion in relief under the Consolidated Appropriations for FY 2021.

Raising the Grade for America's Transit Systems

Given the clear and convincing benefits of sound transit systems, a grade of D- is totally unacceptable. ASCE suggests the following steps to improve overall performance:

- State and local governments as well as the private sector must increase investment to reduce the backlog of rehabilitation needs and increase transit mode share.

- Federal government must increase investment in grant programs to improve and support capital development.
- Encourage the ongoing implementation of new technology to leverage innovation and mobility options to provide better access for all communities.
- Congress should fix the Highway Trust Fund by increasing the gas tax by 25 cents over the next five years. Index future increases using accepted indicators, such as the Producer Price Index or Consumer Price Index.
- Communities must place transit at the forefront when increasing surface transportation system capacity and developing multimodal connectivity. Communities should integrate transit and micromobility options that offer equitable access for all.
- Apply asset management best practices to minimize long-term lifecycle costs and improve the system's overall condition.

Safe, efficient, and reasonably priced mass transit is essential to the smooth functioning of urban centers. It's time for leaders at all levels of government to develop intelligent, far-sighted plans that maximize the public benefits of these indispensable systems.

CHAPTER 11:

Space | Why Space Tech Needs to Take Off

"Space-based services and technologies are key in understanding climate change... . . . among countless applications to which space can contribute."
*—**United Nations**, Sustainable Development Goals document*

As we explore Mars and prepare for the first civilian missions to space, not everyone realizes just how crucial the development of space infrastructure is for the future of humanity. As of March 2021, American, Chinese, and United Arab Emirates vehicles are exploring the surface of Mars. The Chinese Tianwen-1 mission entered the red planet's orbit on February 10, one day after the arrival of the UAE's Hope mission, while NASA's Perseverance mission landed on February 18.

During a conference sponsored by Beyond Earth in March 2021, NASA's Kathy Lueders emphasized the connection between space missions and the technology that has enabled us to live wiser on Earth. Efficient water purification and food sources are some of the most salient examples of how technology developed for space missions can help us navigate the challenges of climate change.

According to Lueders, an Associate Administrator of Human Exploration and Operations at NASA, everybody on Earth is a space person, and every company is a space company; they just don't know it yet. Thus, space infrastructure is Earth infrastructure. And if our government fails to invest enough to develop and maintain that infrastructure, America will pay dearly for it.

In line with Lueders' views, I envision the creation of an infrastructure akin to that of the iPhone. Just like Apple had no inkling of all the apps that could be developed for that platform, we won't know what private companies will be able to achieve if NASA succeeds in developing an infrastructure capable of fostering innovation.

By the end of the decade, small communities of contractors and scientists will likely be living in space. NASA's vision is to use lower orbit missions as a testing ground to prepare to colonize the moon and then use our experience on the moon to prepare to colonize Mars. For former astronaut Dr. Janet L. Kavandi, who is Executive VP of Space Systems at the Sierra Nevada Corporation, the ultimate goal is for us to become "a very successful interplanetary species."

Once a subject matter only fit for science fiction novels, space tourism and lunar colonization are just around the corner. People seldom think about how space exploration affects them, but without satellites, for example, we wouldn't have GPS technology. As China, Russia, and others invest heavily in the space race, it is important to understand that lagging behind cannot only impact the lives of astronauts but of every human being on our planet.

NASA's Infrastructure Failures

On February 18, 2021, a NASA Safety Panel recommended that the agency focus on space infrastructure and strategically develop its workforce. During NASA's Aerospace Safety Advisory Panel (ASAP) meeting, former astronaut Sandy Magnus stated, "The agency must define clearly its central role, authorities, and responsibilities, and the approach that NASA chooses to take should inform not only the skill sets and the workforce of the future but also the acquisition strategy, the operational posture should establish and the infrastructure that should be available."[262]

As NASA's operations involve an increasing number of strategic partnerships and new operational paradigms, hiring should be based on clear strategic guidelines. The agency's workforce is one of the central elements of its space program, and the Safety Panel expressed concerns in its last annual report. "It is not clear to the Panel that NASA is deliberately addressing certain workforce issues at the strategic level," the document states. "Failing to do so could result in blurred responsibilities and the directly related concern that some risks may not be actively or adequately managed."[263]

During the NASA Panel meeting, Magnus referred specifically to infrastructure, stating that the agency has "an opportunity to align [its] infrastructure to [its] long-term strategy. The workforce, the infrastructure, and the strategic direction are all linked."

One of the central issues today involves excessive fixed costs and maintenance of facilities that are no longer critical to NASA's programs. Likewise, the permanent workforce should be reduced, thus freeing resources to hire needed personnel for the duration of specific projects. If the agency's resources are not speedily optimized, I believe space infrastructure will suffer.

Safety review is also failing at NASA. A proposed safety culture audit has been long delayed. Panel members have repeatedly pointed to "lingering systemic issues related to risk management, quality, and safety."

---

262 Foust, J. (2021). Safety Panel Recommends NASA Develop Strategy for Workforce and Infrastructure | SpaceNews. Retrieved 4 June 2021, from https://spacenews.com/safety-panel-recommends-nasa-develops-strategy-for-workforce-and-infrastructure/

263 Aerospace Safety Advisory Panel — Nasa. (2020). Retrieved 4 June 2021, from https://ufdcimages.uflib.ufl.edu/AA/00/05/83/52/00015/2020_pdf.txt

The Story of The Infamous SLS

NASA has spent approximately $20 billion on developing a heavy-lift rocket, the Space Launch System (SLS), which is expected to bring astronauts to Mars. Despite the exorbitant expense, the project is "years behind schedule, relies on outdated technology, suffers by comparison to private-sector alternatives, and has little justification to begin with," a recent Bloomberg editorial stated.[264]

According to NASA's Inspector General, the SLS project, which was initiated in 2011, has endured "rising costs and delays," "shortcomings in quality control," "challenges with program management," "infrastructure issues," "technical issues," "development issues," and "performance issues."

In January 2021, a test of the SLS failed due to an initially unidentified anomaly. One of the rocket's biggest problems is that its core stage can only be loaded with super-low-temperature fuel nine times. This means that if tests continue to fail, there won't be much margin for error when a mission to the moon is finally launched. The whole project seems quite absurd considering the private tech companies like SpaceX and Axiom Space are developing today. For example, SpaceX and Blue Origin are developing reusable rockets while NASA continues to spend hundreds of millions on the disposable SLS.

As innovators and governments project a sustainable human presence on the moon, it seems to make little sense to spend massive amounts of taxpayer dollars on developing a single-use rocket.

The January test was only one in the SLS's long list of disappointments. The rocket's onboard systems activated an automatic abort after about a minute. Originally, the SLS was supposed to fly for the first time in 2016 and

264 Bloomberg Editorial. (2021). Scrap The Space Launch System. Retrieved 4 June 2021, from https://www.bloomberg.com/opinion/articles/2021-02-18/scrap-nasa-s-space-launch-system

to reach Mars sometime in the 2030s. Yet the 2016 date was pushed back all the way to 2020, and Mars seems further away than ever before for NASA's infamous rocket.

Preparing for Cybersecurity Threats in Space

Critical infrastructure on Earth depends on space-based assets to function on a daily basis. Communications, trade, defense, meteorology, and transport rely on satellites, ground stations, and complex data networks. All of these critical assets can be vulnerable to cyberattacks. If successful, these attacks can negatively impact the global economy and compromise vital infrastructure both in space and on Earth.

As space exploration transitions from an activity reserved for government agencies to a commercial industry, these vulnerabilities increase. NASA has saved millions of dollars by partnering with private companies to provide spacecraft and other services, but these savings may come at a cost. With more and more spacecraft connected with critical assets on the ground, opportunities for cyberattacks increase.

According to the Aerospace Corporation, space infrastructure is in dire need of security upgrades in four specific areas:

- Spacecraft vulnerability to command intrusions
- Potential system overload
- Malware attacks on ground control centers
- Malicious intrusions in communications between ground and spacecraft

If we allow terrorists and other criminals to exploit these vulnerabilities, the consequences could be devastating. For example, it would be fairly easy to attack satellite communications and get GPS to calculate incorrect military positions. In many scenarios, this could put lives at risk.

The National Oceanic and Atmospheric Administration and Space Policy Directive 5 have created an incipient framework for safeguarding space infrastructure. Despite its name, however, the Directive does not mandate anything, merely introducing a number of guidelines, and many vulnerabilities still need to be firmly addressed.

As regulators hesitate between creating hurdles for innovation and preventing cyberattacks, the U.S. must create sustainable legal frameworks to mitigate long-term risks.

Space Sector Challenges

There are three key areas in space infrastructure and services:

1. Earth-to-Space (E2S): infrastructure/services developed on Earth for use in space
2. Space-to-Earth (S2E): space-based services used on Earth, including satellite communication and GPS
3. Space-to-Space (S2S): services delivered in space, for example, catering to in-orbit locations, including space tourism

When we consider private-sector innovators, all three segments face numerous challenges, including inadequate access to funding, regulatory barriers, ROI and market readiness issues, and slow technological innovations. The government must mitigate some of these problems, creating an environment more conducive to innovation and success. If cutting-edge space innovators and spacecraft developers cannot find a sustainable business model, space infrastructure will likely suffer due to NASA's outdated methods.

Space Debris

As of early 2020, there were 5,500 satellites in orbit, 3,200 of them defunct. Rocket explosions and other anomalous events have produced thousands of objects that pose a threat to active satellites. With nearly a million objects larger than one centimeter traveling at high speed in the Earth's orbit, the threat is only too real.[265]

Space debris becomes even more challenging as S2E services require large networks of operating satellites. Although there is surveillance and tracking of larger objects in space, it is not nearly enough, and critical space infrastructure is at risk.

As we launch more and more satellites, we will need seamless space traffic management systems to prevent collisions. Meanwhile, nations continue to test anti-satellite weapons, thus creating more dangerous debris. And the existing debris mitigation policies consist of guidelines and lax frameworks rather than enforceable rules.

Near Earth Objects also pose a threat to our planet. Though smaller meteors burn through the Earth's atmosphere on a daily basis, larger ones could hit the surface of our planet and cause significant damage.

NASA has established a Planetary Defense Coordination Office and launched asteroid redirection missions, but its efforts are insufficient. Unless our country focuses more vigorously—in coordination with other nations—on mitigating the risks posed by space debris in the Earth's lower orbit, many tragedies could befall us.

265 Space Debris by The Numbers. (2021). Retrieved 4 June 2021, from https://www.esa.int/Safety_Security/Space_Debris/Space_debris_by_the_numbers

Propulsion Technology

Propulsion system performance will be vital for the development of the next generation of spacecraft. Launch vehicle technology has made minimal advances over the last 20 years. Although we now use superior materials and manufacturing techniques, propellant performance has not changed substantially.[266]

A welcome development, reusable launchers have not sufficiently reduced costs. Hypersonic engines are promising, but we need to develop more prototypes that can land like airplanes, reducing the cost and time of service between missions. Hybrid in-space propulsion holds equal promise.

If we want to send manned spacecraft to other planets, we need higher-performance propulsion systems to enable faster travel and larger payload delivery.

Human Life Sustainability in Space

Developing the technology to create sustainable environments for humans in space poses enormous challenges. We need to create artificial ecosystems that foster both physical and mental health. Among other things, we need to build resource replenishing and waste minimization systems.

LSS

Although several organizations have focused on developing Large Space Structures (LSS), we have observed little progress. If we want to build

266 Aglietti, G. (2020). Current Challenges and Opportunities for Space Technologies. *Frontiers In Space Technologies, 1*. doi: 10.3389/frspt.2020.00001

space bases on the moon or other planets, we need to be able to deploy LSS. Satellite solar power, for example, will require the deployment of massive structures. Meanwhile, the deployment of smaller instruments like telescopes and antennas is still too costly. Our ability to develop lightweight, efficiently packaged, and easily deployable equipment will be vital for space infrastructure.

Robotic In-Orbit Servicing

Satellite servicing and debris removal can be carried out with the help of advanced robotic technologies. While this is nothing new, the challenge we face today involves improving performance and reducing costs.

Defense Challenges

In 2007, when a Chinese missile hit a weather satellite, our country's status as a dominant space power was challenged in a way that had never seemed possible. Since then, Russia has created several additional threats. And our nation is still struggling to regain its leadership. Dominating space is vital for national defense because it has significant implications for warfare on Earth. Military operations, for instance, rely heavily on space-supported technology.

In August 2020, in an address before the National Defense Industrial Association, U.S. Space Command mobilization assistant, Army National Guard Maj. Gen. Tim Lawson warned, "Adversaries don't have to dominate space, they merely need to have the capability to disrupt space operations."[267]

Major threats:

267 Space Challenges Prompt DOD Response, Space Superiority. (2020). Retrieved 4 June 2021, from https://www.defense.gov/Explore/News/Article/Article/2321670/space-challenges-prompt-dod-response-space-superiority

- Interference in communications
- Anti-satellite lasers
- Nuclear explosions in space
- Ground station attacks

To deflect these threats, the U.S. needs to deploy resilient satellite networks and expand its partnerships with allied governments and private space companies. These challenges are not only a matter of national security, but also of global security.

Space Sector Priorities

Space systems are vital instruments of sovereignty; these include autonomous launch capability, civil observation, and space-based military systems. On the other hand, the space sector represents a rapidly growing share of our economy. Therefore, understanding the sector's priorities is key to developing the space infrastructure that can facilitate the technological and scientific advances the Earth will need over the next decades.

Earth Observation

Earth observation is central to security and defense. Over the next few years, our government must develop and acquire new data and analytics systems to support these types of operations.

Satcom

Satellite communications are continually evolving. Demand for new technology is growing, especially in the areas of mobility, IoT, and Machine to Machine (M2M) communications. Significant investments are needed to ensure the U.S. infrastructure doesn't lag behind that of our competitors.

Navigation

GNSS, the satellite navigation tech on which GPS is based, has seen many advances recently. Centimeter-level accuracy in real time is an attainable goal. Precise Point Positioning (PPP) and Real-Time Kinematic (RTK) are central to the functioning of high-precision applications. Our country must focus on developing these technologies, as well as Space-Based Augmentation Systems (SBAS).

Spacecraft Launch

Cost-to-orbit has decreased significantly over the last few years. Today, competition is fierce among sovereign nations, with more and more countries developing launch capabilities. Whether NASA collaborates with private companies or develops its own projects, the agency will have to modernize its launch technology.

Space Traffic Management

The large number of satellites and new space missions underway has created a demand for much more advanced space traffic management than we have today.

Exploration

From lower-orbit missions to lunar colonization and crewed missions to

Mars, exploration will continue to demand an infrastructure that is not yet in place.

Mobility and Logistics

The U.S. military should be making larger investments in mobility and logistics technology to support activities in space.

Although there is currently no need to deploy troops in space, we should be ready. "As we move forward, we're going to want to find ways to be more mobile in space," U.S. Space Command deputy commander Lt. Gen. John Shaw said during a virtual roundtable held in February 2021. "If we don't address those requirements, that would be shutting a door that we need to keep open," he said.[268]

Logistics should enable the military "to replenish space assets rapidly from the Earth's surface or elsewhere in orbit," according to Shaw. "I cannot imagine operations in space in the decades and centuries to come without mobility and logistics underpinning all of this, like they have in the other domains."

While the Space Force has announced it will enter into various partnerships with private companies to accelerate technological developments for space mobility and logistics, it is not moving fast enough.

Weather Capabilities

Weather capabilities are critical to the success of military operations. In Iraq, for example, being able to predict dust storms could save lives. But as the Air

268 Erwin, S. (2021). U.S. Space Command to Recommend Investments in Space Infrastructure | SpaceNews. Retrieved 4 June 2021, from https://spacenews.com/u-s-space-command-to-recommend-investments-in-space-infrastructure/

Force's Defense Meteorological Satellite Program (DMSP) comes to a close, the lack of a substitute is putting our military's meteorological capabilities at risk.

Once a pioneer in weather prediction on a global level, the DMSP program was terminated in 2015. According to *Space News*, "Decisions made over the years by DoD, the National Oceanic and Atmospheric Administration (NOAA), and NASA have led to the very real possibility of significant gaps in cloud characterization and theater weather imagery, specifically over portions of the Middle East and Southeast Asia."[269]

Journalists have referred to the Air Force and NASA's failed attempts to create a substitute for the DMSP as a "broken architecture." As the Space Force reactivates a decommissioned satellite and resorts to private contractors to address the most pressing defense weather needs, it is uncertain, as of February 2021, whether the issue is going to be efficiently managed.

Threats on a Global Scale

After the Space Shuttle was retired in 2011, NASA was unable to send astronauts into orbit for almost 10 years. Later on, our country started paying Russia $82 million per seat on its Soyuz capsule. As early as 2010, two Apollo astronauts warned that U.S. leadership that the space sector was suffering. During a Senate hearing, Neil Armstrong said, "If the leadership we have acquired through our investment is simply allowed to fade away, other nations will surely step in where we have faltered. I do not believe that this would be in our best interests."[270]

---

269 Mineiro, S. (2021). Op-ed | DoD Weather Capabilities Have Lagged; Space Force Can Turn That Around | SpaceNews. Retrieved 4 June 2021, from https://spacenews.com/op-ed-dod-weather-capabilities-have-lagged-space-force-can-turn-that-around/

270 Neil Armstrong Criticizes Obama Space Plan. (2010). Retrieved 4 June 2021, from https://www.npr.org/templates/

Over the last decade, our government has been trying to remedy infrastructure failings through industry partnerships, but this tactic is not appropriate for all types of space programs. According to influential astrophysicist Neil deGrasse Tyson, private companies can provide routine space flight services but are unlikely to make uncertain long-term investments on risky projects that can advance the space frontier.

In a February 2021 TV interview, deGrasse Tyson said, "my read of history tells me [Elon Musk] is not sending [his Starship] rocket anywhere first because that's expensive and [the idea would result in] a very short venture capitalist meeting: What do you wanna do? / Send humans to Mars. / How much does it cost? / I don't know, trillions [of dollars] maybe / Will people die? / Probably. That's a five-minute meeting."[271]

"I can tell you that the first people to do really expensive things where they are dangerous and people could die, those are not business people, those are governments," deGrasse Tyson said in a 2020 interview. When Europeans discovered the American continent, it was not an effort led by the Dutch East India Trading Company, "it was Columbus, funded by Spain," the astrophysicist explained. "Then he draws the maps, here's the trade winds, here's where the hostiles are and the friendlies, here's where you find the fruit that you can eat. Then you can make a business case for it, otherwise it's a really short meeting. . . someone has got to go out there with the long view, longer than the quarterly report view. Once the patents are awarded and you establish what's dangerous and what's safe, then you make the business case."[272]

---

story/story.php?storyId=126775979

271 *Late Show with Stephen Colbert feat. Neil deGrasse Tyson*. (2021). [Video]. Retrieved from https://www.youtube.com/watch?v=v9IztZpE0Lo

272 Hoare, C. (2020). Elon Musk: DeGrasse Tyson's 'Sceptical' Claim Over 'Five-Minute' Mars Meeting Revealed. Retrieved 4 June 2021, from https://www.express.co.uk/news/science/1229968/elon-musk-neil-degrasse-tyson-nasa-spacex-mars-mission-larry-king-tesla-spt

Based on this historical perspective and considering the enormous risks involved in a crewed mission to Mars, the need for our government to invest in space infrastructure becomes abundantly clear.

NASA maintains numerous collaborations with the private sector. Its Artemis program, whose goal is a 2024 lunar mission featuring a female astronaut, involves partnerships with Elon Musk's SpaceX and Jeff Bezos' Blue Origin.

Today, space exploration relies heavily on collaborations with private companies. Likewise, the private sector has largely benefited from technological advances derived from space exploration. While developing new materials and manufacturing techniques to build spacecraft, NASA has driven many engineering advances. Bluetooth headphones, memory foam mattresses, and programmable ovens rely on technology first developed by the space agency, among many other everyday products.

Today, NASA faces significant challenges. As its infrastructure becomes obsolete and its budget fails to adjust to our nation's growing exploration needs, competition from foreign countries increases and leadership is lacking.

More than eight years ago, former National Space Council Executive Secretary Scott Pace referred to "the fundamental disconnects. . . between the policies and programs and budgets" and other programmatic challenges. "There's never enough money; there's never enough time, Pace said during a talk titled "The Future of U.S. Space Policy."[273]

"What you have on the human space flight is an existential problem," Pace added. The lack of policy directions he complained about was reminiscent of the 1970s. Unfortunately, not much has changed since the current head of the Space Policy Institute uttered those words.

273 Fallows, J., Pace, S., & Walker, R. (2013). The Future of U.S. Space Policy. Retrieved 4 June 2021, from https://www.cfr.org/event/future-us-space-policy-0

In an age when innovation is the distinctive sign of world-leading nations, space is central as a source of knowledge and potential resources. Without scientific and technological advances derived from space exploration, it is unlikely that our civilization will attain sustainability and overcome the climate crisis. And without clear policy directions and substantial budget increases, it will be impossible to succeed.

Space 4.0

The space sector faces both difficult challenges and promising opportunities. A combination of Cloud, Blockchain, and Machine Learning technologies has heralded a new era of space exploration. Today's advanced manufacturing systems enable us to build cheaper rockets with a longer useful life, faster. The 3D printing market for the space sector is expected to be valued at USD $5.5 billion by 2027, and space-related investments are booming.

With automated systems, miniaturized electronics, and global supply chains, costs are decreasing as capabilities increase. Space technology developers can find scalable business models, cloud computing democratizes access for startups, blockchain can support cybersecurity and the financing of space missions, and machine learning enables innovators to develop space-based applications for a variety of markets.

In spite of fierce competition and massive challenges, if our government makes the necessary investments in space infrastructure today, America will thrive in the next era of space exploration.

CHAPTER 12:

Cyber Infrastructure | Invisible War Lords

"It takes 20 years to build a reputation and few minutes of cyber-incident to ruin it."
—Stephane Nappo

In our networked world, cyber attacks pose a tremendous threat to governments, private companies, and individuals alike.

Our societies have become tremendously dependent on information and communications infrastructure. Both private and public institutions depend on cyber infrastructure to function efficiently. Energy, transportation, communications, and financial services depend on IT systems, and they are all at risk.

Failing technology, unauthorized access, data manipulation, and system breakdown threaten the integrity of our society. Hacking anything from elections to national banks, cybercriminals have caused tremendous damage over the last few years.

Delinquent governments have notably initiated large-scale, politically and financially motivated attacks on numerous countries, including the U.S. North Korea's government stands alone as the only nation to focus on hacking for monetary gain. Its military intelligence division, the Reconnaissance General Bureau (RGB), actively trains hackers to attack foreign banks and other financial institutions worldwide. Recently, American journalists conducted a lengthy investigation that revealed the RGB's inner workings.[274]

China, North Korea, and Russia are home to some of the world's most brilliant coders, and those talents are routinely weaponized to harm our nation's interests.

In North Korea, children who excel at mathematics are recruited at an early age and put into special programs that lead to a position in the RGB. According to *The New Yorker*, this results in a life of virtual slavery for young men who are qualified enough to get some of the most coveted positions in technology companies.[275]

The magazine referred to North Korea's cybercrime program as "hydra-headed," focusing on everything from hacking banks to stealing millions of dollars worth of cryptocurrency from online exchanges. According to a United Nations report that made headlines in 2019, North Korea's criminal cyber attacks have "generated an estimated $2 billion for its weapons of mass destruction programs."[276]

Meanwhile, China has done its share of stealing patents, and Russia has been accused of attempting to influence elections in several countries, including the U.S.

China was allegedly behind one of the largest data breaches in history. Between 2014 and 2018, Marriott International's system was hacked, compromising personal and financial information about 500 million customers. *The New York Times* attributed the attack to "a Chinese

---

274 Caesar, E. (2021). The Incredible Rise of North Korea's Hacking Army. Retrieved 24 May 2021, from https://www.newyorker.com/magazine/2021/04/26/the-incredible-rise-of-north-koreas-hacking-army

275 Caesar, E. (2021). The Incredible Rise of North Korea's Hacking Army. Retrieved 24 May 2021, from https://www.newyorker.com/magazine/2021/04/26/the-incredible-rise-of-north-koreas-hacking-army

276 Nichols, M. (2021). North Korea Took $2 Billion in Cyberattacks to Fund Weapons Program: U.N. Report. Retrieved 24 May 2021, from https://www.reuters.com/article/us-northkorea-cyber-un/north-korea-took-2-billion-in-cyberattacks- to-fund-weapons- program-u-n-report-idUSKCN1UV1ZX

intelligence-gathering effort that also hacked health insurers and the security clearance files of millions more Americans."[277] In 2018, the newspaper spoke to intelligence officials who said the government-sponsored Chinese hackers had been working to build a database of U.S. government officials with security clearances.

Since the Marriott hack was discovered, threats have only escalated, especially during the COVID-19 pandemic. In this scenario, catastrophic cyber threats are more pressing than ever.

With enough knowledge and resources, hackers could plunge whole cities into darkness or tamper with water supplies and shut down critical pipelines. In fact, some of these things have already happened on U.S. soil, and unless we ramp up our cybersecurity efforts, they are not going to stop.

America vs. Cyber Threats

America currently faces serious national security threats on several fronts. Terrorism is rampant around the world, armed conflicts put our interests at risk, and various foreign nations are developing weapons of mass destruction. Money laundering and fraud affect Americans and drain U.S. taxpayer dollars, while drug trafficking spreads violence and death across our nation.

Dealing with these threats costs billions of dollars every year, yet the fastest, most invisible threat does not involve weapons, killing, or hostage situations. Cyber threats have the potential to cause a financial collapse, health crises, and influence local elections. Countries like China and Russia have already demonstrated they have armies of hackers at their disposal.

277 Marriott Data Breach Is Traced to Chinese Hackers as U.S. Readies Crackdown on Beijing (Published 2018). (2021). Retrieved 24 May 2021, from https://www.nytimes.com/2018/12/11/us/politics/trump-china-trade.html

Terrorists and hostile governments alike could hack into government networks and leave entire cities without power. They could hack into financial institution networks and completely disrupt finance. Beyond Earth, they could potentially cause satellites to crash and rockets to change their course.

In the popular French TV show, The Bureau, a group of Russian hackers stationed in Cambodia hack into European networks. Among other things, they render an entire German hospital's systems useless. Unable to use life signs monitoring, doctors fear that patients could die if administrators do not regain access to their computers.

In the end, a security expert fixes the problem, but the hackers have already cloned the hospital's system without leaving a trace. The only thing in the episode that seemed unrealistic is that a single security expert could quickly fix the issue. The rest is frighteningly real.

Innovation has changed the face of the Earth over the last decade, but our increasing reliance on the Internet has also made us vulnerable. The cyber attacks we have already endured have proved that we are not doing enough to secure our government networks and data. We are losing billions of dollars to cybercrime every year, and there is no telling how far a malicious attack could undermine our national security.

U.S. politicians have often disagreed about how to deal with cyber threats. While some lobby for more stringent federal rules, others argue that regulations are not dynamic enough to respond to fast-changing threats. The danger of implementing hard rules, the latter believe, is that it could create a false sense of security, thus making organizations more vulnerable to sophisticated attacks. This mindset doesn't seem very helpful in the light of the latest, devastating attacks. Considering the dangers that loom on the horizon, doing nothing is not an option.

In February 2021, a bipartisan group of legislators introduced the Cyber Diplomacy Act of 2021, which proposes an approach that greatly differs from the Trump administration's strategies to counter cyber threats. The Act vows to promote U.S. leadership in the cybersecurity field, establishing an Office of International Cyberspace Policy within the State Department.

According to one of its sponsors, House Democrat Jim Langevin (RI), the bill will "best position the United States to reclaim its role as a global leader inside the diplomacy realm, which is very particularly urgent given the ever-changing array of threats that we face."[278]

Rep. Langevin and his co-sponsors believe that diplomacy is a vital tool to combat cyber threats. According to former State Department cybersecurity coordinator Christopher Painter, the legislation aims to "shape a more positive environment."[279] While these efforts seem commendable, they are insufficient; it is unlikely that diplomacy will work with the likes of North Korea.

A History of Hacks

Major international cyber attacks in recent history include:

2015-2016 — Russia purportedly attempted to hack the Democratic National Committee.

2015 — Russian cyber attacks left various Ukrainian regions without electricity.

---

278 Brumfield, C., Fiscutean, A., Korolov, M., Edwards, J., & Fruhlinger, J. (2021). CSO. Retrieved 24 May 2021, from https://www.csoonline.com/article/3609518/cyber-diplomacy-act-aims-to-elevate-americas-global-cybersecurity-standing .html

279 Brumfield, C., Fiscutean, A., Korolov, M., Edwards, J., & Fruhlinger, J. (2021). CSO. Retrieved 24 May 2021, from https://www.csoonline.com/article/3609518/cyber-diplomacy-act-aims-to-elevate-americas-global-cybersecurity-standing .html

2015 — Suspected Chinese hack into the Office of Personnel Management (OPM), which compromised 20 million federal employee records.

2012 — Iranian hackers allegedly infected Saudi oil company ARAMCO's systems with a virus called "Shamoon," destroying 30,000 computers.

2014 — North Korean hack against Sony Entertainment after the company produced a less than flattering film about the country's totalitarian regime.

The last couple of years have been quite prolific for international hackers. The Center for Strategic and International Studies, a nonprofit policy research organization, keeps a record of significant cyber incidents. The lengthy list of events recorded in 2020 and 2021 includes some of the most egregious attacks by state-sponsored hackers to date.

The nonprofit defines significant cyber incidents as "cyber attacks on government agencies, defense and high-tech companies, or economic crimes with losses of more than a million dollars."[280]

From national banks and airlines to the Vatican, cybercriminals have hacked it all. Between 2020 and April 2021, recorded incidents have included:

April 2021 — Hackers took control of the social media accounts of Polish officials, later using them to spread anti-NATO propaganda.

April 2021 — Malware caused an outage on a network comprising 20 airline reservation systems.

280 Significant Cyber Incidents | Center for Strategic and International Studies. (2021). Retrieved 24 May 2021, from https://www.csis.org/programs/strategic-technologies-program/significant-cyber-incidents

April 2021 — Chinese hack on Vietnamese government agencies.

March 2021 — North Korean hackers targeted cybersecurity researchers.

March 2021 — Suspected Russian hackers stole thousands of emails from the U.S. State Department's server.[281]

March 2021 — Suspected Russian hackers attempted to interfere in Germany's national elections.

March 2021 — Chinese hackers sent malicious links to Uyghur activists living abroad. (Several media and human rights organizations have denounced a genocide against Uyghurs in north-western China).

March 2021 — Russian hackers 'briefly took over' Poland's National Atomic Energy Agency and Health Ministry websites, spreading a false radioactive threat alert.

March 2021 — Russian and Chinese intelligence services stole COVID-19 vaccine data from the European Medicines Agency.

March 2021 — A Russian hack used Lithuanian official accounts to target organizations involved in COVID-19 vaccine development.

281 Morgan, R. (2021). Suspected Russian hackers stole thousands of US State Dept. emails, report says. Retrieved 24 May 2021, from https://americanmilitarynews.com/2021/03/suspected-russian-hackers-stole-thousands-of-us-state-dept-emails-report-says/

March 2021— Suspected Iranian hackers targeted numerous public and private organizations in Azerbaijan, Bahrain, Israel, Saudi Arabia, and the UAE.

March 2021 — China-backed criminals hacked enterprise email software to steal data from more than 30,000 organizations in several countries, including government entities, defense contractors, and COVID-19 researchers.

February 2021 — North Korean operators hacked into defense firm systems in over 12 countries as part of a large-scale espionage campaign.

February 2021 — The DOJ indicted three North Korean hackers in connection with a conspiracy to steal over $1.3 billion in cash and digital currencies.

February 2021 — North Korean attempt to break into Pfizer's systems, targeting COVID-19 vaccine data.

February 2021 — Suspected Indian hackers targeted mobile phones belonging to 150 individuals across several countries, including some with links to the Pakistan Atomic Energy Commission and the Pakistan Air Force.

February 2021 — A gang of 10 cybercriminals stole over $100 million in cryptocurrencies after tricking mobile companies into assigning celebrity numbers to new devices. They were subsequently arrested.

January 2021 — Suspected Indian hackers active since 2012 attacked businesses and governments across South and East Asia, with a particular emphasis on military and government organizations in Pakistan, China, Nepal, and Afghanistan, and businesses involved in defense technology, scientific research, finance, energy, and mining.

January 2021 — Unknown hackers broke into New Zealand's central bank's systems.

December 2020 — Chinese hackers took control of the email accounts of several Finnish parliament members.

December 2020 — Saudi and UAE hackers used Israeli spyware to hack Al Jazeera journalists' phones.

December 2020 — Iranian hackers stole data from over 40 Israeli companies.

December 2020 — "Unknown state-sponsored hackers" targeted the Nepali Army and Ministry of Defense, the Sri Lankan Ministry of Defense, the Afghan National security Council, and other government entities across South Asia.

December 2020 — Several U.S. government entities and other organizations from around the world were hacked using SolarWinds software.

November 2020 — North Korean hackers infected AstraZeneca employee devices with malware, using fake job offers.

November 2020 — Chinese hack into numerous Japanese organizations in the U.S. and elsewhere.

November 2020 — Russian and North Korean hacking groups attacked several companies engaged in COVID-19 vaccine development.

October 2020 — Iranian hackers attempted to interfere in the U.S. election by targeting state election websites.

September 2020 — A German hospital suffered a ransomware attack, possibly leading to the death of an agonizing patient who had to be taken to a more distant hospital, much like in the episode of The Bureau.

September 2020 — Suspected Russian hackers targeted the email accounts of Norwegian parliament members.

August 2020 — North Korean hackers targeted United Nations officials, including members of the UN Security Council.

August 2020 — An unidentified DDoS attack against New Zealand's stock exchange disrupted its normal functioning over several days.

August 2020 — North Korean government hackers engaged in a global campaign to steal cash from ATMs.

August 2020 — Taiwanese semiconductor makers denounced an attack by Chinese government hackers to secure proprietary information, including source code and chip design data.

July 2020 — Israel prevented two cyber attacks targeting its water infrastructure.

July 2020 — Chinese government-sponsored hackers launched an attack on the Vatican to conduct espionage as authorities prepared to appoint bishops and negotiate the status of churches in China.

July 2020 — After an investigation, the U.K. concluded that Russia had attempted to interfere in its 2019 general election by stealing and leaking sensitive documents.

June 2020 — China allegedly used mandatory tax reporting software to hack into the systems of international companies operating in the country.

June 2020 — Spyware attack on human rights activists in India.

June 2020 — North Korean state-sponsored hackers sent phishing emails related to COVID-19 to over five million individuals and companies in several countries, including the U.S. and the U.K., in an effort to steal financial and personal information.

June 2020 — Unknown state-sponsored hackers targeted Australian government agencies.

June 2020 — China allegedly used DDoS attacks to target India as tensions over a border dispute escalated in the Galwan Valley.

May 2020 — A Russian hack compromised Germany's energy, water, and power networks.

May 2020 — Chinese hackers gained access to records belonging to nine million EasyJet customers.

May 2020 — Recently re-elected Taiwanese President Tsai Ing-wen was hacked. The hackers leaked potentially damaging documents to undermine his nascent administration.

May 2020 — Japan announced it was investigating a cyberattack against Mitsubishi that may have compromised missile design information.

May 2020 — Israel launched an attack that disrupted operations at an Iranian port.

April 2020 — Suspected state-sponsored operators hacked into Chinese government systems.

April 2020 — Iranian government-sponsored hackers targeted WHO staffer accounts in the context of the COVID-19 pandemic.

Cybersecurity Trends

The 2020 pandemic forced millions of individuals to work remotely, thus increasing their vulnerability to cyber attacks. The majority of last year's attacks involved ransomware. And some of the most vulnerable areas were points where public and private networks meet.

Unfortunately, the COVID-19 crisis has had a catastrophic impact on cybersecurity. In France, for instance, researchers found that cyber attacks hitting strategic businesses increased fourfold during the pandemic.

2021 Trends

- Work-from-home attacks will continue.
- Brute Force attacks make a comeback. Distributed denial-of-service (DDoS) attacks rose by 12 percent in 2020, and they will continue.
- Fileless malware and ransomware attacks will target service providers.
- Old fashioned attacks involving Trojans and botnets are not going anywhere.
- Phishing attacks, using fake COVID-19 and vaccination info as bait.

Risk Assessment

Based on the latest available report on cybersecurity risks from the United States Government Accountability Office (GAO), U.S. government agencies face immense risk in several areas.

Findings on Cybersecurity Risks across the Federal Government 2019

- Limited situational awareness — Agencies often lack timely information regarding the tactics, techniques, and procedures that threat actors use to exploit government information systems.
- Lack of standardized IT capabilities — Agencies lack standardized cybersecurity processes and IT capabilities, which impacts their ability to combat threats effectively.[282]

---

282 TechCrunch. (2021). Retrieved 24 May 2021, from https://techcrunch.com/2018/05/30/government-investigation-finds-federal-agencies-failing-at-cybersecurity-basics/

- Limited network visibility — Agencies lack visibility into what is occurring on their networks to detect data exfiltration attempts and respond to cybersecurity incidents effectively.
- Lack of accountability for managing risks — Agency leadership above the chief information officer level may not be engaged in cybersecurity risk management, and agencies do not possess robust risk management programs or consistent methods of notifying leadership of cybersecurity risks.

GAO has made about 3,000 recommendations to federal agencies. By September 2020, 600 of them, including 75 considered high priority, had not been fully implemented. This means that our government has failed to protect federal IT systems and data despite knowing where susceptibilities lie.

Financial Sector Risks

The financial services sector is one of the most critical to our country's infrastructure. Comprising banks, securities managers, and mutual funds, the sector holds more than $108 trillion in assets, making it a frequent target for international hackers.[283]

GAO has identified three critical cyber risks[284] for the U.S. financial sector:

1. Increasing access to financial records through IT service providers

283 Critical Infrastructure Protection: Treasury Needs to Improve Tracking of Financial Sector Cybersecurity Risk Mitigation Efforts. (2021). Retrieved 24 May 2021, from https://www.gao.gov/products/gao-20-631

284 Critical Infrastructure Protection: Treasury Needs to Improve Tracking of Financial Sector Cybersecurity Risk Mitigation Efforts. (2021). Retrieved 24 May 2021, from https://www.gao.gov/products/gao-20-631

and supply chain partners

2. Increasingly sophisticated malware
3. Growth of interconnectivity and data flow through networks, mobile apps, and the cloud

A report published in March 2021 highlighted the lack of transparency about cybersecurity risks in the private sector. Titled *The State of Cyber-Risk Disclosures of Public Companies*, the report states that the SolarWinds hack exposed numerous vulnerabilities involving supply-chain security, including operational disruption, sensitive customer data loss, intellectual property theft, and email scams.[285]

According to former SEC Commissioner Robert J. Jackson Jr., failing to explain to investors how companies try to mitigate cybersecurity risks is "the most pressing issue in corporate governance today."[286]

Lessons Learned from The SolarWinds Hack

Texas-based SolarWinds is a major IT company operating in the U.S., servicing 300,000 customers. Suspected Russian hackers launched a cyberattack against it that spread to the company's clients and their associates, including the Department of Homeland Security and the Treasury Department.

The cyberattack was initiated in early 2020. By adding malicious code into the company's Orion software, the hackers gained access to SolarWinds' clients' systems.

285 The State of Cyber-Risk Disclosures of Public Companies. (2021). Retrieved 24 May 2021, from https://s3.amazonaws.com/ssc-corporate-website-production/documents/resources/the-state-of-cyber-risk-disclosures-of-public-companies.pdf

286 The State of Cyber-Risk Disclosures of Public Companies. (2021). Retrieved 24 May 2021, from https://s3.amazonaws.com/ssc-corporate-website-production/documents/resources/the-state-of-cyber-risk-disclosures-of-public-companies.pdf

When SolarWinds sent software updates to its customers, it was unwittingly introducing hacked code into their systems. The hackers then used a backdoor to spy on thousands of companies and government organizations.

The hack's 18,000 corporate victims included Fortune 500 companies and federal agencies. A congressional hearing revealed that 80 percent of the victims were NGOs.[287]

The government agencies attacked included the Pentagon, the Department of Homeland Security, the State Department, the Department of Energy, the Treasury, and the National Nuclear Security Administration.

Major players in the global IT arena were affected by the hack, including Microsoft, Cisco, Intel, and Deloitte. The systems of the California Department of State Hospitals and Kent State University were also compromised.

A federal investigation concluded that the organization behind the hack was likely Russia's Foreign Intelligence Service (SVR). Donald Trump once dismissed this accusation, attributing the attack to China. On the other hand, the Biden administration has indicated that it might impose sanctions on Russia over the hack.

But the story of the attack is not over. In an Op-Ed column titled "I Was the Homeland Security Adviser to Trump. We're Being Hacked," Thomas P. Bossert wrote, "While the Russians did not have the time to gain complete control over every network they hacked, they most certainly did gain it over hundreds of them. It will take years to know for certain which networks the Russians control and which ones they just occupy."[288]

---

287 Canales, K. (2021). The US Is Readying Sanctions Against Russia over The Solarwinds Cyber Attack. Retrieved 24 May 2021, from https://www.businessinsider.com/solarwinds-hack-explained-government-agencies-cyber-security-2020-12

288 Opinion | I Was the Homeland Security Adviser to Trump. We're Being Hacked. (2021). Retrieved 24 May 2021, from https://www.nytimes.com/2020/12/16/opinion/fireeye-solarwinds-russia-hack.html

Bossert and other analysts believe that because the Russians have gained control of critical networks, they could potentially impersonate high-ranking officials and manipulate sensitive data.

Writing in December 2021, Bossert asked President Trump to collaborate with elected President Biden to deal with the crisis. "This moment requires unity, purpose, and discipline," he wrote. "An intrusion so brazen and of this size and scope cannot be tolerated by any sovereign nation. We are sick, distracted, and now under cyberattack."[289]

The scope of the SolarWinds attack appears all the more shocking, considering the U.S. Cyber Command spends billions of dollars to prevent precisely this type of attack. In fact, it was not the government but FireEye, a private company, that detected the breach.

In light of the attack's circumstances, it has become clear that the federal government needs to collaborate with the cybersecurity industry if it wants to secure our country's cyber infrastructure. The way organizations deal with these types of threats must also change. Rather than merely securing systems to prevent attacks, they must now assume attacks are possibly underway, taking a more active role in dealing with rapidly evolving hacking strategies and targets.

One unintended consequence of the hack was a spike in share prices for some of the top cybersecurity companies in the country. FireEye shares increased by 32.8 percent, while stocks for Proofpoint, CyberArk Software, and Qualys rose by 11.5-17.4 percent.[290]

SolarWinds was unique because of its scope and motivation. The

---

289 Opinion | I Was the Homeland Security Adviser to Trump. We're Being Hacked. (2021). Retrieved 24 May 2021, from https://www.nytimes.com/2020/12/16/opinion/fireeye-solarwinds-russia-hack.html

290 Bylund, A. (2021). Why Cybersecurity Stocks Soared and SolarWinds Shares Crashed on Friday | The Motley Fool. Retrieved 24 May 2021, from https://www.fool.com/investing/2020/12/18/why-cybersecurity-stocks-soared-and-solarwinds-sha/

consequences of the attack are still unfolding today. According to federal Chief Information Security Officer Chris DeRusha, one thing the administration has learned from the breach is that it must keep an "open door" with the industry and put cybersecurity at the center of its national security efforts. "Society hasn't unpacked fully what types of risks we're facing," DeRusha said; "industry and government need to partner closely so we can educate not just the American public but our workforces."[291]

DeRusha believes the only way forward involves shifting to a "zero trust model," in other words, assuming every online contact is untrustworthy until proven otherwise. Of course, this is a hard notion to sell to some industry players, who may be reluctant to invest more in cybersecurity. "We've got to get really good at being compelling, how we're communicating these risks," DeRusha advises, "We've got to do a better job explaining ROI."[292]

One of the top cybersecurity experts contributing to the conversation has been David A. Wheeler, the Director of Open Source Supply Chain Security at the Linux Foundation. Wheeler compiled a list of best practices for the industry to prevent the next SolarWinds.

His recommendations[293] include:

- Hardening build environments. (A build environment comprises all the tools and data required to build a software project, including compilers, scripting tools, code generators, test suites, scripts, libraries, configuration files, metadata, etc.)

---

291 Johnson, B. (2021). SolarWinds Hack Imparted Lessons to Work Across Silos and Not 'Victim Blame,' Says Federal CISO. Retrieved 24 May 2021, from https://www.hstoday.us/subject-matter-areas/infrastructure-security/solarwinds-hack-imparted- lessons-to- work-across-silos-and-not-victim-blame-says-federal-ciso/

292 Johnson, B. (2021). SolarWinds Hack Imparted Lessons to Work Across Silos and Not 'Victim Blame,' Says Federal CISO. Retrieved 24 May 2021, from https://www.hstoday.us/subject-matter-areas/infrastructure-security/solarwinds-hack-imparted- lessons-to- work-across-silos-and-not-victim-blame-says-federal-ciso/

293 Preventing Supply Chain Attacks like SolarWinds - Linux Foundation. (2021). Retrieved 24 May 2021, from https://linuxfoundation.org/en/blog/preventing-supply-chain-attacks-like-solarwinds/

- Switching to verified reproducible builds
- Changing tools and interfaces to reduce unintentional vulnerabilities
- Providing cybersecurity training for developers
- Using efficient vulnerability detection tools through the software development process
- Improving widely-used OSS
- Providing/requesting a software bill of materials (SBOMs) as part of every software acquisition. (The SBOM is a list of all open-source and third-party components present in a codebase, including license, version, and patch status information.)
- Investigating subcomponents to detect any known vulnerabilities
- Implementing OpenChain (An open-source distributed ledger technology, Openchain allows organizations to "issue and manage digital assets in a robust, secure and scalable way.")

"Let's make it much harder to exploit the future systems we all depend on," Wheeler said. "Those who do not learn from history are often doomed to repeat it."[294]

DeRusha agrees with Wheeler in that SolarWinds is "an enduring wake-up call." One of the problems he has pointed out is victim-blaming, which shifts responsibility instead of acknowledging the vulnerabilities that exist throughout the industry.

While cybersecurity experts tend to agree on the diagnosis, this doesn't make the path forward any easier. Joseph Menn, author of *Cult of the Dead Cow: How the Original Hacking Supergroup Might Just Save the World*, has expressed concern about how disconnected the establishment is from the

---

294 Preventing Supply Chain Attacks like SolarWinds - Linux Foundation. (2021). Retrieved 24 May 2021, from https://linuxfoundation.org/en/blog/preventing-supply-chain-attacks-like-solarwinds/

challenges we currently face. “The four-star generals, the people running intelligence agencies, people in the White House,” he told *The Verge*, “still think of warfare and intelligence in the old terms and don’t get into questions of the private sector versus the public sector stuff because there aren’t really straightforward answers.”[295]

Menn recalls how the Chamber of Commerce was outraged when the Department of Energy tried to issue guidelines to protect power plants, including nuclear plants, from hackers. Imagine how outraged they would be if actual regulations, rather than voluntary guidelines, were implemented. Where we stand today, it is safe to say that state-sponsored groups could eventually hack our nuclear plants. And unless we take action right away, we are putting lives and assets at tremendous risk.

As Capitol Hill discusses implementing mandatory security breach reporting, legislators have been evaluating a bill that would require SEC-registered companies to disclose information about their board members’ cybersecurity expertise levels.

Like the financial sector, national defense is a critical area that needs to be specially protected. According to GAO’s report, the Department of Defense has often failed to include cybersecurity requirements in weapons contracts.

Today, our military operations are vulnerable, our water supplies, nuclear plants, and cryptocurrency exchanges are vulnerable, and so are our hospitals. A ransomware attack on a healthcare facility could lead to the loss of many lives. Massive computer networks could be rendered useless. Billions of dollars could be stolen from banks and federal funds, and whole regions could go dark.

---

295 Hard lessons of the SolarWinds hack. (2021). Retrieved 24 May 2021, from https://www.theverge.com/2021/1/26/22248631/solarwinds-hack-cybersecurity-us-menn-decoder-podcast

National Infrastructure Vulnerabilities

As the response to SolarWinds was still underway, in May 2021, a ransomware attack shut down a major refined products pipeline, exposing our national infrastructure's persistent vulnerability to cyber attacks.

Linking Texas with New York, the Colonial Pipeline moves nearly half of all diesel, gasoline, and jet fuel consumed on the East Coast. Powerless in front of the attack, administrators were forced to take their systems offline, completely shutting down operations.

It takes a combination of sophisticated hackers and insufficiently secured systems for such cyber attacks to succeed. If hackers can deprive one of the planet's most affluent regions in the world of fuel, what else are they capable of?

If cyber attacks continue to increase at the rate we have observed over the last two years, many more pipelines, water supplies, police departments, federal agencies, and private companies will face catastrophic threats. There is, in fact, still much to be done to protect our nation's cyber infrastructure, but there is also some hope on the horizon.

New Rules

Our government appears to be finally giving cybersecurity the high-priority status it merits. The White House has introduced a cybersecurity executive order to strengthen requirements for companies that handle government projects. There is also a bipartisan effort to create a civilian cybersecurity expert group that can develop advanced cyber defense measures.

The White House's eagerly awaited executive order will include plans to investigate cyber events more systematically and standardize software development. Proposing a "black box approach," the executive order envisions a future where each attack will be thoroughly analyzed and where contractors will be required to disclose information about any existing vulnerabilities.

Featuring about a dozen actions, the new legislation vows to incentivize secure software development while putting controls in place to keep developers in check and learn from past mistakes.

National Security Adviser Jake Sullivan said the government hopes to become "a leader, not a laggard" in cybersecurity. In the current geopolitical scenario, cybersecurity leaders will thrive, and laggards will be bombarded with devastating attacks. If there is one area where our country is in dire need of more investments and a more efficient regulatory framework, it is cybersecurity.

CHAPTER 13:

Environmental Infrastructure | Future- Forward Infrastructure

"Conservation has been practiced for many decades and preached for many more, yet only in recent years has it become plain that we cannot afford to conserve in a haphazard or piecemeal manner. No part of our conservation program can be slighted if we want to make full use of our resources and have full protection against future emergencies."

—President Harry S. Truman

Traditionally, the term environmental infrastructure has referred to structures and facilities that moderated human use of natural resources. These would include drinking water systems, wastewater treatment plants, energy production centers, and waste disposal facilities. This infrastructure provides the necessities for human life, while reducing the impact of the human population on the larger ecosystem.

Yet, in our environmentally conscious age, there has been a concerted push to expand the definition of environmental infrastructure to include everything from office towers to residential rental units, and even to encompass, according to Sen. Kirsten Gillibrand of New York, "paid leave. . . childcare. . . [and] caregiving"[296] But while Sen. Gillibrand "may be

296 Brooks, E. (2021). 'Child care is infrastructure': Democrats mocked for expanded definition beyond roads and bridges. Retrieved 5 July 2021, from https://www.msn.com/en-us/news/politics/child-care-is-infrastructure-

going to a bridge too far," pun intended, it is not outlandish to suggest that all hard infrastructure is environmental.

Whether we're talking about bridges, highways, tunnels, or water treatment facilities and power plants, every piece of hard infrastructure alters the environment in which it is built and becomes a major force in the new environment it has created. Therefore, builders must weigh the environmental impact of projects and adjust plans to accommodate nature.

Pollution, noise, and other disruptions to the ecosystem are to be minimized to strike a reasonable balance for our own sake as well as nature's. Unfortunately, reasonable balance is a casualty of the politically polarized time in which we live. We see extremists, making perfect the mortal enemy of the good, thwart progress in the name thereof, inviting the inevitable erosion of the very environment they claim to hold dear. Fortunately, while extremists savage each other in Beltway salons, practical minds are at work in the field, producing solutions that deliver incremental yet impactful results.

The Traditional Approach to U.S. Environmental Infrastructure

Under our federal system of governance, the states have exercised a great deal of autonomy in developing their natural resources. Waterways that impact numerous states have been an exception. The federal government has acted in areas such as the navigability of river systems and flood control, delegating oversight of such projects to the U.S. Army Corps of Engineers, with mixed results (see Chapter 18). As interest in environmental infrastructure has

democrats-mocked-for-expanded-definition-beyond-roads-and-bridges/ar-BB1fpeu5

increased on the federal level, Congress has often designated USACE, or the Corps, to take the lead on such projects.

In a January 2021 report, titled *Army Corps of Engineers: Environmental Infrastructure Assistance*, the Congressional Research Service explains that what the U.S. Army Corps of Engineers broadly labels environmental infrastructure, or EI, encompasses water "distribution and collection works, stormwater collection and recycled water distribution, and surface water protection and development projects."[297]

USACE provides assistance to publicly owned and operated plants in the areas of "planning, design, and construction of municipal drinking water and wastewater infrastructure projects in specified communities, counties, and states."[298] This work complements the Corps' traditional role related to "navigation, flood control, and ecosystem restoration," tasks which are authorized under various Water Resource Development Acts.

According to CRS, the Corps has provided EI assistance "in at least 44 states, the District of Columbia, Puerto Rico, U.S. Virgin Islands, and the Northern Mariana Islands."[299] The states where CRS did not find authorizations for Corps EI work were Delaware, Hawaii, Iowa, Maine, Nebraska, and Washington.

Where the Corps is involved in a project, there is cost sharing, generally at a rate of 75 percent federal and 25 percent nonfederal. However, some projects have shared at 65 percent federal and 35 percent nonfederal. After a project is completed, operations and maintenance are the sole province of the nonfederal party. Municipalities generally pay for the upkeep of

297 Army Corps of Engineers: Environmental Infrastructure Assistance. (2021). Retrieved 5 July 2021, from https://crsreports.congress.gov/product/pdf/IF/IF11184

298 Army Corps of Engineers: Environmental Infrastructure Assistance. (2021). Retrieved 5 July 2021, from https://crsreports.congress.gov/product/pdf/IF/IF11184

299 Army Corps of Engineers: Environmental Infrastructure Assistance. (2021). Retrieved 5 July 2021, from https://crsreports.congress.gov/product/pdf/IF/IF11184

environmental infrastructure through their general funds and stormwater fees.

Since 1992, Congress has authorized $5 billion in EI assistance from the Corps to more than 350 projects. Amounts of individual authorizations vary widely from $100,000 for a water monitoring station to $585 million for the six-state Western Rural Water program. The Corps has also given design assistance for 18 projects, and design and construction assistance for six more.

The report notes that the Congressional ban on earmarking seems to have played a role in reducing the number of authorizations for EI projects. However, Congress has exercised its power to amend authorizations to add funding for projects. But while traditional environmental infrastructure has been built on a large, sometimes staggeringly expensive scale, recent innovations have led to many smaller-scale strategies that are cost-efficient and impactful.

The Current State of American Stormwater Infrastructure

Stormwater systems represent a major segment of traditional environmental infrastructure in the United States. The American Society of Civil Engineers describes these systems as comprising everything "from large concrete storm sewers, roadside ditches, and flood control reservoirs to rain gardens and natural riverine systems."[300] In its 2021 Infrastructure Report Card, ASCE notes that while stormwater utility systems are expanding, so are

300 Infrastructure Report Card | Stormwater. (2021). Retrieved 5 July 2021, from https://infrastructurereportcard.org/cat-item/stormwater/

"the impervious surfaces in cities and suburbs."[301] The result is $9 billion in damages annually, as stormwater floods cause erosion and pollution.[302]

It may seem counterintuitive, but stormwater that is heavy rainfall is a significant source of water pollution in urban areas. That's because, in urban areas, rainfall bypasses nature's filtration systems. Instead of soaking into the soil where impurities and particulates are filtered out, stormwater falls on roofs and paved surfaces, carrying off various pollutants, as well as bacteria, and depositing them in engineered collection systems, from which the stormwater is discharged into local bodies of water.

According to the U.S. EPA, "Higher flows resulting from heavy rains also can cause erosion and flooding in urban streams, damaging habitat, property, and infrastructure."[303] ASCE notes that "nearly 600,000 miles of rivers and streams and more than 13 million acres of lakes, reservoirs, and ponds are considered impaired."[304] Given the poor performance, it's no wonder ASCE gives this infrastructure category an overall grade of D.

The grade is based on criteria which include:[305]

- Capacity — While ASCE concedes it is operating with limited data, what data exists supports the conclusion that capacity is inadequate. Increased urbanization and changes in storm patterns and storm intensity have also changed the way communities must judge system capacity. Cities operating with centuries-old systems, such

301 Infrastructure Report Card | Stormwater. (2021). Retrieved 5 July 2021, from https://infrastructurereportcard.org/cat-item/stormwater/

302 Infrastructure Report Card | Stormwater. (2021). Retrieved 5 July 2021, from https://infrastructurereportcard.org/cat-item/stormwater/

303 What is Green Infrastructure? | US EPA. (2021). Retrieved 5 July 2021, from https://www.epa.gov/green-infrastructure/what-green-infrastructure#downspoutdisconnection

304 Infrastructure Report Card | Stormwater. (2021). Retrieved 5 July 2021, from https://infrastructurereportcard.org/cat-item/stormwater/

305 Infrastructure Report Card | Stormwater. (2021). Retrieved 5 July 2021, from https://infrastructurereportcard.org/cat-item/stormwater/

as Chicago and Philadelphia, "are now struggling with the high cost of retrofits that are needed to accommodate these changes." ASCE notes that "upgrading large networks of aging systems" involves "significant costs and engineering challenges."[306]

- Condition — Again, data is limited, but many locals depend on stormwater conveyance systems more than 100 years old. This puts them at the outer limits of their expected lifecycle. Meanwhile, storage and treatment systems are expected to serve 20 to 30 years, making any systems constructed before the 1980s functionally obsolete. Furthermore, much has been learned in the last few decades about the impact of stormwater systems on local bodies of water. A public demanding pure water is not well served by a stormwater system that enables increased levels of river contamination. Here, ASCE observes that "from 2010 to 2018, the length of impaired rivers and streams increased from about 424,000 miles to more than 588,000 miles."[307]
- Funding and future need — Noting that the federal government provides about $250 million in funding annually, ASCE estimates there is an $8 billion funding gap given the need for expansion and retrofitting.
- Public safety — As we discuss in our chapter on levees, flooding is a potentially catastrophic event. At the same time, flooding is a regular event, as seen from 2004 to 2014, when annual damages totaled $9 billion and caused 71 deaths. The effects of overwhelmed stormwater systems on communities include erosion, sinkholes,

306 Infrastructure Report Card | Stormwater. (2021). Retrieved 5 July 2021, from https://infrastructurereportcard.org/cat-item/stormwater/

307 Infrastructure Report Card | Stormwater. (2021). Retrieved 5 July 2021, from https://infrastructurereportcard.org/cat-item/stormwater/

collapsed roadways, stripped vegetation, extensive property damage, and polluted waterways.

The nation's stormwater dilemma is a classic example of the fiscal dog chasing its tail. The failure to meet an estimated $8 billion in need results in annual losses of $9 billion in property damages. How long can this cycle repeat itself? As dog owners have long observed, before it ever catches its tail, the dog inevitably gives up in frustration. But for communities throughout the country, for whom surrender is not an option, ASCE has suggestions for improving stormwater infrastructure:

- Educate stakeholders and decision makers by fully funding and disseminating information from the EPA's Clean Watersheds Needs Survey. Compile a national database by eliciting more information about maintenance, repair, pollution prevention, and urban flooding from stormwater utilities.
- Develop a stormwater-specific funding and financing program modeled on the existing Clean Water State Revolving Fund.
- States should form peer-to-peer partnerships that empower local governments to create and manage stormwater utilities that sustainably fund, operate, maintain, assess, and, when necessary, expand stormwater infrastructure.
- Educate the public on the efficacy of stormwater infrastructure investments.
- Promote and fund 21st-century technical career training for "green-collar jobs" in the stormwater sector.
- Emphasize climate variability in codes and standards for the design, operation, maintenance, and expansion of stormwater infrastructure.
- Make stormwater infrastructure eligible for federal funding related

to the nation's drinking water and wastewater systems.

- Communities should structure stormwater utilities rates that reflect the true cost of treating and managing stormwater.
- Stormwater management systems should combine gray, green, and natural infrastructure. Innovations should be mainstreamed in urban planning and development.
- Regional coordination of efforts to address point source and nonpoint source pollution.

Taken together, these steps to "raise the grade" form a comprehensive program to remediate an underappreciated problem. But while these steps require a top-down approach from the upper echelons, green innovations provide opportunities for smaller communities and even individual property owners to ease the burden on traditional infrastructure.

From "Environmental Infrastructure" to "Green Infrastructure"

The Clean Water Act, passed in 1972, built on the Federal Water Pollution Control Act of 1948 to expand the federal government's power to regulate the discharge of pollutants into U.S. waters and to regulate quality standards for surface waters. Within the general definitions of CWA, we find the term "green infrastructure," which is defined as "the range of measures that use plant or soil systems, permeable pavement or other permeable surfaces or substrates, stormwater harvest, and reuse, or landscaping to store, infiltrate, or evapotranspirate stormwater and reduce flows to sewer systems or to surface waters."[308] In other words, this category of environmental infrastructure engineers natural processes to manage excess rainfall.

The conventional way of managing stormwater is a standard piped drainage and water treatment system, which removes the water from the urban environment. By contrast, green infrastructure aims to manage and treat stormwater at its source. The EPA describes green infrastructure as "a cost-effective, resilient approach to managing wet weather impacts that provides many community benefits."

Green infrastructure mimics nature. It uses vegetation, soil layers, and other elements to soak up, clean, and store water. Operating on a neighborhood, city, or country scale, green infrastructure is often designed as "a patchwork of natural areas that provides habitat, flood protection, cleaner air, and cleaner water."

Elements of green infrastructure include:

- **Downspout disconnection** — This simple strategy reroutes rooftop drainage pipes from a storm sewer into rain barrels and cisterns for storage, or permeable areas for natural filtration.
- **Rainwater harvesting** — These systems store rainwater for use later, and are especially useful in arid areas with infrequent rainfall.
- **Rain gardens** — Also known as bioretention or biofiltration cells, these shallow, vegetated basins are suitable for any unpaved surface. Rain gardens can collect and absorb stormwater runoff and mimic natural hydrology.
- **Planter boxes** — These "streetscaping" elements collect and absorb

308 What is Green Infrastructure? | US EPA. (2021). Retrieved 5 July 2021, from https://www.epa.gov/green-infrastructure/what-green-infrastructure#downspoutdisconnection

runoff from sidewalks, parking lots, and streets in urban areas. These mini rain gardens have vertical walls to retain runoff for filtration and evaporation.

- **Bioswales** — These elongated channels, often seen alongside roads or parking lots, are vegetated, mulched, or xeriscaped to slow, infiltrate and retain stormwater.
- **Permeable pavements** — Made of pervious concrete, porous asphalt, or permeable interlocking pavers, these surfaces allow stormwater to penetrate, preventing accumulation that could lead to flooding, hydroplaning of vehicles, and ice buildup.
- **Green streets and alleys** — By combining the elements of green infrastructure discussed above, communities can store, infiltrate, and evapotranspire stormwater throughout their neighborhoods.
- **Green parking** — Surface parking lots are rich environments for stormwater contamination. Pollutants on the surface, such as motor oil, rise with rainwater and are carried away into storm drains. Blacktopped lots also put out a lot of radiant heat in the summer, creating what is known as an "urban heat island." By integrating green infrastructure elements into parking lot designs, such as permeable pavements, rain gardens, and bioswales, communities can mitigate damage and create a more comfortable and aesthetically pleasing atmosphere.
- **Green roofs** — Covering surfaces with vegetation enables rainfall infiltration and evapotranspiration. Green roofs are cost-effective in dense urban areas and on large industrial or office buildings where expenses related to stormwater management are often high. Not only do green roofs reduce runoff volumes, but they also regulate building temperatures, reduce the urban heat island effect, and provide urban wildlife habitat. Plant species can be selected for various features, including carbon sequestration potential.

- **Urban tree canopy** — When it comes to stormwater, trees are great interceptors, collecting precipitation in their leaves and branches. Planting trees also beautifies the urban environment, relieves summer heat with much-needed shade, dampens neighborhood noise, and supports biodiversity.
- **Land conservation** — Communities can address water quality and flooding impacts by protecting open spaces and sensitive natural areas, such as wetlands, in their locale. Open spaces provide recreational opportunities for city dwellers, as well as healthy, refreshing respites from the urban grind.

To recap, green infrastructure is cost-effective and can be scaled to individual buildings, lots, streets, or neighborhoods. Green infrastructure reduces the negative impact of stormwater while conferring a range of benefits that includes water conservation; reduction of urban heat islands for greater comfort; beautification of the urban landscape; and enhanced biodiversity in developed settings, especially among bird species and insects necessary for pollination.

Green infrastructure also supports climate resiliency by mitigating erosion, replenishing groundwater reserves, reducing the need to import potable water, reducing the energy needed to cool buildings in summer, and reducing the workload of water treatment facilities.

How Effective is Green Infrastructure?

As noted, traditional stormwater management, known today as "gray infrastructure," is not inexpensive. In 2008, the U.S. EPA conducted a survey of 22 percent of "regulated municipal separate storm sewer systems," or MS4s. The EPA found $100 billion in water infrastructure needs, comprised of "$63.6 billion for combined sewer overflow control" and "$42.3 billion for stormwater management."[309] Now, extrapolate that amount to cover the entire country. That's roughly $500 billion.

That was 13 years ago. As we know, a lot has happened in that time. Infrastructure ages and must be upgraded and rehabilitated. Demographics shift, altering the level of need in various communities. The 2020 U.S. Census shows heavy migration from states such as California, Illinois, Michigan, New York, and Ohio to destinations like Texas, Colorado, Florida, Montana, North Carolina, and Oregon.[310]

As communities grow, they must make choices about meeting the clean water needs of their residents. Integrating green infrastructure strategies into the urban environment can take the pressure off traditional, expensive stormwater infrastructure.

Communities that adopt green infrastructure strategies can expect a reduction in expenses related to site grading, paving, and landscaping due to reduced erosion. Communities can also make do with smaller stormwater piping and detention facilities. By combining green and gray approaches, communities can reduce public expenditures on stormwater infrastructure.

But green infrastructure also confers tangible benefits related to:[311]

- **Air quality** — Green infrastructure can reduce ground-level ozone, commonly called smog, which can cause respiratory problems, including coughing, inflammation of airways, and asthma attacks.[312]

309 Benefits of Green Infrastructure |US EPA. (2021). Retrieved 5 July 2021, from https://www.epa.gov/green-infrastructure/benefits-green-infrastructure

310 Blake, A. (2021). Which states gain and lose in the new census report? Here are 3 takeaways. Retrieved 5 July 2021, from https://www.washingtonpost.com/politics/2021/04/26/3-takeaways-which-states-gain-lose-new-census-report/

311 Benefits of Green Infrastructure | US EPA. (2021). Retrieved 5 July 2021, from https://www.epa.gov/green-infrastructure/benefits-green-infrastructure

312 Health Effects of Ozone Pollution. Retrieved 5 July 2021, from https://www.epa.gov/ground-level-ozone-pollution/

Vegetation ameliorates smog by reducing air temperatures, alleviating the need for air conditioning which causes spikes in power plant emissions during the summer, and by removing air pollutants. Vegetation reduces particulate pollution by absorbing and filtering out tiny bits of dust, chemicals, and metals suspended in the air. Poor air quality has been linked to chronic lung ailments that degrade people's health and even cause premature death. The EPA notes that a study conducted by the City of Philadelphia found that increased tree canopy could substantially reduce "mortality, hospital admissions, and work loss days."

- **Habitat and wildlife** — Vegetation supports biodiversity by providing habitat for birds, mammals, amphibians, reptiles, and insects. Moreover, "by reducing erosion and sedimentation, green infrastructure also improves habitat in small streams and washes." Communities that have built "greenways systems" have supported species by facilitating wildlife movement between formerly isolated habitats.
- **More vibrant communities** — By improving health standards, reducing infrastructure costs, and beautifying the urban landscape, green infrastructure can revive communities. The EPA also suggests that green infrastructure can "promote economic growth, and create construction and maintenance jobs." Shopping and dining on tree-lined streets is certainly more pleasant than on barren avenues with the sun beating down. The promotion and preservation of open spaces can change the character of a community, as residents find it easier to take recreation or simply relax and enjoy their surroundings.

---

health-effects-ozone-pollution

> Vegetation is also a natural dampener of urban noise that can have an insidious effect on residents' nerves. Finally, beautiful streets raise home values benefiting residents and developers.

In short, green infrastructure means more livable communities, which are naturally peaceful and prosperous.

Barriers to Implementing Green Infrastructure

Green infrastructure presents a wealth of opportunities to "think globally and act locally." Unfortunately, government entities are so used to thinking on a grand scale, that measured steps are often undervalued. The "go big or go home" attitude can prevent communities from taking initiatives that deliver benefits at home and could make solid contributions to global efforts.

Communities must also take responsibility for funding their green initiatives since federal programs are focused on more costly, traditional "gray" infrastructure. The EPA identifies several barriers facing municipalities, such as:

- **Perception that green-infrastructure performance is unknown** — Many local governments are skeptical of what they see as emerging technologies with a limited track record, especially as they relate to their location, soil composition, and climate.
- **Perception of higher costs** — Integrating green infrastructure into capital projects comes at a cost, which may be higher in the short term than conventional approaches, particularly when long-term maintenance costs are speculative. Some funding in the form of loans and grants is available at the federal level for smaller, local projects.
- **Perception of resistance within the regulatory community** — Civic leaders may be unaware of the extent to which the EPA has embraced

green infrastructure and is willing to work with communities on feasible plans.

- **Perception of conflict with smart growth principles** — Smart growth is a strategy to limit sprawl and develop vibrant, sustainable communities by concentrating growth in existing cities and suburbs with compact builds combining housing, transportation, and employment opportunities. Civic leaders who advocate for smart growth might believe that managing stormwater at its source requires areas of open land too large to enable compact development. However, as we have seen, green infrastructure strategies can be incorporated into a confined urban environment.
- **Potential conflict with water rights law** — In western states where water has historically been treated as a limited resource, water rights are subject to a complex set of laws, mostly based on the doctrine of "prior appropriation." In some jurisdictions, stormwater collection can be viewed as appropriation contrary to existing law. Green infrastructure projects may require special permits.
- **Conflicting codes and ordinances** — Municipal codes based on gray infrastructure may inhibit green projects. But codes can be re-written if they've become obsolete.
- **Lack of government staff capacity and resources** — Transitioning to green infrastructure can require a change in development codes, education of developers and contractors, and on-site inspections. This generally means authorizing additional expenditures, such as hiring consultants to shepherd personnel through the transition. These additional expenditures must be weighed against the benefits of green planning.

Developers can also be reticent when it comes to incorporating green infrastructure into new builds. Municipalities that want the benefit of green builds must find ways to incentivize developers. We are indeed fortunate that green infrastructure gives us a path forward. The question is whether we have the collective will to walk that path. As President Truman said, "haphazard or piecemeal" approaches will not get the job done. To paraphrase "Give 'em Hell Harry," the buck stops with each of us.

CHAPTER 14:

Sports Arenas | Whose Dime Is It Anyway?

Does it make sense to use public funds to attract and retain sports franchises? When considering the quality-of-life benefits, one can often justify the large public spending. . . It is hard to argue, though, that one main benefit of a new sports facility comes from the improved quality of life of the surrounding community."[313]

—Robby Robertson

Michael Lander should have been hailed as an American hero. A former combat pilot, he'd spent years in an enemy POW camp enduring unspeakable torture before gaining his release. But his war had been Vietnam, so he returned to an ungrateful nation to face accusations and a bitter court martial that stripped him of his remaining dignity. After his marriage failed, Lander spiraled into depression, a brooding psychotic fantasizing about suicide and revenge. That's when Lander met Dahlia Iyad, an operative from the Palestinian terrorist group Black September, who was plotting an ambitious strike against a high-profile target within the United States. Together, the two formulated a scheme to achieve their twisted, grandiose dreams: Lander, flying the blimp over the Super Bowl at Tulane Stadium, would detonate

313 Robertson, R. *The Economic Impact of Sports Facilities* | *The Sport Digest*. Thesportdigest.com. Retrieved 31 August 2021, from http://thesportdigest.com/archive/article/economic-impact-sports-facilities.

weapons supplied by Iyad, inflicting massive carnage on the crowd before the eyes of the entire nation.

This is the plot of a 1974 novel, *Black Sunday*, the first effort of Thomas Harris, who went on to pen *The Silence of the Lambs*. The book was moderately successful and was adapted to film in 1977 by John Frankenheimer, who had previously directed *The Exorcist* and *The French Connection*. The film garnered mixed but generally favorable reviews. Mr. Harris said he had gotten the idea for the book from the terrorist attacks on the Munich Olympics in 1972.

At the XX Olympiad, eight members of the terrorist group Black September had killed two members of the Israeli squad and taken nine more hostage. The hostage crisis dragged on for two days before German police launched an ill-fated rescue attempt. When the smoke cleared, the nine Israeli hostages were dead, as were five members of Black September and one police officer.

The Munich Massacre led to increased security for athletes at major sporting events, but Harris' book opened a new area of concern: the audience. Yet, in the 1970s, a brazen attack against thousands of American civilians to raise public awareness about the plight of Palestinians (or any political cause) seemed far-fetched. It was inconceivable that a small band of guerillas would antagonize the greatest military power on earth. American audiences could comfortably dismiss *Black Sunday* as a wild fantasy.

That zone of comfort was dented in Atlanta in July 1996, when a nail-laden pipe bomb exploded in Centennial Olympic Park, killing one woman and injuring 100 more, "including a Turkish cameraman who suffered a fatal heart attack after the blast."[314] The comfort zone's remnants were dismantled completely on September 11, 2001.

314 Bombing at Centennial Olympic Park. (2010). Retrieved 16 June 2021, from https://www.history.com/this-day-in-history/bombing-at-centennial-olympic-park

Terrorist Threats Against U.S. Stadiums

On September 13, 2006, the Office of Infrastructure Protection in the Risk Management Division of the U.S. Department of Homeland Security issued a report on Stadiums and Arenas.[315] The report begins by noting, "There are more than 1,300 stadiums and arenas in the United States. . . located in every region and state" ranging in capacity from "a few hundred people. . . to over 100,000 spectators," hosting "sporting events, concerts, religious gatherings, university/high school graduations, political conventions, and circuses." Terrorist groups pose "specific threats" to these venues, such as:

- Indiscriminate shooting of patrons
- Hostage-taking
- Explosives (e.g., car bomb, suicide bomber)
- Biological/chemical/radiological agents introduced into the facility
- Arson (e.g., firebombing, using accelerants)

However, the good news is that terrorist activity has "indicators," which the report calls "observable anomalies or incidents that may precede a terrorist attack." Knowledge of the indicators can help authorities prevent "imminent attack" by taking immediate action. Indicators of an incoming attack may include:

- Persons in crowded areas (e.g., facility common areas, food courts) wearing unusually bulky clothing that might conceal suicide explosives or automatic weapons

315 Infrastructure Protection Report: Stadiums and Arenas. (2009). Retrieved 16 June 2021, from https://publicintelligence.net/infrastructure-protection-report-stadiums-and-arenas/

- Unattended packages (e.g., backpacks, briefcases, boxes) that might contain explosives (packages may be left in open areas or might be hidden in trash receptacles, lockers, or similar containers)
- Vehicles approaching the facility at unusually high speeds and/or steering around barriers and traffic controls
- Vehicles (e.g., cars, motorcycles, trucks, boats, or aircraft) illegally parked near facility buildings or near places where large numbers of people gather (the larger the vehicle, the greater the quantity of explosives that might be loaded into it)

In addition, there are observable anomalies that often indicate "potential surveillance by terrorists," which include:

- Persons discovered with facility maps, photos, or diagrams with critical assets highlighted or notes regarding infrastructure or listing of personnel
- Persons questioning facility employees off site about practices pertaining to the facility and its operations, or an increase in personal emails, telephone calls, faxes, or postal mail requesting information about the facility or one of its key assets
- Facility employees using video/camera/observation equipment that is not job-related
- An increase in threats from unidentified sources by telephone, postal mail, or the e-mail system and/or an increase in reports of threats from outside known, reliable sources
- Unfamiliar cleaning crews or other contract workers with passable credentials, or crews or contract workers attempting to access unauthorized areas

When facility security and rank-and-file workers are trained to "see something, say something," authorities can stay one or two steps ahead of the bad guys.

Homeland Security also observed that U.S. stadiums and arenas have common vulnerabilities which need to be addressed, such as:

- Large number of people entering the facility for events with varying levels of inspection of the items carried in.
- Little or no control or inspection of vehicles entering parking areas adjacent to the facility.
- Little or no inspection of items carried in by event participants, vendors, contractors, and maintenance and janitorial personnel.
- Limited security of facility (e.g., lockdowns, patrols, inspections) between events.
- Large number of people present at scheduled and publicized events, providing easy targets.

These vulnerabilities require protective measures which "include equipment, personnel, and procedures designed to protect a facility against threats and to mitigate the effects of an attack." The protective measures the report recommends are:

- Planning and preparedness — Developing a comprehensive security plan and emergency response plan for the facility; establishing liaison and regular communication with local law enforcement and emergency responders; conducting regular exercises with facility employees; reviewing available threat information to determine whether events should be canceled on the basis of this information.
- Personnel — Conducting background checks on all employees (more

detailed checks should be conducted on those who will have access to critical assets); maintaining an adequately sized, equipped, and trained security force for all events; conducting continuous roving security patrols during special events; expand roving/motorized patrols to outer perimeter.

- Access control — Establishing a process for controlling access and egress to the facility, including designated, monitored points of entry; establishing a buffer zone and perimeter around the facility and a process for controlling access; defining and securing controlled areas that require extra security; controlling employee and concessionaire identification and access through the use of photo identification badges; formally identifying gathering areas for tailgate parties and other such gatherings in locations with natural surveillance and access; making informal areas off limits and subject to automatic scrutiny.
- Barriers — Increasing the number of temporary venue barriers and placing them to guide the flow of vehicles; offsetting vehicle entrances from the direction of a vehicle's approach to force a reduction in speed.
- Communication and notification — Maintaining contact numbers and checklists to follow in the event of a security-related incident; during events, maintaining instantaneous communication capability with local, state, or federal law enforcement and emergency responders.
- Monitoring, surveillance, and inspection — Ensuring that the venue has an intrusion detection system; providing video surveillance systems on venue grounds; at the beginning and end of each event, inspecting the interior and exterior of facility; requiring screening of all patrons before they are allowed to enter the facility's

perimeter; requiring screening of all employees, concessionaires, event participants, and delivery and emergency service personnel before they are allowed to enter the facility's perimeter for special events; checking outdoor air intakes of heating, ventilation, and air conditioning (HVAC) systems to ensure that they are protected.

- Infrastructure interdependencies — Providing 24/7 guard at utility supply points starting 24 hours before a special event until its conclusion; ensuring that an emergency power source is provided for critical systems; ensuring that dumpsters are secured and enclosed.
- Cybersecurity — Minimizing the number of people with authorized access to computer systems; increasing computer security levels to maximum.
- Incident response — Ensuring that multiple evacuation routes and rallying points are available; inspecting all available emergency equipment prior to any event to ensure that it will operate during crisis situations; assigning specific staff members the responsibility of turning off the gas, electricity, water, and alarm systems in the event of an emergency.

In the 15 years since the release of this report, stadium and arena managers have implemented these recommendations with barriers and protocols to keep their attendees safe. Spectators have adapted to new prohibitions and procedures which they perceive as reasonable given the potential for a devastating event.

Stadium Events as Super-Spreader Threats

Since the first shutdowns in response to the COVID-19 pandemic, Americans have wondered when normality would return. For most Americans, normal means going to a ballgame or a concert and sitting shoulder-to-shoulder with other fans, who are often complete strangers. Many of us wonder if we can ever so innocently do that again. Certainly, the COVID-19 emergency will pass; pandemics always do. But even before the COVID threat has waned, vocal and influential people, such as Bill Gates, are warning that another pandemic is "almost inevitable in an increasingly globalized world."[316]

Given the disruption that the sports and entertainment industries have suffered, their self-interest, let alone broader humanitarian interest, lies in reducing the threat of spread within their facilities. In the short term, venues will only operate at a sharply reduced capacity to allow for social distancing. Once facilities are allowed to reopen fully, any adjustments that might allay the public's fear would certainly help attendance recover to pre-COVID levels. But what exactly can the venues do?

"Managing a highly communicable disease in a large stadium is a complex process," writes Leander Schaerlaeckens for *Yahoo! Sports.*[317] In response to fan concerns, Bruce Miller, "the managing director of Populous, a firm that has designed more than 1,300 sports venues, including 21 new or remodeled NFL stadiums," launched a study of "touchpoints, working out which surfaces in stadiums are touched the most by customers."

Miller states that "All of those touch-points can be changed and streamlined, so that we minimize the touch-points that are required to attend an event." Then, perhaps the task of sanitizing those touchpoints becomes manageable. Touchpoints can also be constructed of materials, such as copper, which are less hospitable to viruses.

316 Gittins, W. (2020). Bill Gates Predicts When The Next Pandemic Will Arrive. Retrieved 16 June 2021, from https://en.as.com/en/2020/11/24/latest_news/1606228590_532670.html

317 Schaerlaeckens, L. (2020). The Future of Stadiums: How Will America's Sports Venues Be Transformed by The Pandemic? Retrieved 16 June 2021, from https://www.msn.com/en-us/news/technology/the-future-of-stadiums-how-will-americas-sports-venues-be-transformed-by-the-pandemic/ar-BB15zvcX

However, the greatest change might come as pandemic fears accelerate the trend towards smaller venues. Over the last few decades, Major League Baseball has opened numerous parks, all with drastically lower fan capacity than the older facilities. Here are some before and after numbers from around the big leagues:[318]

- New York Mets — from 57,333 to 41,992
- New York Yankees — from 56,936 to 47,309
- Atlanta Braves — from 49,586 to 41,084
- Texas Rangers — from 48,114 to 40,300
- Miami Marlins — from 47,662 to 36,742
- Minnesota Twins — from 46,584 to 38,544

In the NBA, where teams generate 70 to 80 percent of their attendance revenue from the first 20 rows, teams are amenable to downsizing if it provides fans with a more intimate experience.[319] Bill Johnson of HOK, the global design and engineering firm that is remodeling the Phoenix Suns' arena, told Schaerlaeckens that "A lot of these buildings were at a point where it was time to change them anyway. Now we've had to take a hard look at it. If we're going to decrease capacity, how do we create that social experience when we're trying to stay six feet away from each other?"[320]

With venue capacities reduced, the average fan is likely to be priced out of the market. Even now, the cost of tickets, parking, and concessions can

318 Schaerlaeckens, L. (2020). The Future of Stadiums: How Will America's Sports Venues Be Transformed by The Pandemic? Retrieved 16 June 2021, from https://www.msn.com/en-us/news/technology/the-future-of-stadiums-how-will-americas-sports-venues-be-transformed-by-the-pandemic/ar-BB15zvcX

319 Muret, D. (2017). Venues 3.0: Smarter. Smaller. Social. Retrieved 16 June 2021, from https://www.sportsbusinessjournal.com/Journal/Issues/2017/01/16/In-Depth/Downsizing.aspx

320 Schaerlaeckens, L. (2020). The Future of Stadiums: How Will America's Sports Venues Be Transformed by The Pandemic? Retrieved 16 June 2021, from https://www.msn.com/en-us/news/technology/the-future-of-stadiums-how-will-americas-sports-venues-be-transformed-by-the-pandemic/ar-BB15zvcX

be prohibitive for a family outing. Fans of modest means will have to settle for the virtual experience on the sofa in front of their own TV, where at least they'll be safe from any virus.

Towards More Sustainable Venues

Sustainability is a major concern for emerging infrastructure, but especially for hubs of human activity where the worst practices of our disposable society are often on display. Stadiums and arenas, which attract spectators in the tens of thousands for three-hour events (sometimes more), can generate excessive amounts of waste in the form of plastic cups and straws, paper napkins, plastic eating utensils, and cardboard trays.

There are also the electrical demands for illumination, sound, climate control, facility operation, and the water necessary for grounds maintenance and sanitation. Taken altogether, your typical ballpark is an environmentalist's nightmare. So, while no one is advocating for the primitive conditions of Woodstock, a great many minds are hard at work seeking solutions to sustainability issues.

Writing for *Greenmatters.com*, Kristin Hunt explored a range of eco-friendly developments at stadiums throughout the country, starting with the solar power pavilion at Chase Field in Phoenix, Arizona. The Arizona Diamondbacks built the dual-purpose structure to offer fans "some shade near the entrance, all while generating clean energy for the grid."[321]

Other green features at Chase Field include LED concourse lights, low-flow sinks, and EV charging stations. As for recycling efforts, the Chase concessions crew converts fryer grease into "a biodegradable diesel fuel."

321 Hunt, K. (2019). How Sports Stadiums Are Becoming More Sustainable. Retrieved 16 June 2021, from https://www.greenmatters.com/travel/2018/07/31/2f5fvD/sports-stadiums-sustainable-design

Other sporting venues are engaged in the green movement as well. Notably, the Mercedes-Benz Stadium in Georgia, home of the NFL's Atlanta Falcons and the Atlanta United FC of MLS, was "the first outdoor stadium to win LEED Platinum certification in the U.S." LEED, meaning Leadership in Energy and Environmental Design, is a program of the U.S. Green Building Council (USGBC).

Founded in 1993, USGBC is a private 501(c)3 membership-based non-profit organization that promotes sustainability in building design, construction, and operation. USGBC awards certification on four levels (Certified, Silver, Gold, and Platinum) based on a point system. The LEED system has been used to incentivize eco-friendly construction all over the world.[322]

Noteworthy LEED-certified entertainment venues include:

- Pittsburgh's David L. Lawrence Convention Center — Gold
- Levi's Stadium in Santa Clara, home of the NFL's 49ers — Gold
- Apogee Stadium of the University of North Texas — Platinum
- Soldier Field in Chicago, home of the Chicago Bears — Certified

The LEED system has been criticized for adding expense to structures, causing builders to divert funds that could be used to add sustainability features to the project. Critics also caution that a new LEED-certified building in the middle of nowhere is not necessarily more eco-friendly than an existing structure in the center of town. The new building's environmental impact must consider the commute its tenants' employees must make out to the worksite, as opposed to the downtown office building that workers

322 Schendler, A. (2005). Top Green-Building System Is in Desperate Need of Repair. Retrieved 16 June 2021, from https://grist.org/article/leed/

can access through mass transit or at least a shorter drive. Applying that criticism to stadiums and arenas, we can see the importance of transportation infrastructure supporting the venue.

How Stadiums Add to the Toll of Traffic Congestion

Traffic congestion is the bane of urban living, adding to air and noise pollution, lengthening commutes, wasting fuel, and causing unnecessary aggravation that often leads to traffic accidents. In short, congestion adds to the cost of living while diminishing quality of life. The miseries of traffic congestion are very evident when it comes to ingress and egress around stadiums and arenas. Traffic jams not only add to pollution; they can ruin the fan experience. Fans arrive late for games irritated and must often leave early to avoid traffic on the way out, so they don't get the complete game experience.

The traffic jams going into and out of Dodger Stadium are legendary. Apparently, the committee that chose Chavez Ravine as the new ballpark site had not considered traffic flow. The terrain is much like a box canyon from an old Western film: only one way in and one way out. According to *LAObserved.com*, the day before the Dodgers' first game at the new stadium in 1962, "Los Angeles Police Chief William Parker issued this warning to fans, 'It will take two hours to get into Dodger Stadium at Chavez Ravine and two hours to get out.'"[323]

The *Los Angeles Times* reported that "75 percent of the spectators left before the ninth inning, and this was motivated by a desire to avoid a

323 Timmermann, B. (2012). 51 years of trying to beat the traffic at Dodger Stadium. Retrieved 16 June 2021, from http://www.laobserved.com/intell/2012/10/51_years_of_trying_to_beat_the.php

tieup."[324] Over the succeeding decades, fear of the commute home had been so ingrained in the psyches of Dodger fans that by the bottom of the ninth inning of the first game of the 1988 World Series, many thousands of fans were already in their cars, mired in traffic, when pinch-hitter Kirk Gibson dragged his wounded leg to the plate. Those fans never saw his historic game-winning homerun, though most of them would probably still claim they had been there.

Fast-forward 59 years, Los Angeles still has not solved the dreaded Dodger Stadium commute. A rejected proposal envisioned an aerial gondola connecting Union Station, a major transit hub, to the ballpark. [325]Critics said the project lacked the capacity to make an impact and that limited usage would not justify the cost.

The latest thoughts on the matter have come from Elon Musk, the CEO of Tesla and SpaceX. His newest venture is The Boring Company, which aims to make tunneling for transit more cost-effective. The company has almost finished a high-speed tunnel that would allow passengers to travel from LA to Las Vegas in under 45 minutes.[326] This technology is abundantly described in Chapter 26. Musk has suggested a private subway line running under Sunset Boulevard to Dodger Stadium, but critics question whether his scheme would relieve congestion by more than a few percent.

Los Angeles might be the worst-case scenario, but sports fans all across the country are feeling the pain of traffic congestion. *U.S. News* and *World Report* recently published the list of the 10 American cities with the worst

324 Timmermann, B. (2012). 51 years of trying to beat the traffic at Dodger Stadium. Retrieved 16 June 2021, from http://www.laobserved.com/intell/2012/10/51_years_of_trying_to_beat_the.php

325 Sharp, S. (2018). Proposed Gondola System Could Link Dodger Stadium to Union Station. Retrieved 16 June 2021, from https://urbanize.city/la/post/proposed-gondola-system-could-link-dodger-stadium-union-station

326 Cao, S. (2020). Elon Musk's Tunnel Under Las Vegas for Self-Driving Cars Is Almost Complete. Retrieved 16 June 2021, from https://observer.com/2020/09/elon-musk-boring-company-tunnel-las-vegas-near-completion/

traffic.[327] Every city on the list has at least one major league sports franchise. Nine of the 10 are MLB cities, and three of those towns have two franchises. Nine of the cities have, at least nominal, NFL franchises, although several of those teams play at venues outside the city limits. The NBA and NHL are also active in most of those cities. Adding stadium traffic to an already brutal commute is not healthy for people or the environment.

The traffic dilemma punctuates just how important it is for sports and entertainment venues to be supported by road and transit infrastructure. Without smooth and efficient egress, even a LEED Platinum stadium can be an ecological liability.

Who Pays for Sports Stadiums and Arenas?

Building a stadium or arena is a costly undertaking, and the financing is often controversial. Fiscal purists view sports venues as private ventures that should be privately funded. At the same time, those with Keynesian leanings look at the broader picture of economic impact and are more open to public financing.

Michael Farren, writing for *Medium.com*, observes that "Until the 1950s, publicly-owned stadiums were nearly unheard of."[328] The turning point came in 1984 when Baltimore officials refused financing for a new Colts stadium, and the owner abruptly moved the team to Indianapolis. With the threat of a lost franchise hanging overhead, local authorities became more compliant. "By 1992, 77 percent of all U.S. professional sports stadiums had been paid

---

327 Friedman, J. (2020). The 10 Most Congested Cities in The U.S. Boston Is Once Again The U.S. City Where Commuters Spend The Most Time in Traffic. By. Retrieved 16 June 2021, from https://www.usnews.com/news/cities/articles/10-cities-with-the-worst-traffic-in-the-us

328 Farren, M. (2017). The Hidden Costs of Stadium Subsidies. Retrieved 17 June 2021, from https://medium.com/concentrated-benefits/the-hidden-costs-of-stadium-subsidies-fbc079f335f3

for, at least in part, by taxpayer funds." Subsidies for stadiums come in many forms, such as cash payments, grants of land (often taken through eminent domain), tax credits and abatements, and loan guarantees.

Critics of public funding rightly point out that when the government dedicates resources to stadium construction, it cannot use those funds for civic purposes. Farren offers the example of the NFL's Raiders deal for a stadium in Las Vegas: "the $750 million subsidy that Nevada will provide to the Raiders football franchise for construction of their new stadium could instead have provided a year's worth of education to nearly 100,000 public school students or built hundreds of miles of highways. In fact, because Nevada only has 5,692 miles of state-controlled highway, the Raiders' subsidy could have funded all state highway rehabilitation costs in the state for 6.5 years."[329]

In addition, the fiscal benefits to the community are often exaggerated. While building a stadium does encourage fans to spend money on sports entertainment, this might not be extra spending but money taken away from other entertainment options, such as theatre, cinema, restaurants, and shopping. Farren points out that "If the professional sports entertainment option does not cause substantial new spending by local residents, then it probably will not actually increase municipal tax receipts in any meaningful way."

Of course, once the venue has been built, it must be maintained. Maintaining the facility means maintaining a relationship with the primary occupant. This is not always an easy proposition. When the City of Oakland wouldn't build the Raiders a new stadium, owner Al Davis moved the

329 Farren, M. (2017). The Hidden Costs of Stadium Subsidies. Retrieved 17 June 2021, from https://medium.com/concentrated-benefits/the-hidden-costs-of-stadium-subsidies-fbc079f335f3

franchise to Los Angeles.[330] When LA dragged its feet on a new stadium, Davis brought his team back to Oakland, which committed to extensive renovations of its Coliseum.

When the Raiders and the NFL decided that, even with the renovations, the Coliseum was not adequate for professional football, the Raiders again looked to Los Angeles. When the NFL disallowed that move, the Raiders set their sights on Sin City, where they received a promise of $750 in public funding for a new stadium.

The City of Oakland still has the Athletics playing baseball at the Coliseum in the summer. The situation is worse in St. Louis, where the NFL's Rams had been playing before moving back to Los Angeles. Having lost the Cardinals in 1987, St. Louis city leaders had been so eager to lure another NFL franchise to the banks of Old Muddy that they promised team ownership the moon. The Rams moved from Los Angeles in 1995 and spent 20 years in St. Louis, winning the franchise's and the city's first and only Super Bowl in 2000. When the Rams pulled out of St. Louis in 2015, the team "left behind more than bitterness. . . it left a stadium saddled with about $144 million in debt and maintenance costs."[331]

But even before the Rams left, revenues from the stadium had not been covering costs. This is not a unique problem for large venues built for specialized and necessarily limited use. NFL stadiums are designed for professional football. Unless they are shared, as in the New York Giants and New York Jets' unique agreement, these billion-dollar facilities are open for their intended purpose eight times a year. That reality puts pressure on

---

330 Greer, J. (2020). Why did the Raiders move to Las Vegas? Explaining franchise's 2020 shift from Oakland to Sin City. Retrieved 17 June 2021, from https://www.sportingnews.com/us/nfl/news/raiders-las-vegas-move-explained/26kge720q0dv1stx8mwfqij0q

331 Respaut, R. (2018). With NFL Rams gone, St. Louis still stuck with stadium debt. Retrieved 17 June 2021, from https://www.reuters.com/article/us-sports-nfl-stadiums-insight-idUSKCN0VC0EP

management to find alternate uses. Unfortunately, there are a limited number of spectacles that can be expected to draw 50,000 plus ticket-buyers.

So, what does the future look like for U.S. stadiums and arenas? Going forward, developers must be prudent about expenses they might not be able to recover. Simultaneously, designers must endeavor to balance the myriad factors that impact the fan experience, maintenance challenges, environmental sustainability, and the economic bottom line.

CHAPTER 15:

Aviation | Terminal Rehab and Restructure

"The Wright Brothers created the single greatest cultural force since the invention of writing. The airplane became the first World Wide Web, bringing people, languages, ideas, and values together."

—Bill Gates

The Flight to Nowhere

The ability to fly commercially across the North American continent in under five hours is nothing short of phenomenal. So, if our plane is a few minutes late on takeoff or arrival, we tend to take the inconvenience in stride. We are, after all, eons ahead of our ancestors who relied on wagon trains and the iron horse. Still, infrastructure must be judged in the context of its time, and that's where our aviation industry comes up short.

Just ask the passengers of United 1293. That flight from John Wayne Santa Ana Airport in California to Newark Liberty International Airport in New Jersey took place on November 15, 2018. Crossing the continent was totally routine, with touchdown in the Garden State around the five-hour mark. The plane was somehow delayed three hours and 51 minutes on Newark's tarmac before passengers could disembark.

Anyone who has ever flown commercially knows how cramped the cabins are, how little leg room is afforded passengers, and how limited the restroom facilities are. We accept these discomforts as part of the price we must pay to get from point A to point B. But the discomforts become torturous when they're not getting us anywhere. You don't have to be claustrophobic to start clawing at the walls after an hour or more of sitting for no apparent reason, often with no communication from your captors, with the terminal in easy view just a hundred yards away.

That day in November 2018 was miserable for Newark Liberty, which also recorded tarmac delays of three hours and 45 minutes for Spirit Airlines flight 524 from Fort Lauderdale, and three hours and 41 minutes for United Airlines flight 4954 from Newark to Albany, New York. But those were just the domestic flights. Delays were even worse for three international flights. Air Canada flight 549 to Vancouver, Canada, sat for six hours and 18 minutes before departing; United Airlines flight 1473 from Santo Domingo, Dominican Republic, was delayed five hours and 36 minutes upon arrival at Newark; and British Airways flight 189 also from Santo Domingo to Newark waited on the tarmac for five hours and 24 minutes.

Though definitely the worst offender, Newark Liberty was hardly alone in 2018, which turned out to be a banner year from tarmac delays. According to *Forbes.com*, "The number of tarmac delays lasting more than three hours. . . increased sevenfold from 34 in 2010 to 244 during the first 11 months of 2018."[332] A milestone in tarmac delays occurred in 2007 and is known in the aviation industry as the Valentine's Day Crisis. As retold by *Thepointsguy.com*, "a serious ice storm lead [sic] to cancellations and delays at New York's JFK airport," stranding "hundreds of passengers … inside JetBlue aircraft on the tarmac, some for more than 10 hours."[333]

332 Stoller, G. (2019). Passengers Get Stuck on Tarmac More Than 3 Hours on 22 Flights per Month. Retrieved 9 June 2021, from https://www.forbes.com/sites/garystoller/2019/02/21/passengers-get-stuck-on-tarmac-more-than-3-hours-on-22-flights-per-month/?sh=33f377a33a67

333 Dorsey, B. (2019). TPG Exclusive: Airlines Stranding Record Number of Passengers on Tarmacs. Retrieved 9 June

The consumer response was to produce a "Passenger's Bill of Rights" that prompted "U.S. government action." In 2010, the Department of Transportation began imposing severe fines of "up to $27,500 per passenger, for delays on the tarmac that lasted longer than three hours for domestic flights or four hours for international flights."[334]

The fine system showed some early returns. Tarmac delays dipped a bit. But over time, airlines found loopholes in the law. Also, the DOT was loathing to impose huge fines "for rule violations unless they [were] 'egregious or repetitive.'"[335] But airline malfeasance was not the root cause of tarmac delays. Nor were the companies unjustly enriching themselves by allowing tarmac delays, which had been cutting into the companies' bottom lines even before the fines.

The predominant reasons for nightmare-length tarmac delays are severe weather and inadequate infrastructure. Or rather, infrastructure that is not adequate to cope with severe weather.

Infrastructure Inadequate to Meet The Demands of The Flying Public

In its 2021 Infrastructure Report Card for U.S.Aviation, the American Society of Civil Engineers notes that "Prior to the onset of the COVID-19 pandemic, the nation's airports were facing growing capacity challenges. Over a two-year period, passenger travel steadily increased from 964.7 million to 1.2

2021, from https://thepointsguy.com/news/tpg-exclusive-airlines-stranding-record-number-of-passengers-on-tarmacs/

334 Dorsey, B. (2019). TPG Exclusive: Airlines Stranding Record Number of Passengers on Tarmacs. Retrieved 9 June 2021, from https://thepointsguy.com/news/tpg-exclusive-airlines-stranding-record-number-of-passengers-on-tarmacs/

335 Dorsey, B. (2019). TPG Exclusive: Airlines Stranding Record Number of Passengers on Tarmacs. Retrieved 9 June 2021, from https://thepointsguy.com/news/tpg-exclusive-airlines-stranding-record-number-of-passengers-on-tarmacs/

billion per year, yet flight service only increased from 9.7 to 10.2 million flights per year—contributing in part to a total of nearly 96 million delay minutes for airline passengers in 2019."[336] The fact that the conditions and capacities of our nation's airports are not accommodating industry growth weighed heavily in the assignment of a disappointing grade of D+.[337]

Because COVID-19 restrictions decimated passenger air travel (while increasing freight traffic due to increased e-commerce), ASCE treats 2020 as an anomaly, focusing its analysis on the years 2017-2019, when "passenger travel outpaced available flights, delays in the aviation sector grew, and the percentage of flights with 'on-time' performance decreased slightly from 80.1 percent to 79.2 percent." Perhaps the most telling statistic is the increase in "total time passengers were delayed," which is calculated by multiplying the length of the delay by the number of passengers to get passenger minutes. That figure went "from 65.8 million [passenger] minutes in 2017 to 95.8 million [passenger] minutes in 2019."[338] That's thirty million extra minutes, which is a little more than 57 years. Imagine a toddler sitting with his tray table raised and his seat back in the upright position until he qualifies for AARP.

Investment Needs for Our Nation's Airports

According to ASCE's analysis of data from the Airports Council International—North America (ACI-NA), aviation infrastructure needs fall into four main categories:[339]

336 ASCE's 2021 Infrastructure Report Card | Aviation. (2021). Retrieved 9 June 2021, from https://infrastructurereportcard.org/cat-item/aviation/

337 ASCE's 2021 Infrastructure Report Card | Aviation. (2021). Retrieved 9 June 2021, from https://infrastructurereportcard.org/cat-item/aviation/

338 ASCE's 2021 Infrastructure Report Card | Aviation. (2021). Retrieved 9 June 2021, from https://infrastructurereportcard.org/cat-item/aviation/

339 ASCE's 2021 Infrastructure Report Card | Aviation. (2021). Retrieved 9 June 2021, from https://infrastructurereportcard.org/cat-item/aviation/

- Terminal buildings
- Reconstruction needs
- Capacity needs
- Access to terminals

The greatest need, whether the facility is classified as a large, medium, or small hub airport, is for terminal buildings, and this need is continuing to increase. "Since 2019, forecasts for airport needs to expand or rehabilitate terminal buildings ballooned by 62 percent" and "capital needs for terminal buildings grew from nearly $4.1 billion to more than $6.6 billion." The need for improved access to airports is naturally greatest for the large hubs, whose traffic flow can overwhelm major arteries in host cities. Improvements to manage increased capacity also rose significantly, as ACI-NA estimates that growth at 31 percent, the cost of which went "from $3.1 billion to around $4.1 billion."[340]

If there is good news in ACI-NA's data collection, it relates to the condition of airport runways, which are so crucial to flight safety. Although "pavement reconstruction needs increased by 28 percent," and the price tag for "reconstruction projects increased from around $13.1 billion to nearly $16.9 billion," runways are being maintained. "The FAA sets system performance goals to ensure that a minimum of 93 percent of paved runways. . . are maintained in excellent, good, or fair condition." According to data for FY 2019, "97.9 percent of runways. . . are rated as excellent, good, or fair, including 97.8 percent of commercial service airport runways." This represents a slight increase from FY 2017.[341]

340 ASCE's 2021 Infrastructure Report Card | Aviation. (2021). Retrieved 9 June 2021, from https://infrastructurereportcard.org/cat-item/aviation/

341 ASCE's 2021 Infrastructure Report Card | Aviation. (2021). Retrieved 9 June 2021, from https://infrastructurereportcard.org/cat-item/aviation/

"Terminal Illness"

Writing about the world's worst airports for the travel website *Frommers.com*, Sascha Segan describes "most airports" as "awful... at best joyless econoboxes, at worst purgatorial warehouses of stalled lives." Under the subheading of "Terminal Illness," he lists nine airports that "deserve special condemnation," noting that "in some cases, they deserve to be literally condemned." The U.S. airports towards which Mr. Segan directs his scorn include:[342]

- Chicago Midway — Notorious "as the nation's worst for on-time departures in the federal Bureau of Transportation Statistics data," Midway "isn't a bad place to hang out, with a new food court and a frequent subway connection to downtown Chicago," which Mr. Segan points out is "an improvement from the past few decades." Yet, "any airport is the worst airport if you're stuck there, and you aren't getting on a plane."
- Newark Airport Terminal B — "The nation's worst airport for on-time arrivals according to the Bureau of Transportation Statistics data" is also "an awfully dull airport to wait for a flight in." Additionally, "its outdated design idiotically puts security before individual piers in Terminals A and B, which means that rather than have a whole terminal's food and shopping to entertain you once you clear security, you're stuck out on a single pier."
- LaGuardia Airport US Airways Terminal — Also serving greater New York City, the airport named after the Big Apple's most beloved mayor "was recently rated the worst major airport in America by

342 The World's Worst Airport Terminals. Retrieved 9 June 2021, from https://www.frommers.com/slideshows/825013-the-world-s-worst-airport-terminals

> both JD Power and Associates and Zagat Survey." Supporting infrastructure is lacking, as "LaGuardia has no rail link to anywhere—even between its own terminals—and regularly suffers from congestion, overcrowding, and delays."
>
> The facility might adequately serve "a mid-sized city like Kansas City," but "faced with the traffic, demand, and tourist expectations of New York City, LaGuardia just doesn't measure up." The terminals are "smaller and with fewer services than you'd expect from an airport at one of the top tourist destinations in the world." But while "the central terminal has an atrium and the Delta terminal just got some new food options," the US Airways terminal "is dull and sad."

A separate *Frommers.com* essay places the third New York-area airport on the *worst of* list. "Terminal 3" of the John F. Kennedy International airport, we're told, "is known for endless immigration lines in a dank basement, an utter lack of food and shopping options, three crowded and confusing entry points, and hallways that could have been designed by M.C Escher for vomiting international travelers out onto an underground sidewalk with no cabs available." As for sanitation, "There's also a sense that the cleaning crew gave up in despair a while ago."[343]

It's worth mentioning, as Mr. Segan does in his article, that "All three major New York City airports are on this list, in large part because they're run by the Port Authority of New York and New Jersey, a hideously mismanaged money sink. . . that does a poor job of responding to air travelers' needs." That agency, known for grand-scale perfidy, is also charged with maintaining

343 Stoller, G. (2012). Travel Guide Ranks Best, Worst Airport Terminals. Retrieved 9 June 2021, from https://abcnews.go.com/Travel/travel-guide-ranks-best-worst-airport-terminals/story?id=15373892

numerous bridges and tunnels, the PATH rail system, and the port infrastructure surrounding New York Harbor. Summing up the triumvirate of substandard airports in greater New York, *Frommers.com* concludes, "let's be clear: None of them is worthy of the metropolis they serve."[344]

Common passenger complaints about airport terminals include:

- Traffic congestion on approach
- Slow passage through security
- Slow baggage claim and mishandled baggage
- Poor food and beverage options in waiting areas
- Poor air quality and odors
- Not enough charging stations for electronics
- Inadequate, uncomfortable seating in waiting areas
- Inadequate, cramped, poorly maintained restrooms

Yet, passenger comfort is not the most pressing issue. If airports could manage the check-in and security processes more efficiently, passengers would not have to spend as much time at the airport prior to their flights. Yet even these stress points are not as problematic as the lack of gate access that delays equipment which often has a domino effect on departures.

The Effects of Gate-Wait Delay on Airline Performance

Scheduling problems often arise over issues of gate assignment. So often, in fact, that the aviation industry has an acronym for Gate Assignment Problem,

344 The 10 Worst Airports in The U.S. Retrieved 9 June 2021, from https://www.frommers.com/slideshows/848240-the-10-worst-airports-in-the-u-s

i.e., GAP. A GAP occurs when a plane cannot get to a gate or cannot leave a gate because of a variety of circumstances:

- High aircraft arrival rates and long gate-occupancy times
- Gates only handle flights for their assigned airlines
- Due to safety regulations, certain gates only handle flights from certain origins or to certain destinations
- Airline overscheduling of gates

When a plane cannot get to its assigned gate, it either waits for the gate to open, or it may be reassigned to another gate, sometimes at another terminal. This requires all waiting passengers to make their way to the alternate gate. Airlines must then allow time for what can be a lengthy walk, adding to the flight delay.

In their report, entitled *Analysis of Gate-waiting Delays at Major US Airports*, researchers for the Center for Air Transportation Systems Research at George Mason University expound on the problems of gate-waiting delays as follows:[345]

> "First, gate-waiting delay increases the cost of operating a flight, including fuel burn, crew cost, aircraft life, and engine life. Gate waiting can also affect surface operations if airports do not have enough space to hold aircraft waiting for a gate. For example, BOS does not have holding pads where aircraft can wait for gates, so held aircraft may contribute to surface congestion. Gate-waiting delay usually leads to arrival delay. Arrival delay may have a propagation

345 Wang, J., Shortle, J., Wang, J., & Sherry, L. (2009). Analysis of Gate-waiting Delays at Major US Airports. 9Th AIAA Aviation Technology, Integration, And Operations Conference (ATIO). doi: 10.2514/6.2009-7085, from https://catsr.vse.gmu.edu/pubs/9thATIO_GateAnalysis.pdf

effect on an aircraft's next departure and on other aircraft's departure due to crew and passenger connections. If the airport is the passenger's final destination, the passenger trip delay is equal to this flight's arrival delay. But if gate-waiting delay causes passengers to miss their connections, the passenger trip delay will be much higher than the gate-waiting delay."

The George Mason team suggests that airlines can "mitigate gate-waiting delays by decreasing schedule volume and implementing more efficient gate assignment algorithms." Of course, decreasing the number of flights does not help carriers meet public demand for their services or earn the profits their shareholders expect. The researchers also contend that "Airports can mitigate gate-waiting delays by reserving more common gates, encouraging gate usage exchange among carriers, and using hard stands."[346]

But while airports can try to solve GAPs with decreased service, complex analytics, and carrier cooperation, the root problem is one of infrastructure. When gates can accommodate planes of all sizes, airports have more flexibility in their assignments. When large planes can comfortably park side-by-side, gates don't stand empty and unusable. Terminals must be designed for maximum use and efficiency, or they will not keep pace with passenger demand.

Advances in Operational Efficiency

ASCE assures us that "Technological advancements are playing a critical

346 Wang, J., Shortle, J., Wang, J., & Sherry, L. (2009). Analysis of Gate-waiting Delays at Major US Airports. 9Th AIAA Aviation Technology, Integration, And Operations Conference (ATIO). doi: 10.2514/6.2009-7085, from https://catsr.vse.gmu.edu/pubs/9thATIO_GateAnalysis.pdf

role in improving airport service flexibility and efficiency." The Federal Aviation Administration is halfway through a "multi-year investment and implementation plan," that has introduced "its Next Generation Air Transportation System" designed to improve "air travel safety, efficiency, and predictability" to 30 of the nation's largest airports.[347]

NextGen transitions flight control "from a radar-based to satellite-based system, replaces radio communications with data exchange and automation." The result should be a reduction in the amount of information a flight crew must process, thereby shortening routes which will "save time and fuel, minimize traffic delays, increase capacity, and permit controllers to monitor and manage aircraft, leading to greater safety." The FAA has already reported that improved reroutes have saved 15,000 hours by avoiding delays, as well as 25,000 hours of communication time, as delays have averaged "less than 17 minutes per flight, despite increased reports of severe weather and traffic."[348]

Yet, despite these quantifiable improvements, "NextGen investments are taking about four years longer than expected to translate into foundational infrastructure that supports the new technology."[349]

Public Safety and Resilience at Our Nation's Airports

No single event has had a greater impact on the aviation industry than the hijacking of four planes on September 11, 2001. Since that fateful day, when terrorists took control of and deliberately crashed four jet airliners, the federal government has created the Transportation Security Administration,

347 ASCE's 2021 Infrastructure Report Card | Aviation. (2021). Retrieved 9 June 2021, from https://infrastructurereportcard.org/cat-item/aviation/

348 ASCE's 2021 Infrastructure Report Card | Aviation. (2021). Retrieved 9 June 2021, from https://infrastructurereportcard.org/cat-item/aviation/

349 ASCE's 2021 Infrastructure Report Card | Aviation. (2021). Retrieved 9 June 2021, from https://infrastructurereportcard.org/cat-item/aviation/

airports have instituted enhanced security measures, and passengers have willingly suffered the additional inconvenience of longer lines and TSA checkpoints.

But has TSA made flying safer? Not if you believe the rumors that TSA fails up to 95 percent of its own internal tests. Results are classified, but hearsay is damning,[350] as was a report from the nonpartisan Government Accountability Office released to the public in April 2019.[351] GOA examined the results of covert testing TSA had conducted to identify vulnerabilities and fix the system to ensure greater safety. But while TSA uncovered a wealth of deficiencies, GOA found TSA had not used a "risk-informed approach" to select test scenarios, and therefore could not be sure the tests were "targeting the most likely threats."

TSA also failed spectacularly in remedying the problems it did find, primarily due to lack of effort. On the latter issue, the GOA report states, "In 2015, TSA established the Security Vulnerability Management Process to leverage agency-wide resources to address systemic vulnerabilities; however, this process has not yet resolved any identified security vulnerabilities. Since 2015, Inspection officials submitted nine security vulnerabilities identified through covert tests for mitigation, and as of September 2018, none had been formally resolved through this process."[352] In the 20 years of its existence, TSA's record has been appalling, eliciting cries for privatization of airport security from conservatives and liberals alike.

ASCE notes that since the COVID-19 pandemic, TSA has assumed even more responsibility for passenger safety. "In February 2021, TSA implemented

350 Campbell, A. (2015). TSA Fails 95 Percent of Undercover Security Tests: Report. Retrieved 9 June 2021, from https://www.huffpost.com/entry/tsa-fails-95-percent-tests-homeland-security_n_7485558

351 TSA Improved Covert Testing but Needs to Conduct More Risk-Informed Tests and Address Vulnerabilities. (2019). Retrieved 9 June 2021, from https://oversight.house.gov/sites/democrats.oversight.house.gov/files/TJkJ_d19374.pdf

352 GAO Aviation Security Report Highlights. (2019). Retrieved 9 June 2021, from https://www.gao.gov/assets/gao-19-374-highlights.pdf

an executive order requiring individuals to wear a mask at TSA screening checkpoints and throughout the commercial and public transportation systems until at least May 2021."[353] However, given that ridership dropped to a mere five percent of normal, this additional mandate could hardly prove burdensome to TSA's core mission.

As for federal support of passenger safety efforts, ASCE reports the U.S. government spent $4.9 million on airport security in FY 2020, which was "consistent with federal spending since FY 2017." However, the need for security spending is growing, and ASCE anticipates the cost will reach "$1.6 billion, or nearly 4 percent of overall airport funding needs".

How safe are our skies? "In 2018, the FAA reported 395 deaths caused by U.S. airplanes—an increase from 347 the previous year." These deaths are compiled from fatalities "on U.S. air carriers, commuter carriers, on-demand air taxis, and general aviation operations." While mechanical failures are the responsibility of individuals and corporations charged with maintaining aircrafts, deaths due to faulty infrastructure are also a concern. "Maintaining safe conditions through establishing runway safety areas, practicing runway incursion mitigation, and implementing wildlife hazard mitigation improves public safety by minimizing the risk of serious accidents."[354]

Cybersecurity also has a role to play in making the skies safer. "Specifically," according to ASCE, "aviation communication and passenger services, like ticketing, are highly dependent on a strong cybersecurity network, so ensuring safeguards to this system ensures traveler safety and system resilience." Aviation can also play a significant role in the event of a natural disaster or other emergencies, and airport infrastructure should

353 ASCE's 2021 Infrastructure Report Card | Aviation. (2021). Retrieved 9 June 2021, from https://infrastructurereportcard.org/cat-item/aviation/

354 ASCE's 2021 Infrastructure Report Card | Aviation. (2021). Retrieved 9 June 2021, from https://infrastructurereportcard.org/cat-item/aviation/

support those efforts. ASCE rightly points out that "airports play a major role as a gateway for urgent relief and access to critical supplies."[355]

However, an airport might be permanently sidelined during rescue and recovery efforts if, for instance, it lies in an earthquake zone, is not seismically resilient, and becomes a casualty of a massive quake that damages the community it serves. Therefore, our airports must have built-in resilience to "exercise rapid facilities assessments and recovery strategies that can be efficiently and effectively implemented after these types of events."[356] The sooner our airports recover, the sooner aid for threatened areas can flow, reaching those who desperately need it.

ASCE Recommendations for Raising the Grade

A D+ is not an acceptable grade for a nation whose population relies heavily on air travel and air freight for its sense of freedom and its standard of living. We must raise the grade on aviation infrastructure to keep pace with demand, enhance safety and comfort, and prevent the awful waste of time, money, and fuel. To reach these goals, ASCE suggests the following steps be taken:[357]

- Airport authorities should develop plans to improve resilience to potentially catastrophic events, whether it be seismic incidents, weather-related disasters, cybersecurity threats, or global pandemics. Strong revenue mechanisms must be developed that can withstand changes in passenger travel and provide long-term revenue certainty.

355 ASCE's 2021 Infrastructure Report Card | Aviation. (2021). Retrieved 9 June 2021, from https://infrastructurereportcard.org/cat-item/aviation/

356 ASCE's 2021 Infrastructure Report Card | Aviation. (2021). Retrieved 9 June 2021, from https://infrastructurereportcard.org/cat-item/aviation/

357 ASCE's 2021 Infrastructure Report Card | Aviation. (2021). Retrieved 9 June 2021, from https://infrastructurereportcard.org/cat-item/aviation/

- Airports should continue to invest in capacity enhancements that will accommodate projected capacity needs based on pre-COVID-19 pandemic trends.
- Raise or eliminate the cap on the Passenger Facility Charge (PFC) to allow airports the needed revenue to invest in their infrastructure.
- Support efforts to increase federal funding for the Airport Improvement Program (AIP) and continue to support user fee mechanisms that fund the Airport and Airway Trust Fund and maintain budgetary firewalls.
- Explore the use of public-private partnerships (P3s) to support existing funding efforts.
- Support innovative technology, like NextGen, that offers the ability to reduce congestion and improve capacity.
- Continue to recognize that there needs to be a strategic balance between infrastructure investment, enhanced safety measures, and technology improvements, both in investment and long-term planning.

In addition to ASCE's recommendations, busy airports must demand improvements and expansion of transportation infrastructure to allow easy ingress and egress to prevent wasteful congestion. The American hunger for air travel may take time to rebound from the COVID scare, but it will eventually recover. Facilities should take advantage of this lull in demand to address shortcomings and make solid plans for the future.

CHAPTER 16:

Hazardous Waste | Legacy Pollutants

"There is no excuse—and we should call a spade a spade—for chemical companies and oil refineries using our major rivers as pipelines for toxic waste. There is no excuse for communities to use other people's rivers as a dump for their raw sewage."
—Lyndon B. Johnson

William T. Love was a visionary. A Progressive of The Gilded Age, Love perceived that urban electrification was the key to eradicating the squalor of overcrowded slums to achieve the Puritan dream of a shining City Upon a Hill. As Richard S. Newman explains, Love was an industrial reformer who believed that efficient urban planning and management could produce "a model environment of clean streets, efficient sanitation services, and little graft or crime."[358]

Love chose Niagara Falls as the site of his experiment because of the potential for hydroelectric power to support industry and subsidize living. The rushing waters and abundant land for development formed the ideal setting for an "urban-industrial empire" built around a Model City, "a megalopolis that would dominate the region from Lake Ontario to Lake Erie." But more important than industrial might would be establishing an

358 Newman, R. (2016). Making Love Canal. Retrieved 25 June 2021, from https://www.laphamsquarterly.org/roundtable/making-love-canal

egalitarian community that actually cared for its common residents.

Hydroelectricity would bridge the gap between rich and poor. At a time when few homes or businesses had electrical power or telephone, gas, water, and sewer services, Love's Model City would provide modern amenities for all. What's more, "with businesses profiting from cheap power, and Model City leaders supporting low rents for workers, Love's town would avoid the squalor, discontent, and rebellion associated with New York City, Chicago, and Pittsburgh."

Love was not alone in his sentiments. Hydroelectric producers, such as the Niagara Power Company and the Hydraulic Power Company, were able to lure hundreds of industrial enterprises to the region by the early 1900s. In 1897, Nikolai Tesla, the rival of Thomas Edison and the Father of Alternating Current, saw Niagara as "the subjugation of natural forces to man" and a testimony to the power of the American will.

Yet Love had bigger plans. Conceding that the natural force of Niagara Falls provided the "greatest waterpower in the world," Love believed an artificial waterfall could produce double the power. Having secured a land grant of 10,000 acres over which he wielded unchecked sovereignty, Love planned to divert water inland over the Lewiston Ledge. Thus, water would pass from the Upper Niagara to the Lower Niagara by an alternate route that he would control. On May 23, 1894 at Lasalle, workers broke ground on what would become Love Canal.

But by August 1896, Love's great plan was doomed. Expenses had skyrocketed as land prices soared. Love needed the rights to additional undeveloped land to provide a return for his investors. Because he had only secured short-term options to buy land from farmers, he had to repurchase options at higher prices later. Eventually, his business plan inadvertently morphed into a Ponzi scheme with no hope of profit and no chance to secure more capital. Love's efforts were further undercut by Tesla, whose discovery of a means to transport electricity over large distances using alternating current devalued Niagara's unique potential.

The partially dug canal lay idle. A 1908 map of Lasalle shows the old power canal being used by the Niagara County Irrigation and Water Supply Company to divert water to area farmers. Development around the abandoned canal zone was sparse over the next few decades. Locals would swim in the canal in summer and skate on it in winter.

For William T. Love, the saga of the canal was personally ruinous. For his investors, it was prodigiously wasteful. But the greatest tragedy, and horror, was the perversion of Love's dream, as ruthless polluters began using his canal as a dumping ground for toxins that poisoned the unsuspecting residents of the surrounding community.

In the 1920s, Love Canal was turned into a municipal dumpsite, and local companies began to deposit industrial waste. It eventually wound up in the hands of the Hooker Chemical Company, which operated as a military defense contractor during World War II and dumped an estimated 21,000 tons of toxic chemicals in the canal.

Malcolm Logan reports that Hooker was more responsible than previous dumpers in that "They drained the canal and lined it with thick clay, and then, after filling the cavity with stacked barrels, they covered it up. They took care to bury the most potentially dangerous chemicals twenty-two feet deep and purchased the 70-foot-wide banks on either side of the canal as a buffer zone."[359]

Hooker did not go looking for a sucker to take the despoiled property off its hands. But the Niagara Falls City School District was eager to expand and too busy to perform due diligence on the property. When the district

359 The Messy Truth About Love Canal, NY. (2021). Retrieved 25 June 2021, from https://myamericanodyssey.com/the-messy-truth-about-love-canal-ny/

threatened to use eminent domain to seize the land in 1952, Hooker donated the site for one dollar. A school was constructed at the site for 400 children. In the first year of the school's operation, Logan writes, "a twenty-five-foot area crumbled, exposing toxic chemical drums, which then filled with rainwater and overflowed. Children were observed playing in the puddles."[360]

When the school board later decided to sell part of the land to developers who planned to build a subdivision of modest, working-class homes, an attorney for Hooker tried to dissuade them. Hooker's legal department had done its best to shield the company from liability for the toxic mess it had left behind but feared that excavation would rupture the clay containment walls. In fact, by 1957, the city was already excavating to install a new sewer system and had breached the clay. Five years later, construction of the LaSalle Expressway would again punch holes in the protective cap. Rainwater seeped through carrying toxic chemicals into the adjacent neighborhood.

The sale went through and about 800 homes were constructed. But because those homes were not built directly over the former dump site, new residents were not informed of potential danger. Thus, toxic waste permeated a pristine residential neighborhood, like a ticking time bomb, which finally exploded into the nation's consciousness on the first day of August 1978. The lead story for *The New York Times* that day began:

> "NIAGARA FALLS, NY — Twenty-five years after the Hooker Chemical Company stopped using the Love Canal here as an industrial dump, 82 different compounds, 11 of them suspected carcinogens, have been percolating upward through the soil, their drum containers rotting and leaching their contents into the

360 The Messy Truth About Love Canal, NY. (2021). Retrieved 25 June 2021, from https://myamericanodyssey.com/the-messy-truth-about-love-canal-ny/

backyards and basements of 100 homes and a public school built on the banks of the canal."[361]

The New York Times story was not exactly a daring exposé. Rather, the Paper of Record had finally decided the story had become too big to ignore. Months earlier, Eckardt C. Beck had visited the area on assignment for *EPA Journal*, and had observed:

> "Corroding waste-disposal drums could be seen breaking up through the grounds of backyards. Trees and gardens were turning black and dying. One entire swimming pool had been popped up from its foundation, afloat now on a small sea of chemicals. Puddles of noxious substances were pointed out to me by the residents. Some of these puddles were in their yards, some were in their basements, others yet were on the school grounds. Everywhere the air had a faint, choking smell. Children returned from play with burns on their hands and faces."[362]

It wasn't until the following summer that the nation learned of the years of silent suffering in the Love Canal community. It was a mournful tale of miscarriages, stillbirths, crib deaths, and birth defects, including children with three ears, two rows of teeth, and mental retardation. Parents had nervous breakdowns, while children suffered from hyperactivity, epilepsy, and urinary tract disorders.

President Jimmy Carter tasked the U.S. Environmental Protection

361 Upstate Waste Site May Endanger Lives. (1978). Retrieved 25 June 2021, from https://www.nytimes.com/1978/08/02/archives/upstate-waste-site-may-endanger-lives-abandoned-dump-in-niagara.html

362 The Love Canal Tragedy. (1979). Retrieved 25 June 2021, from https://archive.epa.gov/epa/aboutepa/love-canal-tragedy.html

Agency, then eight years old, to work with the Federal Disaster Assistance Agency (precursor to the Federal Emergency Management Agency) to address the crisis.

In 1980, Congress passed the Comprehensive Environmental Response, Compensation, and Liability Act of 1980. Informally known as the Superfund Act, CERCLA empowered the EPA to investigate and remediate contaminated sites. CERCLA also gives the EPA the power to identify potentially responsible parties who can be held liable for cleanup expenses as well as harm to persons and property.

In 1995, after much litigation in federal court, Occidental Petroleum Company, which had acquired Hooker Chemical in 1968, agreed to pay the EPA $129 million as reimbursement for site remediation, which is estimated to have cost more than $230 million.[363] The U.S. Department of Defense ponied up $8 million. OPC also reached a $20 million settlement with 1,300 Love Canal residents. The City of Niagara Falls and the school district were never held accountable for their gross negligence.[364]

In 2016, Lois Gibbs, a mother who founded the Love Canal Homeowners Association in 1978 and led the fight for relocation of affected families, revisited her old neighborhood. She told a local news affiliate that, "They did not clean up Love Canal. At best, they put a trench around it. There are still 20,000 tons of chemicals in the center of that site."[365] Thus, more than 40 years later, residents who were not party to the original settlement continue their fight in court.

It would be comforting to imagine that Love Canal was an aberration.

363 U.S. V. Occidental Chem. Corp. (2015). Retrieved 25 June 2021, from https://www.justice.gov/enrd/us-v-occidental-chem-corp

364 U.S. V. Occidental Chem. Corp. (2015). Retrieved 25 June 2021, from https://www.justice.gov/enrd/us-v-occidental-chem-corp

365 Williams, J. (2016). Love Canal Lawsuits Continue 40 Years Later. Retrieved 25 June 2021, from https://www.wivb.com/news/love-canal-lawsuits-continue-40-years-later/

Unfortunately, as of March 2021, 1,317 sites on the Superfund list are classified as national priorities.[366] States with the most Superfund sites are New Jersey (114), California (97), and Pennsylvania (95).[367]

Deficiencies of Theory, Policy, and Infrastructure in Hazardous Waste Management

Clearly, Hooker Chemical's plan to dispose of hazardous industrial waste did not protect the public. Yet, by the standards of its time, Hooker's conduct was exemplary. Americans with long memories can recall unfiltered waste going directly into rivers and streams, containers being dumped in isolated, undesirable tracts of land and waste simply being incinerated. We were a country of polluted waterways, foul landfills, and toxic plumes rising from towering smokestacks.

Water pollution in the Great Lakes region was so bad that sediment from steel mills, factories, tanneries, breweries, paper mills, coal plants, and countless other industries was blackening the water and contaminating recreational beaches and wildlife habitat. But when waterways used for dumping started to actually catch fire, America had had enough.

On June 22, 1969, sparks from a train running along Cleveland's Cuyahoga River, which empties into Lake Erie, ignited industrial waste floating on the surface of the water and started a conflagration with flames soaring 50 feet into the air. The city, dubbed "The Mistake on the Lake" by standup comedians who wrung dark humor from Cleveland's sad decline, was again a national laughingstock. Yet, the average Clevelander

366 Johnson, D. (2017). Do You Live Near Toxic Waste? See 1,317 of The Most Polluted Spots in The U.S. Retrieved 25 June 2021, from https://time.com/4695109/superfund-sites-toxic-waste-locations/

367 Johnson, D. (2017). Do You Live Near Toxic Waste? See 1,317 of The Most Polluted Spots in The U.S. Retrieved 25 June 2021, from https://time.com/4695109/superfund-sites-toxic-waste-locations/

hardly batted an eye. After all, as Erin Blakemore, writing for *History.com*, notes, "Between 1868 and 1952, [the river] burned nine times. The 1952 fire racked up $1.5 million in damage. But by most, occasional fires and pollution were seen as the cost of the industry—a price no one was willing to dispute."[368]

Nevertheless, disputants arose from other quarters, vociferously demanding environmental protections. By 1970, President Richard Nixon had signed legislation to create the EPA. In 1972, Congress followed up with the Clean Water Act, overriding a veto based on the president's concern for its $24.6-billion price tag.[369] Of that appropriation, $18 billion was in grants to states and municipalities for sewage plants. This expenditure recognized that if the federal government was going to make it illegal to discharge pollutants into a waterway without a permit, compliance would be virtually impossible without improved infrastructure.[370]

However, infrastructure is only part of the puzzle. Sound public policy requires an understanding of the science of waste management, which itself relies on theories of proper amelioration, storage, and containment. We need to understand the hazardous properties of various types of waste, the dynamics of groundwater hydrology, and causal links between land disposal of industrial waste and groundwater contamination.

Technology must also exist to meet policy goals. Building disposal infrastructure around an erroneous theory or obsolete technology would hardly solve the problem. In the decades since the first wave of anti-pollution legislation, the waste disposal industry has faced a steep learning curve.

368 Blakemore, E. (2020). The Shocking River Fire That Fueled The Creation of The EPA. Retrieved 25 June 2021, from https://history.com/news/epa-earth-day-cleveland-cuyahoga-river-fire-clean-water-act

369 Kenworthy, E. (1972). President Vetoes Clean Water Bill. Retrieved 25 June 2021, from https://www.nytimes.com/1972/10/18/archives/president-vetoes-clean-water-bill-nixon-acts-despite-strong.html

370 Kenworthy, E. (1972). President Vetoes Clean Water Bill. Retrieved 25 June 2021, from https://www.nytimes.com/1972/10/18/archives/president-vetoes-clean-water-bill-nixon-acts-despite-strong.html

Undeniable progress has been made. Our society is far from pristine, but neither are our rivers bursting into flame.

Living Down a Legacy of Rampant Pollution

In its 2021 Infrastructure Report Card for Hazardous Waste, the American Society of Civil Engineers awards a grade of D+. ASCE notes that even though the United States produces more than 35 million tons of toxic waste annually, we have adequate capacity to manage that waste up to 2044. In the interim, we can expect advances in technology to both mitigate waste production and improve disposal methods.[371]

So, why the low grade? Because we are still struggling to clean up the "legacy sites," where decades of inadequate storage and reckless dumping have made remediation expensive and time-consuming. ASCE points to "approximately 1,300 Superfund sites where cleanup activities are either incomplete or not yet begun," which is "roughly the same number as four years ago." In other words, the remediation task is huge and seems to be stalled.[372]

Moreover, resilience is an issue for existing hazardous waste storage sites. Recalling how construction around the Love Canal containment zone breached the protective walls and cap, we must ensure that other sites do not suffer damage from human activity or natural phenomena.

Issues of hazardous waste infrastructure that ASCE finds compelling include:[373]

371 Infrastructure Report Card | Hazardous Waste. Retrieved 25 June 2021, from https://infrastructurereportcard.org/cat-item/hazardous-waste/

372 Infrastructure Report Card | Hazardous Waste. Retrieved 25 June 2021, from https://infrastructurereportcard.org/cat-item/hazardous-waste/

373 Infrastructure Report Card | Hazardous Waste. Retrieved 25 June 2021, from https://infrastructurereportcard.org/cat-item/hazardous-waste/

- Capacity and condition — In 2019, the U.S. EPA issued a National Capacity Assessment Report acknowledging 25 years worth of capacity, but warning there had been "significant consolidation of commercial hazardous waste management facilities" at the same time that "the number of hazardous waste generators has increased." In fact, the number of facilities declined from 2,100 to 964 from 2001 to 2019.

  Fortunately, the increase in "waste generators" was primarily due to increased compliance with federal reporting requirements and did not equate to increased hazardous waste. Production of hazardous waste requiring long-term storage actually decreased by 22 percent over the preceding two decades from 45 million tons in 2001 to 35 million tons in 2019. Recycling played only a small role in this reduction, as 1.5 million tons were processed in this manner.
- Superfund limitations — The good news is that the Superfund program has proven successful in returning hundreds of toxic sites to commercial use, "supporting 8,690 businesses that provided 195,465 jobs, resulting in $13.3 billion in estimated annual employment income and $52.4 billion in annual sales." These economic benefits far exceed EPA expenditures on the projects. Additionally, 59 former Superfund sites are now home to renewable energy plants.

  But even though the Superfund has been successful in remediating many toxic waste sites and deterring ongoing waste, the program is simply inadequate to the task. As we have noted, there are more than 1,300 current Superfund sites. Since its inception, the Superfund has only successfully remediated 424 to the point where they could be deleted from the National Priorities List. There is a backlog of identified projects that have remained unfunded for years. ASCE also anticipates the number of contaminated sites will continue to grow.

ASCE points to the more than 500,000 abandoned mines throughout the country, which "pose health risks like radiation exposure, poisoned fish, and contaminated soil, water, and air." Unless remediated, these mines become a source for heavy metals and acid that interact with rainwater, contaminating streams, soil, and groundwater. With abandoned uranium mines, the threat of radiation exposure produces additional health concerns.

- Resource Conservation and Recovery Act — RCRA regulates hazardous waste from the point of generation to final disposal. RCRA charges the U.S. EPA with oversight of more than 45,000 facilities producing large quantities of hazardous waste, and roughly 1,200 waste management facilities and 8,000 recycling centers. The RCRA Corrective Action program also manages the cleanup of 3,779 contaminated sites, covering over 18 million acres to protect populations from exposure to toxins. Like the Superfund, RCRA has been effective, but it is not large enough to address the full scope of need.
- Brownfields — A brownfield is a contaminated property, where the level of hazardous waste poses a problem for human use but is not sufficient to make the Superfund list. Today, there are more than 450,000 brownfields in the U.S. These sites lie idle, suppressing economic development. Cleaning up brownfield sites "increases local tax bases, facilitates job growth, utilizes existing infrastructure, reduces development pressures from open land, and both improves and protects the environment."

  Federal grant programs that fund brownfield cleanup have returned two million acres to productive use since 2006, stimulating local economies. But the remaining acreage that requires remediation could cover the state of South Carolina.
- Public safety — ASCE concedes that infrastructure built to protect

the public by containing hazardous waste is generally fit for the purpose. However, the organization has concerns about resiliency. ASCE sites a 2019 Government Accountability Office report found that roughly 60 percent of all non-federal NPL sites are "in areas that may be impacted by flooding, storm surge, wildfires, or sea-level rise related to climate change effects."

ASCE notes that in 2017, when the excessive rain and storm surge from Hurricane Harvey damaged several Superfund sites, including the San Jacinto River Waste Pits near Houston, where "floodwaters eroded the containment structure, releasing highly toxic wastes including dioxins into the river." Then, in 2018, the Carr Fire in California almost destroyed the water treatment system at the Iron Mountain Mine site near Redding.

Additionally, fire consumed high-density propylene lines causing an explosion inside the mine. ASCE also notes that the waste sector of the U.S. economy accounts for two percent of the nation's greenhouse gas emissions, linked to climate change.

Yet, one slippery substance could have a huge impact on these assessments.

The Sticky Issue of Teflon

In 1938, Dr. Roy J. Plunkett, a research chemist working at the DuPont Jackson Laboratory in Deepwater, New Jersey, made an accidental discovery that would start a culinary revolution. Plunkett created a waxy substance that turned out to be both heat-resistant and stick-resistant. [374]

374 PFOS and PFOA Timeline. Compiled by Fluoride Action Network Pesticide Project. (2005). Retrieved 25 June 2021, from http://www.fluoridealert.org/wp-content/pesticides/effect.pfos.class.timeline.htm

After 10 years of development, DuPont introduced Teflon and soon produced two million pounds of the substance per year. In 1951, DuPont began using ammonium perfluorooctanoate, also called C8, to smooth out the lumpiness in Teflon at its Washington Works plant near Parkersburg, West Virginia. The Minnesota Mining and Manufacturing, or 3M, produced the chemical for DuPont. It became a major manufacturer of non-stick, stain-resistant, and waterproof consumer products employing the trademark Scotchgard. By 1954, DuPont workers were already raising concerns about the toxicity of C8, but that didn't stop the FDA from giving final approval for Teflon cookware in 1962.

By the 1970s, DuPont and 3M began to understand that C8 was building up in the blood of their workers and might have toxic effects. In 1981, DuPont ordered all female workers out of its Teflon division after two pregnant workers gave birth to children with birth defects. One child was born with a single nostril and other facial deformities. Then, in 1984, DuPont began secretly testing the water in the area, asking their employees to bring in samples from their homes. The results confirmed fears that C8 had leached into the public drinking supply. There was a high-level concern that C8 contamination could damage the DuPont brand and expose the company to severe liability.[375]

Those concerns turned out to be well-founded. C8 has been linked to numerous maladies, including:[376]

- Endocrine disruption

375 Kelly, S. (2016). Teflon's Toxic Legacy: DuPont Knew for Decades It Was Contaminating Water Supplies. Retrieved 25 June 2021, from https://www.ecowatch.com/teflons-toxic-legacy-dupont-knew-for-decades-it-was-contaminating-wate-1882142514.html

376 What Are PFAS Chemicals, and Where Are They Found? Retrieved 25 June 2021, from https://www.ewg.org/pfaschemicals/what-are-forever-chemicals.html

- Increased cholesterol
- Low birth weight
- Reproductive problems
- Testicular, kidney, liver, and pancreatic cancer
- Weakened childhood immunity
- Weight gain in children and dieting adults

After decades of litigation alleging DuPont had contaminated drinking water supplies in West Virginia and Ohio, the company finally agreed to settle its liability for $343 million.

The EPA has not yet determined that per- and polyfluoroalkyl substances (PFAS) are hazardous substances within the meaning of CERCLA. But there has been much hinting to that effect, and such a determination is much more likely under the current administration. If that ruling comes down, we can expect to see many more sites added to the Superfund program. This would undoubtedly strain the program since PFAS compounds were widely used for decades (3M phased out C8 in 2002) and are regarded as "forever chemicals" because they do not biodegrade. Remediation of PFAS contamination would be difficult and costly.

Raising the Grade for Hazardous Waste Infrastructure

As one might guess, the central issue around hazardous waste management is funding. ASCE urges additional resources for:

- A designated funding source for mining site cleanup, separate from the Superfund, which would also provide research on more sustainable, cost-effective remedial approaches

- Expanded brownfields competitive grant programs
- Investments in technology to improve groundwater treatment systems
- PFAS research
- Staff shortages, training gaps, and contracting delays in the Superfund program
- Superfund backlog

However, there is also a social justice component to ASCE's recommendation since too many Superfund and RCRA Corrective Action sites are located near historically disadvantaged, low-income communities, which have been disproportionately harmed by exposure to contamination. For struggling communities, the added burden of a toxic environment is unjust and must be redressed.

CHAPTER 17:

Levees | Let History Be Thy Guide

"If it keeps on rainin' levee's goin' to break.
If it keeps on rainin' levee's goin' to break.
And all these people will have no place to stay."
—Kansas Joe McCoy & Memphis Minnie
When the Levee Breaks (1929)

The U.S. Army Corps of Engineers assured a worried public that the levee system would hold. After all, the Corps had built the levees to confine Old Muddy and protect the Crescent City, so the public could have every confidence. If the river swelled to a dangerous level, there were outlets to divert water into the Atchafalaya River, the Gulf, or Lake Pontchartrain just above New Orleans. There was no reason to panic.

This might sound familiar, like the prelude to an account of the Hurricane Katrina disaster of 2005. But that would be getting way ahead of the historical narrative. Imagine instead we're in the spring of 1927, the year of the Great Flood, which then U.S. Secretary of Commerce Herbert Hoover would call "the greatest peace-time calamity in the history of the country."

After epic rainfall from the Appalachians to the Rockies from August 1926 through the winter of 1926-1927, the Ohio River had overflown its banks, and the Mississippi River had risen mightily, gaining immense strength. Some estimates set the rainfall totals at 10 times the yearly average.

Levees from southern Illinois to Louisiana were threatened. The Corps raised levees from their normal height of two to seven-and-a-half feet to as high as 38 feet in some areas. Still, the rains came.

On April 15, 1927, Good Friday, the Memphis Commercial Appeal warned: "The roaring Mississippi River, bank and levee full from St. Louis to New Orleans, is believed to be on its mightiest rampage. . . All along the Mississippi considerable fear is felt over the prospects for the greatest flood in history." That day, more than 14 inches of rain fell on New Orleans, disabling the pumps used to drain the city, and "more than 20,000 men were put to work sandbagging levees between Baton Rouge and New Orleans."[377]

Despite the Corps' assurances, Louisiana state officials knew the levees would crumble under the pressure. The question was, where? If they broke below the city, a breech would relieve pressure, but massive floods would put as much as 80 percent of the city underwater if the break occurred upstream. Thus, over the strenuous objections of downstate residents, officials devised a plan to use dynamite to blast a crevasse in the levee below the town.

Engineers selected a westward loop in the river at Caernarvon as the site for the blasting, which commenced on April 29. Prior to blasting, some 10,000 residents were evacuated, since their homes and businesses would be washed away. Residents were promised full compensation for their losses, based on estimates of $2 to 6 million. But when actual losses rose to $35 million, displaced parties ultimately received little to nothing. For 10 days, engineers used 39 tons of dynamite to blast open a "channel that released 250,000 cubic feet of water per second from the river."

Yet, amazingly, pressure continued to build upstream. On the Atchafalaya River, a Mississippi tributary northwest of Baton Rouge, the levee broke on

377 Bradshaw, J. (2021). Great Flood of 1927. Retrieved 25 May 2021, from https://64parishes.org/entry/great-flood-of-1927

May 17. A breach of the Bayou des Glaises levee added to what became a massive flood inundating several parishes and displacing 60,000 residents. "Thousands of cattle drowned, and farm crops were wiped out as southern Louisiana turned into a lake 200 miles long and 50 to 100 miles wide." It wasn't until mid-June that the flood waters started to recede into the Gulf.

But Louisiana was not the only area where disaster struck. On April 21, the river broke through the levees to the north. Major John C. H. Lee, the Army district engineer at Vicksburg, wired the chief of the Corps of Engineers, General Edwin Jadwin, "Levee broke... crevasse will overflow the entire Mississippi Delta."[378] The breach occurred upriver of Greenville and it was huge, releasing a channel 100 feet deep and half a mile across. The rate of flow was twice that of Niagara Falls. Within 10 days, more than one million acres were under 10 feet of water. The channel continued to feed the pool for months.

Historian Stephen Ambrose notes that, "Twenty-seven thousand square miles were inundated. This was about equal to the combined size of Massachusetts, Connecticut, New Hampshire, and Vermont." At this time in U.S. history, the Mississippi River Delta had been the most fertile farmland in the country but was now a watery wasteland.

The National Museum of African American History and Culture at the Smithsonian reports that "The flood inundated 16 million acres of land, displacing nearly 640,000 people in states from Illinois to Louisiana."[379] Roughly half a million of those displaced were poor, Black agricultural workers, kept in a semi-slave state under an oppressive Jim Crow regime that

378 The Mounds Levee Landing Break | PBS. Retrieved 28 May 2021, from https://www.pbs.org/wgbh/americanexperience/features/flood-levee/

379 Man vs. Nature: The Great Mississippi Flood of 1927. National Geographic. (2021). Retrieved 25 May 2021, from https://www.nationalgeographic.com/culture/article/mississippi-river-flood-culture

catered to the cotton plantations' need for cheap labor. They lived for months in what could only be described as concentration camps, as plantation owners worried that if workers were relocated, they would never return to the fields. Nevertheless, the Great Flood was a historical turning point that accelerated the Great Migration to the northern cities.

A Predictable Failure of Infrastructure

Hindsight, as we know, is 20-20, and so it might be unfair to criticize authorities for failing to recognize a millennial disaster in the making. However, at least one prominent civil engineer had known a day would come when the levees would fail, and the outlets would be inadequate to divert the troubling volume of water. He had advised authorities on precautions he believed would permanently lower the river level and make floods impossible. They did not listen.

James Buchanan Eads knew the Mississippi intimately. He had built the first railroad bridge over the river at St. Louis from 1867 to 1874. At the time, the Eads Bridge was the longest arch bridge in the world and the first to be constructed with steel as the primary material. In 1876, Louisiana called upon Eads to solve a problem plaguing the 100-mile stretch from the port of New Orleans to the Gulf of Mexico. The buildup of silt was constantly shifting and frequently making outlets unnavigable to the point of stranding ships. Eads constructed a system of wooden jetties that narrowed and focused the main outlet, so the flow of water accelerated and carved out the silt in its path, digging a deeper channel for commercial traffic.

A subsequent flood in 1890 raised the idea of a jetty system for the entire Mississippi Valley. Eads believed that concentrating the river's force would naturally lower the riverbed, accelerating flow. Eads declared, "floods can be permanently lowered," making levees unnecessary. But Eads' plan was not adopted, nor was an alternative idea of building reservoirs along various tributaries to regulate flow. The Mississippi Delta and its residents would rely entirely on levees. It was a tragic lack of foresight that invited disaster.

New Orleans Levee Failure of 2005

Louisiana and the U.S. government, which had assumed more and more control over the levee system through a series of Flood Control Acts, had 68 years from the Great Flood to Katrina to figure out a better way to protect the City of New Orleans. In the interim, the city suffered through Hurricane Betsy, which rampaged along the Gulf Coast, killing 81 people, and slamming New Orleans on September 9, 1965. As the storm surge reached Lake Pontchartrain, the levees along some canals failed. More than 160,000 homes, mostly in the Lower Ninth Ward, were flooded and remained underwater for more than 10 days.

As a result, a new levee remediation effort began in 1965, dubbed HPS or Hurricane Protection System. It was expected to be completed in 2015. But the plan itself was inadequate for remediating a system that was demonstrably, historically inadequate.

According to the American Society of Civil Engineers, the plan was based on U.S. Congress instructions to "Design for the most severe storm that is considered reasonably characteristic of a region."[380] Under that criterion, the U.S. Army Corps of Engineers used the "storm of record" within the 1900-1959 timeframe, which had winds of 101 mph. For some reason, they ignored the fact that Hurricane Betsy's top wind speed had been 140 mph. So, even

380 Roth, L. (2021). The New Orleans Levees: The Worst Engineering Catastrophe in U.S. History — What Went Wrong and Why. Retrieved 25 May 2021, from https://biotech.law.lsu.edu/climate/ocean-rise/against-the-deluge/01-new_orleans_levees.pdf

before work began, the plan was doomed to fail because it was not adequate to protect against the worst known threat.

But design is only part of the failure. We must also consider construction. Levees are ancient technology. They can be simple earthen mounds, a mere enhancement of the natural process of the river itself, which washes mud up onto the shore as it floods, depositing it as the water ebbs. But a river moving swiftly in full flood can erode an earthen levee in short order. For that reason, levees are fortified in various ways. Robust fortification requires solid foundations and materials.

The New Orleans HPS levees were composed mostly of soil surrounding an I-wall, a thin metal barrier composed of sheet piling. In 1993, these were in desperate need of repair. A contract was awarded to Pittman Construction to basically pour concrete over the soil and sheet piling to create flood walls. By 1998, Pittman complained that the soil was weak and the flimsy sheet piling "lacked structural integrity." Pittman also told the Corps of Engineers that "the soil and foundation for the walls were not of sufficient strength, rigidity, and stability to build on."[381]

For whatever reason, no officials in the notoriously corrupt state or city government, or within the Army Corps of Engineers, seemed sufficiently concerned to halt work and re-evaluate the plan. Thus, on August 28, 2005, when Katrina strengthened from a low-end Category 3 hurricane to a Cat 5, extending 200 nautical miles from its center with winds reaching 145 knots, New Orleans was on a collision course with a monster it was not prepared to face.

The monster generated a surge that greatly exceeded the design, let alone the feeble construction, of the HPS. In all, 50 major breaches occurred

381 New Orleans' Levee System. (2021). Retrieved 25 May 2021, from https://sites.google.com/site/neworleanlevee/about-us

during Katrina. According to ASCE, all but four were caused by overtopping and erosion, meaning the storm surge was higher than the barrier, so water overflowed and wore away the structure. Of the four breaches that occurred without overtopping, ASCE blamed these factors for the failure:

- Wall deformation, which opened a water-filled gap on the flood side
- Variability in soil strength
- Critical water pressures beneath the levees

Not everyone agreed. A team of researchers from U.C. Berkeley conducted an independent investigation of the HPS failure, issuing a report in May 2006. The Berkeley team disputed the notion that the storm had simply overwhelmed the system. Raymond Seed, professor of civil and environmental engineering, said, "These levees were not overtopped, they failed, primarily as a result of human error. The hurricane wasn't much bigger than the levees were designed for."[382] Instead, faulty construction was to blame. The report cites "a large number of engineering errors and poor judgments" that contributed to the structural failures. These were problems the report calls "somewhat pervasive."

One of the key findings in the Berkeley report echoed the Pittman complaint, saying the 17th Street Canal levee was "doomed to fail because of three weaknesses in the soil. . . which should have been foreseen." Rising floodwaters had tipped the floodwall, then water had flowed into a gap at its base, cutting the levee in two. Under pressure, "the outer half of the levee then slid horizontally along a weak layer of flocculated clay with a jelly-like consistency." According to Prof. Seed, the weakness of the soil meant that

382 UC Berkeley-led levee investigation team releases final report at public meeting in New Orleans. (2021). Retrieved 25 May 2021, from https://www.berkeley.edu/news/media/releases/2006/05/24_leveereport.shtml

"The levee was going to fail anytime the water got up to eight or nine feet on the flood wall."

Another failed levee had been composed of "highly erodible material, including shell sand." Seed said such material "should never have been used in a levee." The Berkeley team found another levee at London Avenue South had failed due to water seepage through porous materials. One or more trees that should have been removed, but had been allowed to remain on the levee, probably contributed to the seepage and breakup of the levee.

Bob Bea, professor of civil and environmental engineering and co-author of the Berkeley report, pointed the finger at "dysfunctional organizations." The Corps did not provide adequate oversight of the entire levee system, instead allowing local levee districts to build and maintain portions of it. Thus, there were flood walls and levees built to different standards that didn't mesh. This resulted in weak links that easily snapped.

The Corps, under "mandates by the White House, Congress and the state to be better, faster, and cheaper," had also laid off many of its geotechnical engineers. As Bea describes it, "They took the engineering out of the Corps of Engineers." They also watered down the influence the Corps could bring to bear on the project. The Corps fought for floodgates on the three major canals, but "couldn't sway the local Levee Board or Water and Sewerage Board." Lack of flood gates meant there was no way to release the pressure generated by the storm. To prevent future calamities, Bea argued, "The Corps needs to be modernized, and federal and state oversight of flood control restructured, because they can't build a safe levee with current processes."

The failure of preparedness came with a high price. When the levees gave out, whole communities were destroyed as 80 percent of the city was placed under 10 to 15 feet of water, trapping people in their homes and attics until help arrived. Property damage and business losses exceeded $100 billion. More than 1,100 people were killed, and 400,000 people fled New Orleans, never to return. Job losses were estimated at 125,000. It is, therefore, no exaggeration when ASCE calls the Katrina debacle "the worst engineering catastrophe in U.S. history."

The State of America's Levees Today

Although New Orleans is the most egregious example of serial levee failure, it is not the only trouble spot in the United States. As recently as 2019, record-breaking winter run-off caused the Missouri, Mississippi, and Arkansas Rivers and their tributaries to flood, inundating millions of homes across the Midwest.[383] Beginning in early spring and lasting through late fall, floodwaters submerged acreage from the Dakotas down to Missouri, impacting an estimated 14 million people and causing $6.2 billion in property damage. Eleven levees failed by breaching or overtopping along the Missouri River alone.[384]

They say experience is the best teacher. Yet, a cursory glance at ASCE's 2021 Infrastructure Report Card for levees suggests this nation has not learned from the Great Flood, Hurricane Betsy, Hurricane Katrina, or the Flood of 2019. The grade is a disappointing D, based on the average age and primitive composition of the structures, and the sparse oversight and inspection given to critical levees protecting lives and property.

ASCE reports that 97 percent of all levees are simple earthen embankments, prone to fatal weakening through erosion, while only 3 percent comprise concrete, rock, or steel floodwalls. The average age of an American levee is 50

383 Powell, M. (2021). The Insidious Damage of Inland Flooding| National Flood Services. Retrieved 25 May 2021, from https://nationalfloodservices.com/blog/the-2019-midwestern-floods-the-insidious-damage-of-inland-flooding/

384 10 Failed Levees in Midwest Flood Zone Were Not Inspected by Federal Government. (2021). Retrieved 25 May 2021, from https://www.kcur.org/news/2019-03-24/10-failed-levees-in-midwest-flood-zone-were-not-inspected-by-federal-government

years, and many were built under much less rigorous engineering standards than are employed today. The grade is truly disconcerting when we consider that these levees directly protect more than 11 million people.

So, what are the problems? First, making a complete assessment of the nation's levees is virtually impossible. Congress passed the National Levee Safety Act as part of the Water Resources Development Act of 2007, creating the National Levee Database (NLD) and authorizing the inventory, inspection, and risk assessment of all levees within the U.S. Army Corps of Engineers' portfolio.

To date, the Corps has inventoried about 30,000 miles of levees. Still, there remain an estimated 10,000 miles of levees the Corps has difficulty accessing, "due to the diverse public and private entities that own, operate, and maintain them."[385] The good news is, these levees are thought to be protecting fewer than 100 people each, so the risk is low. The bad news is, it will be years before we know the condition of 25 percent of the nation's levees.

Of the levees the Corps has inventoried, less than 4 percent are characterized as high or very high risk (an improvement over five percent in 2017), 9 percent are moderate risk, 60 percent are low risk. The remaining 27 percent of the levees in the portfolio have not been assessed. This brings us to a total of 52 percent of the nation's levees about which we have insufficient information to assess safety. Making matters worse, about 45 percent of the population immediately at risk from levee failure lives or works behind the high- or very high-risk levees. Moreover, 80 percent of the high- or very high-risk levees were found with "one or more levee performance concerns that would likely result in a breach prior to overtopping."

Levees certified safe by the federal government nevertheless seem to

385 Infrastructure Report Card. (2021). Retrieved 25 May 2021, from https://infrastructurereportcard.org/wp-content/uploads/2017/01/Levees-2021.pdf

suffer from deficiencies. The National Flood Insurance Act of 1968 authorizes the Federal Emergency Management Agency to establish a National Flood Insurance Program so that businesses and individuals in at-risk areas can purchase flood insurance. As part of that program, FEMA has accredited about 500 levee systems, about 270 of which are in the Corps' portfolio. For accreditation, a levee must be certified by an engineer as meeting NFIA minimum standards for design, operation, and maintenance.

Accreditation does not set the bar very high; such levees are only expected "to provide a 1 percent annual chance of flood risk reduction." Yet, 30 percent of accredited levees in the Corps' portfolio are rated moderate, high, or very high risk, despite safeguarding about 3.6 million people and $400 billion of property.

The 2019 Midwest Floods demonstrated the tragic consequences of *de minimis* oversight of the nation's levees. Kansas City public radio station KCUR reports that 10 of the 11 failed levees on the Missouri River had not been inspected within a year by the Army Corps of Engineers.[386] In the early 2010s, seven of the 11 levees had been found to be "minimally acceptable," but there were no records of inspections for three others. One of the failed levees had been built by the federal government back in 1953, so it was 66 years old when it breached. The rest had been constructed by local districts that are charged with oversight.

A Problem of Our Own Making?

One issue that arose out of the 2019 Midwest Floods is whether rapid, severe flooding is not simply the price of progress. Bob Criss, emeritus professor

386 10 Failed Levees in Midwest Flood Zone Were Not Inspected by Federal Government. (2021). Retrieved 25 May 2021, from https://www.kcur.org/news/2019-03-24/10-failed-levees-in-midwest-flood-zone-were-not-inspected-by-federal-government

of hydrogeology at Washington University in St. Louis, blames the Corps' work, which has reshaped the historically shallow, multi-channel wide river into a slim channel that runs too high and floods too easily. Today's Missouri is "narrow and featureless," according to Criss. "That is not what Lewis and Clark saw." As a result, when a river floods, there isn't a gradual rise of slow-moving water, but a furious torrent of higher volume and higher velocity.

Thus, the very force that James Buchanan Eads hoped would carve out silt and deepen the riverbed would instead, in a different geologic setting, cause rising and overtopping of the levees. Tom Waters, chair of the Missouri Levee and Drainage District Association, concedes that, as the character of the river has changed, "we haven't done anything with the flood control infrastructure to compensate for that."

How to Raise the Grade and Build a Safer Levee System

ASCE has numerous suggestions for improving the nation's levee infrastructure, including:

- Working within communities to reduce the number of new developments behind levees through zoning restrictions and land development regulations.
- Increasing the number of levees with an emergency action plan and flood warning plan.
- Increasing resources, education, and outreach to communities that live and work behind levees to communicate the risks and consequences of levee failure.
- Fully funding the National Levee Safety Program at $79 million a year to identify and inventory the location and condition of all the

nation's levees and complete the National Levee Database.

- Encouraging property owners, when appropriate, to purchase flood insurance, even if behind an NFIP-accredited levee.
- Encouraging states to assume authority to regulate levee safety.
- Deploying more broadly innovative, efficient technologies, such as LIDAR, to quickly assess levees and identify problems.
- Adopting a risk-based approach when designing new levees and evaluating existing levees.

In deciding how to move forward with levee infrastructure, we might reflect on the words of Heraclitus, a philosopher in the fifth century B.C. He wrote, "You cannot step twice into the same river, for other waters are continually flowing on." Knowing the waters will always flow, and that we cannot retake the same steps, we should at least endeavor not to make the same missteps.

CHAPTER 18:

Taming Nature | Inland Waterways and the Lifeblood of Commerce

"Nothing is softer or more flexible than water, yet nothing can resist it."
—Lao Tzu

In 1783, George Washington returned from touring the Mohawk Valley and wrote this about the country's natural waterway system to a friend:

> "Prompted by these actual observations, I could not help taking a more extensive view of the vast inland navigation of these United States and importance of it, and with the goodness of that Providence, which has dealt its favors to us with so profuse a hand. Would to God we had the wisdom enough to improve them."[387]

When we think of infrastructure, most people tend to think of manmade structures, but traditional infrastructure is made up of the four Rs: roads, railways, runways, and rivers. Inland waterways are a vital part of America's

387 Fourth "R": Support Higher Funding Levels for River Infrastructure. (2021). Retrieved 17 June 2021, from https://www.waterwayscouncil.org/key-issues/profile/fourth-r-support-higher-funding-levels-for-river-infrastructure

infrastructure. Still, the majority of them are rivers created by nature, with 25,000 miles of waterway currently existing in the U.S.[388] Because the basis of the system is naturally occurring, people tend to overlook waterways when thinking about infrastructure.[389] However, crucial parts of those waterways that make them navigable are manmade locks, ports, canals, and other supporting structures that control and direct the water flow. These manmade structures require a tremendous amount of maintenance and repair to remain functional.

It is important to note that dams are part of the American inland waterway system (separately covered in Chapter 5). Locks and dams must be considered in tandem in many instances because they function side-by-side and because improvements to the inland waterway system are accomplished by replacing locks with a dam.

The importance of the inland waterway system is often undervalued. Billions of dollars of trade and commerce hinge on regular access to and use of this system. The waterway system is entirely inland, but it serves the function of connecting inland locations with ports from which ships are bound for international destinations, so domestic and international trade is dependent on the smooth workings of the inland waterway system.

Understanding the Inland Waterway System

While rivers are natural formations, they become manageable with the addition of ports, locks, and canals. Here are some helpful key concepts to understand the workings of the inland waterway system:

388 ASCE's 2021 Infrastructure Report Card | Inland Waterways. (2021). Retrieved 17 June 2021, from https://infrastructurereportcard.org/cat-item/inland-waterways/

389 Toohey, M. (2016). Why Congress Must Fully Fund Waterway Projects. Retrieved 17 June 2021, from https://www.politico.com/agenda/story/2016/03/americas-water-infrastructure-rivers-fund-obama-000065/

- Ports are made up of the structures and equipment that allow ships and barges to dock and load and unload their cargo. The inland waterway ports are essential for trade.
- A lock is essentially an elevator, transporting a ship or barge from a lower waterway to a higher waterway (or vice versa) by closing the ship into a confined area and raising or lowering the water to that of the destination. A lock allows ships to move between waterways that would otherwise be inaccessible to each other. There are 241 locks in the inland waterways system managed by the USACE, not including those in the St. Lawrence Seaway.[390]
- Canals are manmade waterways that connect two natural waterways, enabling ships and barges to get from one to the other. For example, Sturgeon Bay Canal connects Green Bay with Lake Michigan in Wisconsin.

The majority of this chapter discusses the maintenance and work that needs to be done to the locks, but it is important to keep in mind that the rivers themselves also require some maintenance to maintain the depth of nine feet required for the passage of the vessels on the rivers.[391]

Although inland waterways are a key factor in the economy, the network of waterways exists in just 38 states, concentrated in the Midwest and eastern part of the country. Small segments do occur in the West (such as the Port of Seattle and the waterway system surrounding it). The inland waterway system is managed by USACE.[392]

390 Funding and Managing The U.S. Inland Waterways System: What Policy Makers Need to Know. (2015), 15. doi: 10.17226/21763

391 Prioritizing Waterway Lock Projects: Barge Traffic Change. (2018). Retrieved 17 June 2021, from https://crsreports.congress.gov/product/pdf/R/R45211

392 ASCE's 2021 Infrastructure Report Card | Inland Waterways. (2021). Retrieved 17 June 2021, from https://infrastructurereportcard.org/cat-item/inland-waterways/

The inland waterway system is part of the national watershed system, as well as part of the freight transportation system, bringing it under the purview of several federal agencies and federal laws. One such law is the Water Resources Development Act (WRDA), which allows Congress to authorize capital projects. However, most of the inland waterway system is already developed and at this point needs only maintenance and repairs, not further development.[393]

Importance of Inland Waterways

The waterway system within the U.S. is a key part of the economy, with 14 percent of all domestic freight carried over American's inland waterways. Each year, 600 million tons of cargo valued at over $200 billion makes its way through our inland waterways.[394]

Notably, the freight that passes through is not only domestic freight, but also freight bound for international destinations or freight that originated outside of the country and is bound for domestic destinations. Sixty percent of grain exports, 22 percent of domestic petroleum and petroleum related products, and 20 percent of coal for electricity generation is transported by barge over inland waterways. In 2014, 73 percent of all agricultural exports and 65 percent of agricultural imports were transported via inland waterways.[395]

The system is also responsible for transporting steel, soybeans, iron, agricultural inputs, chemicals, and other crucial materials in and out of the

393 Funding and Managing the U.S. Inland Waterways System: What Policy Makers Need to Know. (2015), 67. doi: 10.17226/21763

394 ASCE's 2021 Infrastructure Report Card | Inland Waterways. (2021). Retrieved 17 June 2021, from https://infrastructurereportcard.org/cat-item/inland-waterways/

395 ASCE's 2021 Infrastructure Report Card | Inland Waterways. (2021). Retrieved 17 June 2021, from https://infrastructurereportcard.org/cat-item/inland-waterways/

country's more diverse areas. It is important to note that while coal barges are decreasing (with the shift away from coal as fuel), other barge traffic is on the rise, with increases in corn and soybean expected in coming years.[396]

These waterways are responsible for maintaining more than 500,000 jobs for Americans. These jobs are worth more than $29 billion in the American economy. This industry is also far safer than other transport industries with employee safety records that are 18 times safer than rail jobs and 132 times safer than trucking jobs per ton-miles moved. Furthermore, inland waterways have room for employment growth—10,000 to 15,000 new jobs could be added just for needed construction alone.[397]

One of the important reasons that inland waterways serve as the pathway for significant cargo is because moving freight over water is more fuel-efficient than other methods. Barges achieve four times more distance per gallon of fuel in comparison to trucks,[398] making them four times more fuel-efficient. In fact, shipping freight via barges pulled by towboats has the lowest emissions rate of any freight transportation.[399]

Shipping goods via inland waterways saves $23.37 per cargo ton when compared to shipping via other methods, a total yearly savings of $12.3 billion, which is felt by those shipping the goods as well as those consuming them.[400]

Sending freight by water also keeps traffic off the highway and railway systems because barges carry far more freight than any truck or railroad

396 ASCE's 2021 Infrastructure Report Card | Inland Waterways. (2021). Retrieved 17 June 2021, from https://infrastructurereportcard.org/cat-item/inland-waterways/

397 Toohey, M. (2016). Why Congress Must Fully Fund Waterway Projects. Retrieved 17 June 2021, from https://www.politico.com/agenda/story/2016/03/americas-water-infrastructure-rivers-fund-obama-000065/

398 ASCE's 2021 Infrastructure Report Card | Inland Waterways. (2021). Retrieved 17 June 2021, from https://www.infrastructurereportcard.org/inland-waterways/

399 Toohey, M. (2016). Why Congress Must Fully Fund Waterway Projects. Retrieved 17 June 2021, from https://www.politico.com/agenda/story/2016/03/americas-water-infrastructure-rivers-fund-obama-000065/

400 Toohey, M. (2016). Why Congress must Fully Fund Waterway Projects. Retrieved 17 June 2021, from https://www.politico.com/agenda/story/2016/03/americas-water-infrastructure-rivers-fund-obama-000065/

can. Barges are connected to each other and towed through the waterways, consolidating many freight units in one trip. One tanker barge carrying petroleum can move enough gas in one trip to fuel 2,500 cars for one whole year.[401]

Since inland waterways are such a crucial segment of the freight distribution channel, disruption of their operation can cause significant economic damage. The USACE indicated that if the Charleroi Lock in Pittsburgh fails, for example, the result would be an estimated $1 billion of economic damage to the western part of Pennsylvania—and that's just the failure of one lock. The entire system is central to the country's economic health.[402]

The main competition for waterway transport is railroads, which are generally faster but much less fuel-efficient. Pipelines are the primary competition for the transportation of petroleum. However, they are costly to build and do not have as extensive a reach as waterways. Furthermore, most of the shippers who rely on barge transport over inland waterways have located their facilities at or near the ports on the rivers and remain committed to this transportation method.[403]

The highest use waterways for commercial shipping are the Upper Mississippi River and the Upper Ohio River systems.[404] Fifty percent of barge traffic in the U.S. occurs on just 16 percent of the inland waterways. After the upper Mississippi and upper Ohio Rivers, the Illinois river, lower Mississippi and Columbia Rivers are the most trafficked areas.[405]

401 Toohey, M. (2016). Why Congress Must Fully Fund Waterway Projects. Retrieved 17 June 2021, from https://www.politico.com/agenda/story/2016/03/americas-water-infrastructure-rivers-fund-obama-000065/

402 Toohey, M. (2016). Why Congress Must Fully Fund Waterway Projects. Retrieved 17 June 2021, from https://www.politico.com/agenda/story/2016/03/americas-water-infrastructure-rivers-fund-obama-000065/

403 Prioritizing Waterway Lock Projects: Barge Traffic Change. (2018). Retrieved 17 June 2021, from https://crsreports.congress.gov/product/pdf/R/R45211

404 Funding and Managing The U.S. Inland Waterways System: What Policy Makers Need to Know. (2015), 42. doi: 10.17226/21763

405 Funding and Managing The U.S. Inland Waterways System: What Policy Makers Need to Know. (2015), 59. doi: 10.17226/21763

Problems with Inland Waterways

Significant problems with inland waterways make the system far less efficient and reliable than it could be and pose real dangers not only to human life but to the ongoing viability of the system itself and all the trade that hinges on it.

Interestingly, the technology for locks has not c hanged much since the system was built, so the science behind the locks (essentially gravity) remains valid. The problem, however, is the structures themselves, which have aged and fallen into disrepair.

The most significant issue at play is the age of the system. Most of the locks within the system are more than 50 years old and were designed with just a 50-year lifespan, which means the entire system has surpassed its expected lifespan.[406] In 2014, a study determined that the average age of a lock in the system was 59 years. Because of their deterioration, many no longer function correctly.[407]

By 2014 the average delay per lock in the system was 121 minutes. Overall, 49 percent of the vessels using the inland waterways system had to deal with delays on their journeys. But because there is no standardized reporting mechanism in place, the reasons for the delays are not tracked, making it challenging to address the issues causing them.[408]

The system is in such disrepair that the American Society of Civil Engineers rated the inland waterways with a D grade due to delays and desperate conditions.[409]

---

406 Inland Waterway Navigation. (2000). Retrieved 17 June 2021, from https://www.mvp.usace.army.mil/Portals/57/docs/Navigation/InlandWaterways-Value.pdf

407 Sents, N. (2019). Boatloads of Water Problems. Retrieved 17 June 2021, from https://www.agriculture.com/news/business/boatloads-of-water-problems

408 ASCE's 2021 Infrastructure Report Card | Inland Waterways. (2021). Retrieved 17 June 2021, from https://infrastructurereportcard.org/cat-item/inland-waterways/

409 Jones, M. (2018). The Mississippi River Lock and Dam System Is Critical to The Economy. But It's Falling Apart Fast. Retrieved 17 June 2021, from https://www.jsonline.com/story/news/local/wisconsin/2018/06/01/critical-

Because of the funding problems associated with locks, the USACE is placed in the position of having to decide what repairs are most urgent, often leaving maintenance at the bottom of the to-do list.[410] This creates a cycle in which only the most pressing repairs are handled, and more long-term maintenance is constantly delayed, which then leads to more urgent repairs that were preventable.

The lack of funding means that the USACE is always playing catch up when it comes to repairing locks. They are so far behind they use a "fix as fail" system, only repairing things that become unusable and never being able to move ahead to preventive maintenance.[411] This also means that closures happen on an emergency basis, with no planning. A lock suddenly breaks down and barges then sometimes wait months at times for the repair to be completed.

Twenty percent of the delays along the system are due to outages (both scheduled and unscheduled). In 2013, USACE data showed that 49 percent of barges being towed through the highest-tonnage locks had a delay of 3.8 hours.[412] These outages and delays cannot be anticipated by the vessel operators and leave the operators in positions where they continuously have to try to minimize or absorb the costs of the problems they encounter while moving cargo.[413]

Many of the locks have no auxiliary locks to fall back on when there are delays or outages. One such lock on the Columbia-Snake River waterway has

---

mississippi-river-lock-and-dam-system-crumbling/573693002/

410 Inland and Intracoastal Waterways. Twenty-year capital investment strategy. (2016). Retrieved 17 June 2021, from https://www.iwr.usace.army.mil/Portals/70/docs/IWUB/WRRDA_2014_Capital_Investment_Strategy_Final_31Mar16.pdf

411 Toohey, M. (2016). Why Congress Must Fully Fund Waterway Projects. Retrieved 17 June 2021, from https://www.politico.com/agenda/story/2016/03/americas-water-infrastructure-rivers-fund-obama-000065/

412 Funding and Managing The U.S. Inland Waterways System: What Policy Makers Need to Know. (2015), 55. doi: 10.17226/21763

413 Toohey, M. (2016). Why Congress Must Fully Fund Waterway Projects. Retrieved 17 June 2021, from https://www.politico.com/agenda/story/2016/03/americas-water-infrastructure-rivers-fund-obama-000065/

managed this problem by closing the lock each year for the same two weeks, allowing barge operators to plan for the shutdown and factor it into their schedules and costs.[414] But this method is not applied across the board in any planned way.

Lock size is another problem that leads to delays. Most of the locks in the system that are 600 feet long were built in the 1930s or earlier. Locks that are 600 feet in length cannot accommodate the common barge groupings of 12 barges per tow.[415] These groupings have to be separated into two groups to pass through the locks. This contributes to lock backlog and long wait times.

The inland waterway system is at the mercy of climate change. Drought lowers the water levels, causing many waterways to no longer be deep enough for the ships that need to pass through them.[416] On the other hand, floods can also make the system unnavigable while damaging the manmade infrastructure of locks and ports. This impacts the entire inland waterway system.

Examples of the Damaged System

The Olmstead Dam Project is the most expensive and largest inland waterway project ever begun in the U.S. The project is estimated to have cost $3 billion. It was technically finished and became operational in 2018, although aspects of the project have still not fully been completed, and it is not 100 percent operational. The project involved building a dam to replace two locks on the

414 Inland and Intracoastal Waterways. Twenty-Year Capital Investment Strategy. (2016). Retrieved 17 June 2021, from https://www.iwr.usace.army.mil/Portals/70/docs/IWUB/WRRDA_2014_Capital_Investment_Strategy_Final_31Mar16.pdf

415 Inland Waterway Navigation. (2000). Retrieved 17 June 2021, from https://www.mvp.usace.army.mil/Portals/57/docs/Navigation/InlandWaterways-Value.pdf

416 Navigable Inland Waterways | Global Climate Change Impacts in The United States 2009 Report. (2009). Retrieved 17 June 2021, from https://nca2009.globalchange.gov/navigable-inland-waterways/index.html

Ohio River. The project was characterized by massive delays (it took 30 years to complete) and out of control costs. [417]

The USACE attempted to build the project using an "in the wet" method instead of a more traditional approach of erecting temporary dams. In addition to the billions of dollars spent on the project, it resulted in the loss of four lives and the loss of millions of dollars to the barge operators and the sellers and purchasers of the products carried through the two locks that were replaced. This is the poster child for how poorly planned improvements are, and how budgets are drastically underestimated for inland waterway projects.[418]

The LaGrange Lock in Versailles, Illinois is one of the locks currently in the worst condition. The lock was built in 1939. The electrical and mechanical systems are outdated. Frequent flooding, freezing/thawing cycles, and high traffic regularly create problems with the lock's functionality. [419]

The lock is only 600 feet long and cannot handle large barge groupings. Sections of the concrete have been removed so they won't fall off into the river. A 2005 report estimated $72.6 million were needed to repair the lock. This project is part of the Navigation and Ecosystem Sustainability Program (NESP). Work began but was suspended when there was not enough funding to complete the project in 2011. The poor condition of the lock results in long delays for barges that need to move through it. [420]

A study by the University of Tennessee and Vanderbilt University found that unplanned closures of this lock impact commerce in 18 states and costs

417 Kelley, T. (2016). Choke Point of a Nation: The High Cost of an Aging River Lock. Retrieved 17 June 2021, from https://www.nytimes.com/2016/11/23/business/economy/desperately-plugging-holes-in-an-87-year-old-dam.html

418 McLaughlin, E. (2021). 30 years and $3 billion Later, One of America's Largest Civil Works Projects Set to Open on Ohio River. Retrieved 17 June 2021, from https://abcnews.go.com/US/30-years-billion-americas-largest-civil-works-projects/story?id=57505266

419 Glass, P. (2017). Lockdown: Inside America's Decaying Waterways Infrastructure. Retrieved 17 June 2021, from https://www.workboat.com/coastal-inland-waterways/lockdown-decaying-inland-waterways-infrastructure

420 Glass, P. (2017). Lockdown: Inside America's Decaying Waterways Infrastructure. Retrieved 17 June 2021, from https://www.workboat.com/coastal-inland-waterways/lockdown-decaying-inland-waterways-infrastructure

$17 billion for alternate transportation. It also reduces farm incomes by $2.1 billion.[421]

It is important to note that most of the barges that pass through this area traverse the entire Mississippi River system, so a delay or closure here impacts the entire system negatively.[422]

Another part of the system in need of repair is the Inner Harbor Navigation Canal (IHNC) in New Orleans, which connects the Gulf Intracoastal Waterway (GIWW) and the Mississippi River. The canal involves locks and drawbridges. Petroleum and chemicals are the two primary products shipped through this area.[423]

The lock needs to be widened to allow two barges to move through it simultaneously. Currently, there is a 12 to 24-hour wait for a barge to pass through. In 2016 the lock was closed 185 days of the year for repairs. The USACE estimates the cost of expansion at $1.4 billion.[424] The community around the canal is currently opposing the project, which has been discussed in public meetings.

Funding Issues

Bringing American waterway infrastructure up to modern expectations is costly. Before considering solutions, it is helpful to understand how the waterway management is funded. There are two types of costs involved, and they are funded differently:

---

421 Moore, K. (2017). Study Finds Lock and Dam Breakdowns Cost Billions. Retrieved 17 June 2021, from https://www.workboat.com/coastal-inland-waterways/study-finds-lock-breakdowns-drain-billions-from-economy

422 Moore, K. (2017). Study Finds Lock and Dam Breakdowns Cost Billions. Retrieved 17 June 2021, from https://www.workboat.com/coastal-inland-waterways/study-finds-lock-breakdowns-drain-billions-from-economy

423 Prioritizing Waterway Lock Projects: Barge Traffic Change. (2018). Retrieved 17 June 2021, from https://crsreports.congress.gov/product/pdf/R/R45211

424 Prioritizing Waterway Lock Projects: Barge Traffic Change . (2018). Retrieved 17 June 2021, from https://crsreports.congress.gov/product/pdf/R/R45211

1. Construction and rehabilitation — Construction and maintenance are funded 65 percent by the federal government's general funds and 35 percent through the Inland Waterways Trust Fund, which users fund (note that until the 2021 fiscal year, the split was 50/50). The Inland Waterways Trust Fund is funded through a tax on barge fuel (set at 29 cents per gallon[425]).[426]
2. Operation and maintenance — The cost of operation and maintenance is paid for completely by the federal government.[427]

The estimated overall cost of repairing and upgrading the system is $4.9 billion over the coming 20 years, according to the USACE.[428] Individual lock repair projects run between $300 million and $800 million per project, while the total annual funding available has totaled only $200 million in past years.[429]

What is important to note is that the more funding the system has access to, the more quickly projects that are languishing can be completed. For example, because of increased funding, projects that were planned for 2090 completion have now received revised completion dates of 2038.[430]

As with all federal projects, improvements and repairs fluctuate depending on the government's budget and allocations. The Trump administration cut

425 26 U.S. Code § 4042 — Tax on Fuel Used in Commercial Transportation on Inland Waterways. Retrieved 17 June 2021, from https://www.law.cornell.edu/uscode/text/26/4042

426 ASCE's 2021 Infrastructure Report Card | Inland Waterways. (2021). Retrieved 17 June 2021, from https://infrastructurereportcard.org/cat-item/inland-waterways/

427 ASCE's 2021 Infrastructure Report Card | Inland Waterways. (2021). Retrieved 17 June 2021, from https://infrastructurereportcard.org/cat-item/inland-waterways/

428 ASCE's 2021 Infrastructure Report Card | Inland Waterways. (2021). Retrieved 17 June 2021, from https://infrastructurereportcard.org/cat-item/inland-waterways/

429 Prioritizing Waterway Lock Projects: Barge Traffic Change. (2018). Retrieved 17 June 2021, from https://crsreports.congress.gov/product/pdf/R/R45211

430 ASCE's 2021 Infrastructure Report Card | Inland Waterways. (2021). Retrieved 17 June 2021, from https://infrastructurereportcard.org/cat-item/inland-waterways/

funds for this system in 2016, and money in the Trust was diverted to general government funds, leaving even less money available to repair and upgrade the system.[431]

In 2019, President Trump signed 2020 spending bills, which included $765 billion for USACE's civil works projects, which includes but is not limited to inland waterways.[432] Additionally, the bill also allows full use of all the funds in the Trust, opening up $317 million for operation and maintenance on the system.[433] It remains to be seen how the current administration will allocate funds for the inland waterways system.

Another problem with the funding model is that the barge industry provides part of the funds for operation and maintenance of locks (through the barge fuel tax) yet has no seat at the table to influence upkeep, maintenance, and operation of the system.[434] So, the companies and people who are most familiar with the system and its issues have no input or even an advisory capacity when it comes to maintenance.[435]

Solutions

The USACE has published *Technologies to Extend the Life of Existing Infrastructures: Volume 1 Navigation Infrastructure,* [436] which lays out a

431 Toohey, M. (2016). Why Congress Must Fully Fund Waterway Projects. Retrieved 17 June 2021, from https://www.politico.com/agenda/story/2016/03/americas-water-infrastructure-rivers-fund-obama-000065/

432 Kenn, M. (2020). 2020 Spending Bill Gives Money to Aging US Waterways; Is It Enough?. Retrieved 17 June 2021, from https://www.dtnpf.com/agriculture/web/ag/columns/cash-market-moves/article/2020/01/13/2020-spending-bill-gives-money-aging-2

433 Kenn, M. (2020). 2020 Spending Bill Gives Money to Aging US Waterways; Is It Enough?. Retrieved 17 June 2021, from https://www.dtnpf.com/agriculture/web/ag/columns/cash-market-moves/article/2020/01/13/2020-spending-bill-gives-money-aging-2

434 America's Locks & Dams: "A Ticking Time Bomb for Agriculture? (2011). Retrieved 17 June 2021, from https://static.tti.tamu.edu/tti.tamu.edu/documents/TTI-2011-9.pdf

435 Toohey, M. (2016). Why Congress Must Fully Fund Waterway Projects. Retrieved 17 June 2021, from https://www.politico.com/agenda/story/2016/03/americas-water-infrastructure-rivers-fund-obama-000065/

436 Technologies to Extend The Life of Existing Infrastructure. Volume 1: Navigation infrastructure. (2016). Retrieved 17 June 2021, from https://operations.erdc.dren.mil/pdfs/TechExtLife1.pdf

comprehensive plan to repair and maintain existing waterways infrastructure which suggests the following actions:

- Give USACE the authority to contract for projects. Currently, it does not have that authority, and this results in a stop-and-go construction process which hinges on appropriations.
- Congress should regularly provide funding for inland waterways by passing a WRDA every two years to ensure that funding is consistently available so that projects can proceed and be planned for. According to the USACE, WRDA funding is crucial for support of the inland waterways to allow the USACE to do the projects necessary to keep the waterways flowing.[437] WRDA bills consistently have bipartisan support in Congress.
- Congress should continue to appropriate all of the funds in the Trust so it can be used and increase the funding available for operations and maintenance each year.
- The government should find alternative funding methods, including public-private partnerships, to increase the amount of funds available for the system.
- A standardized system is needed to record, explain, and evaluate the delays across the system and the reasons for those delays so that changes can be made to address the reasons for the delays.[438]

The recommendations from the USACE should be front and center for

437 Council, W. Support Biennial Water Resources Development Acts (WRDA). Retrieved 17 June 2021, from https://www.waterwayscouncil.org/key-issues/profile/support-biennial-water-resources-development-acts-wrda

438 Funding and Managing the U.S. Inland Waterways System: What Policy Makers Need to Know. (2015), 54. doi: 10.17226/21763

any changes to the system. In addition to those recommendations, there are other improvements that could be made:

- Change the management of the repair system — Locks that are in need of repair and maintenance, which would cause the largest amount of disruption from outages, should be prioritized. [439]
- Create a new funding strategy — Since operation and maintenance costs are paid directly by the federal government (in contrast to construction and maintenance costs, which in part are funded by the tax paid into the Trust), lock projects compete directly with other infrastructure projects for funding.[440]

  Due to the age and disrepair of the inland waterway system, the repairs needed now make up about 75 percent of the requested budget. A new funding strategy is needed to ensure funds are allocated to these much-needed repairs.[441] A new system that supports these costs through the system beneficiaries could solve this problem. A study is needed to assess if increased user charges or increased barge fuel tax is a feasible option and how it could help to alleviate the lack of funding needed. The study would need to assess the economic value of the system to commercial users and the assets needed to improve the system so that it can be reliable in the future. [442]

  Funding through the WRDA may no longer make sense for the waterway system since it is already developed. Instead, funding

439 Funding and Managing the U.S. Inland Waterways System: What Policy Makers Need to Know. (2015), 2. doi: 10.17226/21763

440 Funding and Managing the U.S. Inland Waterways System: What Policy Makers Need to Know. (2015), 2. doi: 10.17226/21763

441 Funding and Managing the U.S. Inland Waterways System: What Policy Makers Need to Know. (2015), 2. doi: 10.17226/21763

442 Funding and Managing the U.S. Inland Waterways System: What Policy Makers Need to Know. (2015), 2. doi: 10.17226/21763

could come from a source that focuses on maintenance and development.[443] At the very least, this option should be considered and studied.

- Create a new system for lock traffic — Key planning is needed to reduce lock congestion through changes in availability at peak demand time and to revamp lock design to decrease congestion and wait times.[444]
- Implement an asset management system — This would use standardized methods for assessing the maintenance necessary for the system to function in connection with a revised budget, which would allow for maintenance to be done where and when it is needed on a regular schedule.[445] The USACE has begun to do this, but it is not implemented on a national basis.[446]

  Risk-informed management of the inland waterways will allow the USACE to isolate and then address the locks with the highest risk of closure and with the highest level of deterioration, and funding can then be channeled to the projects with the highest need.[447]
- Implement a system of regularly scheduled maintenance — A maintenance system that is planned years in advance, so that vessel operators can schedule around closures and factor the delays into their costs would make the system more reliable. This would allow

443 Funding and Managing the U.S. Inland Waterways System: What Policy Makers Need to Know. (2015), 67. doi: 10.17226/21763

444 Funding and Managing the U.S. Inland Waterways System: What Policy Makers Need to Know. (2015), 57. doi: 10.17226/21763

445 Funding and Managing the U.S. Inland Waterways System: What Policy Makers Need to Know. (2015), 2. doi: 10.17226/21763

446 Funding and Managing the U.S. Inland Waterways System: What Policy Makers Need to Know. (2015), 2. doi: 10.17226/21763

447 Inland and intracoastal waterways. Twenty-year capital investment strategy. (2016). Retrieved 17 June 2021, from https://www.iwr.usace.army.mil/Portals/70/docs/IWUB/WRRDA_2014_Capital_Investment_Strategy_Final_31Mar16.pdf

the USACE time to do regular maintenance that would prevent unscheduled closures.[448]

- Increase lock size — As repairs and maintenance are done, 600-foot locks should be increased to 1200-feet, to allow the common barge size to pass through them without uncoupling. This would reduce delays and allow for smoother traffic flow.
- Create a capital investment strategy for the entire waterway system — This is desperately needed so that funds and project scheduling can be allocated in a way that addresses the neediest elements of the system first to avoid the delays from unexpected closures.[449]

The inland waterway system is crucial to the nation's economy but is currently poorly operated, maintained, and repaired. Changes in funding, monitoring, spending allocation, scheduled repairs, and traffic management would greatly improve the inland waterway system and allow it to function at peak levels for years to come.

448 Inland and intracoastal waterways. Twenty-year capital investment strategy. (2016). Retrieved 17 June 2021, from https://www.iwr.usace.army.mil/Portals/70/docs/IWUB/WRRDA_2014_Capital_Investment_Strategy_Final_31Mar16.pdf

449 Inland and intracoastal waterways. Twenty-year capital investment strategy. (2016). Retrieved 17 June 2021, from https://www.iwr.usace.army.mil/Portals/70/docs/IWUB/WRRDA_2014_Capital_Investment_Strategy_Final_31Mar16.pdf

CHAPTER 19:

Public Parks | Our Partnership with the Planet

"A national park is not a playground. it's a sanctuary for nature and for humans who will accept nature on nature's own terms."

—Michael Frome

The United States has a long-standing commitment to parks and recreation areas, including National Parks, state parks, and local park and recreation areas. These areas play a key role in the health and well-being of the nation, with more than one billion visits per year.[450] These areas are crucial for supporting biodiversity, protecting the environment from climate change, and supporting the economy.

They also play an important role in mental and physical health and social and community connections. The park systems have received recent attention and financial support, but there is still a gigantic deficit that must be addressed if the system is to maintain itself, let alone blossom in the future. Climate change is a real and significant danger to the parks, threatening their very existence, and this must be addressed if they are to continue and to thrive.

450 Get to Know America's State Parks. Retrieved 26 June 2021, from Get to Know America's State Parks. Retrieved 26 June 2021, from https://www.stateparks.org/about-us/

History of the Park System

The National Park System had its beginnings on March 1, 1872, when Yellowstone Park was established as a public park in the Territories of Montana and Wyoming by an act of Congress. In 1916, President Woodrow Wilson established the National Park Service (NPS), which was given control of the existing 35 national parks and monuments under the Department of the Interior. In 1933 an executive order transferred management of national monuments and military sites from the Forestry Service to the NPS. Today the NPS manages more than 400 areas with more than 84 million acres in all 50 states and many U.S. territories. The NPS employs 20,000 employees.[451]

The United States was the first country to create a national park, spurring on more than 100 other countries that have now established more than 1,200 national parks or preserves.[452] It's important to note that although most people think of green space when they think of National Parks, the NPS, in fact, manages not just what we think of as parks, such as open areas like Yosemite, but significant cultural and historical sites and National Monuments like the Statue of Liberty, Antietam battlefield, Independence Hall, Abraham Lincoln's birthplace, John F. Kennedy Historic Site, Mount Rushmore, and many, more places that are essential parts of America's past.[453]

Preserving the National Parks is about more than maintaining fields and mountains; it is also about preserving and protecting history and culture for future generations.

The U.S. Army Corps of Engineers (USACE) manages 400 lakes, rivers,

451 Quick History of The National Park Service. Retrieved 26 June 2021, from https://www.nps.gov/articles/quick-nps-history.htm

452 Quick History of The National Park Service. Retrieved 26 June 2021, from https://www.nps.gov/articles/quick-nps-history.htm

453 National Park System. Retrieved 26 June 2021, from https://www.nps.gov/aboutus/national-park-system.htm

and recreation areas across the country and works in tandem with the NPS to manage and maintain structures in the National Parks.[454] The USACE sees 270 million visitors per year to its facilities, 90 percent of which are within 50 miles of major metropolitan areas.[455]

National Parks are an important part of the system of parks in our country, but they are not alone. State parks include 6,792 sites over 14 million acres of land[456] with more than 813 million visitors each year (roughly twice as many as to National Parks). The first state park in the nation was Niagara Falls State Park, established in 1885.[457] City parks in the 100 largest U.S. cities encompass 2.1 million acres over 22,764 parks, and 70 percent of people living in those cities live within a 10-minute walk to a park.[458] Today in the National, state, and local park systems there are ten acres of public park acreage for every 1000 residents.[459]

Importance of the Park System

The nation's parks provide a wide variety of benefits and necessary roles, many of which most people are unaware of.

The most obvious benefit of the park system is health. Many studies have supported the links between spending time outdoors and mental and physical health.[460] Providing areas for citizens to reap those benefits

454 Williamson, E. (2016). 100-year-old National Park Service. Retrieved 26 June 2021, from https://www.nwo.usace.army.mil/Media/News-Stories/Article/945299/100-year-old-national-park-services-roots-go-deeper-with-us-army/

455 Infrastructure Report Card | Public Parks. Retrieved 26 June 2021, from https://infrastructurereportcard.org/cat-item/public-parks/

456 Walls, M. (2009). Parks and Recreation in The United States. Retrieved 26 June 2021, from https://media.rff.org/documents/RFF-BCK-ORRG_State20Parks.pdf

457 Get to Know America's State Parks. Retrieved 26 June 2021, from https://www.stateparks.org/about-us/

458 2018 City Park Facts. (2018). Retrieved 26 June 2021, from https://www.tpl.org/sites/default/files/CityParkFacts2018.8_13_18finLO.pdf

459 Infrastructure Report Card | Public Parks. Retrieved 26 June 2021, from https://infrastructurereportcard.org/cat-item/public-parks/

460 Healthy Parks Healthy People Resources. (2021). Retrieved 26 June 2021, from https://www.nps.gov/subjects/

is a key responsibility of the government. Creating and maintaining green spaces is a great social equalizer, providing health benefits to citizens of all socioeconomic statuses.[461]

It has been estimated that parks and protected areas have a $9 trillion impact on worldwide mental health.

Americans take great advantage of the parks available to them, visiting on average twice per month.[462] National park visits have increased 13 percent in the last ten years.[463] The COVID-19 pandemic initially shuttered National Parks, but attendance soared past previous records once they reopened.[464]

The park system is essential to national and local economies. Visitors to parks spent $21 billion in 2019 and overall, parks generated $41.7 billion for the national economy and supported 340,500 jobs in 2019.[465] Visitor spending increased by $1 billion in just one year from 2018 and $4.1 billion over the previous five years, growing its impact on the national economy by $9.7 billion.[466]

There are 278,000 jobs in gateway communities (those within 60 miles of a park) supported by the parks they are near. Local parks are responsible for eight full-time park jobs per 10,000 residents, as well as gateway jobs in the surrounding community.[467]

The parks provide a wide variety of other benefits which are less

---

healthandsafety/healthy-parks-healthy-people-resources.htm

461 Healthy Parks Healthy People Resources. (2021). Retrieved 26 June 2021, from https://www.nps.gov/subjects/healthandsafety/healthy-parks-healthy-people-resources.htm

462 Infrastructure Report Card | Public Parks. Retrieved 26 June 2021, from https://infrastructurereportcard.org/cat-item/public-parks/

463 Infrastructure Report Card | Public Parks. Retrieved 26 June 2021, from https://infrastructurereportcard.org/cat-item/public-parks/

464 Michael J. Coren, D. (2020). Once Again, A Pandemic Has Stoked Americans' Love for National Parks. Retrieved 26 June 2021, from https://qz.com/1908674/covid-19-has-americans-visiting-national-parks-in-record-numbers/

465 Infrastructure Report Card | Public Parks. Retrieved 26 June 2021, from https://infrastructurereportcard.org/cat-item/public-parks/

466 Infrastructure Report Card | Public Parks. Retrieved 26 June 2021, from https://infrastructurereportcard.org/cat-item/public-parks/

467 Infrastructure Report Card | Public Parks. Retrieved 26 June 2021, from https://infrastructurereportcard.org/cat-item/public-parks/

well-known. Parks are central to the health of the earth itself, supporting biodiversity, which is important not only for protecting and maintaining the natural resources of the planet, but for the sustainability of all species, including humans.[468]

Parks increase nearby property values by up to 20 percent because of the aesthetic benefits they provide to communities.[469] Parks also have important environmental impacts that most people are unaware of. Parks help reduce combined sewer overflows from extreme weather events, which send untreated wastewater, toxic substances, and agricultural runoff into bodies of water.[470] Parks are used as rain gardens to manage stormwater and avoid these detrimental occurrences.

Additionally, parks filter rain, helping to reduce pollution and protect drinking water. Parks also filter air, creating $3.8 billion in savings on air pollution.[471] And parks reduce the heat island effect of cities (wherein cities maintain higher temperatures than surrounding areas), helping to keep them cooler, reducing cooling costs for buildings in the cities.

Parks do this by increasing wind patterns through cities, trapping carbon, and providing an area of lower temperatures within the city.[472] Many parks have made an effort to return areas to their natural state, which creates a buffer between bodies of water and human-inhabited areas, allowing wildlife to thrive.[473]

---

468 Buttke, D., Allen, D., & Higgins, C. (2018). Benefits of Biodiversity to Human Health and Well-being. Retrieved 26 June 2021, from https://www.nps.gov/articles/parksciencev31-n1_buttke_etal-htm.htm

469 Infrastructure Report Card | Public Parks. Retrieved 26 June 2021, from https://infrastructurereportcard.org/cat-item/public-parks/

470 Infrastructure Report Card | Public Parks. Retrieved 26 June 2021, from https://infrastructurereportcard.org/cat-item/public-parks/

471 Infrastructure Report Card | Public Parks. Retrieved 26 June 2021, from https://infrastructurereportcard.org/cat-item/public-parks/

472 Bristow R., Blackie R., Brown N. (2010). Parks and The Urban Heat Island: A Longitudinal Study in Westfield, Massachusetts. Northeastern Recreation Research Symposium 2010:224—230.

473 Infrastructure Report Card | Public Parks. Retrieved 26 June 2021, from https://infrastructurereportcard.org/cat-item/public-parks/

Park Maintenance Needs

The greatest concern for National Parks and state and local parks is their deferred maintenance backlog. The parks have huge projects that need attention and funding in order to do necessary repairs, yet they do not receive enough money to handle all the projects. Projects are then deferred, creating a giant backlog of projects that need funding but are on hold.

The National Parks deferred maintenance backlog grew 9 percent in the last decade and is currently at $11.92 billion. State parks have $5.6 billion in deferred maintenance, while local parks have $60 billion. The average state park faces $143.7 million in deferred maintenance.[474]

The trails, bridges, parking areas, and drinking water systems in the National Parks are all part of the giant deferred maintenance backlog. Dangerous trails and damaged water systems directly impact human health and can, in some instances, cause the deaths of visitors. The NPS also has more than 75,000 constructed assets (such as buildings), and more than half of those need repairs.[475]

Half of the infrastructure repair backlog at National Parks is for roadways. Motor vehicle crashes account for the second largest category of deaths in National Parks, indicating that roadway maintenance is important.[476] Other significant deferred maintenance projects include Mesa Verde National Park, which is in need of $6 million in deferred repairs to buildings, and Yosemite, which is in need of $582 million in repairs, including $20 million in repairs to hiking trails.[477]

---

474 Infrastructure Report Card | Public Parks. Retrieved 26 June 2021, from https://infrastructurereportcard.org/cat-item/public-parks/

475 Infrastructure Report Card | Making The Grade. Retrieved 26 June 2021, from https://infrastructurereportcard.org/making-the-grade/

476 Most Dangerous National Parks in The U.S. | Fatal Accident Statistics. (2020). Retrieved 26 June 2021, from https://www.psblaw.com/nevada/deaths-in-us-national-parks/

477 Historic Park Funding Bill Becomes Law. (2020). Retrieved 26 June 2021, from https://www.npca.org/advocacy/62-historic-park-funding-bill-becomes-law

Drilling and Mining

The impact of drilling and mining on National Parks cannot be understated. The Trump administration increased leasing and eliminated many environmental protections that have left National Parks open to exploitation. More than 19 million acres were offered for leasing for oil and gas during the administration.[478] As an example of the dangers of these policies, gas and oil leasing in Yellowstone and Grand Teton National Parks endangers the wildlife travel corridors, placing migratory animals at great risk.[479]

The administration opened up close to a million acres of land (more than 85 percent of the land set aside by the Obama administration) in the Grand Staircase-Escalante National Monument and Bears Ears area to leasing by removing it from NPS management.[480] Because of drilling, Chaco Park is currently the largest methane hotspot in the U.S.[481] with a methane cloud the size of Delaware now covering the park and surrounding areas.[482]

Pressing Dangers at Parks

In addition to the vast maintenance and protection issues facing national and local parks, there are also severe dangers lurking that must be addressed to preserve the parks and the benefits they create.

---

478 Spoiled Parks: Top 12 National Parks Threatened by Trump Administration's Energy Agenda. (2019). Retrieved 26 June 2021, from https://www.npca.org/articles/2324-spoiled-parks-top-12-national-parks-threatened-by-trump-administration-s

479 Spoiled Parks: Top 12 National Parks Threatened by Trump Administration's Energy Agenda. (2019). Retrieved 26 June 2021, from https://www.npca.org/articles/2324-spoiled-parks-top-12-national-parks-threatened-by-trump-administration-s

480 Davenport, C. (2020). Trump Opens National Monument Land to Energy Exploration. Retrieved 26 June 2021, from https://www.nytimes.com/2020/02/06/climate/trump-grand-staircase-monument.html

481 Chaco Culture National Historical Park. Retrieved 26 June 2021, from https://www.npca.org/case-studies/chaco-culture-national-historical-park

482 Chaco Culture National Historical Park. Retrieved 26 June 2021, from https://www.npca.org/case-studies/chaco-culture-national-historical-park

Wildfires

Wildfires[483] are an increasing, dangerous concern for many parks. Climate change has resulted in hotter, drier summers, increasing the risks of wildfires. Additionally, many years of fire suppression strategies have actually led to denser forests which result in more intense wildfires when those forests do burn. Wildfires not only destroy wildlife and damage park assets but they also create air pollution. In fact, 96 percent of National Parks have air pollution problems, many resulting from wildfires. The smoke from wildfires is dangerous to visitors with asthma and pulmonary illnesses. The fires also create carbon monoxide, which worsens climate change.

As an example, the Ferguson Fire in 2019, and the 2013 Rim Fire greatly impacted Yosemite and killed two people, injured 29, and burned 350,000 acres. Fires are not limited to Western states. A 2016 fire in the Great Smoky Mountain Park killed 14 people, damaged or destroyed 2,500 homes, and burned 11,000 acres of the park.

Fires like this are becoming more and more common. Yellowstone, Glacier, and Ricky Mountain Parks are expected to have the most significant increase in wildfires in the coming years, but as warmer temperatures increase, parks in the south are also at risk. Future forest fires could kill the biggest trees in the park, some of which are more than 2,000 years old. Additionally, the NPS predicts that wildfires could lead to destabilization and erosion of the Ancient Pueblo Historic Site.[484]

---

483 Hotter, Drier Summers and Increasingly Intense Wildfire Seasons Could Change The Makeup of Park Forests and Dramatically Affect Visitor Health. Retrieved 26 June 2021, from https://www.npca.org/case-studies/fire

484 Rising Ocean Levels and Intensifying Storms Threaten to Inundate and Destroy Irreplaceable Park Structures and Artifacts Across The Country. Retrieved 26 June 2021, from https://www.npca.org/case-studies/history-and-culture

Climate Change

Climate change is a major contributing factor to wildfires, but also is responsible for other dangers in the parks. A majority of the western parks in the system are predicted to suffer from climate change by 2050. Warmer temperatures cause droughts which impact the flora and fauna of the parks. For example, due to temperature changes in Saguaro National Park, no new saguaro trees have grown since the 1990s. Drought in Everglades National Park has led to an increase in sea level (USACE predicts that sea levels will rise 26 inches in this park by 2050) and saltwater inundation within the park, negatively impacting native birds and fish.[485]

Since 1895, National Parks have experienced rising temperatures at a rate that is twice faster than the rest of the country on average because many of the parks are located in areas of extreme environment.[486]

Another impact of climate change is ice and snow melt. In Glacier and Mount Rainier Parks, snowmelt has led to an intrusion of trees into meadow areas. Flooding is another outcome of the change to the earth's climate. Flooding impacts trails as well as roads and parking areas in parks and leads to a decrease in visitors.[487]

Sea level rise and storm surges are another danger. According to the NPS, 24 of the parks in the Pacific Northwest are in particular danger from this.[488] The Dry Tortugas Park will be completely submerged if sea levels reach a rise of three feet.

485 Climate Impact | Drought and Water Availability. Retrieved 26 June 2021, from https://www.npca.org/case-studies/drought-and-water-availability

486 Climate Impact | Drought and Water Availability. Retrieved 26 June 2021, from https://www.npca.org/case-studies/drought-and-water-availability

487 Climate Impact | Recreation and Visitation. Retrieved 26 June 2021, from https://www.npca.org/case-studies/recreation-and-visitation

488 Rising Sea Levels. Retrieved 26 June 2021, from https://www.npca.org/case-studies/rising-sea-levels

Additionally, the National Mall in Washington, D.C., floods often and is in danger of becoming submerged with rising sea levels. Recent events have shown how dangerous flooding can be. Hurricane Sandy in 2012 submerged 75 percent of Liberty Island (where the Statue of Liberty stands) as well as most of Ellis Island, including the main administration building, with damage totaling $59 million. Archaeological digs at Historic Jamestown are endangered by coastal flooding.[489]

Funding

The park system in the United States derives its funding from a wide variety of sources.

Roads and bridges inside National Parks are funded by the Department of Transportation, as well as fees that are collected in the parks. Department of Transportation grants and discretionary appropriations also contribute.[490]

The rest of the funding for National Parks comes from federal discretionary funds, which have increased 52 percent in the last decade. The 2020 funding from this was $572 million. There was $510 million in mandatory funding for the deferred maintenance backlog, which makes up 26 percent of the NPS budget. Discretionary funding for maintenance has increased 52 percent in the past ten years.[491]

One dramatic change has meant good news for the National Parks. The Great American Outdoors Act of 2020 created a National Parks, and Public Land Legacy Restoration Fund. This funnels up to $9.5 billion over five

489 Rising Ocean Levels and Intensifying Storms Threaten to Inundate and Destroy Irreplaceable Park Structures and Artifacts Across The Country. Retrieved 26 June 2021, from https://www.npca.org/case-studies/history-and-culture

490 Infrastructure Report Card 2020 | Public Parks. (2021). Retrieved 26 June 2021, from https://infrastructurereportcard.org/wp-content/uploads/2020/12/Public-Parks-2021.pdf

491 Infrastructure Report Card 2020 | Public Parks. (2021). Retrieved 26 June 2021, from https://infrastructurereportcard.org/wp-content/uploads/2020/12/Public-Parks-2021.pdf

years from federal mineral revenues.[492] The funds are to be used for deferred maintenance backlogs in the National Parks as well as other public lands.

State park funding is derived from user fees (about 45 percent of funds come from this) and state general funds.[493] In the past ten years, state parks' operating expenditures have been driven down more than half a billion dollars. The inconsistent nature of funding makes it challenging for local parks to create budgets and handle all the necessary maintenance their assets need.

State and local parks use 40 percent of their funding just for maintenance, which does not leave enough to handle the significant backlog of repairs.[494] The Land and Water Conservation Fund (LWCF) provides funding to local parks and 98 percent of counties have a park that receives this funding. The fund is supported by offshore oil and gas energy revenue, with revenue of over $900 million per year. However, of the $40.9 billion in the fund, less than half has been appropriated. The Great American Outdoors Act permanently and fully funded the LWCF.[495]

City park agencies are chronically underfunded, and when they do receive the funding, it is generally for new capital projects, not for deferred maintenance (capital spending has increased 23 percent in the past five years while operations and management budgets have ticked up only 2 to 3 percent).[496]

---

492 Infrastructure Report Card 2020 | Public Parks. (2021). Retrieved 26 June 2021, from https://infrastructurereportcard.org/wp-content/uploads/2020/12/Public-Parks-2021.pdf

493 Infrastructure Report Card 2020 | Public Parks. (2021). Retrieved 26 June 2021, from https://infrastructurereportcard.org/wp-content/uploads/2020/12/Public-Parks-2021.pdf

494 Infrastructure Report Card 2020 | Public Parks. (2021). Retrieved 26 June 2021, from https://infrastructurereportcard.org/wp-content/uploads/2020/12/Public-Parks-2021.pdf

495 Infrastructure Report Card 2020 | Public Parks. (2021). Retrieved 26 June 2021, from https://infrastructurereportcard.org/wp-content/uploads/2020/12/Public-Parks-2021.pdf

496 2018 City Park Facts. (2018). Retrieved 26 June 2021, from https://www.tpl.org/sites/default/files/CityParkFacts2018.8_13_18finLO.pdf

Solutions

Although the Great American Outdoors Act has increased the funding available for National Park maintenance, the deferred maintenance necessary remains astronomical. However, this Act must be fully funded for it to have the impact desired. Increased funding is a fast and direct way to give the parks the resources necessary to preserve and protect their assets and repair those that are damaged.

Polls show Americans strongly support National Parks and want them to be funded.[497] Four out of five Americans think that local parks are worth the approximately $70 they pay in local taxes, and 30 percent think they are actually worth more. Ninety-one percent of Americans think parks and recreation are a government service that is important.[498] Based on this, a small tax increase to fund parks would likely be accepted by the majority of Americans.

Establishing dedicated funding that National and local parks can rely on will allow them to create plans for maintenance and repairs. Currently, funding is always in question, and providing dedicated funds will give parks the opportunity to create reliable fiscal strategies. An additional funding solution would be to mandate that user fees collected in a park remain in that park for its own use. Currently, funding is collated and then redistributed.

Creative funding options would greatly increase the monies parks could have at their disposal. For state and local parks, these could include[499]:

497 Support Increased National Park Funding. Retrieved 26 June 2021, from https://www.npca.org/advocacy/21-support-increased-national-park-funding

498 Infrastructure Report Card 2020 | Public Parks. (2021). Retrieved 26 June 2021, from https://infrastructurereportcard.org/wp-content/uploads/2020/12/Public-Parks-2021.pdf

499 Infrastructure Report Card 2020 | Public Parks. (2021). Retrieved 26 June 2021, from https://infrastructurereportcard.org/wp-content/uploads/2020/12/Public-Parks-2021.pdf

- Lottery proceeds
- Sporting goods sales tax proceeds
- Real estate tax proceeds

Another important avenue that should be explored is outsourcing some of the maintenance needed to maintain the parks. Currently, the NPS does have partnerships wherein non-governmental organizations handle asset maintenance and situations in which the NPS leases assets to organizations and requires them to maintain and repair the assets.[500] This avenue should be explored more deeply as it ensures that necessary maintenance occurs with very little cost to the parks themselves.

Another very promising avenue is the reliance on volunteers. NPS already uses some volunteer organizations for maintenance and projects, and it is estimated that if they increase the number of volunteers to 600,000 by 2028, it would culminate in 40 million labor hours worth $802.6 million over 10 years.[501] City parks in the U.S. top 100 cities benefit from 501(c)(3) park conservancy organizations, which have spent more than $500 million in the parks in these cities in the last five years.

Additionally, volunteer work contributed a value of $433 million to those parks in the past year. Partnerships for Parks programs are a central organizing element for volunteer and charitable support for city parks. This is an approach that could be implemented nationally and locally with a huge impact.[502]

Geographic Information Systems (GIS) are used to track projects in

500 Infrastructure Report Card 2020 | Public Parks. (2021). Retrieved 26 June 2021, from https://infrastructurereportcard.org/wp-content/uploads/2020/12/Public-Parks-2021.pdf

501 Infrastructure Report Card 2020 | Public Parks. (2021). Retrieved 26 June 2021, from https://infrastructurereportcard.org/wp-content/uploads/2020/12/Public-Parks-2021.pdf

502 2018 City Park Facts. (2018). Retrieved 26 June 2021, from https://www.tpl.org/sites/default/files/CityParkFacts2018.8_13_18finLO.pdf

the parks. This allows the park management to manage assets, track tasks, revenue and infrastructure age, and assess return on investment.[503] Across the board, implementation of GIS in national, state, and local parks would create a more efficient management strategy and allow for clearer strategizing for future projects.

In addition to solving funding and maintenance issues, there are specific improvement and changes[504] which would make parks more accessible, more useful, and more beneficial to the entire population. These include:

- Make park assets and facilities more accessible to all Americans regardless of disabilities.
- Provide better public transportation to parks.
- Increase multiple uses of parks by adding walking loops, dog park areas, playgrounds, etc.
- Expand park programs to include child care/daycare, music and cultural events, and intergenerational activities
- Add facilities for sports of growing interest, including pickleball, bike paths, and disc golf.[505]

Large scale climate change initiatives are necessary to protect National, state, and local parks from severe damage in the future. The NPS has already created and implemented the Climate Friendly Parks Program, which guides parks in measuring greenhouse gas emissions from the parks and offers

503 Infrastructure Report Card 2020 | Public Parks. (2021). Retrieved 26 June 2021, from https://infrastructurereportcard.org/wp-content/uploads/2020/12/Public-Parks-2021.pdf

504 Infrastructure Report Card 2020 | Public Parks. (2021). Retrieved 26 June 2021, from https://infrastructurereportcard.org/wp-content/uploads/2020/12/Public-Parks-2021.pdf

505 2018 City Park Facts. (2018). Retrieved 26 June 2021, from https://www.tpl.org/sites/default/files/CityParkFacts2018.8_13_18finLO.pdf

response initiatives they can apply.[506] Additionally, the NPS has a managed relocation program in place that is meant to help relocate species to prevent extinction resulting from climate change.

These are positive steps and programs that need more funding. However, the bulk of climate change causes don't come from inside the parks themselves, so global and national initiatives are needed to reduce climate change and protect the parks from wildfires, snow melt, flooding, and sea-level rise, which will eventually create widespread destruction of the parks. *Yale Climate Connections* reports that acting quickly to reduce carbon pollution would likely cut the projected temperature increases in National Parks by two-thirds.[507]

The parks themselves must be protected from extensive drilling and mining, which not only destroy the natural beauty of the parks but contributes to species extinction and climate change. At the very minimum, rules that expanded leasing, drilling, and mining should be rolled back. Other rules that exposed the Parks to damage (there are more than 100 environmental safeguards the last administration removed) must be re-implemented.[508] The NPS created the 9B Rules in 1978 to provide guidelines for protecting the parks from these invasions. The rules were updated in 2016, and these rules, created by the very people who manage the parks, should be incorporated and implemented by the federal government to protect the parks.[509]

National, state, and local parks are a crucial part of the nation's

506 Climate Friendly Parks Program. Retrieved 16 June 2021, from https://www.nps.gov/subjects/climatechange/cfpprogram.htm

507 Swift action on climate change could help protect national parks » Yale Climate Connections. (2020). Retrieved 16 June 2021, from https://yaleclimateconnections.org/2020/06/swift-action-on-climate-change-could-help-protect-national-parks/

508 Lund, N. (2017). The Facts on Oil and Gas Drilling in National Parks. Retrieved 16 June 2021, from https://www.npca.org/articles/1471-the-facts-on-oil-and-gas-drilling-in-national-parks

509 Lund, N. (2017). The Facts on Oil and Gas Drilling in National Parks. Retrieved 16 June 2021, from https://www.npca.org/articles/1471-the-facts-on-oil-and-gas-drilling-in-national-parks

infrastructure that directly impacts citizen's personal health and happiness and offers environmental benefits that affect the entire planet. Providing needed funding, expanding environmental protections, and reducing climate change will ensure that the parks provide benefits for future generations.

CHAPTER 20:

Rails | Positive Train Control - That's the Ticket

"Neither a wise man nor a brave man lies down on the tracks of history to wait for the train of the future to run over him."
—Dwight D. Eisenhower

The early years of the 21st century were not kind to railways and their passengers. Several commuter train crashes claimed lives due to human error, design flaws, maintenance problems, and the failure to implement current safety technology.

One such crash occurred at 9:23 pm on May 12, 2015. Amtrak Northeast Regional Train 188 from Washington, D.C., traveling the Northeast Corridor on its way to New York City, derailed and wrecked near the Kensington neighborhood in northeastern Philadelphia. The train carried 238 passengers and five crewmembers, of whom eight were killed and more than 200 injured, 11 critically. As many as 200 police officers and 120 firefighters responded to the scene and began to free trapped passengers.[510]

The injured were sent to at least four area hospitals, while city buses transported individuals who were not seriously injured. Visiting the crash

510 Amtrak Train Was Going at Least 100 MPH Before Crash. (2021). Retrieved 27 May 2021, from https://nymag.com/intelligencer/2015/05/amtrak-train-derails-philadelphia.html

scene, Philadelphia Mayor Michael Nutter declared the site "an absolute disastrous mess. I've never seen anything like this in my life."

In its investigation, the National Transportation Safety Board focused on the train's excessive speed; it was recorded going 104 miles per hour on a stretch of track zoned for 50 miles per hour.[511] The speed, NTSB concluded, was due to "human error." The human who committed the error was engineer Brandon Bostian, whom NTSB investigator Ted Turpin described as "a concerned operator" with an excellent record and "no past performance issues."

An NTSB board member described Bostian as "extremely cooperative," but the engineer testified that since he had suffered a concussion in the crash, he had only the barest, "dream-like" recollection of the critical moments before the crash. At some point, he realized his locomotive had gone into the curve too fast, so he hit the brakes as the train started to tip over. "I remember holding onto the controls tightly and feeling like, okay well this is it, I'm going over," Bostian told the NTSB.[512] He tried to brace himself, and saw "objects fly in front of me, kind of a bluish tint to them."

Descriptions given by passengers seem to support Bostian's hazy memory. According to a report in *New York* magazine, Paul Cheung, an *Associated Press* manager, said he felt the train decelerate, as if someone had jammed on the brake.[513] "Then suddenly you could see everything starting to shake," he said. "You could see people's stuff flying over me." Michael Black, another passenger, stated that, "All of a sudden it felt like the brakes were hit hard and then our car. . . just slowly started going over to the side."

---

511 Human Error and High Speed Blamed for Deadly Philadelphia Amtrak Crash. (2021). Retrieved 27 May 2021, from https://www.nbcnews.com/storyline/amtrak-crash/human-error-blame-deadly-philadelphia-amtrak-crash-n575341

512 Amtrak Engineer Recalls 'Dream-Like' Memory Before Deadly Crash. (2021). Retrieved 27 May 2021, from https://www.nbcnews.com/storyline/amtrak-crash/amtrak-engineer-recalls-dream-memory-deadly-philedalphia-crash-n508691

513 Amtrak Train Was Going at Least 100 MPH Before Crash. (2021). Retrieved 27 May 2021, from https://nymag.com/intelligencer/2015/05/amtrak-train-derails-philadelphia.html

NTSB concluded Bostian may have been distracted by radio chatter. However, he did recall hearing dispatches about a rock hitting a SEPTA train. Stephen Jenner, a National Transportation Safety Board investigator, suggested that Bostian may have been distracted by that report and "may have lost situational awareness of where he was." There were no indications that Bostian had been impaired by drugs or alcohol or used a cellphone prior to the crash. For whatever reason, Jenner concluded, "The engineer lost track of where he was before he accelerated to a high rate of speed."

Two years later, just before the statute of limitations for reckless endangerment cases expired, Bostian faced eight charges of involuntary manslaughter, one charge of causing a catastrophe, and numerous counts of reckless endangerment. In the years since, charges have been dismissed and reinstated several times. On May 15, 2020, Superior Court Judge Victor Stabile overturned a lower court's decision to dismiss charges and reinstated counts of the involuntary manslaughter and reckless endangerment against Bostian.[514] For its part, Amtrack agreed to pay $265 million to settle claims filed by victims and their families.

Perhaps the most consequential finding to come out of the NTSB investigation was that the stretch of track where the train derailed lacked state-of-the-art safety technology. NTSB reported that "a contributing factor was that Amtrak 188 was not yet equipped with a positive train control device that would have automatically slowed the train down when it exceeded the speed limit."

In 2008, Congress had mandated PTC for 57,536 miles of Class I freight and passenger railways by the end of 2015. This stretch of the Northeast

514 Judge Reinstates Charges Against Brandon Bostian in Deadly Philadelphia Amtrak Crash. (2021). Retrieved 27 May 2021, from https://philadelphia.cbslocal.com/2020/05/15/judge-reinstates-charges-against-brandon-bostian-in-deadly-philadelphia-amtrak-crash/

Corridor was included among the mandated routes, but installation had not begun. Where safety technology exists, it becomes a moral imperative to employ it since, as NTSB Chairman Christopher Hart stated regarding Amtrak 188, "An engineer who is not fatigued, distracted, or impaired is not infallible on their best day."

Hart's assessment is certainly borne out by examples of catastrophic crashes within the public's recent memory. For example, on September 12, 2008, in one of the worst train accidents in Southern California history, a Metrolink passenger train carrying 225 passengers collided with a Union Pacific freight train on a sharp curve.[515] Twenty-five people were killed and more than 135 were injured. One theory of the crash was that the Metrolink engineer, Robert Sanchez, who had a history of texting while operating trains, may have missed a red stop signal, because he was texting at the time. However, a surviving crew member testified the signal was green, and investigators concluded a red signal at that juncture might not have been clearly visible. If Sanchez was at fault, he paid the ultimate price, dying of severe bodily trauma.

Five years later, on December 1, 2013, a southbound Metro-North passenger train derailed after going into a sharp curve at 82 miles per hour, at a point where the speed limit drops abruptly from 70 to 30 miles per hour.[516] Four people were killed and more than 60 were injured. The engineer, William Rockefeller, reportedly told investigators he had "zoned out" and snapped out of "a daze" too late to slow down. NTSB found he had fallen asleep "due to undiagnosed severe obstructive sleep apnea exacerbated by a recent circadian rhythm shift required by his work schedule." In classic

---

515 Full coverage of September 2008 Metrolink Crash and Aftermath. (2021). Retrieved 27 May 2021, from https://www.latimes.com/local/la-me-traincrash-sg-storygallery.html

516 A Look at Other Recent Train Deadly Train Crashes. (2021). Retrieved 27 May 2021, from https://www.nbcnews.com/news/us-news/deadliest-train-crashes-u-s-over-past-25-years-n656826

closing-the-barn-door style, the Metropolitan Transportation Authority responded to the Metro-North derailment by installing an automatic braking system on that stretch of the route.

Sleep apnea was also a factor in a deadly New Jersey Transit commuter rail crash in Hoboken on the morning of September 29, 2016.[517] The NTSB found that the engineer, Thomas Gallagher, had an undiagnosed case of sleep apnea that had caused him to doze off at the helm. As the train approached the station, it sped up to 21 miles an hour, more than twice the posted limit, and crashed into the concrete barrier at the end of the track.

The impact knocked loose a section of ceiling that fell, killing a young mother who had been waiting on the platform. The crash injured 108 other people and caused $6 million in property damage. Gallagher was found unconscious in the cab and claimed to have no memory of the crash. NSTB also ruled that the absence of positive train control allowed the crash to happen.

Clearly, human error or incapacity cannot be entirely eliminated throughout a nationwide rail system of approximately 137,000 miles. To avert disasters, the system must be designed to compensate for human frailties. What is the current state of railroad safety technology? And how far behind are our nation's railroads in adopting that tech?

What is Positive Train Control?

Movie fans may recall *The Taking of Pelham 1 2 3*, a suspense thriller based on the best-selling novel by John Godey about the hijacking of a New York City subway train. In the original 1974 film, Robert Shaw leads a team of

517 NJ Transit Settles Lawsuits From Fatal 2016 Hoboken Train Crash. (2021). Retrieved 27 May 2021, from https://www.nj.com/news/2021/05/nj-transit-settles-lawsuits-from-fatal-2016-hoboken-train-crash.html

hostage-takers, who threaten to kill one strap-hanger every minute past the appointed time to deliver $1 million. Walter Matthau, playing a dour police lieutenant, doesn't understand how Shaw expects to get away with his crime since his team is trapped underground.

They can't hope to decoy the police by jumping out of the moving train, because a safety device known as "the dead man's feature" will grind the train to a halt. Installed in the event of a motorman's heart attack, the device requires the pressure of the motorman's hand to move the train. No pressure, no movement. But Shaw has an insider on his team, a former MTA motorman, who has designed a mechanical fix to override the dead man's feature.

The dead man's feature was an early attempt at what today we call positive train control: a fail-safe device that compensates for human frailty. *Pelham* also features another fail-safe: automatic braking triggered when the train runs a red signal. But while these are mechanical responses, technology has advanced to the point where sensors collecting data can anticipate problems and prompt the train to react well in advance of trouble. PTC is specifically designed to prevent crashes like that of Amtrak 188, the Metrolink, and Metro-North.

Positive train control[518] is a three-part network, consisting of:

- A centralized office dispatch system
- An on-board train computer
- Trackside monitors or "ping points"

518 Brueck, H. (2021). How 'Positive Train Control' Works & How It Could Make Rail Travel Safer. Retrieved 27 May 2021, from https://www.forbes.com/sites/hilarybrueck/2015/05/20/how-positive-train-control-works-how-it-could-make-rail-travel-safer/?sh=22398a647e9d

The dispatch system feeds movement authority and speed restriction into the on-board computer, so the train cannot move without authorization or exceed the set speed. The on-board computer downloads route information before the journey and applies this data along the route to ensure compliance. As it travels, the train maintains contact with the dispatch system via signaling devices, some of which are actually embedded in the track. These devices also inform the dispatcher about the train movement, including its speed at various points. If the train is moving too fast, the on-board computer will alert the engineer. In an emergency, the computer can override the engineer.

PTC does more than regulate speed. Since the system has a global view of train traffic, it can prevent collisions between trains, keep trains out of work zones, and stop trains that may have been cleared to move by errant signals.

PTC had been on the NTSB's wish list since 1990. But it wasn't until the Metrolink crash that Congress felt sufficient urgency to appropriate funds and compel widespread adoption. The Rail Safety Improvement Act of 2008[519] was signed into law on October 20, 2008. The law originally mandated compliance by 2015 for 41 passenger and commuter railways named in the 315-page bill. However, the process suffered a severe setback in June of 2009. On June 22, a computer-driven Metrorail train in Washington, D.C., rear-ended another train near the Fort Totten station. The crash killed six people, injured 70 others, and called into question the safety of computer reliance.

Eighteen months later, in December 2010, the U.S. Government Accountability Office reported that Amtrak and other mandated railroads were still developing software and would probably not complete PTC installation by the 2015 deadline. Publicly funded railroads were also struggling to find sources of funding for the projects. In October 2015, with

519 Positive Train Control (PTC) | FRA. (2021). Retrieved 27 May 2021, from https://railroads.dot.gov/train-control/ptc/positive-train-control-ptc

the deadline looming, Congress passed an extension until December 31, 2018. Nevertheless, only four railroads met the extended deadline, prompting Congress to extend it again, until December 31, 2020, for the remaining 37. The Federal Railroad Administration was finally able to announce on December 29, 2020, that "PTC technology is in operation on all 57,536 required freight and passenger railroad route miles, prior to the December 31, 2020, statutory deadline set forth by Congress."

Cynics might reply that only in government work can entities that are five years late claim to be two days early. But let us be grateful that the PTC dreams of 1990 are at long last coming to fruition. For example, by the time civil litigation over the Hoboken station crash had settled for undisclosed sums,[520] New Jersey Transit had announced the installation of PTC in compliance with the federal mandate. Nevertheless, PTC is not operable on more than 70,000 remaining miles of track. Safety demands that this work continue.

The Overall State of America's Railways

In its Infrastructure Report Card for 2021, the American Society of Civil Engineers gives our nation's railways, estimated to contain 140,000 miles of track, an overall grade of B. However, this grade should be bifurcated, since there are really two overlapping systems, one for freight and another for passengers. ASCE notes that the freight system "maintains a strong network largely through direct shipper fees," transporting more than 1.7 million ton-miles of goods per day. This user-pays system enables investment of more than $260,000 per mile of track for maintenance.

520 NJ Transit Settles Lawsuits From Fatal 2016 Hoboken Train Crash. (2021). Retrieved 27 May 2021, from https://www.nj.com/news/2021/05/nj-transit-settles-lawsuits-from-fatal-2016-hoboken-train-crash.html

On the other hand, Amtrak and other passenger rail services are heavily subsidized by the government to keep rider fees affordable. This "government investment" has not been adequate for maintenance and improvements, leading to a "repair backlog at $45.2 billion," despite Amtrak spending about $713 million on projects between 2017 and 2019.

Passenger rail problems are most acute within the Northeast Corridor, the most traveled passenger rail route. Here, "infrastructure-related issues caused 328,000 train-delay minutes, or the equivalent of roughly 700 Northeast Regional train trips from Boston, Massachusetts, to Washington, D.C."[521]

The Condition and Capacity of America's Rail System

America's railways are divided into six component[522] classes:

- Class I Freight Carrier — The Surface Transportation Board, an advisory and adjudicatory group within the U.S. Department of Transportation, defines a Class I freight railway as one earning annual revenue of more than $250 million. The seven Class I freighters in the United States comprise a large majority of the nation's operable tracks, and include Canadian Pacific Railway, Norfolk Southern Railway and CSX, Union Pacific, BNSF, Canadian National, and Kansas City Southern. These companies own and maintain their tracks. The largest is the BNSF Railroad with $23.4 billion in annual revenue.

---

521 Infrastructure Report Card: Rail. (2021). Retrieved 27 May 2021, from https://infrastructurereportcard.org/cat-item/rail/

522 Types of Common Rail Systems - VRE. Retrieved 27 May 2021, from https://www.vre.org/about/blog/types-of-common-rail-systems/

- Class II Freight Carriers — These regional railroads are smaller in terms of track-miles and revenue, earning between $20.5 million and $250 million per year. Regional railways often own mainline tracks, and networks of slower speed secondary tracks that connect with industries. Regional railroads are conduits for freight traffic accessing Class I railroads. The nation's 22 regional carriers include the Reading & Northern Railroad, Wheeling & Lake Erie and the Maine, Montreal & Atlantic System.
- Class III Freight Carriers — Also known as short-line railways, these 584 carriers consist of spurs covering short distances and generating less than $20 million revenue annually. Short-line railways allow penetration into less trafficked industrial areas, where producers need access to the regional and Class I networks. Short-line railroads include the Lehigh Railway, Towanda Monroeton Shippers Lifeline, and Delaware-Lackawanna.
- Class I National Passenger Carrier — The U.S. government founded the National Railroad Passenger Corporation, or Amtrak, in 1971 because Class I railroads wanted out of the passenger business, which was suffering after the creation of the Interstate Highway System and the growth of air travel. Amtrak comprises 21,400 miles of track, 70 percent of which are owned by other railroads, 93 percent of which are freight lines.[523] ASCE reports that Amtrak carried 32.5 million passengers in 2019 to more than 500 destinations across 46 states and the District of Columbia. The daily average was about "89,100 trips on more than 300 Amtrak trains." Amtrak qualifies as a Class I

523 Infrastructure Report Card: Rail. (2021). Retrieved 27 May 2021, from https://infrastructurereportcard.org/cat-item/rail/

carrier based on revenue, even though it lost $171 million in 2018,[524] and receives federal grants of about $1.4 billion annually.[525]

Amtrak requested a grant of $1.8 billion in 2020 "to support the Northeast Corridor and National Network accounts." The Northeast Corridor connecting Washington, D.C., with Baltimore, MD; Wilmington, DE (famously Pres. Biden's home station); Trenton and Newark, NJ; New York City; Hartford, CT; Providence, RI; and Boston, MA is the most heavily trafficked passenger route in the country, accounting for "18.8 million trips to 12.5 million riders in 2019."

Amtrak owns most of the NEC which has identified investment needs for FY 2020-2024 of $32.2 billion. Of that amount, "$18 billion [is] available, $7.6 billion [is] being requested through existing federal grant programs, and $6.6 billion [is] currently unfunded."

- Regional Commuter Carrier — Commonly referred to as a commuter rail, these carriers are found in dense urban areas, operate on networks of privately held tracks or over host railroads. Regional commuter lines generally operate under partnerships with transit authorities and government agencies. Examples include the SEPTA Regional Rail Division, serving the suburbs of Philadelphia, and New Jersey Transit Regional Rail, connecting points throughout northern New Jersey with New York City.
- Closed System Rapid Transit — This category covers rail systems operating within a single city or between two major population

524 Amtrak Annual Report. (2021). Retrieved 27 May 2021, from https://www.amtrak.com/content/dam/projects/dotcom/english/public/documents/corporate/reports/Amtrak-General-Legislative-Annual-Report-FY2020-Grant-Request.pdf

525 Federal Grants to Amtrak. (2021). Retrieved 27 May 2021, from https://railroads.dot.gov/grants-loans/directed-grant-programs/federal-grants-amtrak

centers. As the name implies, these systems are for the exclusive use of their own equipment, which frequently runs through a network of closely placed destinations. Trains run on the surface, underground, or on elevated tracks, usually via electric power. Examples include Washington, DC's Metro, the railways of the Chicago Transit Authority, and New York's MTA.

Despite their mechanical similarities, these categories serve diverse purposes. Therefore, they face different challenges and require different solutions.

Funding Needs for the Nation's Railways

As mentioned earlier, the freight system, which is privately owned and operates under a user-pays model, is substantially healthy. Private rails have spent about $700 billion over the last 40 years to develop their current network, including $24.9 billion in 2018. This expenditure comes to more than $260,000 per mile.

We have also noted that Class I freight railroads generate substantial revenue; they also reinvest about 20 percent of that revenue on infrastructure. For example, in 2017, Class I freighters budgeted $11.5 billion for capital expenditures. These lines prioritize projects under two categories: mission-critical and potentially funded/optional projects. According to ASCE, "Mission-critical projects include scheduled maintenance and unscheduled repairs. Potentially funded or optional projects include those that reduce bottlenecking, line extensions, information technology solutions, and related capital investments."

Class II and III railroads reinvest at an even higher rate, recycling "an average of 25 percent to 33 percent of annual revenues" for capital improvements and maintenance. Nevertheless, "funding for capital projects is very challenging." A federal tax credit enacted in 2005, allows railways to claim "$0.50 on every dollar spent up to $3,500 per mile on track and bridge improvements." This has spurred about $4 billion in investments. Among freight carriers, short lines face the greatest shortfall. ASCE notes that "the short-line industry reports a $10 billion shortfall for the state of good repair projects needed to retain a strong connection to the Class I network."

Passenger rails are a different story altogether. Amtrak has been a lightning rod for criticism since its creation. It has always lost money, due in large part to the fact that it is generally more expensive and time consuming than driving or taking a plane. Efforts to make Amtrak competitive with the airline industry, such as Acela trains designed to travel 150 miles per hour, have not succeeded. But ASCE states that, "prior to the pandemic, Amtrak was projected to require no federal funding support to cover operating costs in FY 2020." Still, Amtrak received $1 billion in direct aid through the CARES Act and $1 billion more from a subsequent COVID-19 relief act.

Critics also point out that Amtrak serves a very small segment of the population who are frequent riders, so the benefits are not evenly shared among the taxpayers footing the bill. This criticism is borne out when we compare expenditures for the Northeast Corridor with funds allotted for the rest of the national network: CARES contained $492 million for the NEC and $526 million for the national network.

In comparison, H.R. 133 sent $655 million to NEC and $345 million to the national network. Amtrak also receives funds from 18 state governments, totaling $234.2 million in FY 2019. The question of whether the states served should take total responsibility for Amtrak funding is legitimate.

Closed system transit also faces financial challenges. New York's MTA, which received $3.7 billion in COVID-19 relief in 2020, was still facing a shortfall of $4.4-$8 billion after that money rolled in.[526] But even before COVID, the MTA was in trouble, anticipating a shortfall of $20 billion.

With passenger rail systems being such a money pit, federal and state governments may have to make some difficult choices about which systems to subsidize. Cities like New York, Chicago and Washington, D.C., cannot live without their metro systems, but critics of Amtrak assert that, other than certain members of Congress, even Northeast Corridor residents wouldn't miss Amtrak.

In the immediate future, funding for passenger rail must be concentrated in dense population centers. It should also address additional public safety concerns, such as the danger to motor vehicles at crossings and the openness of railroad right-of-way to trespassers who are easily struck and killed.

America will always rely on freight railways. But unless ways can be found to make passenger rail travel affordable, it may be necessary to concede this mode of transportation belongs to a bygone century.

526 Report: MTA Will Need ANOTHER $4-8 Billion in Fed Funding. (2021). Retrieved 27 May 2021, from https://nyc.streetsblog.org/2020/04/15/report-mta-will-need-another-4-8-billion-in-fed-funding/

CHAPTER 21:

Ports in Peril

"U.S. seaports are showing signs of neglect, a disturbing prospect as the nation competes in an increasingly dynamic global economy. Many aspects of port infrastructure and management are mid-century relics. And while ports throughout Europe and Asia are becoming more modern and productive, many U.S. ports will soon become obsolete without significant upgrading and investment."[527]

—Charles Bookmore

It was early in the morning on June 6, 1993, when police responded to an emergency near Fort Tilden on Breezy Point, a narrow strip of land separating the Rockaway Inlet from the Atlantic Ocean. A rusty freighter, ironically named the Golden Venture, had run aground, and hundreds of passengers were fighting their way through the bone-chilling water to the shore.

Twenty-five years later, the first first-responder on the scene, U.S. Park Police Sergeant David Somma told *The Rockaway Times*, "I remember the blood-curdling screams and the hair standing on the back of my neck. I can hear it like it happened five minutes ago."[528]

At approximately 1:45 a.m., Somma was riding patrol with a partner down Shore Parkway on the grounds of Fort Tilden and saw a light on top

---

527 Bookman, C. (October 01, 1996). U.S. Seaports: At the Crossroads of the Global Economy. *Issues in Science and Technology, 13*, 1, 71-77.

528 McFadden, K. (2018). The Golden Venture: 25 Years Later. Retrieved 16 June 2021, from http://rockawaytimes.com/index.php/columns/3917-the-golden-venture-25-years-later

of a mast that seemed oddly close to shore. Although he knew immediately "something wasn't right," Somma said he "couldn't grasp the magnitude of the whole thing because it was so dark that all you could see was the dark shape of the hull."

He climbed over a dune and ran toward shore, where he "saw people standing on the entire top deck and others beginning to jump into the water." Somma ran back to his car and put in a call for massive backup. Then the two officers returned to the beach, entering the water to retrieve refugees, laboring alone for "about 20 minutes."

Their efforts were frustrated by a nasty riptide and the inordinate dead weight of the slight people they were attempting to rescue. Somma said of the first man he encountered, "I couldn't understand why he was so heavy. These were small, emaciated people. As I'm pulling him in, the waves were crashing over my head. When I finally got to a spot where I could stand him up, I realized he had a rope tied around him, which was tied to a canvas bag with all his belongings, wrapped in plastic. I finally got him to shore, and then we kept going back in as another person appeared through the darkness, and then another, and then another."

The next responder to reach the scene was USPP officer Daniel McFadden, who also dashed into the water to assist. He was concerned the tide would take helpless swimmers out past Breezy Point, where they'd be lost in Lower New York Bay. At one point, McFadden recalled turning back to shore and seeing "the people that we had first brought to shore, opening up their bags, taking off their clothes, and changing into dry clothes, and then they started running over the dune." McFadden said. At that point, he realized, "This was a smuggling operation."

As the word went out across the police band that "aliens [were] landing at Rockaway," responders poured in. Don Morgan, a 101st Precinct NYPD Officer, was on patrol on Beach 19th Street. He and his partner responded, and "saw bodies floating in the water and along the shoreline." On closer inspection, Morgan saw, "They had plastic bags tied together and swung across their neck, and they were jumping out of the boat with all of their belongings. I think that's what caused some of them to drown."

With daybreak, the facts began to take shape. A total of 282 Asian nationals, mostly from China, had paid human traffickers, known as "snake heads," to smuggle them into the United States for what they'd hoped would be a better life.[529] The desperate migrants "had been at sea for 112 days with little food and lots of abuse." Twenty-five years later, roughly 30 were still in the United States, according to *The New York Daily News*. Most, numbering about 140, were deported to China, and "about 50 more were sent to other countries." The death toll from drowning and hypothermia was 10.

The saga of the Golden Venture shocked the nation, especially coming as it did less than two weeks after a similar high-profile human trafficking story. A freighter had dropped off a large number of Chinese nationals under the Golden Gate Bridge.

The public learned that migrants were paying up to $40,000 to be smuggled into the United States, putting down a $5,000 deposit and promising to work off the balance as indentured servants. In other words, a slave network was operating within U.S. borders. Incredibly, the Golden Venture was the "24th Chinese refugee ship to be seized since August 1991."[530] If that many ships had been interdicted, how many more had gotten through? That question has never been satisfactorily answered.

Yet, as the Golden Venture faded from the headlines and from

529 O'Shaughnessy, P. (2008). The Golden Venture Tragedy: From Hell At Sea to The American Dream. Retrieved 16 June 2021, from https://www.nydailynews.com/news/golden-venture-tragedy-hell-sea-american-dream-article-1.294299

530 Goldman, J. (1993). Chinese Flee Smuggling Ship; 7 Die : Rescue: Swarms of Illegal Immigrants Leap into Ocean After Freighter Runs Aground off A New York City Beach. Another Group of Chinese Men Detained in Huntington Beach. Retrieved 16 June 2021, from https://www.latimes.com/archives/la-xpm-1993-06-07-mn-630-story.html

America's consciousness, similar if less spectacular stories continued to pop up occasionally. In 2000, *CBC* in Canada reported that authorities had discovered "18 illegal migrants inside a cargo container on a ship from Hong Kong. . . Three of them were dead."[531] It was the fourth such incident in a few weeks at Seattle-area ports, involving around 60 more migrants, all suffering from severe malnutrition and dehydration.

China's cooperation on this issue, along with an increased standard of living in China over the last couple of decades, would seem to have diminished this problem. However, desperate migrants are still using shipping containers to escape impoverished nations. In 2014, according to *The New York Daily News*, "one man died and another 34 people were found inside a shipping container" on board a freighter in transit between Belgium and the U.K.[532]

The migrants had only been in the container about 12 hours, or many more might have succumbed. They were believed to have come originally from India. In March of 2020, the UN's International Organization for Migration reported that "The bodies of 64 male migrants were discovered Tuesday in a sealed shipping container at a checkpoint in Tete, Mozambique."[533] There were 14 survivors.

Such incidents are most importantly a humanitarian concern, but they are also indicative of a serious security threat.

A Snapshot of U.S. Port Security

U.S. port security falls under the aegis of U.S. Customs and Border Protection,

531 Three Illegal Migrants Die in Shipping Container. (2000). Retrieved 16 June 2021, from https://www.cbc.ca/news/world/three-illegal-migrants-die-in-shipping-container-1.209697

532 Harding, D. (2014). Illegal Immigrants Discovered in Shipping Container, One Dead. Retrieved 16 June 2021, from https://www.nydailynews.com/news/world/illegal-immigrants-found-shipping-container-dead-article-1.1905666

533 Picheta, R. (2020). 64 Bodies Found in A Shipping Container In Mozambique. Retrieved 16 June 2021, from http://edition.cnn.com/2020/03/24/africa/mozambique-migrants-found-dead-intl/index.html

and the Department of Homeland Security. It's a huge job to secure 320 U.S. ports of entry, encompassing seaports, international airports, and land crossings, and the agency has finite resources. On a typical day, CBP will process:[534]

- 650,178 passengers and pedestrians
- 169,842 incoming international air passengers and crew
- 35,795 passengers and crew on arriving ship/boat
- 444,541 incoming land travelers
- 187,049 incoming privately owned vehicles
- 77,895 truck, rail, and sea containers
- $6.64 billion worth of imported goods

In the course of this activity, CBP will also:

- Conduct 1,107 apprehensions at U.S. ports of entry.
- Arrest 39 wanted criminals at U.S. ports of entry.
- Encounter 634 inadmissible persons at U.S. ports of entry.
- Discover 250 pests at U.S. ports of entry and 3,091 materials for quarantine, including plants, meat, animal byproduct, and soil.
- Seize various contraband, including 3,677 pounds of narcotics, $386,195 undeclared or illicit currency, $3.6 million worth of products with Intellectual Property rights violations (pirated merchandise, counterfeits, or "knock offs").

Yet, for all the interdiction, smugglers keep smuggling, whether it's

534 A Summary of CBP Facts and Figures. (2021). Retrieved 16 June 2021, from http://www.cbp.gov/sites/default/files/assets/documents/2021-Mar/cbp-snapshot-web-032021.pdf

narcotics, human beings, or counterfeit merchandise. The risks are high—Lee Peng Fei, the mastermind behind the Golden Venture, was sentenced to 20 years in prison, while an investor in the scheme, Chen Chui Ping, a notorious snakehead from New York's Chinatown, was sentenced to 35 years and died of cancer in a Texas prison—so the rewards must be astronomical.[535] We can only speculate as to how much contraband moves successfully through America's ports of entry, but it is certainly enough for cartels to treat seized goods as an expense item, merely the cost of doing business.

Narrowing our discussion to our nation's seaports, we note that ocean shipping accounts for 90 percent of world trade.[536] Yet only 2 to 10 percent of shipping containers are ever physically inspected. Smugglers keep trying because they are succeeding. They are succeeding because the magnitude of shipping volume overwhelms the regulatory system. This creates a threat to U.S. commerce from counterfeit merchandise, a threat to health and welfare from the illicit drug trade, and a threat to national security from illegal entries and potential terrorist attacks.

Are U.S. Ports Vulnerable to a 9/11 Type Attack?

There are two very real and very frightening scenarios for a terrorist attack on U.S. seaports. The first involves a rogue nation or a terrorist cell transporting a nuclear device undetected in a shipping container and detonating the device either at the port or at a targeted destination within the country. Such an attack could devastate a major coastal city, such as New York, Los Angeles, or Seattle. While Kim Jung-Un has gotten global attention for his threats

535 McFadden, K. (2018). The Golden Venture: 25 Years Later. Retrieved 16 June 2021, from http://rockawaytimes.com/index.php/columns/3917-the-golden-venture-25-years-later

536 Fun Fact #1: Shipping Accounts for 90% of World Trade. Retrieved 16 June 2021, from https://www.icontainers.com/us/2016/10/28/friday-fun-fact-1-shipping-accounts-for-90-of-world-trade/

to launch missiles at Hawaii or the West Coast of the United States, rocket attacks are probably not as big a threat as an atomic mail bomb.

Within months of the terrorist attacks on September 11, 2001, the U.S. Customs Service launched the Container Security Initiative (CSI) to prevent shipping containers from being used as weapons of mass destruction. The Initiative is comprised of three core elements:[537]

- Identifying high-risk containers — "CBP uses automated targeting tools to identify containers that pose a potential risk for terrorism, based on advance information and strategic intelligence."
- Prescreening and evaluating containers prior to shipping — "Containers are screened as early in the supply chain as possible, generally at the port of departure."
- Rapid prescreening of high-risk containers — This process employs "large-scale X-ray and gamma ray machines and radiation detection devices."

Selling CSI to foreign nations was an important hurdle, since successful prescreening requires foreign government participation. Ports in developed nations that valued trade with the United States were quick to comply, but expanding the program to developing nations presented obstacles. To even be eligible to participate in CSI, a candidate nation "must commit" to certain "minimum standards," which include:[538]

- Allowing the U.S. Customs Administration "to inspect cargo

537 CSI: Container Security Initiative. Retrieved 16 June 2021, from https://www.cbp.gov/border-security/ports-entry/cargo-security/csi/csi-brief

538 Container Security Initiative (CSI) Fact Sheet. (2005). Retrieved 16 June 2021, from https://www.ait.org.tw/container-security-initiative-csi-fact-sheet/

originating, transiting, exiting, or being transshipped through" the country.

- Establishing an automated risk management system to identify potentially high-risk containers.
- Sharing "critical data, intelligence, and risk management information with the United States Customs and Border Protection."

The nation must also have a seaport with "regular, direct, and substantial container traffic to ports in the United States." This would seem to create a loophole where countries with insubstantial traffic could avoid prescreening requirements.

Prescreening is an added expense for developing nations, which may be hoping to increase trade with the United States but may not have the resources to meet the standards. However, the program does offer incentives, such as expedited processing through U.S. Customs, which might be sufficient inducement to make the investment. As of 2011, 58 ports had signed on to CSI.

In 2011 Matthew Wallin, writing for *AmericanSecurityProject.org*, revisited the issue of shipping container security.[539] Calling containers the "poor man's ICBM," Wallin warned of "60,000 people dead—instantly. 150,000 more exposed to hazardous radiation. All ships and infrastructure at the Ports of Los Angeles and Long Beach were destroyed. An exodus of six million people from the greater Los Angeles region. Initial costs of $1 trillion. This is exactly the scenario considered in a 2006 RAND Corporation study of the effects of a possible detonation of a 10-kiloton nuclear device

539 Wallin, M. (2011). Shipping Containers: The Poor Man's ICBM. Retrieved 16 June 2021, from https://www.americansecurityproject.org/shipping-containers-the-poor-mans-icbm/

hidden in a standard 20-foot shipping container. In 2010 alone, these ports received a combined total of over 7.2 million 20-foot equivalent containers. Haystack indeed."

Successive U.S. presidents had been aware of the problem and had taken steps to mitigate risk. Wallin explains that "Under the [George W.] Bush Administration, th.S. US began equipping American ports with radiation detection devices designed to detect nuclear materials, such as those that could be used in the detonation of a 'dirty bomb.'"

During the Obama Administration, the National Nuclear Security Administration initiated its Second Line of Defense Program, "a two-part project, including the 'Core Program' to equip 650 sites in 30 countries around the world with detection equipment, and the 'Megaports Initiative' to equip more than 100 seaports with radiation equipment by 2018." The goal was to train foreign operators to enable "scanning of around 50 percent of global shipping traffic by 2018."

As of 2011, Wallin was not impressed with the effectiveness of the program. He noted that "The innate problem with nuclear material detection is that nuclear weapons aren't inherently radioactive. In fact, the sensitivity level required to detect nuclear weapons is so great, that cat litter, ceramic tiles, and people have been known to regularly set off the detection equipment."

Fast forward 10 years, and where are we in dealing with this threat today? The CBP claims that their radiation detection systems scan "over 99 percent of arriving sea containers."[540] But what of that other one percent? And what about the "innate problem" Wallin describes? Is the fact that a container nuke hasn't been detonated evidence that the system is working, or simply proof the type of attack hasn't been tried yet?

---

540 Homeland Security, Cargo Screening. Retrieved 16 June 2021, from https://www.dhs.gov/cargo-screening

Cybersecurity at U.S. Ports

If a nuclear attack on U.S. ports sounds far-fetched, the second major threat, that of hacking a port's computer network, should fall more within the realm of possibility. As Commander Joseph Kramek, USCG Executive Fellow, explained in a 2013 policy paper, "U.S. port facilities rely as much upon networked computer and control systems as they do upon stevedores to ensure the flow of maritime commerce that the economy, homeland, and national security depend upon."[541]

Yet, as we might expect from a paper entitled *The Critical Infrastructure Gap: U.S. Port Facilities and Cyber Vulnerabilities*, Cmdr. Kramek was concerned about deficiencies in the security of the network and the consequences a breach would have for American commerce. Cmdr. Kramek writes that "No cybersecurity standards have been promulgated for U.S. ports, nor has the U.S. Coast Guard, the lead federal agency for maritime security, been granted cybersecurity authorities to regulate ports or other areas of maritime critical infrastructure."

Kramek cites a warning from a then-recent National Intelligence Estimate (NIE) that "the next terrorist attack on U.S. Critical Infrastructure and Key Resources (CIKR) is just as likely to be a cyber-attack as a kinetic attack."

What would be the result of a scrambled cyber network? "The potential consequences of even a minimal disruption of the flow of goods in U.S. ports would be high. The zero-inventory, just-in-time delivery system that sustains the flow of U.S. commerce would grind to a halt in a matter of days; shelves at grocery stores and gas tanks at service stations would run empty. In certain ports, a cyber disruption affecting energy supplies would

541 The Critical Infrastructure Gap: U.S. Port Facilities and Cyber Vulnerabilities. (2013). Retrieved 16 June 2021, from https://www.brookings.edu/wp-content/uploads/2016/06/03-cyber-port-security-kramek.pdf

likely send not just a ripple but a shockwave through the U.S. and even global economy."

Any Port in a Storm: Enabling a Potent Response to Disasters

Another area of concern with our ports is emergency response. When cities sustain damage from natural disasters, such as a hurricane, an earthquake, or the nuclear scenario discussed above, a robust response is necessary to treat the injured and stave off secondary harm, such as starvation or exposure.

The United States, relying heavily on our Navy, has a proud tradition of humanitarian assistance all over the globe, including Operation United Response, following the 7.0 earthquake that devastated Haiti in 2010; Operation Tomodachi, following the Japanese earthquake and tsunami in 2011 that damaged the Fukushima nuclear reactor; and Operation United Assistance bringing medical support to Liberia during the deadly Ebola outbreak of 2014-2015.

The Navy has also been instrumental in facilitating humanitarian assistance from the Federal Emergency Management Agency in coordination with the U.S. Department of Defense after natural disasters, such as Hurricane Katrina in 2005.

Most recently, the Navy and the Army Corps of Engineers responded to calls for assistance with managing the COVID-19 pandemic. Anticipating an influx of patients that would overwhelm New York City's hospital system, President Trump sent the USNS Comfort, a 1,000-bed hospital ship, to New York Harbor.[542] The ship's medical team "treated a total of 182 patients over

542 Fuentes, G. (2020). Hospital Ship Comfort Ends NYC COVID-19 Mission After Treating 182 Patients. USNI News. Retrieved 16 June 2021, from https://news.usni.org/2020/04/27/hospital-ship-comfort-ends-nyc-covid-19-mission-after-treating-182-patients

a three-and-a-half week period," which was much fewer than anticipated due to Governor Cuomo's ill-fated decision to send COVID patients to nursing homes. The military's mission also included converting the Jacob Javits Convention Center in Manhattan into a hospital where 1,100 patients received treatment.

The ability of the Navy to play a role in disaster response depends on port infrastructure. Leading commercial ports, such as New York and Los Angeles, have the capacity to accommodate Navy ships for extended stays. But since there's no reason to think disasters would discriminate against smaller ports, what can we say about their capacity and readiness?

Grading U.S. Port Infrastructure

The American Society of Industrial Engineers examined U.S. port infrastructure as part of its 2021 Infrastructure Report Card.[543] Noting that "more than 300 coastal and inland ports are significant drivers of the U.S. economy," ASCE lamented "a funding gap of $15.5 billion for waterside infrastructure such as dredging over the next 10 years, with additional billions needed for landside infrastructure."

An additional problem lies with a port's dependence on the infrastructure outside its gates, "which is often congested or in poor condition." Nevertheless, ACSE grades the port system at B-. ASCE breaks down its concerns into these categories:

- Capacity and condition — ASCE notes that "all ports are challenged to maintain their infrastructure in harsh marine environments.

543 ASCE's 2021 Infrastructure Report Card | Ports. (2021). Retrieved 16 June 2021, from https://infrastructurereportcard.org/cat-item/ports/

Corrosion from saltwater and de-icing salts, constant wet and dry cycles, temperature variations, and more accelerate the rate of decline of everything from cranes to wharfs." This explains, though it does not excuse, the fact that only 9 percent of ports were rated good or very good in this category. Many ports also require retrofits to accommodate today's larger vessels.

- Operations and maintenance — The U.S. Department of Transportation Strategic Plan stresses lifecycle and preventive maintenance to keep infrastructure in good repair. An internal review by the Maritime Administration in 2017 "found that ongoing planning frequently fails to target state-of-good-repair projects and could be better at considering resiliency to threats like weather and earthquakes."
- Funding and future need — Ports obtain funding "from a variety of sources, including federal, state, and local funding," as well as the private sector. The federal Harbor Maintenance Trust Fund pays for dredging from funds it obtains "through a 0.125 percent user fee on the value of the cargo," which roughly comes to "$15 per container box." A recent ASCE economic study estimates "that unmet waterside infrastructure needs at coastal ports will be $12.3 billion over the next 10 years." As for landside development, the American Association of Port Authorities identified $32.03 billion in needs in 2018.
- Public safety and resilience — ASCE notes that "Ports have a key role to play in helping a community recover from a natural or manmade disaster," but completely ignores the threat port vulnerabilities pose to public safety. As for resilience, ASCE mentions the need to fortify ports against "sea level rise."
- Innovation — Automation and advanced analytics are driving

improved performance at many of our nation's ports. "Long Beach and Los Angeles each have one fully automated terminal. Three semi-automated terminals can be found in Virginia and New Jersey." Automation increases capacity and delivers safety benefits. Advanced analytics also increase efficiencies to "ensure flexible, responsive, and adaptive management amid highly complex and dynamic scenarios."

Deficiencies in the port system could have a deleterious effect on the entire U.S. economy, while security blind spots could bring disaster. Simply accepting the status quo, thereby allowing the port system to slowly decline, is not an option.

Raising the Infrastructure Grade for America's Ports

ASCE suggests numerous steps the federal government and port authorities can take to improve the state of port infrastructure. These include:

- Remove the multimodal cap on INFRA funds and increase overall investment in the INFRA and BUILD programs to ensure ports can effectively distribute and receive goods as ships continue to grow in size.
- Appropriate funds to the Congressionally authorized projects to ensure that projects crucial to freight movement are completed promptly.
- Adopt new technologies to reduce wait times at docks, boost efficiency, improve resilience, and increase security.
- Improve freight and landside connections to strengthen the entire freight system and reduce congestion that is costly to the economy when moving goods.

- Ensure that ports are a part of comprehensive disaster planning. Ports play a critical role in the aftermath of a disaster, facilitating the movement of people and the delivery of supplies. Integrating ports into a holistic disaster recovery plan—one that is developed with all stakeholders and is based on the data and data sharing—is vital to ensuring a community can quickly recover.
- Port owners and operators should utilize asset management to prioritize limited funding and pinpoint needed repairs.
- Ensure smaller ports can compete in existing and new competitive grant programs.

These actions are vitally important to ensure the safe, steady flow of goods in and out of the country. However, the need for robust security dwarfs all other concerns. Improved methods of screening containers must be developed, along with hardened cybersecurity, to prevent a potentially crippling attack that could have a ripple effect throughout the country.

CHAPTER 22:

Solid Waste | Fight Dirty

"It made Daniel think. The people who had the least were the most willing to share. He outlined a dictum that he would believe the rest of his life: the more people have, the less they give. Similarly, generous cultures produce less waste because excess is shared, whereas stingy nations fill their landfills with leftovers."

—Mark Sundeen

Perhaps the most successful one-minute public service announcement in television history aired starting on Earth Day in 1971. Sponsored by the "Keep America Beautiful" campaign, the spot depicts an American Indian, portrayed by "Iron Eyes" Cody, an actor who had already established himself in film and TV Westerns as the very image of the "Noble Savage." The Indian paddles a canoe from a pristine wilderness stream to a river littered with floating trash.

After passing smoky factories, he pulls his canoe onto a mud bank strewn with garbage. He walks to a crowded highway and stoically watches the speeding traffic. We hear the rich bass voice of one of radio and television's great narrators, William Conrad, say, "Some people have a deep, abiding respect for the natural beauty of this country." A passing driver tosses a plastic bag of garbage out of his window. It bursts at the feet of the Indian, as Conrad continues, "And some people don't." The Indian turns slowly toward the camera as the narrator states firmly, "People start pollution. People can stop it." The final image is a closeup of the noble Indian as a single tear falls from his right eye.

Dubbed *The Crying Indian*, the spot won two Clio Awards, the Oscars for advertising.[544] The PSA was so effective—supported by billboards and magazine ads—at shaming Americans to change their thoughtless habits, the campaign is credited with reducing litter by 88 percent across 38 states.[545] The campaign even earned Iron Eyes Cody a star on the Hollywood Walk of Fame. However, that fame came at a price after Native American groups discovered that the actor with the striking indigenous looks and a vividly detailed Cherokee and Cree origin story was actually Espera Oscar de Corti, a second-generation American of 100 percent Italian descent. Nevertheless, Iron Eyes maintained his identification with the Native American community, working as an advocate for Indian causes until his death in 1999 at the age of 91.[546]

The Crying Indian was a seminal moment in the environmental movement, galvanizing the nation in the fight against litter. According to statistics from "Keep America Beautiful", in the 40 years from 1969 to 2009, "visible litter" on U.S. roadways has decreased approximately 61 percent.[547] Paper, metal, glass, and beverage container litter has decreased by 74.4 percent.[548] These gains have been accomplished despite a 340 percent per capita increase in the use of plastic packaging during that time.

Still, KAB reminds us that litter remains a persistent problem for our communities and our environment. KAB conducted what it claims was the nation's largest litter survey, in 2009, and found that more than 51 billion pieces of litter appear on U.S. roadways each year.[549]

544 Crockett, Z. The True Story of 'The Crying Indian'. Retrieved 25 June 2021, from https://priceonomics.com/the-true-story-of-the-crying-indian/

545 Crockett, Z. The True Story of 'The Crying Indian'. Retrieved 25 June 2021, from https://priceonomics.com/the-true-story-of-the-crying-indian/

546 Keep America Beautiful. Retrieved 25 June 2021, from https://kab.org

547 Keep America Beautiful. Retrieved 25 June 2021, from https://kab.org

548 Keep America Beautiful. Retrieved 25 June 2021, from https://kab.org

549 2009 National Visible Litter Survey and Litter Cost Study. (2009). Retrieved 25 June 2021, from https://kab.org/wp-

Although 91 percent of that trash comprises articles less than four inches in length, those 46.6 billion pieces of litter constitute 6,729 items per roadway mile. Those small items are primarily tobacco products, such as discarded cigarette butts, which make up about 38 percent of all U.S. roadway litter, as well as paper and plastic articles, at 22 and 19 percent, respectively. Of those litter items greater than four inches in length, packaging comprises 46 percent, and includes discarded wrappings and containers for fast food, snacks, tobacco, and other products.[550]

KAB explains the cost of litter is more than aesthetic. Litter cleanup costs more than $11.5 billion each year. Although businesses pay the lion's share ($9.1 billion), they naturally pass on that cost of doing business to their customers. Local and state governments, schools, and other organizations pick up the remaining costs, for which they bill taxpayers.[551]

The indirect costs of litter can also be seen in the impact on property values. Sixty percent of property appraisers state that the presence of litter reduces a home's value, though how much is open for debate. Fifty-five percent of realtors surveyed claimed the drop in value would be about nine percent, but 40 percent of homeowners thought their losses would be more like 10 to 24 percent.[552]

The onset of the COVID-19 pandemic produced new concerns about litter, prompting KAB to warn that "the masks and gloves we wear to the store, the hand sanitizer bottle we keep handy, and the wipes we use incessantly, all belong in the trash and not on the ground."[553] Even conscientious mask-

content/uploads/2019/08/News-Info_Research_2009_NationalVisibleLitterSurveyandCostStudy_Final.pdf

550 2009 National Visible Litter Survey and Litter Cost Study. (2009). Retrieved 25 June 2021, from https://kab.org/wp-content/uploads/2019/08/News-Info_Research_2009_NationalVisibleLitterSurveyandCostStudy_Final.pdf

551 2009 National Visible Litter Survey and Litter Cost Study. (2009). Retrieved 25 June 2021, from https://kab.org/wp-content/uploads/2019/08/News-Info_Research_2009_NationalVisibleLitterSurveyandCostStudy_Final.pdf

552 2009 National Visible Litter Survey and Litter Cost Study. (2009). Retrieved 25 June 2021, from https://kab.org/wp-content/uploads/2019/08/News-Info_Research_2009_NationalVisibleLitterSurveyandCostStudy_Final.pdf

553 Managing Used PPE: Gloves, Wipes, and Masks - Keep America Beautiful. Retrieved 25 June 2021, from https://kab.

wearers were confused about protocols, prompting KAB to state, "These items are not recyclable and should not be placed in recycling collection bins." Yet, even though these items were used to guard against a presumably deadly and highly contagious disease, they soon became as common as gum wrappers on some neighborhood streets. If Iron Eyes had not left us two decades ago, he'd have ample reason to weep today.

Litter might be the most odious form of solid waste we encounter daily, but it is only a small portion of American's solid waste management problem. According to the U.S. EPA, total municipal solid waste (MSW) generation in 2018 was 292.4 million tons, increasing approximately 23.7 million tons from 2017, but 84.1 million tons more than in 1990.[554]

The breakdown of materials was as follows[555]:

- Paper and paperboard — 23.05 percent
- Glass — 4.19 percent
- Metals — 8.76 percent
- Plastics — 12.20 percent
- Yard trimmings — 12.11 percent
- Food — 21.59 percent
- Wood — 6.19 percent
- Rubber and leather — 3.13 percent
- Textiles — 5.83 percent
- Other — 1.56 percent

org/managing-used-ppe/

554 National Overview: Facts and Figures on Materials, Wastes and Recycling | US EPA. (2020). Retrieved 25 June 2021, from https://www.epa.gov/facts-and-figures-about-materials-waste-and-recycling/national-overview-facts-and-figures-materials

555 National Overview: Facts and Figures on Materials, Wastes and Recycling | US EPA. (2020). Retrieved 25 June 2021, from https://www.epa.gov/facts-and-figures-about-materials-waste-and-recycling/national-overview-facts-and-figures-materials

- Miscellaneous inorganic wastes — 1.39 percent

The EPA notes that although the generation of paper and paperboard fluctuates annually, the trend is downward, decreasing from 87.7 million tons in 2000 to 67.4 million tons in 2018. On the other hand, generation of yard trimmings and food waste has increased since 2000. Notably, overall MSW generation increased from 1960 to 2005, then declined from 2005 to 2010, only to rise again from 2010 to 2018.

Recent Trends in Municipal Solid Waste Management

MSW management falls into four categories: recycling, composting (and other food management), combustion with energy recovery, and landfilling.

Recycling dispensed with more than 69 million tons in 2018, which accounted for about 32 percent of all MSW generated. This represents significant growth from 1990, when only 15 percent of MSW was recycled. However, the growth in recycling has slowed in recent years. Paper and paperboard accounted for about two-thirds of that 2018 total, followed by metals comprising about 13 percent, while glass, plastic, and wood amounted to between 4 and 5 percent.[556]

In 2018, the most-recycled products and materials[557] were as follows:

- Corrugated boxes — 32.1 million tons

556 National Overview: Facts and Figures on Materials, Wastes and Recycling | US EPA. (2020). Retrieved 25 June 2021, from https://www.epa.gov/facts-and-figures-about-materials-waste-and-recycling/national-overview-facts-and-figures-materials

557 National Overview: Facts and Figures on Materials, Wastes and Recycling | U.S. EPA. (2020). Retrieved 25 June 2021, from https://www.epa.gov/facts-and-figures-about-materials-waste-and-recycling/national-overview-facts-and-figures-materials

- Mixed nondurable paper products — 8.8 million tons
- Newspapers/mechanical papers — 3.3 million tons
- Lead-acid batteries — 2.9 million tons
- Major appliances — 3.1 million tons
- Wood packaging — 3.1 million tons
- Glass containers — 3 million tons
- Tires — 2.6 million tons
- Mixed paper containers and packaging — 1.8 million tons
- Selected consumer electronics — 1 million tons

These top products accounted for 90 percent of total MSW recycled in 2018.

Also in 2018, composting dispensed 25 million tons of MSW, which included roughly 22.3 million tons of yard trimmings and 2.6 million tons of food waste, which was only a tiny fraction (4.1 percent) of the nation's wasted food.[558] In addition to composting, the EPA measured what it calls "other methods of food management" for the first time in 2018. That year, 17.7 million tons of food, which the EPA estimates to have been 28.1 percent of wasted food across the country, was "managed through animal feed, co-digestion/anaerobic digestion, bio-based materials/biochemical processing, donation, land application and sewer/wastewater treatment."[559]

Rapid growth in recycling and composting is encouraging. Consider the following percentages of products either recycled or composted in 1960 and then in 2018:

---

558 Arendt, K. (2020). Boulder County proposes new compost facility off Hwy. 287. Retrieved 25 June 2021, from https://www.lhvc.com/story/2020/12/02/news/boulder-county-proposes-new-compost-facility-off-hwy-287/5882.html

559 Funding Opportunities and EPA Programs Related to the Food System. Retrieved 25 June 2021, from https://www.epa.gov/sustainable-management-food/funding-opportunities-and-epa-programs-related-food-system

- Paper and paperboard — 17 percent increasing to 68 percent
- Glass — 2 percent increasing to 25 percent
- Plastics — Negligible fraction (*i.e.,* less than 0.05 percent) growing to 9 percent
- Yard trimmings — Negligible fraction growing to 63 percent
- Lead-acid batteries — Negligible fraction increasing to 99 percent

Food composting as a whole was negligible in 1990 and has shown awfully slow growth. The process reached its apex in 2017 when 6.3 percent was reported. The EPA explains the drop-off in 2018 to 4.1 percent due to a different counting methodology, leading to higher estimated food waste generation.

It's interesting to consider how much of this waste the average American accounts for. The EPA reports the following per capita rates[560] for 2018:

- Recycling — 1.16 pounds per person per day
- Composting — 0.42 pounds per person per day
- Other food management — 0.30 pounds per person per day

Another way to dispose of solid waste is to burn it. In bygone days, garbage incinerators were common. Inner city apartment buildings burned trash, so less would have to be carted away. Needless to say, the consequences for air quality were appalling. Unregulated burning of indiscriminate waste belched toxins, such as lead and carbon monoxide, into the air to the detriment of public health and the environment.

560 National Overview: Facts and Figures on Materials, Wastes and Recycling | U.S. EPA. (2020). Retrieved 25 June 2021, from https://www.epa.gov/facts-and-figures-about-materials-waste-and-recycling/national-overview-facts-and-figures-materials

Today, the process is heavily regulated to minimize environmental damage and allow for "energy recovery." Key benefits of this method, according to the EPA, are "offsetting the need for energy from fossil sources and reduc[ing] methane generation from landfills."[561]

Changes in burning practices began with the advent of the Clean Air Act in 1970. Existing incinerators had to implement new standards that prohibited uncontrolled burning and placed restrictions on particulate emissions. Those facilities that could not meet the new requirements were forced to close.

Still, the EPA reports that combustion of MSW increased in the 1980s, and by the early 1990s, the country was burning more than 15 percent of its MSW. By this time, most non-hazardous waste incinerators were recovering energy and had installed pollution control equipment. Yet additional facilities had to be retrofitted or closed when the EPA imposed Maximum Achievable Control Technology regulations in response to "newly recognized threats posed by mercury and dioxin emissions."

The EPA reports that 34.6 million tons of MSW were combusted with energy recovery in 2018.[562] The largest category of products to be burned was food which accounted for around 22 percent. Rubber, leather, and textiles made up more than 16 percent, while plastics comprised roughly 16 percent, and paper and paperboard made up about 12 percent.[563]

The final core method of processing MSW is landfilling. In 2018, about 146.1 million tons of MSW went to what we used to call "the dump." The

561 Benefits of Landfill Gas Energy Projects | U.S. EPA. Retrieved 25 June 2021, from https://www.epa.gov/lmop/benefits-landfill-gas-energy-projects

562 National Overview: Facts and Figures on Materials, Wastes and Recycling | US EPA. (2020). Retrieved 25 June 2021, from https://www.epa.gov/facts-and-figures-about-materials-waste-and-recycling/national-overview-facts-and-figures-materials

563 National Overview: Facts and Figures on Materials, Wastes and Recycling | US EPA. (2020). Retrieved 25 June 2021, from https://www.epa.gov/facts-and-figures-about-materials-waste-and-recycling/national-overview-facts-and-figures-materials

EPA defines a "municipal solid waste landfill" as "a discrete area of land or excavation that receives household waste." However, a MSWLF can also receive other types of nonhazardous waste, including commercial solid waste, nonhazardous sludge, conditionally exempt small quantity generator waste, and industrial nonhazardous solid waste.[564]

In 2009, the contiguous United States had about 1,908 MSWLFs, all under state management. MSWLFs must comply with a litany of federal and state regulations which cover a wide range of issues, including:

- Closure and post-closure care
- Composite liners requirements to protect groundwater and the underlying soil from environmentally damaging leachate releases
- Corrective action provisions to control and clean up landfill releases and achieve groundwater protection standards
- Financial assurance to fund environmental protection during and after landfill
- Groundwater monitoring to determine whether waste materials have escaped
- Leachate collection and removal systems
- Operating practices such as regularly compacting and covering waste with several inches of soil

Many of these practices also help protect public health by reducing the stench, preventing litter from leaving the landfill, and managing insects and rodents.

The EPA reports that landfilling of waste is on the decline proportionate

---

564 Municipal Solid Waste Landfills. Retrieved 25 June 2021, from https://www.epa.gov/landfills/municipal-solid-waste-landfills

to the total generated, decreasing from 94 percent of all MSW in 1960 to about 50 percent in 2018.[565] However, the total level tonnage of MSW being landfilled has remained fairly constant at just under 150 million tons annually since 1990.[566] That consistent dumping of massive volumes of solid waste has led to a quiet crisis in waste management.

Are Our Landfills Getting Too Full?

Writing for *Roadrunner Recycling*, Ryan Deer makes the case that America is running out of landfill space. The United States produces 12 percent of the world's MSW even though we are only four percent of its population. Thus, Deer dares to ask, "How long until we run out of space to bury it all? When does the New York City Metro Area, home to a population of nearly 19 million people, start to look and smell like 15th-century Paris?"[567]

According to a 2015 study done by Dr. Bryan Staley, CEO of the Environmental Research & Education Foundation, the answers seem to be state specific. Stanley finds that "Seven states are looking at running out of landfill space in the next five years, one state will reach capacity in 5 to 10 years, and three states have 11 to 20 years to go. But 22 states have available landfill space for decades to come." Deer concludes it will be only 62 years before all of "our currently operating facilities are stuffed to the gills."[568]

Yet, capacity is not the only problem. Anyone who has ever driven

565 National Overview: Facts and Figures on Materials, Wastes and Recycling | U.S. EPA. (2020). Retrieved 25 June 2021, from https://www.epa.gov/facts-and-figures-about-materials-waste-and-recycling/national-overview-facts-and-figures-materials

566 National Overview: Facts and Figures on Materials, Wastes and Recycling | U.S. EPA. (2020). Retrieved 25 June 2021, from https://www.epa.gov/facts-and-figures-about-materials-waste-and-recycling/national-overview-facts-and-figures-materials

567 Deer, R. (2021). Landfills: We're Running Out of Space. Retrieved 25 June 2021, from https://www.roadrunnerwm.com/blog/landfills-were-running-out-of-space

568 Deer, R. (2021). Landfills: We're Running Out of Space. Retrieved 25 June 2021, from https://www.roadrunnerwm.com/blog/landfills-were-running-out-of-space

past a landfill would probably conclude these sites are not healthy for the environment.

Issues related to landfills[569] include:

- Air pollution — Methane, a potent greenhouse gas, rises naturally from landfills as biodegradable organic matter decays. This unprocessed methane traps up to 20 times more heat in the atmosphere than does carbon dioxide. However, technology exists to use this naturally occurring methane to produce fairly clean energy with more eco-friendly carbon dioxide as a by-product. This process also alleviates the terrible, pervasive odor of the landfill.
- Biodiversity — The Romanian Ministry of Environment and Forests reports that the development of a landfill site changes the local ecology to eliminate "approximately 30 to 300 species per hectare."[570] While some species are lost, species that thrive in garbage, such as rats and crows, proliferate, creating an imbalance. The area's vegetation also changes as some plant species replace others.
- Groundwater pollution — Rainfall mixes with dissolving matter to form highly toxic chemicals, such as ammonia, and heavy metals, that can leach into groundwater. The resulting contamination of local groundwater can be disastrous for public health. Such contamination can also de-oxygenate groundwater, which, with or without noxious chemicals, can kill aquatic life in local rivers and streams.
- Soil fertility impact — Toxic substances can also migrate through the soil to areas surrounding a landfill site. This toxicity can further

569 Kent, M. (2017). Can The Effects of Pollution Be Reversed?. Retrieved 25 June 2021, from https://sciencing.com/can-effects-pollution-reversed-23523.html

570 Newton, J. (2018). The Effects of Landfills on the Environment. Retrieved 25 June 2021, from https://sciencing.com/effects-landfills-environment-8662463.html

damage the biodiversity of animals and vegetation.

- Visual and health impacts — No one wants a landfill in their backyard, for obvious reasons. They wreak, and they are eyesores. More importantly, they are bacterial breeding grounds and attract vermin, which can lead to disease outbreaks and chronic poor health for surrounding communities. Exposure to certain toxins can cause chronic respiratory illness and a variety of cancers.

For these reasons, it is extremely difficult to get authorizations for additional landfills near the communities they serve. But building landfills at remote sites incurs greater expense from transporting the waste.

Solutions to the Landfill Methane Gas Issue

Because methane gas buildup poses a health and safety danger and could violate government regulations, facilities are implementing various strategies to collect, control and treat gases, or to use gases to benefit the community, especially to generate electricity and heat for buildings. For example, when a landfill's methane generation is sufficient to make recovery practical, a facility can install a methane gas recovery system.

Methane gas recovery is nothing new. Since 1989, the Ajinomoto Pharmaceutical Company in Raleigh, North Carolina, has used landfill gas to fuel its facility boilers, heat the facility and warm pharmaceutical cultures.[571] This project is credited with preventing pollution equivalent to 23,000 cars on the road. Lucent Technologies in Pittsburgh, Pennsylvania, saves $100,000 annually by using landfill gas to generate steam for space heating and hot

571 ATSDR - Landfill Gas Primer - Chapter 5: Landfill Gas Control Measures. (2001). Retrieved 25 June 2021, from https://www.atsdr.cdc.gov/HAC/landfill/html/ch5.html

water.[572] Meanwhile, by working with Detroit Energy, the City of Riverview, Michigan, generates enough electricity from recovered landfill gas to service more than 3,700 homes.[573] These are but a few examples of the effective use of landfill methane.

Factors that make methane recovery feasible, include:

- A landfill area greater than 35 acres
- An open, active landfill site that will continue to operate for years to come
- More than one million tons of waste at the site
- Waste depth greater than 35 feet and stable enough for well installation.
- Refuse that can generate large quantities of landfill gas composed of 35 percent or more of methane[574]
- A climate, neither severely cold nor very dry, which is conducive to gas production
- Proximity to a community of energy users

Techniques for converting methane to energy include combustion and non-combustion methods. These methods require three basic components:

- A gas collection system
- A gas processing, treatment, and conversion system
- A means to transport the gas or final product to the user

572 ATSDR - Landfill Gas Primer - Chapter 5: Landfill Gas Control Measures. (2001). Retrieved 25 June 2021, from https://www.atsdr.cdc.gov/HAC/landfill/html/ch5.html

573 ATSDR - Landfill Gas Primer - Chapter 5: Landfill Gas Control Measures. (2001). Retrieved 25 June 2021, from https://www.atsdr.cdc.gov/HAC/landfill/html/ch5.html

574 ATSDR - Landfill Gas Primer - Chapter 5: Landfill Gas Control Measures. (2001). Retrieved 25 June 2021, from https://www.atsdr.cdc.gov/HAC/landfill/html/ch5.html

Gas which is collected for direct use in the landfill's own boilers requires minimal treatment. Landfill gas that is injected into a natural gas pipeline requires extensive treatment to remove carbon dioxide and various impurities. Minimally, gas must be filtered to remove particulates and water.

Energy generation from landfills is perhaps the epitome of the old adage that "One man's trash is another man's treasure." It provides a relatively clean source of renewable energy for minimal expense.

How Do Civil Engineers Grade U.S. Solid Waste Infrastructure?

In its 2021 Infrastructure Report Card, the American Society of Civil Engineers grades America's solid waste infrastructure a C+.[575] ASCE concedes there is no national database of solid waste facilities, so its assessment of landfill capacity relies on estimates. ASCE is concerned about the age of the existing landfills, noting that "The average age of landfills is somewhere between 30 and 50 years old."[576] Nor does any "publicly available data exist to characterize the condition of the nation's materials recovery facilities, which sort and process recyclables."[577]

ASCE relies on the U.S. Bureau of Labor Statistics' data, which reports an increase from 906 public and private materials recovery facilities in 2009 to 1,331 such plants in 2020.[578] So, while landfills are aging out, recycling and other modes of recovery continue to increase.

---

575 Infrastructure Report Card | Solid Waste. (2021). Retrieved 25 June 2021, from https://infrastructurereportcard.org/cat-item/solid-waste/

576 Infrastructure Report Card | Solid Waste. (2021). Retrieved 25 June 2021, from https://infrastructurereportcard.org/cat-item/solid-waste/

577 Infrastructure Report Card | Solid Waste. (2021). Retrieved 25 June 2021, from https://infrastructurereportcard.org/cat-item/solid-waste/

578 Infrastructure Report Card | Solid Waste. (2021). Retrieved 25 June 2021, from https://infrastructurereportcard.org/cat-item/solid-waste/

Still, the EPA would like to see more. In 2020, the Agency announced a National Recycling Goal, increasing recycling rates by 50 percent within 10 years.[579] This goal could be particularly difficult to achieve given shifts in international policy regarding imported recyclables. The United States had been sending plastic products back to China for processing, but in 2018, China instituted the National Sword policy.

This measure "halted the import of many types of solid waste, effectively closing off the destination for two-thirds of the world's plastic waste." Thus, "as much as 92 percent of U.S. plastic in the first part of 2018" were re-routed to other Southeast Asian countries for recycling.[580] With the loss of international markets, U.S. recycling will rely more heavily on domestic facilities. Fortunately, new plants are coming online in Orangeburg, South Carolina, and Huntsville, Alabama.

But even with new facilities, accomplishing the EPA's goal will require operational improvements. For example, wrong materials, such as food and other contaminants, too often enter the recycling stream. The process works much more efficiently when recyclables are clean. Correcting this problem will require "clear, consistent public education and outreach."

On the public safety front, ASCE is concerned with the disposal of pharmaceuticals. Prescribers are supposed to warn patients not to flush unused pills down the toilet because the chemicals don't get processed out of the water system and can be detrimental to marine life. Physicians generally instruct patients to dispose of pills as solid waste, making them an issue for landfills.

ASCE also warns against per- and polyfluoroalkyl substances (PFAS),

579 U.S. National Recycling Goal | U.S. EPA. (2021). Retrieved 25 June 2021, from https://www.epa.gov/americarecycles/us-national-recycling-goal

580 U.S. National Recycling Goal | U.S. EPA. (2021). Retrieved 25 June 2021, from https://www.epa.gov/americarecycles/us-national-recycling-goal

pesticides, industrial chemicals, surfactants, and personal care products, which "are consistently being found in groundwater, surface water, wastewater, drinking water, and some food sources."[581]

PFAS are also frequently found in landfill leachate sent to wastewater treatment plants. ASCE notes that the EPA has yet to take action on PFAS, despite expressed concerns for their impact on human health and the environment. As mentioned in the Hazardous Waste chapter, listing PFAS and similar chemicals as hazardous substances is vital and would, theoretically, keep them out of landfills.

So, how can the United States raise its solid waste management grade? ASCE suggests[582] these steps:

- Set standards for the recyclability of materials and address the true cost of waste by implementing deposits on bottles and fees on plastic bags.
- Strengthen domestic markets for recycled materials by supporting companies looking to build domestic reprocessing plastic facilities and reusing plastics.
- Support research for the use of waste as resources, such as aerobic digesters and plasma gasification.
- Oppose federal legislation that would ban the interstate movement of municipal solid waste to regional solid waste facilities.
- Encourage Congress to list PFAS as hazardous substances in the Superfund.

---

581 Infrastructure Report Card | Solid Waste. (2021). Retrieved 25 June 2021, from https://infrastructurereportcard.org/cat-item/solid-waste/

582 Infrastructure Report Card | Solid Waste. (2021). Retrieved 25 June 2021, from https://infrastructurereportcard.org/cat-item/solid-waste/

Much of this will depend on whether Americans change the way they think of solid waste. ASCE warns we must adopt the attitude that "waste is not waste until it is wasted." ASCE envisions the materials we routinely discard as potential resources, and wishes Americans would share this vision. Considering the population growth that awaits, the expansion of urban areas, and the increase of new forms of waste, turning solid waste into valuable resources is the only viable solution on the horizon.

CHAPTER 23:

Wastewater | The Monster Beneath

"It is often forgotten. . . what an important role wastewater treatment plays in protecting the environment and the health of the public. Without it there would be no development and growth; without it our environment and our very lives would be at risk."[583]

—Nicholas Frederick Gray

One of the greatest infrastructure innovations in human history, which enabled us to enjoy long, healthy lives in big, bustling cities, lies mostly beneath our feet. In general, we try to think about it as little as possible. Of course, I'm referring to our wastewater system: the pipes and sewers which secret away the unmentionable byproducts of existence that we swiftly flush down our toilets. Without sewage systems and treatment plants to neutralize nefarious germs and toxins, human beings would quickly contaminate their surroundings with bodily filth. Population centers would become nests of pestilence. In developing countries where wastewater infrastructure is poor or nonexistent, the risks are evident. Horrible diseases such as cholera, dysentery, and typhoid can run rampant, and infant mortality is often higher than in places with modern sanitation.[584]

583 Gray, N. (1992). *Biology of wastewater treatment.* Oxford: Oxford University Press

584 Alemu A. (2017). To What Extent Does Access to Improved Sanitation Explain The Observed Differences in Infant Mortality in Africa?. *African journal of primary health care & family medicine,* 9(1), e1—e9. https://doi.org/10.4102/phcfm.v9i1.1370

On top of those issues, the stench of massive amounts of human excrement and other waste products can seriously impact the quality of life, along with imposing untold negative effects on the local environment. It goes without saying that if you were lucky enough to be born in a part of the world with good sewers, you should be thankful.

Unfortunately, America's wastewater systems are just as strained and hurting for resources as the rest of our public infrastructure. The American Society of Civil Engineers graded wastewater a D+[585] in its 2021 infrastructure report card, just slightly below the grade of "C-" for all infrastructure nationwide.[586] The main problem is that people are connecting to these systems faster than local communities can repair and improve them.

With continued population growth and increases in people upgrading from septic tanks to urban sewage systems, demand for services is expected to rise by 23 percent by 2032, requiring tens of billions of dollars for expansion and upgrades. Yet sewage bills in many communities barely support the ongoing costs, and politicians loathe to raise taxes and fees to pay for improvements, according to the organization.

The consequences of not making adequate investments in wastewater systems can be dire, posing public health threats. The U.S. Environmental Protection Agency has estimated there are anywhere from 23,000 to 75,000 sanitary sewer overflows in the U.S. each year.[587] Blockages, line breaks, defects, power failures, vandalism, and improper design all contribute to overflows, polluting drinking water, flood homes, and other properties, and cause lingering foul smells.

---

585 ASCE's 2021 Infrastructure Report Card | Wastewater. (2019). Retrieved 9 June 2021, from https://infrastructurereportcard.org/cat-item/wastewater/

586 Condon, C. (2021). U.S. Engineers Grade Infrastructure 'C-' Ahead of Biden Plan. Retrieved 9 June 2021, from https://www.bloomberg.com/news/articles/2021-03-03/u-s-engineers-grade-infrastructure-c-ahead-of-biden-plan

587 Sanitary Sewer Overflows (SSOs). Retrieved 9 June 2021, from https://www.epa.gov/npdes/sanitary-sewer-overflows-ssos

Poorer communities and those with heavy minority populations often suffer the worst wastewater system troubles. In Centreville, Illinois, a town in a flood-prone area near the Mississippi River, the nearly all-Black and mostly lower-income population has struggled for years with sewage overflows. Now the town reeks with the odor of excrement, water is considered unsafe to drink, and human waste and toilet paper can be seen in puddles on the grass.

An ongoing lawsuit accuses the local government and the sewer authority of failing to invest in appropriate maintenance and repairs, and it is expected to go to trial in October 2021.

"The system is broken because people have not paid attention," a lawyer for the town's residents, Nicole Nelson, told *The Guardian* in February.[588] "And because of that, there are Black people in Centreville who cannot live in their homes. That is absolutely a class and race issue."

A Brief History of Sewers

As long as people have lived together in permanent communities, they have pined for clean, efficient ways to dispose of bodily waste. According to a 2014 study by an international team of sustainability researchers, sewage and storm drainage systems were developed as early as 6,000 years ago in ancient Mesopotamian cities Ur and Babylon, located in present-day Iraq.[589]

Fueled by a cultural desire for cleanliness, the systems included vaulted sewers, storm drains, drains connected to houses, and gutters for runoff.

---

588 Smith, C. (2021). 'If White People Were Still Here, This Wouldn't Happen': The Majority-Black Town Flooded with Sewage. Retrieved 9 June 2021, from https://www.theguardian.com/us-news/2021/feb/11/centreville-illinois-flooding-sewage-overflow

589 De Feo, G., Antoniou, G., Fardin, H., El-Gohary, F., Zheng, X., Reklaityte, I., … Angelakis, A. (2014). The Historical Development of Sewers Worldwide. Sustainability, 6(6), 3936—3974. doi:10.3390/su6063936

Wealthier homes had small interior rooms that served as latrines, with a hole in the floor and a cesspool under the house—some of these homes and cesspools connected to drains and sewers.

Elsewhere, inhabitants of the ancient Scottish village of Skara Brae are believed to have also connected huts to a planned drainage system, with early toilet facilities, as early as 3200 B.C. Around the same time, the Bronze Age Minoan civilization on the island of Crete developed complex sewer systems using stone and terra-cotta. Palaces included basic versions of flush toilets, which relied on pouring water from large jars to wash waste into sewers.

Likewise, the wealthiest and most powerful individuals in ancient India, Egypt, and China all had access to some form of lavatory that drained into conduits or sewers. Elites in Egypt as far back as 2100 B.C. had bathrooms with limestone toilets, sometimes even with copper pipes that brought in hot and cold water. Their effluent was channeled into nearby rivers or run directly out into the desert.

Always a resource-intensive endeavor, wastewater systems during most of recorded history were usually available only to the rich. To relieve themselves, poor people throughout the world typically squatted in the streets or over pits dug near their homes.

But in ancient Greece and Rome, some common people and the wealthy had access to public water, sewage and sanitation networks. Roman baths were equipped to pipe in water and pipe out waste from public toilets. Some private homes in Rome were also permitted to connect to municipal sewers. Smells could be ghastly, as there were insufficient vents built into the system. That said, it was easy enough for a Roman citizen to find a relatively clean place to do his or her "business." [590]

---

590 How Did The Romans Go to The Toilet?. Retrieved 9 June 2021, from https://www.bbc.co.uk/bitesize/clips/z8xtsbk

With the fall of the Roman empire, Western society became more fragmented and agrarian, clustered around manors, and cities fell into decline.[591] Few large-scale waste and septic systems were built or developed in Europe, apart from at a handful of monasteries.[592] Communities went for centuries without assured sources of clean water or a means of disposing of human waste apart from storing it in latrines or dumping it directly into rivers. When cities such as London and Paris did start to flourish in the high Middle Ages, lack of proper sanitation was a constant headache.

By the 1500s, London Bridge had become[593] a highly coveted address,[594] built up with many shops and homes, partly because sanitation was easier than elsewhere in the city. Toilet facilities could be built directly over the Thames, washing away any noxious substances and smells.

People from the Roman era through the Industrial Revolution tended to assume bad odors caused disease—not an unreasonable association. But simply taking away foul-smelling excrement and dumping it into the surrounding environment didn't necessarily make people healthier. Although praised by historians for their hygienic practices, Romans still suffered from diseases and parasites common in communities without proper wastewater systems.[595]

Things finally got better in the 1800s. Industrialization sparked massive population growth in cities and towns, motivating urban planners to tackle

---

591 Why Are the Middle Ages Often Characterized as Dark or Less Civilized?. (2015). Retrieved 9 June 2021, from https://slate.com/human-interest/2015/01/medieval-history-why-are-the-middle-ages-often-characterized-as-dark-or-less-civilized.html

592 Water Supply and Wastewater Management in The Medieval | Wastewater Treatment. (2020). Retrieved 9 June 2021, from https://www.climate-policy-watcher.org/wastewater-treatment-2/water-supply-and-wastewater-management-in-the-medieval-age.html

593 London Bridge During The Tudor Period. Retrieved 9 June 2021, from https://www.thehistoryoflondon.co.uk/london-bridge-during-the-tudor-period/

594 Public Toilets in the Middle Ages. (2014). Retrieved 9 June 2021, from https://www.medievalists.net/2014/09/public-toilets-middle-ages/

595 Bichell, R. (2016). Friends, Romans, Countrymen, Lend Us Your Toilets (Without Parasites). Retrieved 9 June 2021, from https://www.npr.org/sections/health-shots/2016/01/07/462050193/friends-romans-countrymen-lend-us-your-toilets-without-parasites

the stench. Scientific advances led to the understanding that germs carried by effluent into drinking water caused cholera, among other terrible illnesses. In Europe and the United States, cities developed modern sewers, piped in drinking water from clean sources,[596] and began to implement rudimentary treatment protocols on wastewater before releasing it back into the environment.[597] Life spans and public health significantly improved as a result.

How Modern Wastewater Systems Work

In order for cities and towns to remain relatively free of waterborne diseases and limit pollution to the surrounding environment, they must not only carry away sewage and other waste but also thoroughly treat it to remove toxins. Treatment processes in the U.S. were subject to some degree of variability until the enactment of the Clean Water Act in 1972.[598] Further standards were imposed under the Safe Drinking Water Act in 1974.[599]

The U.S. Environmental Protection Agency issues regulations for the discharge of wastewater to surface waters and sewage treatment plants.[600] Modern waste categories include other contaminants apart from human effluent, including toxic chemicals, pharmaceuticals, wastewater from oil and gas extraction, and other byproducts of industry and our contemporary lifestyles.

Water that is flushed down toilets or "gray water" drained from sinks and showers in cities eventually goes to a wastewater treatment plant, where

---

596 History of New York City's Drinking Water. Retrieved 9 June 2021, from https://www1.nyc.gov/site/dep/water/history-of-new-york-citys-drinking-water.page

597 History of Wastewater Treatment in The U.S. Retrieved 9 June 2021, from http://civil.colorado.edu/~silverst/cven5534/History%20of%20Wastewater%20Treatment%20in%20the%20US.pdf

598 Summary of The Clean Water Act. Retrieved 9 June 2021, from https://www.epa.gov/laws-regulations/summary-clean-water-act

599 Drinking Water Standards and Regulations. (2020). Retrieved 9 June 2021, from https://www.cdc.gov/healthywater/drinking/public/regulations.html

600 Effluent Guidelines. Retrieved 9 June 2021, from https://www.epa.gov/eg

it is put through a series of stages to remove pollutants and bacteria.[601] Typically, large items such as wood, rocks, and animal carcasses are first filtered out and taken to landfills. Then wastewater is aerated with oxygen to encourage chemical processes and the release of dangerous dissolved gasses like hydrogen sulfide. Poisonous, corrosive, and highly flammable hydrogen sulfide is easily recognized as a pungent "rotten egg" smell.

Various components of the wastewater—gritty bits like sand and coffee grounds and "sludge," which is generally excrement and other organic matter—are encouraged to settle and are removed and handled accordingly. Grit is sent to landfills, while sludge is separately processed in holding tanks.

As those heavy solids are removed, grease, soap and other floating pollutants are skimmed from the top. Once collected, this "scum" is processed in the same tanks as the "sludge," where they are heated and broken down into safe material using healthy bacteria. The remaining water is then filtered through sand and sometimes carbon, eliminating any remaining solid parties and most bacteria and lingering odors.

A final step is to chlorinate the water to kill the remaining microorganisms. Sometimes other chemicals are then added to neutralize the chlorine before the water is returned to the environment in order to avoid harming fish and other water-dwelling creatures.

What Happens When Things Go Wrong

Unfortunately, Centreville, Illinois, is far from the only community in America to suffer from poorly maintained, outdated, and overflowing wastewater systems. Many other economically disadvantaged areas have

601 A Visit to A Wastewater Treatment Plant. Retrieved 9 June 2021, from https://www.usgs.gov/special-topic/water-science-school/science/a-visit-a-wastewater-treatment-plant?qt-science_center_objects=0#

insufficient resources for taking care of their existing sewer and treatment facilities, let alone enough funds for capital improvements.

American Indian reservations fall far behind most other communities in terms of water and wastewater infrastructure. The federal government has estimated that 1.6 percent of all American Indians and Alaska Natives lack any form of water supply or wastewater disposal facilities, and 27 percent require substantial improvements.[602]

On a national scale, close to 40 million U.S. residents live in cities with combined sewer systems,[603] which channel stormwater, wastewater, and industrial waste down a single pipe. This design was common when older industrial municipalities in the Northeast and Great Lakes regions were first building sanitary sewers, and not enough of those systems have been upgraded.

After heavy rains, combined systems are prone to overflows, leading to dangerous algae blooms, contaminated beaches, and polluted drinking water. A study in 2010 found that gastrointestinal illness in children tended to spike after rainstorms,[604] while another study in 2015 revealed a connection to combined sewer systems.[605] For years, the EPA has considered overflows from combined sewer systems as one of the biggest wastewater infrastructure problems in the U.S.

Meanwhile, heavy storms and catastrophic flooding, which are becoming

602 Testimony of Bill Sterud, Chairman Puyallup Tribe of Indians Before the House Transportation and Infrastructure Subcommittee on Water Resources and Environment's Hearing on Building Back Better: The Urgent Need for Investment in America's Wastewater Infrastructure. (2021). Retrieved 9 June 2021, from https://transportation.house.gov/imo/media/doc/Sterud%20Testimony.pdf

603 Evans, M. (2015). Flushing the Toilet Has Never Been Riskier. Retrieved 9 June 2021, from https://www.theatlantic.com/technology/archive/2015/09/americas-sewage-crisis-public-health/405541/

604 Drayna, P., McLellan, S., Simpson, P., Li, S., & Gorelick, M. (2010). Association between Rainfall and Pediatric Emergency Department Visits for Acute Gastrointestinal Illness. *Environmental Health Perspectives, 118*(10), 1439-1443. doi: 10.1289/ehp.0901671

605 Jagai, J., Li, Q., Wang, S., Messier, K., Wade, T., & Hilborn, E. (2015). Extreme Precipitation and Emergency Room Visits for Gastrointestinal Illness in Areas with and without Combined Sewer Systems: An Analysis of Massachusetts Data, 2003—2007. *Environmental Health Perspectives, 123*(9), 873-879. doi: 10.1289/ehp.1408971

more prevalent due to climate change, continue to strain many sewage systems. In February 2017, flooding severely damaged a sewage treatment plant near Seattle, causing almost 250 million gallons of untreated waste and stormwater to flow into Puget Sound.[606] Fortunately, the release did not harm the area's water quality, but other communities have not been so lucky.

Hurricanes have wreaked havoc on wastewater systems throughout the Gulf Coast over the past two decades, including after Hurricane Katrina in 2005.[607] More than 200 wastewater treatment plants in Louisiana, Mississippi, and Alabama were affected by the storm, leading to sewage overflows in homes and roads. Drinking water facilities and the largest wastewater treatment plant in New Orleans were submerged under floodwaters for weeks.

Although repairs were eventually made, infrastructure has not been significantly upgraded to better prepare facilities in the region to handle increasingly powerful storms and flooding. During Hurricane Matthew in 2016 and Hurricane Florence in 2018, communities in the Southeast suffered sewage spills from more than 200 treatment systems. A group of insurance experts advised in a report that towns in North Carolina needed help improving their wastewater systems to deal with the effects of climate change, including moving treatment plants out of flood zones.[608]

The consequences of sewage spills have the potential to be severe and long-lasting. They include intestinal diseases, deterioration in quality of life, closures of schools and businesses, and in the long run, decreases in employment and property values.[609] No one wants to live or work in a

606 Mapes, L. (2018). West Point Disaster Sent Raw Sewage into Puget Sound. Surprisingly, the water quality was barely affected. Retrieved 9 June 2021, from https://www.seattletimes.com/seattle-news/environment/west-point-disaster-sent-raw-sewage-into-puget-sound-surprisingly-the-water-quality-was-barely-affected/

607 Chou, B. (2015). Water and Wastewater Systems Are Still At Risk 10 Years after Katrina. Retrieved 9 June 2021, from https://www.nrdc.org/experts/ben-chou/water-and-wastewater-systems-are-still-risk-10-years-after-katrina

608 Bonner, L. (2019). Hurricanes Cause Sewage to Flow into NC Rivers and Burst from Manholes. Can It Be Fixed?. Retrieved 9 June 2021, from https://www.newsobserver.com/news/politics-government/article236869228.html

609 Sewage FAQs. (2014). Retrieved 9 June 2021, from https://dhss.delaware.gov/dhss/dph/files/sewagefaq.pdf

city or town with unsafe drinking water and reeking of raw sewage. Areas contaminated with improperly treated industrial waste and polyfluoroalkyl substances[610] can also have higher cancer rates, birth defects, and other illnesses.[611]

The coronavirus pandemic has added another concern to the mix.[612] Because SARS-CoV-2, which causes COVID-19, can live in the feces of infected people for nearly 50 days, sewage spills may allow the disease to quickly pass from household to household. The presence of COVID-19 in wastewater is so common in areas where people contract the disease that researchers can use it to map the spread, serving as an even more reliable indicator than data collected by healthcare personnel.[613]

"COVID-19 dramatically increases the public health consequences of these combined sewage overflows," said Kyla Bennett, a scientist and attorney formerly with the EPA, in May. "Our aging water infrastructure represents a growing public health vulnerability as these sewage spills become more common."[614]

What Needs to Be Done

With many of our aging sewer and wastewater systems operating near, at, or even above capacity, the need for large-scale improvements is clear. This is especially true as more Americans seek to connect their homes and

---

610 Basic Information on PFAS. Retrieved 9 June 2021, from https://www.epa.gov/pfas/basic-information-pfas

611 Nearly 100 Cancer-Causing Contaminants Found in U.S. Drinking Water. (2019). Retrieved 9 June 2021, from https://www.ewg.org/enviroblog/2017/09/nearly-100-cancer-causing-contaminants-found-us-drinking-water

612 Sewage Spills Pose COVID-19 Risks. (2020). Retrieved 9 June 2021, from https://www.peer.org/sewage-spills-pose-covid-19-risks/

613 Larsen, D., & Wigginton, K. (2020). Tracking COVID-19 with Wastewater. *Nature Biotechnology*, *38*(10), 1151-1153. doi: 10.1038/s41587-020-0690-1

614 Sewage Spills Pose COVID-19 Risks. (2020). Retrieved 9 June 2021, from https://www.peer.org/sewage-spills-pose-covid-19-risks/

businesses to these systems. According to the American Society of Civil Engineers, approximately 20 percent of the country's residents currently rely on septic tanks and other on-site waste systems. Many of these systems are coming to the end of their lifespans, however, and people will be turning to municipal sewers.

Meanwhile, a significant portion of maintenance on municipal sewers is reactive—responding to problems after they occur—rather than proactive. In its report on the current state of wastewater systems, the American Society of Civil Engineers found that 38 percent of maintenance on sewer pipes is performed in response to failures, instead of getting ahead of the problem.[615] This is not surprising considering that the average age of wastewater pipes in the U.S. is 45 years old, with some components in some cities being more than a century old. Most of these pipes were designed to last no more than 50 to 100 years.

At the same time, maintenance needs are increasing, funding for major projects is running short. In the 1970s, the federal government shouldered roughly 63 percent of capital investment in wastewater system improvements. That responsibility has shifted largely to states, municipalities, and local utilities. The federal government handled only about 9 percent of sewage system improvement expenses in 2017, the ASCE said, citing the Congressional Research Service.

Local governments and sewage districts have an uneven track record with raising sufficient revenue, budgeting for improvements, and managing expenses. Politics comes into play, with some officials loathing to raise rates and fees, at the risk of angering the public. The result is that projects and maintenance keep being deferred until disaster strikes. To pay for the cost

615 Infrastructure Report Card | Wastewater D+. (2020). Retrieved 9 June 2021, from https://infrastructurereportcard.org/wp-content/uploads/2020/12/Wastewater-2021.pdf

of addressing an emergency, fees may suddenly spike, creating affordability concerns. The ASCE notes that user costs for sewers vary dramatically from community to community, reflecting this dynamic.

All told, there is an annual gap of $81 billion in water and wastewater-related capital investments. According to the ASCE, the unmet capital investment need in those systems across the U.S. is likely to swell to $434 billion if changes aren't made. As improvements are put off, ongoing costs of keeping wastewater systems functioning are likely to rise as well. This will have implications for the broader economy, especially for water-reliant businesses and the healthcare industry. By 2029, service disruptions could cost water-reliant businesses $111 billion and tack $378 million onto American's healthcare bills, the ASCE said.

Speaking before a Congressional panel in February 2021, the general manager of Buffalo, New York's sewer authority, Oluwole McFoy, described the compounding problems of wastewater issues driving wealthier residents out of the community, leaving mostly poor Black residents to shoulder the financial burden of the system.[616]

New York State's second-largest city, located along the Niagara River at the eastern edge of Lake Erie, used to be a hub for steel production and the automotive industry, but fell into decline since the 1970s. Decaying infrastructure has deepened the downturn, with ratepayers routinely asked to pay more for reduced services.

"These migration patterns, along with a significant drop over time in federal infrastructure support, in many ways helped lay the foundation for the current environmental challenges facing our urban areas today

616 The Subcommittee on Water Resources and Environment hearing on: "Building Back Better: The Urgent Need for Investment in America's Wastewater Infrastructure." Testimony by Oluwole McFoy. (2021). Retrieved 9 June 2021, from https://transportation.house.gov/download/02/23/2021/mcfoy-testimony

around delivery of water and sewer services," McFoy told the Congressional committee.[617]

"As a result, our drinking water and wastewater infrastructure deteriorated, with the word being done on it relegated to mostly maintenance, repairs, and necessary replacements. This has proven to be an unsustainable approach."

Raising the level of resilience in wastewater systems is also a concern, especially in light of climate change and the growing severity of natural disasters. These types of improvements will require a carefully tailored approach, as every geographic location faces unique risk factors. Older treatment plants may also have been placed in areas that did not consider worsening floods, fires and other catastrophes.

"For instance, some wastewater systems are in low-lying areas that are especially prone to the impacts of flooding, while others may be drought-prone regions or areas with increasingly frequent wildfires," the ASCE said in its most recent wastewater infrastructure assessment.

"Rather than continuing to operate under a 'business as usual' framework, some critical infrastructure decision-makings are shifting their efforts from singularly addressing short-term metrics" to incorporating "long-term, resilience-related factors into planning such as sea level rise, frequency, intensity, and likelihood of natural disasters, cybersecurity threats, and post-interruption recovery time."

Wastewater Systems of the Future

But the news isn't all bad. Policymakers at the federal level have become

617 The Subcommittee on Water Resources and Environment hearing on: "Building Back Better: The Urgent Need for Investment in America's Wastewater Infrastructure." Testimony by Oluwole McFoy. (2021). Retrieved 9 June 2021, from https://transportation.house.gov/download/02/23/2021/mcfoy-testimony

increasingly aware of the resource gaps in our wastewater infrastructure, and efforts are underway to provide greater coordination and support for sewer districts. Municipalities are also increasingly bringing in professional asset managers' expertise to better budget and prepare for increasing maintenance costs. And technological and scientific advances have offered opportunities to increase efficiency and revenue in ways that won't hurt users' pocketbooks.

Coming into office with a slogan of "Build Back Better," President Joe Biden has pledged to make infrastructure investment, including wastewater infrastructure investment, a priority. As of March 2021, his administration was working on a potential multi-trillion-dollar package, expected to be taken up by Congress after it handled pandemic relief measures.[618]

Additionally, a Congressional infrastructure committee has introduced the Water Quality Protection and Job Creation Act of 2021, which would devote more federal tax dollars to water and sewer systems.[619] A similar bill was introduced in the Senate, supported by at least 70 Democratic lawmakers and hundreds of advocacy, labor, and faith-based groups.[620]

The United States Conference of Mayors has also called on lawmakers to raise existing federal funding commitments, increase grant funding, and support expansion of water, wastewater, stormwater, and flood protection services. Municipal leaders are further advocating for increased financial

618 Condon, C., & Wasson, E. (2021). Biden's Economic Legacy at Stake as Next Package Takes Shape. Retrieved 9 June 2021, from https://www.bloomberg.com/news/articles/2021-02-21/biden-s-economic-legacy-at-stake-with-next-package-taking-shape

619 The Subcommittee on Water Resources and Environment Hearing on: "Building Back Better: The Urgent Need for Investment in America's Wastewater Infrastructure." (2021). Retrieved 9 June 2021, from https://transportation.house.gov/committee-activity/hearings/building-back-better-the-urgent-need-for-investment-in-americas-wastewater-infrastructure

620 Biden Urged to Back Water Bill Amid Worst US Crisis in Decades. (2021). Retrieved 9 June 2021, from https://www.theguardian.com/us-news/2021/feb/25/joe-biden-water-act-bernie-sanders

flexibility, which would allow cities, counties, and towns to take advantage of asset management options and investment strategies that would lessen the burden on customers.

Another rising hope is that scientific innovation could substantially reduce expenses associated with managing wastewater systems, and even help the systems pay for themselves. Sensors and better data tracking methods have allowed for more targeted operations and proactive maintenance to be performed by a wastewater utility in San Antonio, Texas, according to the ASCE. Similar efforts could be rolled out nationwide, potentially allowing for billions of dollars in savings.[621]

In the future, we may also treat the waste in wastewater as a potential resource.[622] Sludge, which is mostly made up of the organic solids we flush down our toilets, can be chemically treated to produce methane, and methane can be used in place of natural gas to produce electricity.[623]

Theoretically, any organic waste has the capacity to throw off methane. Wastewater plants outfitted to draw methane from sludge, which use it to generate electricity locally, may have the ability to be largely self-sustaining. Electricity is one of the biggest ongoing expenses for wastewater systems, as it is needed for pumps and sewage treatment processes.

An added benefit: Using methane to make electricity prevents it from being released into the environment. Methane is a potent greenhouse gas and a significant contributor to global warming.[624] Much of it comes from

621 Energy Data Management Manual for The Wastewater Treatment Sector. (2017). Retrieved 9 June 2021, from https://www.energy.gov/sites/prod/files/2018/01/f46/WastewaterTreatmentDataGuide_Final_0118.pdf

622 Energy Data Management Manual for The Wastewater Treatment Sector. (2017). Retrieved 9 June 2021, from https://www.energy.gov/sites/prod/files/2018/01/f46/WastewaterTreatmentDataGuide_Final_0118.pdf

623 Fu, X., Schleifer, L., & Zhong, L. (2021). Wastewater: The Best Hidden Energy Source You've Never Heard Of. Retrieved 14 June 2021, from https://www.wri.org/insights/wastewater-best-hidden-energy-source-youve-never-heard

624 Global Greenhouse Gas Emissions Data |US EPA. (2014). Retrieved 14 June 2021, from https://www.epa.gov/ghgemissions/global-greenhouse-gas-emissions-data

agriculture—dairy cows generate significant amounts of methane[625] through their digestive processes—and other industries. But some of it comes directly from us. Although turning this methane into electricity does create carbon dioxide, another greenhouse gas, the end result is much less harmful.

With these developments, there is cause to hope that the wastewater infrastructure of the future will be highly efficient, well-monitored, and capable of powering itself. Sewage overflows and disastrous conditions like we've seen in Centreville, Illinois, could become a legacy of the past. Our cities and towns will be healthier and, in some cases, better smelling. Less raw sewage will pollute our environment, making our beaches and waterways safer for humans and wildlife.

"Across all sizes of wastewater treatment systems, technology and scientific innovations have made significant contributions to addressing the sector's challenges," the ASCE said. The organization further noted that it might also be possible to recover valuable nutrients from sewage.

With renewed and dedicated focus by policymakers on wastewater infrastructure, these innovations could become the norm, and our economic progress would no longer be at risk of being impaired by our "unmentionables."

625 Cows, Methane, and Climate Change. (2020). Retrieved 14 June 2021, from https://letstalkscience.ca/educational-resources/stem-in-context/cows-methane-and-climate-change

PART III:
INFRASTRUCTURE SOLUTIONS

CHAPTER 24:

Economic Impact | Social Values of Impact Projects

"Show me a healthy community with a healthy economy and I will show you a community that has its green infrastructure in order and understands the relationship between the built and the unbuilt environment."
*—**Will Rogers**, Former President of the Trust for Public Land*

As the need to invest in resilient infrastructure becomes more pressing, it is vital to integrate impact into infrastructure investment and development. The utilitarian vision of physical assets that dominated infrastructure in the 20th century has become obsolete. As the world changes, we must adapt our ideas about how we design the hardware that sustains our lives and our livelihoods.

In a warming planet threatened by dwindling arable lands, demographic growth, and zoonotic viruses, the development of high-impact infrastructure is a central challenge to ensuring a sustainable future.

From developing gas supply infrastructure for biogas-powered ships and charging stations for electric cars to building high-performance transit infrastructure and renewable energy plants, the focus of the projects of tomorrow must be on impact.

It is critical to consider impact from two different perspectives. We must take into account the impact of social and environmental changes on assets and the impact of infrastructure assets on society and the environment. It is by understanding this dynamic that we can efficiently design and build projects with true social value.

For investors, both private and public, sustainability is the key to determining the long-term value of infrastructure assets. We can no longer view the interests of end-users and investors as opposites; this obsolete mode of thinking can be equally damaging for both. In this age of massive societal and technological shifts, there are many opportunities to boost infrastructure impacts.

Impact cannot be a vague category, randomly invoked to garner community support. Impact infrastructure requires adequate impact monitoring. Modern technology enables us to measure impact in a multitude of ways, including AI, geolocation, real-time visualization, climate research, lifecycle analysis, and carbon footprints.

The successful integration of impact into infrastructure project planning requires developing a solid strategic framework. Impact roadmaps, relevant metrics, geographical contextualization of expected results, and performance assessments are all valuable tools. Because impact is particular, it must be measured all the way from the micro to the macro level. The impact of a new project on a region must be considered simultaneously with its social value for a town, a neighborhood, a single household, or even an individual.

The global infrastructure investment deficit is close to $100 trillion.[626] It is nearly impossible for mere mortals to conceive such a figure; infrastructure needs appear monstrous before us. But that does not mean the only way to ensure impact is to build large-scale physical infrastructure projects. In reality, we can achieve great impact through small, localized projects that improve the quality of life at the community level, providing efficient transit,

626 *Report: Impact infrastructure.* (2021). Retrieved 9 August 2021, from https://pages.devex.com/impact-infrastructure.html.

clean drinking water, affordable energy, and adequate housing. We need massive infrastructure for huge metropolises, but we must not overlook the potential impact of smaller projects that cater to marginalized communities.

Societal and Environmental Benefits

In a recent poll by Devex and Bechtel, infrastructure development experts said that impact projects require community engagement, using local contractors, and building community capacity. In fact, 69 percent of respondents emphasized that local communities and governments "lack a basic understanding of disaster risk reduction and resilience principles."[627] In other words, to positively impact society, policymakers and other stakeholders must involve the relevant communities from the design stage.

In the past, infrastructure projects were assessed based on their economic impact, but social value has now taken center stage.

Societal and Environmental Benefits of Infrastructure Projects

- Better air quality
- Better distribution of benefits
- Better mental and physical health
- Better social relations
- Better wildlife protection
- Carbon emissions reduction
- Cleaner and safer local environment

627 *Report: Impact infrastructure.* (2021). Retrieved 9 August 2021, from https://pages.devex.com/impact-infrastructure.html.

- Efficient energy use
- Expanded biodiversity
- Higher employment rates
- Improved workplace safety
- Less waste
- Lower crime rates
- More renewable energy
- More skills and knowledge
- Reduced congestion
- Reduction in water use
- Reduction of noise pollution

While many infrastructure projects of the past have negatively impacted some of the areas mentioned above, we can no longer afford to repeat those mistakes. As uncontrollable fires rage through Southern Europe[628] as I am writing this, in the summer of 2021, it has become clear that we need to meet sustainability goals before our planet becomes unlivable.

Environmental and social impacts are intricately interconnected, but they have some differences. To measure social impact, it is important to define what constitutes value for a specific society. An infrastructure project has social value when it directly or indirectly improves the quality of life for the members of a community.

Social Value Analysis

Industry players need to understand the impact of infrastructure on quality

628 *Fires Rage Around The World: Where Are The Worst Blazes?* The Guardian. (2021). Retrieved 9 August 2021, from https://www.theguardian.com/world/2021/aug/09/fires-rage-around-the-world-where-are-the-worst-blazes.

of life to develop a well-rounded perspective that can inform the design and evaluation of new projects.

Of course, infrastructure projects are complex, and they can have a multiplicity of consequences. Policymakers, environmental advisors, and community advocates must prioritize the projects that provide the most benefits for the community. When negative impacts are to be expected, these must be neutralized through other positive-impact projects and activities.

A cost-benefit analysis based on social value propositions is key to developing impact projects. We need to learn how much the project costs and what society is willing to give up on to receive the benefits the new development will bring. We must go beyond a basic financial analysis and include an assessment of perceived social benefits, and losses that are not material.

This type of cost-benefit analysis requires selecting the appropriate indicators to measure impacts, engaging all stakeholders in the discussion, predicting quantitative impacts, and carefully analyzing potential changes (both planned and involuntary).

Indicators that can be used to verify results include cost-utility analysis, cost-effectiveness analysis, multi-criteria analysis, and social return on investment.

Aspects that require consideration when assessing the social value of infrastructure include supply chains, asset life cycle, procurement approaches, measurable outcomes, and "the unique needs of the delivery and assessment of social value to each asset."[629]

---

629 *Measuring Social Value in Infrastructure Projects: Insights from The Public Sector*. Rics.org. (2020). Retrieved 9 August 2021, from https://www.rics.org/globalassets/rics-website/media/knowledge/research/insights/measuring-social-value_1st-edition.pdf.

Infrastructure Assets in Context

Physical infrastructure assets are usually built as units, a new train station, a new bridge or dam, a new highway. But none of these projects exist in isolation. They are part of complex systems and networks, and we cannot evaluate their impacts without considering each system as a whole.

A new transit station can deliver significant social benefits for a local community, but it could negatively impact the rural communities around it. These impacts must be assessed in a wider context. How does a new project impact the local transit network? How does it affect the regional transit system? Who will benefit, who will suffer? Impact infrastructure requires that the maximum number of people and communities benefit, and new activities and sub-projects must be designed to prevent anyone from suffering.

When assets become operational, developers must assess "how interconnected assets and networks support the delivery of the broader economic, social and environmental objectives."[630]

Social Capital

In this elusive concept's origin, social capital was defined as "those tangible assets [that] count for most in the daily lives of people: namely goodwill, fellowship, sympathy, and social intercourse among the individuals and families who make up a social unit." More recently, the Organisation for Economic Co-operation and Development (OECD), an international organization dedicated to building better policies for better lives, has defined

---

630 *Measuring Social Value in Infrastructure Projects: Insights from The Public Sector*. Rics.org. (2020). Retrieved 9 August 2021, from https://www.rics.org/globalassets/rics-website/media/knowledge/research/insights/measuring-social-value_1st-edition.pdf.

social capital as the "networks together with shared norms, values, and understandings that facilitate co-operation within or among groups."

When we build infrastructure projects, we contribute enormously to social capital. "Social capital provides the glue which facilitates co-operation, exchange, and innovation," the OECD stated in a report titled "OECD Insights: Human Capital."[631]

Impact infrastructure fosters collaborative environments by bringing people closer together and laying bridges between different communities. A recent analysis[632] of social infrastructure investments identified three different types of community infrastructure that can contribute to social capital:

- Public places conducive to meetings among people: parks, playgrounds, community halls and centers, squares, etc.
- Places "where people meet informally or are used as meeting places," including bars, cafes, schools, libraries, and churches.
- Services that facilitate access to meeting places: transport, urban design, landscape architecture, etc.

What Works Wellbeing's analysis concluded that community hubs and green spaces foster social interaction and interpersonal bonding, enhance social cohesion, and bridge social capital, especially in marginalized communities.

---

631 *OECD Insights: Human Capital | What Is Social Capital?*. Oecd.org. (2021). Retrieved 9 August 2021, from https://www.oecd.org/insights/37966934.pdf.

632 *Places, Spaces, People and Wellbeing / Community Hubs and Green Space*. What Works Wellbeing. Retrieved 9 August 2021, from https://whatworkswellbeing.org/resources/places-spaces-people-and-wellbeing/.

Social Benefits of Green Spaces

The benefits of green spaces and their contribution to social capital are multi-layered and complex. Based on *What Works Wellbeing*'s findings,[633] they include:

- Bonding and bridging social capital.
- Connecting people from different cultures and socio-economic groups.
- Contributing to individual well-being: "gaining employment and a sense of purpose, a transformative change in some people's lives."
- Development of new partnerships and increased organizational capacity.
- Fostering civic activity.
- Improving family well-being.
- Increasing physical activity and healthy eating.
- Opportunities for social activities, confidence-building connections, community empowerment, and volunteering.
- "Community participation and co-production."
- "Learning processes to gather insights to improve interventions."
- "Multiple and layered interventions developed in response to local need and to reach disadvantaged groups."

What Works Wellbeing has identified similar benefits for blue spaces, i.e., public infrastructure involving fountains, pools, or waterways.

---

633 *Places, Spaces, People and Wellbeing / Community Hubs and Green Space.* What Works Wellbeing. Retrieved 9 August 2021, from https://whatworkswellbeing.org/resources/places-spaces-people-and-wellbeing/.

Social Benefits of Community Hub Projects

- Contributing to the creation of new community groups and overall community empowerment
- Development of informal support networks and training programs
- Facilitating the development of activities and projects that contribute to the community
- Opportunities for social interaction, networking, partnership, and enhanced access to funding
- Reduction of social inequalities

Aside from its multiple societal benefits, a study based on data from 21 European countries[634] concluded that social capital can greatly contribute to economic growth. The researchers' findings confirmed that "bridging social capital is linked to higher levels of regional economic growth" and "bridging social capital is fundamental for stimulating economic growth, especially in low-skilled regions."[635]

The distinction between bridging and bonding is important here. Bridging refers to connections between different communities, people of different ethnicities, and socio-economic levels, while bonding refers to increased connections between individuals belonging to the same group or category. Bonding can be very positive, but bridging has broader social impacts, as it helps create links that did not exist before. The European researchers found that in some cases, bridging social capital can even "replace formal education

634 Muringani, J., Fitjar, R. D., & Rodríguez-Pose, A. (2021). Social Capital and Economic Growth in The Regions of Europe. *Environment and Planning A: Economy and Space*. https://doi.org/10.1177/0308518X211000059

635 Muringani, J., Fitjar, R. D., & Rodríguez-Pose, A. (2021). Social Capital and Economic Growth in The Regions of Europe. *Environment and Planning A: Economy and Space*. https://doi.org/10.1177/0308518X211000059

in driving local economic growth."[636]

Social infrastructure fosters community training initiatives that help develop human capital, and community hubs increase physical capital. Likewise, green and blue spaces increase environmental and natural capital. All of these factors combined are proven drivers of economic growth and social development. The availability of green spaces, in particular, can boost health and reduce mortality rates.[637]

Social capital may be immaterial, but it is a prime catalyst for getting things done in any community. Allowing people to work together gives them access to a variety of benefits from social relationships. The economies of the 21st century cannot function efficiently without focusing on social capital.

A source of influence and power, social capital drives innovation and minimizes risk. As an integral part of human development, it has contributed to progress and innovation since the dawn of humanity. In the words of renowned anthropologist Mary Clark, "The early human species could not have survived without the expanded social bonding beyond parent and offspring needed to protect helpless human infants—a job that mothers alone could not accomplish. Social bonding to one's group was a biological necessity."[638]

We have greatly evolved since then, but the need for human connections and the social capital they develop has remained constant. No matter how advanced our infrastructure might be, if we do not focus on social capital, it will not realize its full potential.

---

636 *Measuring Social Value in Infrastructure Projects: Insights from The Public Sector*. Rics.org. (2020). Retrieved 9 August 2021, from https://www.rics.org/globalassets/rics-website/media/knowledge/research/insights/measuring-social-value_1st-edition.pdf.

637 Dobson, J., Harris, C., Eadson, W., & Gore, T. (2019). *Space to Thrive A Rapid Evidence Review of The Benefits of Parks and Green Spaces for People and Communities*. Heritagefund.org.uk. Retrieved 10 August 2021, from https://www.heritagefund.org.uk/sites/default/files/media/attachments/Space%20to%20thrive_2019-A%20rapid%20evidence%20review%2014102019-accessible.pdf.

638 Korten, D. (2015). *When Corporations Rule The World*.

Defining Impact Over a Project's Life Cycle

It is important not to confuse impact with immediate results. Whether we are evaluating benefits or negative aspects, we need to consider a project's entire life cycle.

Often, our country has built projects capable of delivering valuable economic impacts in the short term and disastrous environmental consequences in the long term. When we assess social value today, we must consider scenarios spanning many decades into the future. What will be the value of our project for human health over the next 50 years? How will it impact the environment by the end of its life cycle? We need to ask questions like these about safety, sustainability, and other vital social impacts.

These aspects need to be considered in the design stage to boost impact and minimize risks. Decisions that affect social value have the most impact when they are made during the earlier stages of design and development.

A report published in London by the Royal Institution of Chartered Surveyors (RICS)[639] details the decreasing impact of decisions throughout the design stage. According to RICS, there are seven project stages, and each one of them must integrate social value assessment and planning.

Stages of Impact Project Design

Stage 0: Collect data from stakeholders and on the terrain.

Stage 1: Establish project requirements and develop social value ideas.

---

639 *Measuring Social Value in Infrastructure Projects: Insights from The Public Sector.* Rics.org. (2020). Retrieved 9 August 2021, from https://www.rics.org/globalassets/rics-website/media/knowledge/research/insights/measuring-social-value_1st-edition.pdf.

Stage 2: Integrate social impact features into the design, consider options and trade-offs.

Stage 3: Align the whole design to social value and evaluate different design options based on impact.

Stage 4: Propagate features through the supply chain, integrate procurement and technical aspects.

Stage 5: Data collection, performance monitoring, facilitate integration with deliverables.

Stage 6: Communicate impact to end users, document lessons learned.

Stage 7: Collect evidence and evaluate impact, continue to monitor till the end of the asset's life cycle.

Impact Opportunities

The social value paradigm can help the infrastructure sector evolve by contributing to the development of new competencies and operational efficiencies. One of the challenges we face in this respect is persuading both industry players and the public that even small projects can be connected to large visions, like that of the United Nations Sustainability Development Goals, and the overall well-being of our societies.

The concept of social value is sometimes vaguely defined. We must be capable of quantifying and measuring benefits, and communicating them in a way that end users can understand. The public sector must also continue researching and developing guidelines that can sustain private companies as they design and develop assets in a high-impact environment.

From investors and engineers to end-users and local authorities, everyone involved in or affected by an infrastructure development needs clear impact assessment frameworks to level the playing field and ensure social values guide decisions from the earliest design stages.

Impact infrastructure can provide valuable opportunities for knowledge acquisition in both the public and the private sectors. If we are to develop, build, and monitor impact projects efficiently, we need qualified personnel throughout the infrastructure development matrix. We need specialized social value analysts and advanced impact infrastructure research. This is both a weakness and an opportunity. We lack these professionals and knowledge today, but as we train individuals and research these issues, the sector will acquire new competencies and capabilities.

Social impact must be integrated into project management tools as a core metric. We now have the technology to process massive amounts of data. As we deploy sensors and capture increasingly detailed satellite images, we can assess the impact of infrastructure in real-time and make any necessary adjustments.

A long-term analysis of this data can inform future projects, mitigate risk, and boost impact. AI and digital models enable us to test multiple aspects of infrastructure developments with a high degree of accuracy. If we profit from these opportunities, we will be able to build the impact infrastructure we will need over the next 50 years.

CHAPTER 25:

What We Can Learn From China

"China's history is marked by thousands of years of world-changing innovations: from the compass and gunpowder to acupuncture and the printing press. No one should be surprised that China has re-emerged as an economic superpower."

—Gary Locke

Westerners have often criticized China's 'creative' interpretation of the concept of intellectual property, but even its harshest critics recognize the Asian superpower's ability to build large-scale infrastructure projects at a breakneck pace.

America does not want to emulate the absolute government control that has allowed China to build futuristic bridges and airports in record time. However, there are still some things we can learn from our biggest global competitor.

The White House itself has invoked China's grand achievements in its quest to secure more infrastructure funding from Congress. The administration believes that the only way to compete with China is to spend at least $2 trillion on upgrading bridges and mass transit, modernizing neighborhoods and airports, and making broadband access universal.[640]

The skylines of China's largest metropolises are nothing short of mesmerizing. Its grand airports and auditoriums amaze tourists and locals

640 Huang, Y. (2021). Biden Wants to Replicate China's Infrastructure Miracle. Retrieved 2 August 2021, from https://foreignpolicy.com/2021/05/05/china-infrastructure-debt-land-prices-biden/

alike. Explore any important Chinese city on Google maps, and you will find a level of modernization in infrastructure that far surpasses American cities of similar size. Scholars have coined the phrase "China envy" to refer to the effects of this phenomenon.[641]

According to urban planning historian Thomas J. Campanella, China is doing the kind of things America used to do: amazing the world with grand structures that push engineering and architecture forward.[642] The question is, if China has emulated us, can we now emulate China?

China Envy

There are some basic differences between the two nations which make emulation difficult. On the one hand, China has leapfrogged from rudimentary infrastructure to suborbital spaceships and bullet trains. America is at a different stage and moves at a different pace. Chinese leaders don't need approval from the opposition in Congress; they have total control. If the Chinese administration wants to build a bridge, they just go ahead and do it. Democracy is a bit more complicated, but we naturally welcome the complexities, considering how stifling the political atmosphere is under communist rule.

Another difference some analysts have pointed out is that the current Chinese President and his predecessor both studied engineering, so they were naturally keen on innovation in their field. Meanwhile, U.S. presidents have seldom had such backgrounds. The American public has more often elected lawyers to rule over our nation.

641 Ovide, S. (2020). America's Internet Has China Envy. Retrieved 21 July 2021, from https://www.nytimes.com/2020/11/16/technology/internet-china.html

642 Areddy, J. (2021). What the U.S. Can Learn from China's Infatuation with Infrastructure. Retrieved 21 July 2021, from https://www.wsj.com/articles/what-the-u-s-can-learn-from-chinas-infatuation-with-infrastructure-11617442201

China envy is understandable. Our competitor is home to 49 of the planet's 100 tallest skyscrapers.[643] It also boasts a million bridges. While the U.S. spends 2.4 percent of GDP on infrastructure, China spends 8 percent.[644] This was an important selling point for the White House's ambitious infrastructure plan.

Located in a mountainous region with over 1,500 rivers, China has built bridges of fantastic proportions to keep urban centers and important agricultural areas connected. The Pingtang Bridge in Guizhou province links two sides of a canyon that are 7,000 feet apart.[645] The spectacular, 7-mile-long Hutong Yangtze River Bridge efficiently provides railway and highway access to Shanghai from Jiangsu province.[646]

As climate change forces us to reevaluate Americans' preference for private cars and the neglect of our railway systems, the inferior car ownership that was once a disadvantage for China is now an advantage. By 2025, high-speed trains will service 98 percent of Chinese cities.[647] Subways are common in many of them. Today, the country boasts a high-speed rail network totaling more than 23,500 miles, or eight times the distance between New York and LA.[648] Chinese workers travel on bullet trains at 215 miles per hour, much faster than their American counterparts.

The gap between China and the U.S. when it comes to infrastructure is one of astronomic proportions. A few years ago, Bill Gates announced

643 100 Tallest Completed Buildings in The World — The Skyscraper Center. Retrieved 21 July 2021, from https://www.skyscrapercenter.com/buildings

644 How Does U.S. Infrastructure Spending Compare Internationally? (2021). Retrieved 21 July 2021, from https://www.brinknews.com/quick-take/how-does-us-infrastructure-compare-internationally/

645 Mega Bridge in SW China's Guizhou Inaugurated. (2019). Retrieved 21 July 2021, from https://news.cgtn.com/news/2019-12-31/Mega-bridge-in-SW-China-s-Guizhou-inaugurated-MRYzD2d5vi/index.html

646 Hutong Yangtze River Bridge. (2020). Retrieved 21 July 2021, from https://structurae.net/en/structures/hutong-yangtze-river-bridge

647 China-Tibet Bullet Trains to Commence Operations Before July. (2021). Retrieved 21 July 2021, from https://www.railway-technology.com/news/china-tibet-bullet-trains-july/

648 Past, Present and Future: The Evolution of China's Incredible High-Speed Rail Network. (2021). Retrieved 21 July 2021, from https://edition.cnn.com/travel/article/china-high-speed-rail-cmd/index.html

that China had used as much cement in three years as the U.S. in 100 years. China currently produces 14 times more steel[649] than the U.S. and about 2.2 gigatons of cement per year, roughly half of the 4.5 gigatons our country used in the 20th century.[650]

In China, city planners have not focused on short-term return on investment, but on broader societal benefits. For example, World Bank officials were not enamored with the idea of creating a subway in Shanghai; the region's geology made the project far too complex. The World Bank suggested buses would be a better solution for the city's transit, but Chinese officials didn't listen and went ahead.[651] Thirty years later, the Shanghai subway has become an example of efficiency, transporting more than 10 million people every day.

It is as if China followed a different logic, one that often pays off. According to Mr. Campanella, "We need a bit of China to be stirred into our game. . . We're over privileging the immediately affected residents. What we don't do is give requisite weight to the larger society."[652]

China's modernization has, however, not been without cost. Accelerated construction creates pollution, and not all the country's massive structures are green or energy efficient. President Xi's country is conscious about pollution, and it has poured significant resources into green infrastructure projects like wind and solar farms.

There is a boldness in China's infrastructure planning, a pioneering spirit that we would do well to imitate. What American jurisdiction would spend

649 World Steel in Figures. (2021). Retrieved 21 July 2021, from https://www.worldsteel.org/en/dam/jcr:96d7a585-e6b2-4d63-b943-4cd9ab621a91/World%2520Steel%2520in%2520Figures%25202019.pdf

650 Mineral Commodity Summaries. (2021). Retrieved 21 July 2021, from https://www.usgs.gov/centers/nmic/mineral-commodity-summaries

651 Areddy, J. China's Building Push Goes Underground. Retrieved 21 July 2021, from https://www.wsj.com/articles/SB10001424052702303482504579177830819719254

652 Areddy, J. (2021). What The U.S. Can Learn From China's Infatuation with Infrastructure. Retrieved 21 July 2021, from https://www.wsj.com/articles/what-the-u-s-can-learn-from-chinas-infatuation-with-infrastructure-11617442201

billions on a new state-of-the-art airport only 50 miles away from a recently modernized one?[653] China has done it in Beijing. In a way, it seems that China is seeing beyond the here and now, planning for tomorrow, and this is something we can definitely learn from our competitors.

How China Funds Infrastructure

China's investment in infrastructure since the last economic crisis has transformed the country. Though foreign analysts have criticized the questionable safety of 'vanity' projects, such as spectacular glass walkways between mountains, it is undeniable that the investments have paid off. Today, China has more high-speed rail lines than the rest of the world combined.[654]

The economic model of China's infrastructure investments relies on capturing the land value of infrastructure improvements. After acquiring cheap land outside a city, the government builds transportation networks and services that boost land prices, and then sells the plots to avid real estate developers, securing sizable profits.[655] In fact, real estate sales have often accounted for nearly a third of the Chinese government's annual revenue.[656]

This model does not translate very well to America, where landowners have more rights. When the Chinese government wanted to create a wine route and develop vineyards in a promising region, they simply forced local farmers to move elsewhere, giving them jobs and homes in another region. It

653 Beijing Daxing International Airport (PKX). Retrieved 21 July 2021, from https://daxing-pkx-airport.com

654 Nunno, R. (2018). Fact Sheet | High Speed Rail Development Worldwide. Retrieved 21 July 2021, from https://www.eesi.org/papers/view/fact-sheet-high-speed-rail-development-worldwide

655 Case Study: How Does China Pay for Her Infrastructure? (2021). Retrieved 21 July 2021, from https://www.rics.org/en-za/wbef/megatrends/markets-geopolitics/case-study-how-does-china-pay-for-her-infrastructure--funding-the-worlds-most-ambitious-megaproject/

656 Zhu, X., Wei, Y., Lai, Y., Li, Y., Zhong, S., & Dai, C. (2019). Empirical Analysis of The Driving Factors of China's 'Land Finance' Mechanism Using Soft Budget Constraint Theory and The PLS-SEM Model. Sustainability, 11(3), 742. doi: 10.3390/su11030742

didn't matter if the farmers wanted to stay. China simply needed to get in on the global wine production and wine tourism business.

In 2018, a villager who was resettled during the wine boom told a *New Yorker* reporter, "For thirty years now, they have herded us from place to place. Tell me, please, how am I different from this sheep?"[657] This type of individual plight is of no consequence to the administration. In the same journalistic report, a government official from the Ningxia wine region explained, "Here's something you have to understand about the Chinese reality: everything is about being bigger and faster. Quality and longevity of an industry are not priorities."[658]

While we cannot dispossess farmers in America, there are certainly opportunities for funding infrastructure through real estate deals. The business model preferred by China has already been successful in several Western countries. Japan's bullet train company Kyushu Railway profits more from developing adjacent real estate than from operating railways.[659] Grand Central Station in New York was partially financed by real estate. There are other successful examples of the practice in England and Australia.[660]

Aside from taking advantage of real estate development opportunities, America can also learn from China that using public funds to improve infrastructure can be beneficial for society. Whether the Chinese are doing it out of vanity or to make life better for their people, they have understood the importance of infrastructure for economic growth.

---

657 Nast, C. (2018). Can Wine Transform China's Countryside? Retrieved 21 July 2021, from https://www.newyorker.com/magazine/2018/03/12/can-wine-transform-chinas-countryside

658 Nast, C. (2018). Can Wine Transform China's Countryside? Retrieved 21 July 2021, from https://www.newyorker.com/magazine/2018/03/12/can-wine-transform-chinas-countryside

659 One Big Chinese Lesson for America's Infrastructure Plan. (2021). Retrieved 21 July 2021, from https://www.bloomberg.com/opinion/articles/2021-04-08/china-has-a-big-lesson-for-biden-and-his-push-to-speed-up-u-s-infrastructure

660 One Big Chinese Lesson for America's Infrastructure Plan. (2021). Retrieved 21 July 2021, from https://www.bloomberg.com/opinion/articles/2021-04-08/china-has-a-big-lesson-for-biden-and-his-push-to-speed-up-u-s-infrastructure

China spends more on fixed assets than any other nation in the world. This is a relatively new phenomenon. In 1982, China's investments in infrastructure accounted for 2.1 percent of the global total; by 2014, they amounted to $4.6 trillion, nearly 25 percent.[661]

China builds faster than America, but they sometimes overlook safety concerns. For example, many of China's spectacular glass-bottom walkways between mountains had to shut down after the glass broke, putting lives at risk.

Researchers have also found that only about a third of China's infrastructure projects were economically productive after a few years of operation.[662] Analysts have established that cost overruns account for about a third of China's national debt.

According to Atif Ansar, who analyzed China's infrastructure investments, "It is a myth that China grew thanks largely to heavy infrastructure investment. It grew due to bold economic liberalization and institutional reforms, and this growth is now threatened by over-investment in low-grade infrastructure. The lesson for other markets is that policymakers should place their attention on software and deep institutional reforms, and exercise far greater caution in diverting scarce resources to large-scale physical infrastructure projects."[663]

While these types of statements can be controversial, there is no question that China's experiences, its failures and successes, should inform infrastructure decision-making in America.

---

661 Ansar, A., & Flyvbjerg, B. (2017). China's Infrastructure Boom Threatens Its Economic Prosperity. Retrieved 21 July 2021, from https://www.jstor.org/stable/resrep23193.6

662 Ansar, A., & Flyvbjerg, B. (2017). China's Infrastructure Boom Threatens Its Economic Prosperity . Retrieved 21 July 2021, from https://www.jstor.org/stable/resrep23193.6

663 Ansar, A., & Flyvbjerg, B. (2017). China's Infrastructure Boom Threatens Its Economic Prosperity. Retrieved 21 July 2021, from https://www.jstor.org/stable/resrep23193.6

Infrastructure Beyond Borders

Over the last 30 years, the skylines of Chinese cities have changed dramatically. Some of the bustling financial districts of today were backward little neighborhoods in the 1980s. Skyscrapers have taken the place of derelict residential buildings. China's economy has become quite dependent on these types of investments.

Today, China's infrastructure sector seems to be in perpetual expansion. The communist government is keen on setting records: the highest railway, the largest water transfer system, the tallest buildings. The rest of the developing world gazes on these magnificent structures in awe. For most developing nations, investing hundreds of millions of dollars in bridges and bullet trains is impossible.

Plagued by debt, the world's smaller economies struggle to make ends meet. China has seen an opportunity in this problem. While some of the projects the communist nation is carrying out on its own territory may appear superfluous, Africa is thirsty for infrastructure to support economic emergence. The same is true of many Asian and Latin American countries.

When President Xi Jinping visited Kazakhstan and Indonesia about a decade ago, the concept of a new silk road was born. Known for his dreams of grandeur, Jinping was thinking big. He projected building railways, ports, and highways connecting 60 countries in Asia and Africa, which are home to more than half of the world's population. By 2027, China may have spent over $1 trillion to realize Xi Jinping's vision.[664]

Chinese infrastructure investments are by far the largest in Africa. One

664 China's $900 Billion New Silk Road. What You Need to Know. (2017). Retrieved 21 July 2021, from https://www.weforum.org/agenda/2017/06/china-new-silk-road-explainer/

of China's strategy problems is that these infrastructure projects on foreign soil often employ Chinese laborers and are financed through Chinese bank loans. In high-unemployment regions like Sub-Saharan Africa, this is not an ideal situation. As the receiving countries become indebted to China, Xi Jinping's influence on local politics rises to unsavory levels.

Angola provides an illustrative example of this complex geopolitical scenario. After Angola received a $10.5 billion loan from China, it was constrained to using Chinese companies on 70 percent of the country's infrastructure projects. Chinese investments continued to expand until China controlled much of Angola's most prized asset: its oil production, through a partnership with the national oil company Sonangol.[665]

China is able to exert this power in the international arena because its infrastructure investment deals are made between its government and foreign governments. This is a model the U.S. can hardly imitate. Yet as China expands its area of influence on the global scene, America loses many strategic economic positions. Unlike China, our country is too busy trying to fix our crumbling infrastructure to try to beat the Chinese at their game.

Comparing America's and China's Solar Capacities

Among its many contradictions, China counts the fact that it has the largest solar power plants in the world and yet continues to be the largest greenhouse gas emitter.[666] While the administration has announced China will reach carbon neutrality as early as 2060, their hope doesn't sound very

665 Zeeshan, M. (2021). A Lesson for India? Why China Invests Heavily in Infrastructure, both at Home and Abroad. Retrieved 21 July 2021, from https://scroll.in/article/985659/a-lesson-for-india-why-china-invests-heavily-in-infrastructure-both-at-home-and-abroad

666 Profiling The Five Largest Solar Power Plants in China. (2021). Retrieved 21 July 2021, from https://www.nsenergybusiness.com/features/largest-solar-plants-china/

realistic.[667] Whatever the outcome, one can't deny China is really focusing on transforming its energy matrix.

In 2021, no other nation in the world can produce as much solar power as China. By 2020, its total installed solar capacity was 240GW, five times more than it had been only five years earlier. In 2025, it could approach 500GW.

Top Solar Plants in China

- Tengger Desert Solar Park — The Tengger Desert Solar Park, also known as the 'Great Wall of Solar,' is one of the five largest solar plants in the world. With a capacity of 1.55GW, it occupies a vast expanse of the Tengger desert and services over 600,000 households.
- Huanghe Hydropower Hainan Solar Park — The Huanghe Hydropower Hainan Solar Park has an installed capacity of 2.2GW. It is the second largest on the planet. It cost the Chinese government $2.31 billion and has been in operation since September 2020.
- Yanchi Ningxia Solar Park — Yanchi Ningxia solar park has an installed capacity of 1GW. With an advanced centralization technology, it is home to a system of photovoltaic modules that function as a single electricity-generating unit. It is operated through cloud computing using the latest smart technology.
- Datong Solar Power Top Runner Base — Located in Shanxi province, the Datong Solar Power Top Runner Base ranks third in size among Chinese solar power plants. It boasts a capacity of 1.1GW, but construction is ongoing, and when it is completed, the plant's

667 Colenbrander, S., Cao, Y., & Pettinotti, L. (2021). Five Expert Views on China's Pledge to Become Carbon Neutral by 2060. Retrieved 21 July 2021, from https://odi.org/en/insights/five-expert-views-on-chinas-pledge-to-become-carbon-neutral-by-2060/

installed capacity will reach 3GW, more than any other solar farm on Earth.[668]

- Longyangxia Dam Solar Park — Perched up on the Tibetan Plateau, Longyangxia was once the largest solar farm in the world. Though it has lost that position over the last few years, it still boasts a remarkable capacity, at 850MW, and ranks among China's five largest solar plants. It services over 200,000 homes.[669]

Top Solar Power Plants in The U.S.

A comparison between the five largest solar plants in China and their counterparts in the U.S. can be rather revealing.[670]

- Solar Star — Solar Star is the largest solar power farm in the U.S. Spanning 13 square kilometers across Kern and LA Counties in California, it is divided into two sections which generate a total of 579 MW. Spectacular in scale, it has millions of solar panels capable of powering more than 255,000 homes.
- Topaz Solar Farm — Like Solar Star, Topaz Solar Farm was completed in 2015. Covering 15 square kilometers of land in California, it could supply electricity for more than 150,000 homes. A study concluded that substituting fossil fuels with Topaz-generated power would reduce carbon emissions equivalent to the environmental cost of having 77,000 cars on U.S. roads.

---

668 Profiling The Five Largest Solar Power Plants in China. (2021). Retrieved 21 July 2021, from https://www.nsenergybusiness.com/features/largest-solar-plants-china/

669 Profiling The Five Largest Solar Power Plants in China. (2021). Retrieved 21 July 2021, from https://www.nsenergybusiness.com/features/largest-solar-plants-china/

670 Chakrabarti, S. (2019). Top 10 Biggest Solar Farms in The USA | SF Magazine. Retrieved 21 July 2021, from https://www.solarfeeds.com/mag/solar-farms-in-the-usa/

- Ivanpah Solar — Ivanpah Solar is also located in California, at the foot of Clark Mountain. The project cost $2.2 billion and has a 392 MW capacity. It comprises more than 300,000 solar panels.
- Agua Caliente Solar Project — Agua Caliente Solar is located in Arizona and has an installed capacity of 290 MW. The facility cost $1.8 billion to build.
- The Crescent Dunes Solar Energy Project — Crescent Dunes is located in Nevada. The project was developed on public land and has a 110MW capacity. It cost $1 billion to build and has its own energy storage technology.

What the U.S. Can Learn from Foreign Solar Power Developments

Over the last decade, our country's solar power output has risen 50-fold, reaching 81GW in 2020. America's solar power plants now have the capacity to provide electricity for over 15 million homes. Policies like the Investment Tax Credit have greatly contributed to this shift. Public policies and incentives have also accelerated solar developments in China and elsewhere, and some of them provide important lessons.[671]

Germany, which indirectly kickstarted China's solar boom, has been offering many incentives for investments in renewable energy since the turn of the century, and the strategy has paid off. By 2030, the Chinese administration expects to reach its 50 percent renewable energy target.[672]

---

671 Comparing Solar Across U.S., China, Germany, and Japan - DG+Design. (2020). Retrieved 21 July 2021, from https://dgplusdesign.com/insights/what-the-u-s-can-learn-from-china-germany-and-japans-solar-energy-markets/

672 Comparing Solar Across U.S., China, Germany, and Japan - DG+Design. (2020). Retrieved 21 July 2021, from https://dgplusdesign.com/insights/what-the-u-s-can-learn-from-china-germany-and-japans-solar-energy-markets/

Though Germany is not the sunniest place in the world, the European nation has managed to become a leader in research and innovation. Clean energy accounts for nearly 40 percent of Germany's energy consumption today.[673]

Meanwhile, China completely dominates the global market for solar panels. When Germany's legislation created a huge demand for photovoltaic panels, China brought in German engineers, borrowed capital, and began producing them at a competitive price. Soon enough, China became the world leader in terms of installed solar capacity. To boost this capacity, China implemented various incentives. By 2020, solar power-related subsidies are estimated at $247.74 million.[674]

Installed capacity can be a meaningless figure if we don't consider capacity per capita. Though China's solar power capacity has far surpassed Germany's and America's, Germany is still the leader in terms of per capita capacity, followed closely by Japan and the U.S., with China in fourth place.

Installed Solar Power Capacity Per Capita 2020

- Germany: 589W
- Japan: 491W
- United States: 231W
- China: 146W[675]

---

673 Comparing Solar Across U.S., China, Germany, and Japan - DG+Design. (2020). Retrieved 21 July 2021, from https://dgplusdesign.com/insights/what-the-u-s-can-learn-from-china-germany-and-japans-solar-energy-markets/

674 Comparing Solar Across U.S., China, Germany, and Japan - DG+Design. (2020). Retrieved 21 July 2021, from https://dgplusdesign.com/insights/what-the-u-s-can-learn-from-china-germany-and-japans-solar-energy-markets/

675 Comparing Solar Across U.S., China, Germany, and Japan - DG+Design. (2020). Retrieved 21 July 2021, from https://dgplusdesign.com/insights/what-the-u-s-can-learn-from-china-germany-and-japans-solar-energy-markets/

As we can see, building massive solar farms is not the answer if the majority of the population has no access to renewable energy. Still, the Chinese can teach America a lesson or two about the shift to clean energy. China, Germany, and Japan have all implemented centralized policies to incentivize solar power plant development. Our federal government, on the other hand, has failed to implement a nationwide clean energy target.

We owe much of the expansion of solar projects in the U.S. to the ITC, but the tax credit system will expire in 2024 unless Congress renews it.[676] As summer temperatures surpass 120 degrees in Canada, it seems that our country's incentive system is too volatile for the current scenario. Bipartisan efforts on a federal scale will be needed to truly transform America's energy infrastructure.

The feed-in-tariff model used in China, Japan, and Germany might be a better solution than the ITC. The U.S. briefly had a similar program, but it was terminated in 2011.[677]

If America wants to become a leader in solar markets and climate policies, we will need a long-term federal policy and nationwide renewable energy targets. We must do it the American way, but certainly our federal government structure cannot get in the way of our global leadership.

China's Smart Roads and Cars

In the city of Jinan, in Eastern China, the local government is building a road paved with solar panels covered in clear concrete. The panels will be placed

676 Marsh, J. (2021). The Solar Tax Credit Explained: Federal Solar Tax Credit 101. Retrieved 21 July 2021, from https://news.energysage.com/solar-tax-credit-explained/

677 Comparing Solar Across U.S., China, Germany, and Japan - DG+Design. (2020). Retrieved 21 July 2021, from https://dgplusdesign.com/insights/what-the-u-s-can-learn-from-china-germany-and-japans-solar-energy-markets/

along one kilometer of a local highway and will generate enough electricity to power 800 homes.[678]

China envisages the creation of a truly 'smart' road. The panels will do much more than collect solar power; they will share traffic and weather data. Eventually, these power-generating roads could also charge electric vehicles on the go.

In 2021, the Chinese government and Huawei have been testing smart road technology combined with driverless vehicles on a 2.5-mile road in Jiangsu province. The road, street signs, and traffic lights all contain sensors, radars, and cameras that communicate with circulating vehicles.[679]

According to Huawei's Jiang Wangcheng, "Autonomous driving is an irresistible trend, but any isolated vehicle alone can't nail it. . . The only solution is to get more information from the roads."[680] There may be some truth to Wangcheng's assertion, considering that autonomous vehicle tests have often failed because the car's sensors 'misread' their surroundings.

In Jiangsu, an autonomous bus controlled by a transit network constantly exchanges information with the system and the surrounding sensors. For example, it can request green traffic lights to ensure it stays on schedule. As the project progresses, Huawei has been chosen to provide the software and communications technology to power China's smart vehicles and roads revolution.[681]

Currently the largest car market on the planet, China has set a target of 50 percent smart vehicle sales for 2025. As stated above, the technology

678 China's Built a Road So Smart It Will Be Able to Charge Your Car. (2018). Retrieved 21 July 2021, from https://www.bloombergquint.com/technology/the-solar-highway-that-can-recharge-electric-cars-on-the-move

679 China's Huawei Develops Smart Roads That Talk to Driverless Cars. (2021). Retrieved 21 July 2021, from https://www.bloomberg.com/news/articles/2021-01-13/china-s-huawei-develops-smart-roads-that-talk-to-driverless-cars

680 China's Huawei Develops Smart Roads That Talk to Driverless Cars. (2021). Retrieved 21 July 2021, from https://www.bloomberg.com/news/articles/2021-01-13/china-s-huawei-develops-smart-roads-that-talk-to-driverless-cars

681 China's Huawei Develops Smart Roads That Talk to Driverless Cars. (2021). Retrieved 21 July 2021, from https://www.bloomberg.com/news/articles/2021-01-13/china-s-huawei-develops-smart-roads-that-talk-to-driverless-cars

will not be complete without massive smart road developments. Smart road infrastructure was mentioned in a technology road map made public by the Chinese government in late 2020. The document outlines China's plans to build roads and vehicles that can provide accurate, real-time information to safety drivers, pedestrians, and traffic authorities.[682]

The War Over Electric Cars

In spite of its ambitious plans, China is not currently the global leader in electric car technology. Recently, a Chinese startup named XPeng unveiled a startling prototype: its P7 model will do 400 miles on a single charge, and will be fully autonomous, typically requiring driver intervention only once every 60 miles, all at a price tag below that of the Tesla Model 3.[683]

Local governments have poured $700 million into Xpeng in the province of Guandong, and the central administration has regaled it with multiple subsidies and tax breaks. This has more than pleased Xpeng's vice chairman, Brian Gu. "The government is actually a lot more open to allow some of the innovative ideas of businesses to push forward with their research and test their technologies," Gu told reporters.[684]

It is unlikely that such a startup would fare as well in the U.S. As China accelerates investments in the autonomous vehicle sector, America is lagging behind. The Asian giant's subsidies are nearly impossible to match for Western democracies. While the U.S. does protect its own, it doesn't

682 Roadmap plots course of China's auto industry. (2020). Retrieved 21 July 2021, from https://global.chinadaily.com.cn/a/202011/02/WS5f9f6791a31024ad0ba82797.html

683 Chinese Tesla rival Xpeng Motors Launches Sedan with New Driverless Features as EV Race Heats Up. (2014). Retrieved 21 July 2021, from https://www.cnbc.com/2021/04/14/xpeng-motors-launches-p5-lidar-electric-car-to-rival-tesla-in-china.html

684 Schuman, M. (2021). The Electric-Car Lesson that China Is Serving Up for America. Retrieved 21 July 2021, from https://www.theatlantic.com/international/archive/2021/05/joe-biden-china-infrastructure/618921/

go anywhere near China's efforts to catapult homegrown companies into global stardom.

In the U.S., the cost of developing an innovative prototype could be the same as in China, but by the time the prototype hits the market, the Chinese product would have gone through so many subsidy rounds, that its retail price would be considerably lower than that of its American competitor.

Another lesson to learn from China is that innovators need more support from the federal government, because global leadership in futuristic technology sectors will eventually benefit us all.

Writing in *The Atlantic*, Michael Schuman recently argued that "the contest over electric cars is a proxy war between the West and China, between their economic models and political ideologies."[685] For Schuman, if China becomes the global leader in the autonomous technology revolution, this will be a terrible blow for America's free-market philosophy.

According to our President's national security adviser, Jake Sullivan, "U.S. firms will continue to lose ground in the competition with Chinese companies if Washington continues to rely so heavily on private sector research and development." The White House's large-scale infrastructure plan is an attempt to bridge that gap and put America on par with China.

A 2020 study estimated that China has poured at least $100 billion into the electric vehicle industry, mainly in the shape of subsidies. The strategy seems to have paid off. Electric vehicle sales in China have gone from 336,000 in 2016 to 1.2 million in 2020. And China is now home to the largest electric vehicle battery manufacturer.[686]

Tesla is still outselling its Chinese competitors, even in China; nevermind

685 Schuman, M. (2021). The Electric-Car Lesson that China Is Serving Up for America. Retrieved 21 July 2021, from https://www.theatlantic.com/international/archive/2021/05/joe-biden-china-infrastructure/618921/

686 Schuman, M. (2021). The Electric-Car Lesson That China Is Serving Up for America. Retrieved 21 July 2021, from https://www.theatlantic.com/international/archive/2021/05/joe-biden-china-infrastructure/618921/

that Elon Musk has accused XPeng of stealing its technology. The U.S., it seems, still has one competitive advantage; it has companies with better brand recognition, and it is still the place where the most disruptive technology is being developed. "Persuading the Chinese to drive a P7 over a [Tesla] Model 3 is difficult enough;" Michael Schuman explains, "wooing Americans, Europeans, and others will be harder."[687]

What we can learn from China, it appears, is that if we support our extraordinary innovators with the infrastructure and funding they require, China will be the one that lags behind.

---

687 Schuman, M. (2021). The Electric-Car Lesson That China Is Serving Up for America. Retrieved 21 July 2021, from https://www.theatlantic.com/international/archive/2021/05/joe-biden-china-infrastructure/618921/

CHAPTER 26:

Possible Scenarios | America 2050

"With every inch of land on Earth now catalogued by our satellites, the stars are the next place we as a species must travel. And with a booming world population that will hit 9.1 billion in 2050, large-scale space travel may become a necessity."

-Ben Parr

Infrastructure is an investment we make to build a better society. When we build bridges and canals, and broadband networks, we are not only solving our communities' problems; we are building for the future. Infrastructure projects are about creating opportunities for future generations.

One of the problems of physical infrastructure is that the longer it has been around, the harder it is to replace it. Societies often become conservative, and regulations don't adapt fast enough to accommodate new technologies.

Governments and private companies alike are often too focused on the short term. If we were perpetually planning for the future, we would be better prepared to face unknown challenges. Although predictions are sometimes proven wrong, we can forecast what our country will look like in 30 years by looking at the technology being developed today.

In today's fast-paced environment, sophisticated technologies are becoming increasingly disruptive. While it used to take decades for certain industries to change, now everything around us can be completely transformed in a matter of years or even months. Infrastructure's life-cycle is getting shorter, and we are about to see change like never before.

Autonomous Vehicles Will Speed Along Intelligent Highways

In an era of massive data flow through every single interaction with infrastructure, it is quite surprising that highways are still disconnected surfaces, exchanging no information with the vehicles on them. In 2050, that will no longer be the case.

Autonomous cars and public transit vehicles will gradually take over American roads. Initially, human drivers will be mandatory, but as the technology continues to improve, it will be safer to opt for driverless vehicles.

To increase safety, cars will need efficient sensors, and road surfaces will have to exchange vital data with vehicles. Onboard computers will receive and share data about road conditions and traffic more than 1,000 times per second. As the AI controlling autonomous vehicles becomes more advanced, cars will function as part of a complex system that includes sensor-packed roads and highways.[688] Eventually, traffic accidents will become a rarity.

With safer traffic, roads will be able to accommodate faster vehicles. Travel speeds will increase, and commute times will be reduced. This will, in turn, transform metropolitan areas, enabling more people to move further away from urban centers.

Intelligent highways will accommodate many more vehicles, potentially 100 times more than they do today.[689] Intelligent cars will detect and report road issues in real-time, and repairs will be faster and more efficient. Smart highway technology will also facilitate driving in extreme weather conditions.

---

688 Toh, C., Sanguesa, J., Cano, J., & Martinez, F. (2020). Advances in Smart Roads for Future Smart Cities. *Proceedings Of The Royal Society A: Mathematical, Physical And Engineering Sciences*, *476*(2233), 20190439. doi: 10.1098/rspa.2019.0439

689 Electric and Autonomous Vehicles: The Future Is Now. Retrieved 19 July 2021, from https://www.bain.com/insights/electric-and-autonomous-vehicles-the-future-is-now/

Big Cities Will Get Even Bigger

According to UN estimates, by 2050, there will be 9.74 billion people living on Earth.[690] Meanwhile, the U.S. population will be 398 million by mid-century. Nearly 70 percent of the global population will live in cities and other urban centers.

This population growth will increase demand for water, food, energy, transport, housing, healthcare services, recreation, and education. If we were to develop traditional infrastructure to satisfy this massive demand, the environment would suffer. The only way to accommodate the inevitable population growth is to grow sustainably. Thus, in 2050, sprawling cities will drive sustainability and technological innovation.

Megacities will dominate the landscape in 2050. In 1990, there were only ten cities in the world with a population of over 10 million. Today, there are more than 30. By 2050, there will be about 50 megacities,[691] the majority of which will be in Asia, South America, and Africa. Twenty percent of the people living in urban centers in 2050 are expected to live in one of these megacities.

We'll Travel by Hyperloop

If you have never heard of Elon Musk's brainchild, it is high time you did. Hyperloops are passenger pods that will propel humans through vacuum tunnels at 750 miles per hour.[692] Because the air has been removed from the tunnels, there is little friction, and the pods can travel faster.

---

690 World Population Prospects - Population Division. (2019). Retrieved 19 July 2021, from https://population.un.org/wpp/Download/Standard/Population/

691 Pope, K., & Hoornweg, D. (2014). Socioeconomic Pathways and Regional Distribution of The World's 101 Largest Cities. Retrieved 19 July 2021, from https://shared.ontariotechu.ca/shared/faculty-sites/sustainability-today/publications/population-predictions-of-the-101-largest-cities-in-the-21st-century.pdf

692 PandoMonthly Presents: A Fireside Chat with Elon Musk. (2012). Retrieved 19 July 2021, from https://pando.com/2012/07/12/pandomonthly-presents-a-fireside-chat-with-elon-musk/

Designed to float using magnetic levitation, hyperloop pods hold enormous promise for intercity traffic. Hyperloop infrastructure could be cheaper to build than railroads. Providing a faster way to move between urban centers, it would reduce pollution from fossil-fuel-powered cars.

While we wait for flying cars to become available, Hyperloop will be an interesting option.

Virgin Group's Hyperloop is already in development in the Nevada desert. According to Virgin Hyperloop's founder, traveling in the passenger pods will feel "like an aircraft at take-off and once you're at speed."[693] Test runs have successfully propelled pods along a 1,640-feet tunnel.[694]

Virgin's pods can accommodate 28 passengers and can also be used for freight. The company estimates that the technology will be operational by 2027.[695]

'Vacuum trains' are an old idea. France tried to develop the technology in the 1960s, but the project died due to lack of funding.[696] In 2013, Elon Musk revived the concept at SpaceX, where one of the heads of the Virgin Hyperloop project used to work.

The infrastructure will be first implemented in places like India and Saudi Arabia, where public transport is either lacking or overloaded.

Analysts estimate that Hyperloop technology could eventually shoot passengers to their destination at up to 4,000 miles per hour.[697] Some

693 Virgin Hyperloop Shows Off The Future: Mass Transport in Floating Magnetic Pods. (2021). Retrieved 19 July 2021, from https://www.reuters.com/lifestyle/science/virgin-hyperloop-shows-off-future-mass-transport-floating-magnetic-pods-2021-05-06/

694 Humans Have Taken Their First Trip Inside a Hyperloop. (2021). Retrieved 19 July 2021, from https://www.popularmechanics.com/technology/infrastructure/a34630407/virgin-hyperloop-first-manned-trip/

695 Virgin Hyperloop Shows Off The Future: Mass Transport in Floating Magnetic Pods. (2021). Retrieved 19 July 2021, from https://www.weforum.org/agenda/2021/05/virgin-hyperloop-future-mass-transport/

696 Timeline: Tracing The Evolution of Hyperloop Rail Technology. (2020). Retrieved 19 July 2021, from https://www.railway-technology.com/features/timeline-tracing-evolution-hyperloop-rail-technology/

697 Christ, G. (2013). Hurtling Toward Hope with The Hyperloop. Retrieved 19 July 2021, from https://www.industryweek.com/innovation/product-development/article/21961681/hurtling-toward-hope-with-the-hyperloop

developers have referred to vacuum tube transportation as "space travel on Earth."[698]

Tube travel requires little power; it is extremely safe and does not pollute the environment. The caveat is that it requires a massive network of tunnels, just like trains require rail networks. Building interlinked Hyperloop tunnels worldwide will be a massive undertaking that will create employment for millions of people, and America will not be the exception.

In July 2020, the U.S. Department of Transportation published a guidance document that proposed a regulatory framework for the Hyperloop system. "These formerly abstract ideas, evocative of science fiction, have now matured into physical prototypes and project proposals," USDOT Secretary Elaine Chao said at the time. "Inventors, investors, and stakeholders are ready to build out these technologies."[699]

Our country was the first to establish regulations for this technology, and companies like LA-based HyperloopTT already have plans for several Hyperloop routes. "Between Boston and New York, or L.A. and San Francisco, or Portland and Seattle, it's not difficult to come up with potential projects based on these high-demand corridors," one of the company's engineers said in an interview.[700]

Based on the private sector's plans and various reports, by 2050, it is likely that Hyperloop corridors will also link:

- Chicago and Cleveland — Known as the "Great Lakes Corridor," this Hyperloop system would connect many large cities in the Great

698 Frey, T. (2017). *EPIPHANY Z - 8 Radical Visions for Transforming Your Future.* New York: Morgan James Publishing.
699 Carpenter, S. (2020). Remember Hyperloop? It's Getting Closer to Reality. Retrieved 19 July 2021, from https://spectrumlocalnews.com/tx/austin/news/2020/08/03/remember-hyperloop--its-getting-closer-to-reality
700 Carpenter, S. (2020). Remember Hyperloop? It's Getting Closer to Reality. Retrieved 19 July 2021, from https://spectrumlocalnews.com/tx/austin/news/2020/08/03/remember-hyperloop--its-getting-closer-to-reality

Lakes region. HyperloopTT is developing a project that will cover this route, with an extension to Pittsburgh and a few stops along the way. The full trip will take a mere 45 minutes.[701]

- New York and Washington, D.C. — Connecting the center of government with the country's largest metropolis, this corridor would also link large urban centers like Philadelphia and Baltimore. It could be expanded to reach Boston, constituting a corridor for the Northeastern Megalopolis.[702]
- Delhi to Mumbai — This 870-mile corridor will link two of the largest cities in India, transporting cargo and passengers from Delhi to Mumbai in about four hours. The trip currently takes more than 15 hours by rail.[703]
- Moscow to St. Petersburg — This corridor will connect the main administrative centers in Russia, spanning 435 miles that will be covered in less than 60 minutes.[704]

We'll Access Untapped Freshwater Sources

As global temperatures rise, freshwater will become increasingly scarce. Today, freshwater makes up a mere 2 percent of the water available on our planet, and we only have access to a fraction of it.[705]

Collecting rainwater is not exactly a new technology. Indigenous South

---

701 Cleveland Hyperloop Benefits Would Justify $29.8 Billion Price Tag: Study. (2019). Retrieved 19 July 2021, from https://www.cleveland.com/news/2019/12/benefits-would-justify-298-billion-cost-of-cleveland-hyperloop-line-according-to-study-to-be-unveiled-monday.html

702 Virgin's Hyperloop Could Mean a 30-Minute New York-to-D.C. Journey. (2020). Retrieved 19 July 2021, from https://www.afar.com/magazine/virgins-hyperloop-now-closer-to-becoming-a-reality

703 Saluja, N. (2020). Virgin Group Reaches Out to Nitin Gadkari for Hyperloop. Retrieved 19 July 2021, from https://economictimes.indiatimes.com/news/economy/infrastructure/richard-branson-reaches-out-to-nitin-gadkari-for-hyperloop/articleshow/74167862.cms

704 Adrien Henni, E. (2016). Russia Considers $12 Billion Hyperloop Project to Link Moscow and St. Petersburg. Retrieved 19 July 2021, from https://venturebeat.com/2016/05/30/russia-considers-12-billion-hyperloop-project-to-link-moscow-and-st-petersburg/

705 Competing for Clean Water Has Led to A Crisis. Retrieved 19 July 2021, from https://www.nationalgeographic.com/environment/article/freshwater-crisis

Americans were doing it in the 15th century, and so were Europeans 2,000 years ago.[706] Naturally, modern technology is much more advanced than the Incas' ancient channel systems. By 2050, there could be homes that generate their own drinking water and crops capable of self-irrigation.

At any given moment, our planet's atmosphere is a reservoir of about 37,500 trillion gallons[707] of freshwater. Innovators have developed clean-powered systems that can harvest that water and distribute it efficiently. By 2050, contamination from aging pipes will be a thing of the past, and communities that suffer from lack of access to drinking water in developing countries will likely see their prayers answered.

We'll Harvest Energy from Space

The Earth's power consumption has grown steadily over the last 50 years. Earth-based energy sources will soon be insufficient to power the ultra-connected cities of 2050, and several nations are already exploring other options.

Following the Fukushima disaster, Japan decided to look beyond nuclear energy to power the next technological revolution. The Japan Aerospace Exploration Agency (JAXA) recently announced plans to build a 1GW solar power plant in space. Construction will take place over the next 25 years.[708]

In 2020, the director of JAXA predicted that by 2050, "space near the Earth will be a part of global society as a place of human activity, and human

706 The History of Rainwater Harvesting. Retrieved 19 July 2021, from https://4perfectwater.com/blog/history-of-rainwater-harvesting

707 Abrar, P. (2019). Addressing Scarcity: Meghdoot Makes Potable Water from Atmospheric Moisture. Retrieved 19 July 2021, from https://www.business-standard.com/article/technology/addressing-scarcity-meghdoot-makes-potable-water-from-atmospheric-moisture-119040301317_1.html

708 Vedda, J., & Jones, K. (2021). Space-based Solar Power, A Near-term Investment Decision. Retrieved 19 July 2021, from https://aerospace.org/sites/default/files/2020-10/Vedda-Jones_SolarPower_20201006_0.pdf

beings will regularly stay on the Moon and Mars, and people will routinely travel to space as tourists."[709]

The concept of space-based solar has been around for more than 50 years, but the sheer scale of implementation has hitherto given it a utopian aura.[710] In 2021, the technology to harvest solar power from space is readily available. If Japan's project succeeds, undoubtedly, many will follow.

In April 2021, the Air Force Research Laboratory (AFRL) announced the U.S. is already developing its own project, known as Space Solar Power Incremental Demonstrations and Research (SSPID).[711] The AFRL plans to develop the technology to harvest solar power in space as soon as possible. By 2050, this project should be well underway.

Precision Farming Will Boost Food Production

Modern technologies are revolutionizing farming. Sensors can provide data about the temperature and acidity of soils, allowing farmers to plan their activities more efficiently. By 2050, optimization will also come from increasingly accurate weather forecasts. The Internet of Things will allow agricultural producers to monitor their machinery, livestock, and crops remotely. Drones will provide real-time data to inform a wide range of decisions.

Farming equipment giant John Deere is developing self-driving tractors, and the ones it commercializes today are already connected to the Internet,

---

709 JAXA Space Exploration Innovation Hub Center. (2021). Retrieved 19 July 2021, from https://www.ihub-tansa.jaxa.jp/english/

710 Moran, S. (2014). We Have Lift-Off: A History of Space-Based Solar Power | Environmental Leadership, Action and Ethics. Retrieved 19 July 2021, from https://edblogs.columbia.edu/scppx3335-001-2014-1/2014/03/12/we-have-lift-off-a-history-of-space-based-solar-power/

711 Space Power Beaming — Air Force Research Laboratory. Retrieved 19 July 2021, from https://afresearchlab.com/technology/successstories/space-power-beaming/

providing multiple metrics about crop yields.[712] By analyzing data gathered by sensors and satellite imagery, it will be easier to boost outputs and minimize costs.

Greenhouses will greatly benefit from smart technology and the IoT, which will enable them to generate a self-regulating microclimate that can better protect crops and increase production.[713]

By 2023, Insider Intelligence predicts, there will be 12 million agricultural sensors installed worldwide. By 2050, a standard farm could yield 500,000 data points every single day, and their statistical analysis could work wonders for productivity and profits.[714]

In February 2020, the USDA's Agriculture Innovation Agenda (AIA) set the goal of "increasing U.S. agricultural production by 40 percent, while cutting the environmental footprint of U.S. agriculture in half by 2050."[715]

To increase production while protecting the environment, AIA relies on a number of technologies and methodologies,[716] including:

- Genomics — The agriculture of the future will increasingly rely on genome design and precision breeding to "improve traits of agriculturally important organisms."
- Automation and IoT — Installing accurate sensors to collect data in real-time, enabling farmers to mitigate risks and maximize efficiency and productivity.
- Prescriptive Intervention — "Applying and integrating data sciences,

712 The Future of Farming Technology | John Deere. Retrieved 19 July 2021, from https://www.deere.co.uk/en/agriculture/future-of-farming/

713 Smart Greenhouse. (2020). Retrieved 19 July 2021, from https://www.designingbuildings.co.uk/wiki/Smart_greenhouse

714 Smart Farming in 2020: How IoT sensors Are Creating A More Efficient Precision Agriculture Industry. (2021). Retrieved 19 July 2021, from https://www.businessinsider.com/smart-farming-iot-agriculture

715 Initiatives and Highlighted Programs. Retrieved 19 July 2021, from https://www.usda.gov/our-agency/initiatives

716 Initiatives and Highlighted Programs. Retrieved 19 July 2021, from https://www.usda.gov/our-agency/initiatives

software tools, and systems models to enable advanced analytics for managing the food and agricultural system."

- Sustainable Farm Management — "Leveraging a systems approach to understand the nature of interactions among different elements of the food and agricultural system to increase overall efficiency, resilience, and sustainability of farm enterprises."

We Will Live in Energy-Efficient Buildings

Buildings are responsible for 33 percent of global carbon emissions and 40 percent of humanity's energy consumption.[717] If we want to address climate change, we need to start by making buildings sustainable and energy efficient.

In 2050, smart buildings will automatically adjust heating and lighting based on occupancy, external conditions, and other data. They will have integrated energy generation systems, like solar panels, and will absorb carbon emissions.

A good example of this type of building is The Edge building in Amsterdam, which features solar panels and thermal energy storage.[718] The Edge is a model green structure, capable of generating all the energy it needs for cooling and heating.

Some of the Edge building's environmental features[719] include:

- Orientation based on the path of the sun.
- Façades designed to suit orientation and purpose, including louvers

717 Buildings — Topics - IEA. Retrieved 19 July 2021, from https://www.iea.org/topics/buildings

718 The Edge, Amsterdam | BREEAM. Retrieved 19 July 2021, from https://www.breeam.com/case-studies/offices/the-edge-amsterdam/

719 Tay, M. (2016). Why Amsterdam's The Edge Is A Model for Green Offices Worldwide. Retrieved 19 July 2021, from https://www.eco-business.com/news/why-amsterdams-the-edge-is-a-model-for-green-offices-worldwide/

adapted to the sun's angles, solar panels capable of powering everything from laptops to electric cars, and a transparent Atrium façade to maximize natural light.

- Smart lighting — LED system featuring 30,000 sensors to adjust energy use based on various measurements.
- Solar panels on façades, roof, and on the nearby University of Amsterdam's roof, totaling 65,000 square feet.
- Energy and rainwater reuse — Rainwater collected on the roof is used to irrigate green spaces and flush toilets. Excess ventilation from offices is used for air-conditioning the atrium.
- Storage of thermal energy from aquifer wells.
- Personalized workspaces allow individuals to set light and temperature levels using a smartphone app.
- A green space separates the structure from the adjacent motorway, functioning as a natural habitat for insects and animals.

By 2050, there will be many buildings like this across America. Aside from protecting the environment, green construction and upgrades will create hundreds of thousands of jobs over the next decades.

Energy-efficient buildings will be beneficial for the environment and human health while also stimulating the economy and benefitting society by creating jobs. Despite the need for substantial investments, both the private and the public sectors will reap the rewards in the long term.

New York's 2019 Climate Mobilization Act has already laid out the plan for transforming the city's buildings.[720] The project has a $4 billion price tag and is expected to be completed between 2030 and 2050. By 2030, it will

720 Climate Mobilization Act. Retrieved 19 July 2021, from https://council.nyc.gov/data/green/

reduce greenhouse gas emissions amounting to 5.3 million metric tons.[721]

The legislation mandates owners of large buildings to cut their carbon emissions by 80 percent by 2050. Policymakers expect it will drive the development of services and products that will enable property owners to comply with these strict rules. According to Urban Green Council's CEO, John Mandyck, "This law could possibly be the largest disruption in our lifetime for the real estate industry in New York City."[722] A number of federal proposals could help landlords pay for the upgrades through weatherization assistance and electrification rebates.

Our Homes Will Be Smart, and Robots Will Do The Housework

In 2050, we will be able to control every aspect of our homes through digital technology. Millions of sensors and geotags will realize the concept of the Internet of Things, making infrastructure more responsive than ever. Household robots will handle cleaning, food preparation, and maintenance, while drones deliver everything imaginable to our doorsteps. AI will control a wide range of smart home functions, enabling us to reduce our energy consumption.

We'll Take Flying Taxis to The Airport

We need not wait thirty years to test out flying taxis. Companies like Uber Air, Volocopter, and Airbus have projects in very advanced stages of development.

721 Climate Mobilization Act: How NYC Buildings Can Avoid Fines, Comply. Retrieved 19 July 2021, from https://greatforest.com/sustainability101/climate-mobilization-act-how-nyc-buildings-can-avoid-fines-comply-with-new-standards/

722 Capps, K. (2019). Can New York Make Buildings Super-Efficient, Fast?. Retrieved 19 July 2021, from https://www.bloomberg.com/news/articles/2019-05-02/can-new-york-make-buildings-super-efficient-fast

Many have operated successful test flights. Airbus, in particular, is currently working with the city of Paris to deploy the first flying taxis there on the occasion of the 2024 Olympics.[723]

By 2050, this new air traffic will make urban airspace much busier than it is today. Electric Vertical Takeoff and Landing vehicles will start offering trips between JFK Airport and Manhattan for about $50 per passenger.[724] Unlike other aircraft, these vehicles can land almost anywhere, but they will require significant developments in terms of EV charging infrastructure and landing pads.

Suborbital Spacecraft Will Take Us Anywhere on Earth in 30 Minutes

By 2050, several companies will be offering suborbital spaceflight services that will eventually make airplanes obsolete. SpaceX plans to offer point-to-point suborbital flights on its Starship craft, with landing and takeoff at offshore platforms. On its webpage, the company states, "With Starship and Super Heavy, most international long-distance trips would be completed in 30 minutes or less. In addition to vastly increased speed, one great benefit to traveling in space outside of Earth's atmosphere is the lack of friction as well as turbulence and weather. Imagine most journeys taking less than 30 minutes with access to anywhere in the world in an hour or less."[725]

SpaceX's competitor Blue Origin is also considering expanding into the

723 Dautreppe, C. (2019). Paris Aims to Beat Olympic Traffic with Flying Taxis. Retrieved 19 July 2021, from https://phys.org/news/2019-06-paris-aims-olympic-traffic-taxis.html

724 Garsten, E. (2021). Archer Aviation Unveils Electric Vertical Takeoff/Landing Air Taxi. Retrieved 19 July 2021, from https://www.forbes.com/sites/edgarsten/2021/06/10/archer-aviation-unveils-electric-vertical-takeofflanding-air-taxi/?sh=1546524e32f9

725 Earth Orbit Experience Our Home Planet from Over 300km Up. Retrieved 19 July 2021, from https://www.spacex.com/human-spaceflight/earth/index.html

sector. Meanwhile, Virgin Galactic's CEO, Richard Branson, says his company will offer suborbital space tourism aboard its SpaceShipTwo.[726] Passengers will get a glimpse of Earth from a 62-mile altitude, crossing the threshold into space, known as the 'Kármán Line.' In time, the SpaceShipTwo fleet will also offer flights between major cities.

Last April, China announced its own plans to enter the race. In a video[727] titled "One Hour Global Arrival in the Space Transportation System," the China Academy of Launch Vehicle Technology unveiled the Asian superpower's plans to offer suborbital point-to-point travel to reach any destination on Earth in an hour or less. Germany's DLR is also developing suborbital flight technology. The European superpower's Aerospace Center claims its SpaceLiner craft could transport 100 people from Europe to California in an hour.[728]

Arcology Will Substitute Architecture

One thing is certain about life in 2050, it will look very different from now. Disruption is on its way, not only due to technological progress, but due to climate change and rising temperatures. As the global environment threatens our survival through constant flooding, desertification, unbearably hot summers, drought, and rising sea levels, technology will move fast to address these problems with renewable energy, innovative water purification systems, green construction, smart cities, and space-based solar power.

---

726 Cameron, M. (2021). Richard Branson's Virgin Galactic Flight Opens Door to Space Tourism. Retrieved 19 July 2021, from https://www.wsj.com/articles/richard-bransons-virgin-galactic-set-for-travel-to-space-in-sunday-flight-11626002209

727 Williams, M. (2021). Chinese Company Claims to Be Working on A Starship-Like Rocket. Retrieved 19 July 2021, from https://www.universetoday.com/151039/chinese-company-claims-to-be-working-on-a-starship-like-rocket/

728 Owano, N. (2015). SpaceLiner: Europe-Australia, 90 Minutes, Europe-US, One Hour. Retrieved 19 July 2021, from https://techxplore.com/news/2015-08-spaceliner-europe-australia-minutes-europe-us-hour.html

Considering trends like urban growth, decentralization, and sinking coastlines, the world's top architects and engineers are already developing the infrastructure of the future. In the world ahead, many of the construction forms we have used so far will become obsolete, and if humanity is to survive, many traditional forms of architecture will perish.

In the 1960s, Italian architect Paolo Soleri came up with the concept of 'arcology.' The result of combining architecture with ecology, arcology is at the center of modern architectural design.[729] As desertification progresses and arable lands dwindle, the urban planners of the future will have to find creative ways to integrate agriculture and greenery into building design and city layouts. The green spaces that serve no purpose today, around shopping malls and residential areas, will have to be converted into integrated energy farms, freshwater harvesting units, and agricultural plots.

Arcologies are integrated into the landscape. They are efficient and sustainable, featuring vertical farms, insect farms, rainwater irrigation, carbon capture systems, and hydroponics. In the cities of the future, building façades will absorb harmful carbon dioxide and transform it into useful bioenergy. Each multiple-home building will possess the infrastructure to grow food and produce power.

Arcology Projects

Abu Dhabi's Masdar City is "a pioneer in sustainability and a hub for research and development, spearheading the innovations to realize greener, more sustainable urban living," according to its official website.[730] A hub

729 What Is Arcology? | Ideology of Paolo Soleri | Arcosanti. Retrieved 19 July 2021, from https://www.arcosanti.org/arcology/

730 Welcome to Masdar City. Retrieved 19 July 2021, from https://masdarcity.ae

for clean-tech companies, the city has reserved prime real estate to house the International Renewable Energy Agency's headquarters.

Masdar is powered by solar and wind power. Smart technology helps reduce energy consumption, rainwater is captured, and up to 80 percent of wastewater can be recycled and reused. The project, which was designed to house 50,000 residents,[731] has only completed one phase of construction. Today, Masdar City accommodates only a few thousand startup employees.

The original urban transit plan for Masdar called for a fleet of underground, driverless pods to keep its streets free of cars, while a light rail line connected it to the airport and other locations in Abu Dhabi.

In 2020, when the United Nations 10th World Urban Forum's attendees walked around Masdar City, they encountered a driverless, electric microbus smoothly gliding along the complex.[732] The pilot eco-urban center is far from being completed, but it offers a glimpse of what 2050's cities could be like. At least $20 billion have been allotted to the realization of this powerful concept.[733]

Once a beacon of hope for urban sustainability, the city was developed by the Masdar company, which is involved in many successful projects. The tech corporation just landed a massive deal to build and operate solar energy plants in Armenia, in a region that boasts high radiation and lacks arable land. The 200MW utility-scale solar project has the potential to boost the Caucasus nation's ailing economy.[734]

731 Jeppesen, H. (2010). Built on Sand: Masdar City to Become Eco-City of The Future. Retrieved 19 July 2021, from https://www.dw.com/en/built-on-sand-masdar-city-to-become-eco-city-of-the-future/a-5488979

732 Puttkamer, L. (2020). Looking Back at WUF10. Retrieved 19 July 2021, from https://medium.com/@lauravonputtkamer/looking-back-at-wuf10-culture-and-innovation-29ccfb77df38

733 Saadi, D. (2021). INTERVIEW: UAE's Masdar Seeks to Double Renewable Capacity in 2-3 Years. Retrieved 19 July 2021, from https://www.spglobal.com/platts/en/market-insights/latest-news/electric-power/042821-interview-uaes-masdar-seeks-to-double-renewable-capacity-in-2-3-years

734 Hall, M. (2021). Masdar Secures Deal to Develop 'Armenia's Biggest Utility Scale Solar Project'. Retrieved 19 July 2021, from https://www.pv-magazine.com/2021/07/06/masdar-secures-deal-to-develop-armenias-biggest-utility-scale-solar-project/

Today, there are still cars on the streets of Masdar City, and many of its clean technologies are not operational yet. Planners hope everything will be up and running, with full carbon neutrality, by 2030.

Floating Cities

A creation of Kevin Schopfer, Boston Arcology is a sustainable, floating mega-structure designed to be built in Boston Harbor. It would be home to 15,000 residents and numerous commercial properties.[735] Powered by clean energy, it would expand the city with massive floating vertical structures, without adding to the environmental impact of urban growth.

Schopfer has also designed a resilient floating city for Haiti. The structure would be anchored to the ocean floor, which would make it less vulnerable to earthquakes. A utopia of tethered floating modules to be installed off the coast of Port-au-Prince, the city could house 30,000 residents and several industrial and agricultural projects.[736]

Vincent Callebaut's Lilypad City[737] concept is a sustainable floating city that is totally self-sufficient, generating enough clean energy to service 50,000 residents through a mix of tidal, solar, wind, and biomass power. The Lilypad's structure would be coated in titanium dioxide to absorb harmful atmospheric CO2.

735 Schopfer Pitches Floating City in Boston Harbor. Retrieved 19 July 2021, from https://northendwaterfront.com/2010/01/schopfer-pitches-floating-city-in-boston-harbor/

736 Harvest City is A Floating Agricultural and Industrial City for Haiti. Retrieved 19 July 2021, from https://www.evolo.us/harvest-city-is-a-floating-agricultural-and-industrial-city-for-haiti/

737 Floating cities, Oasis for The Future. Retrieved 19 July 2021, from https://www.meretdemeures.com/es/news/slides-floating-cities-oasis-for-the-future/

We'll Be Building a City on Mars

In March 2021, ABIBOO architecture studio and The Mars Society unveiled a plan to build a cluster of sustainable cities on Mars.[738]

Named Nüwa city, the capital city will be surrounded by four other urban centers. A vertical structure featuring homes, green areas, and offices, it will be built into the side of a Martian cliff, offering protection from dangerous radiation.

Plants will produce oxygen and solar panels will provide energy. Nüwa has been designed to overcome problems like low gravity and high atmospheric pressure. According to one of ABIBOO's designers, "water is one of the great advantages that Mars offers, it helps to be able to get the proper materials for the construction. Basically, with the water and the Co2, we can generate carbon and with the carbon, we can generate steel."[739] In fact, all the materials to build the cities will be locally sourced.

The urban planners believe they can start building the cities by 2054, and humans could be living there as early as 2100.[740] ABIBOO's plans for Mars have many implications for urban design on Earth. After all, if we can build a sustainable, self-sufficient city in such an inhospitable terrain as Mars, what can we not build on Earth, even taking into account the impact of climate change?

---

738 Nüwa, the First Sustainable City on Mars • ABIBOO Studio. Retrieved 19 July 2021, from https://abiboo.com/projects/nuwa/

739 Plans for the first sustainable city on Mars unveiled. Retrieved 19 July 2021, from https://www.euronews.com/green/2021/03/19/plans-for-the-first-sustainable-city-on-mars-unveiled

740 Khan, S. (2021). ABIBOO Unveiled Plans for Nuwa, The First City in Mars; Would Elon Musk's Vision Come True?. Retrieved 19 July 2021, from https://www.techtimes.com/articles/258250/20210321/nuwa-the-first-city-in-mars-will-be-ready-in-2100-developer-abiboo-reveals-plans-and-function.htm

The Future

As we approach mid-century, new technologies will be developed and implemented to make America and the world more sustainable. The challenges of climate change will force innovators and governments to find solutions. Between 2021 and 2050, we will witness a transformation in infrastructure like humanity has never seen before. We are fortunate to live in this age and to be able to experience it. If our country focuses on the opportunities ahead and creates a favorable environment where innovators can thrive, the future will be as bright as the stellar beams that will power the transformations to come.

CHAPTER 27:

A Modern New Deal

"There can be little doubt that in many ways the story of bridge building is the story of civilization. By it we can readily measure an important part of a people's progress."
—Franklin D Roosevelt

The new administration's plans to upgrade America's infrastructure has put the concept of infrastructure at the center of the political debate. Infrastructure is more than bridges and roads; it's about making societies function efficiently. The White House and Democratic leaders agree that the nation needs a radical overhaul when it comes to anything from water pipes, power grids, and Internet access to healthcare and educational facilities, autonomous vehicle lanes, and cybersecurity technology.

Meanwhile, the opposition has referred to the administration's 'New Deal' as a Trojan horse designed to introduce tax increases and a progressive agenda. For Republican House Minority Leader Kevin McCarthy, aside from 6 percent of spending reserved for bridge and road upgrades, the infrastructure plan is "a 'kitchen sink' of wasteful progressive demands, payoffs for labor unions and radical environmentalists, and job-killing regulations."[741]

It will be very difficult to truly upgrade American infrastructure without bipartisan backing. This is not the first time our country has been locked in a debate about the importance of infrastructure. In the mid 19th century,

---

741 Bidenomics. (2021). Retrieved 5 July 2021, from https://www.republicanleader.gov/bidenomics/

policymakers, and local residents in various regions engaged in heated arguments over plans to build roads and canals.[742] Then and now, the debate had many implications for Americans living in different jurisdictions; it was a debate about the future, and the kind of country different people wanted to live in.

Republicans and Democrats agree about one thing: we need infrastructure upgrades. Their visions differ in terms of which investments will pay off. They particularly disagree about whether stricter environmental regulations and clean energy will benefit our economy. The White House said it wants to invest not only in material things but also in American society, families, workers, scientists, and innovators.[743] According to a 2021 poll by PBS and NPR, 56 percent of Americans support the administration's infrastructure plan.[744]

Commenting on the White House's plan, Microsoft president Brad Smith said technology creates challenges, and only a bold infrastructure plan can "create a springboard for new jobs, sustained competitiveness and broader prosperity. . . to make the most of technology's future."[745]

On the other hand, Republican Senators like Bill Hagerty believe benefits will only come from investing in highways, bridges, waterways, and the like.[746] To form an opinion, it is important to understand what the administration's original Infrastructure Plan entails.

742 White, A. (2012). Infrastructure Policy: Lessons from American History. Retrieved 5 July 2021, from https://www.thenewatlantis.com/publications/infrastructure-policy-lessons-from-american-history

743 Fact Sheet: The American Families Plan | The White House. Retrieved 5 July 2021, from https://www.whitehouse.gov/briefing-room/statements-releases/2021/04/28/fact-sheet-the-american-families-plan/

744 Milligan, S. (2021). A Majority of Americans Support Biden's Infrastructure Plan. Retrieved 5 July 2021, from https://www.usnews.com/news/politics/articles/2021-04-15/a-majority-of-americans-support-bidens-infrastructure-plan

745 Lohrmann, D. (2021). The Broadening of American Infrastructure — Or Not. Retrieved 5 July 2021, from https://www.govtech.com/blogs/lohrmann-on-cybersecurity/the-broadening-of-american-infrastructure-or-not

746 Yu, Y. (2021). Bill Hagerty Criticizes Biden Administration's $2.3T Infrastructure Package During Nashville Trip. Retrieved 5 July 2021, from https://www.tennessean.com/story/news/politics/2021/05/03/bill-hagerty-criticizes-2-3-trillion-infrastructure-package-american-jobs-plan/4920889001/

The American Jobs Plan

One of the most significant components of the President's original Infrastructure Plan is the American Jobs Plan (AJP).[747] Bearing some similarities to Roosevelt's Keynesian inspiration, the AJP proposes infrastructure projects as a means to facilitate job creation.

The AJP's Main Targets

- Upgrade highways, ports, bridges, airports, and transit systems.
- Improve drinking water quality, renew the electric power grid, ensure access to high-speed broadband for all Americans.
- Build two million modern homes and commercial buildings, upgrade educational and child-care facilities, modernize hospitals and federal buildings.
- Improve care economy infrastructure by upgrading wages for caregivers.
- Revitalize the manufacturing industry, secure supply chains in the homeland, increase R&D investments, enhance training programs for "the jobs of the future."
- Create quality employment in safe workplaces, facilitate collective bargaining with employers.

The AJP is the heart of the administration's vision for the next decade of American society. After announcing its plan to invest $2.3 billion in infrastructure, the White House unveiled an additional economic plan

747 FACT SHEET: The American Jobs Plan | The White House. (2021). Retrieved 5 July 2021, from https://www.whitehouse.gov/briefing-room/statements-releases/2021/03/31/fact-sheet-the-american-jobs-plan/

involving $1.8 trillion in new spending and tax cuts over a decade.[748]

A $1.8 Trillion Plan to Benefit American Families

American families stand to benefit from the proposed plan, as it includes tax cuts for families, national paid family and medical leave programs, subsidies to assist with the cost of childcare, and various tax credit expansions.[749]

Education is also part of the ambitious new proposal, which would create universal prekindergarten for 3- and 4-year-olds; free community college for two years; more substantial Pell Grant awards; and an influx of funds into higher education institutions serving minority groups.

The plan would be funded by an increase in taxes for corporations over 15 years.[750] Vulnerable Americans on unemployment would also benefit if the proposal comes to fruition, as it would automatically link the amount and length of benefits to the recipient's economic conditions.

The Importance of Infrastructure Upgrades

One cannot underestimate the importance of safe and reliable infrastructure for the well-being of Americans. "Infrastructure is the physical framework upon which the U.S. economy operates, and our standard of living depends,"[751] the American Society of Civil Engineers said in a 2021 report. "This framework enables us to move goods, power businesses of all sizes,

748 Tankersley, J., & Goldstein, D. (2021). Biden Details $1.8 Trillion Plan for Workers, Students and Families. Retrieved 5 July 2021, from https://www.nytimes.com/2021/04/28/us/politics/biden-american-families-plan.html

749 Fact Sheet: The American Families Plan | The White House. Retrieved 5 July 2021, from https://www.whitehouse.gov/briefing-room/statements-releases/2021/04/28/fact-sheet-the-american-families-plan/

750 Luhby, T., Vazquez, M., & Lobosco, K. (2021). Here's What's In Biden's $1.8 Trillion American Families Plan. Retrieved 5 July 2021, from https://edition.cnn.com/2021/04/28/politics/american-families-plan/index.html

751 Norwood, C. (2021). How Infrastructure Has Historically Promoted Inequality. Retrieved 5 July 2021, from https://www.pbs.org/newshour/politics/how-infrastructure-has-historically-promoted-inequality

connect people to jobs and services, heat and cool office buildings, and enjoy a glass of clean water."

The engineers' collective calculated that if our country does not increase investment in infrastructure improvements, American households stand to lose approximately $3,330[752] every year over the next two decades.

The ASCE's Failure to Act report stated that investing $16.9 billion per year in electricity infrastructure over the next 18 years can "protect 540,000 jobs and $5,800 per household in personal income," and investing in America's water and wastewater infrastructure can prevent "$250 billion in increased costs to businesses by 2039."[753]

The Costs of Poor Infrastructure

Looking at infrastructure in the long term reveals that Americans and the government spend more money when it is failing and not functioning appropriately. The direct and indirect costs of crumbling infrastructure include:

- Poorly maintained roads damage vehicles and increased the cost of car repair and maintenance.
- Hazardous waste in the proximity of communities can cause disease and increase healthcare costs.
- Insufficient transportation lines and lacking infrastructure upgrades can lower property value.
- Lack of rail connections and bridges can prevent individuals from

752 Failing Infrastructure Costing Families $3,300 A Year, New ASCE Report Says. (2021). Retrieved 5 July 2021, from https://source.asce.org/failing-infrastructure-costing-families-3300-a-year-new-asce-report-says/

753 Failure to Act | ASCE. (2021). Retrieved 5 July 2021, from https://www.asce.org/failuretoact/

commuting to higher-paying jobs.

- Transportation infrastructure failures could cost each American household $625 per year. “Losses to households and industries will amount to $677 billion over the 2020—2029 period and $1.3 trillion during the 2030—2039 decade.”[754]

Infrastructure Across the Union

In April 2021, the White House released infrastructure fact sheets for every U.S. state, listing all the bridges and roads in poor condition and needed water and energy infrastructure upgrades.

The fact sheets gave 25 states a grade below C-minus.[755] The states with the highest rating were Georgia and Utah, which received a C+. Next were Florida, Kansas, North Dakota, Washington, Iowa, Maryland, Montana, Nevada, Minnesota, Texas, Vermont, and Wisconsin with a C grade.[756] The rest of the U.S. states, Puerto Rico, and D.C. received grades below C, except for Delaware, Massachusetts, New Mexico, Virginia, Arkansas, Wyoming, South Carolina, and six other states that weren't graded. The administration's report was based on data from the ASCE's infrastructure report card 2021, which gave the nation an overall C-minus score.[757]

The White House highlighted the issues plaguing state infrastructures to emphasize the need for action and promote its large-scale infrastructure overhaul plan. The administration's definition of infrastructure has, as stated

754 Failure to Act Economic Reports. (2021). Retrieved 5 July 2021, from https://infrastructurereportcard.org/resources/failure-to-act-economic-reports/

755 White House Releases State-by-State Fact Sheets to Highlight Nationwide Need for the American Jobs Plan. (2021). Retrieved 5 July 2021, from https://www.whitehouse.gov/briefing-room/statements-releases/2021/04/12/white-house-releases-state-by-state-fact-sheets-to-highlight-nationwide-need-for-the-american-jobs-plan/

756 White House Hits States With Cs And Ds In Its 'Infrastructure Report Cards'. (2021). Retrieved 5 July 2021, from https://www.businessinsider.com/white-house-infrastructure-report-cards-state-grades-2021-4

757 Infrastructure Report Card 2021. (2021). Retrieved 5 July 2021, from https://infrastructurereportcard.org/

above, caused controversy. For some politicians who could block some of the White House's plans, investing in bridges is an investment in infrastructure, but spending taxpayer dollars on broadening access to childcare and community colleges does not belong in the same category.

To understand the administration's vision of infrastructure, it is helpful to look at some of the state fact sheets in detail. Detailed information about issues observed in a highly populated state like California, with a C-minus grade, can offer an interesting perspective on how the White House perceives infrastructure problems and how it plans to remedy them.

California Fact Sheet Highlights

Problems: 1,536 bridges and more than 14,000 miles of highway are in poor condition. Commute times have gone up 14.6 percent since 2011. Poorly maintained roads cost drivers $799 per year.
Proposed Solution: The AJP plans to devote $115 billion to road and bridge repairs across the U.S.[758]

Problems: Californians who use public transportation to reach their workplace spend 66.6 percent more of their time commuting. Sixteen percent of transit vehicles, including trains, are still operating past their useful life.
Proposed Solution: The AJP includes an $85 billion investment in public transit upgrades.

Problem: Over the last decade, California spent over $50 billion to repair

758 The Need for Action in California. (2021). Retrieved 5 July 2021, from https://www.whitehouse.gov/wp-content/uploads/2021/04/AJP-State-Fact-Sheet-CA.pdf

damages from extreme weather events.

Proposed Solution: The presidential project proposes spending $50 billion to improve American infrastructure's resiliency and offer support for communities affected by natural disasters.

Problem: Water infrastructure is failing. Over the next two decades, maintaining it and improving it will demand a $51 billion funding boost.

Proposed Solution: The AJP proposes a $111 billion investment to deliver safe drinking water to all communities throughout the state.

Problem: Inadequate access to affordable housing has caused over three million Californians to spend approximately a third of their income on rent.

Proposed Solution: The infrastructure overhaul plan proposes investing $200 billion to facilitate access to affordable homes and address the crisis.

Problem: 5.5 percent of the state's population lives in areas with insufficient broadband infrastructure. Over half of Californians live in areas where there is only one high-speed Internet provider. For many households, the price of an Internet subscription is inaccessible; only 10 percent of households in the state have this 'luxury.'

Proposed Solution: The AJP proposes investing $100 billion to make high-speed, reliable Internet available to every U.S. household.

Problem: 60 percent of Californians have inadequate access to childcare. School maintenance and upgrades require an additional $3.22 billion investment.

Proposed Solution: The AJP includes a large-scale plan to modernize schools and build new ones all over California and the rest of the country.

Problem: Low-income households in California spend approximately 5 percent of their income on home energy costs "forcing tough choices between paying energy bills and buying food, medicine or other essentials."
Proposed Solution: The AJP proposes upgrading the energy efficiency of low-income homes "through a historic investment in the Weatherization Assistance Program, a new Clean Energy and Sustainability Accelerator to finance building improvements, and expanded tax credits to support home energy upgrades."

Problem: California's 1.68 million veterans receive healthcare services at insufficient and poorly maintained VA facilities.
Proposed Solution: The White House proposes spending $18 billion on improving the infrastructure of VA healthcare facilities nationwide.

Overview of Other States

Fact sheets for the rest of U.S. states are similar in scope. In Michigan, for example, the number of bridges in need of urgent upgrades is 1,219, the White House claims, while 7,300 miles of highway are in poor condition. Michigan's water infrastructure requires upgrades that will cost $13 billion, and half a million residents are rent burdened.[759]

In Florida, an average low-income family spends about 9 percent of their income on energy bills, and nearly 1.5 million home renters spend more than 30 percent of their income on rent.[760]

In Oklahoma, 16 percent of households don't have an Internet

759 The Need for Action in Michigan. (2021). Retrieved 5 July 2021, from https://www.whitehouse.gov/wp-content/uploads/2021/04/AJP-State-Fact-Sheet-MI.pdf

760 The Need for Action in Florida. (2021). Retrieved 5 July 2021, from https://www.whitehouse.gov/wp-content/uploads/2021/04/AJP-State-Fact-Sheet-FL.pdf

subscription.[761] In Georgia, the average low-income family spends between 10 and 12 percent of their income on energy costs. Members of these families spend an extra 74 percent of their time commuting, relying on trains and public transit vehicles that are largely, poorly maintained or past their useful life.[762] In Tennessee, the percentage of transit vehicles circulating beyond their 'expiration date' is a staggering 21 percent.[763]

In Alabama, the lack of resilient infrastructure has resulted in $20 billion worth of damages from extreme weather events, and 60 percent of residents "live in a childcare desert."[764] In Kansas, drivers spend over $500 per year due to damage caused by poorly maintained roads.[765]

Even in states that got a passing grade, infrastructure is crumbling, the administration reports. In Washington, 416 bridges and nearly 5,000 miles of highway are in poor condition.[766] In Utah, commuters spend an additional 103.5 percent of their time getting to work on public transportation, and 17 percent of trains and buses are past their useful life.[767]

There isn't a single U.S. state where infrastructure is in excellent shape. When we look at the bridges, high-speed trains, and renewable energy farms the Chinese are building, we feel we are lagging behind. The picture presented by the state-by-state analyses is a grim one. From Alaska to New York, and from California to Illinois, malfunctioning public transit vehicles, outmoded

---

761 The Need for Action in Oklahoma. (2021). Retrieved 5 July 2021, from https://www.whitehouse.gov/wp-content/uploads/2021/04/AJP-State-Fact-Sheet-OK.pdf

762 The Need for Action in Georgia. (2021). Retrieved 5 July 2021, from https://www.whitehouse.gov/wp-content/uploads/2021/04/AJP-State-Fact-Sheet-GA.pdf

763 The Need for Action in Tennessee. (2021). Retrieved 5 July 2021, from https://www.whitehouse.gov/wp-content/uploads/2021/04/AJP-State-Fact-Sheet-TN.pdf

764 The Need for Action in Alabama. (2021). Retrieved 5 July 2021, from https://www.whitehouse.gov/wp-content/uploads/2021/04/AJP-State-Fact-Sheet-AL.pdf

765 The Need for Action in Kansas. (2021). Retrieved 5 July 2021, from https://www.whitehouse.gov/wp-content/uploads/2021/04/AJP-State-Fact-Sheet-KS.pdf

766 The Need for Action in Washington. (2021). Retrieved 5 July 2021, from https://www.whitehouse.gov/wp-content/uploads/2021/04/AJP-State-Fact-Sheet-WA.pdf

767 The Need for Action in Utah. (2021). Retrieved 5 July 2021, from https://www.whitehouse.gov/wp-content/uploads/2021/04/AJP-State-Fact-Sheet-UT.pdf

ports, and decrepit bridges punctuate the landscape. We still don't know just how many billions of dollars the federal government will actually pour into U.S. infrastructure, but help may be on the way.

The Bipartisan Infrastructure Framework

In late June, 2021, the White House agreed to support a bipartisan infrastructure plan, leaving many of the President's original economic proposals for a future bill. Though the administration had reached a compromise, it said this was only the beginning, and a larger infrastructure package would follow.

The White House's full plan comprised investments totaling over $2.3 trillion, while the bipartisan infrastructure plan proposed investing an additional $579 billion in infrastructure, totaling $1.2 trillion overall, and leaving aside many of the administration's climate-related programs.

"The $1.2 trillion Bipartisan Infrastructure Framework," the White House said in a press release, "is a critical step in implementing [the President's] Build Back Better vision. The Plan makes transformational and historic investments in clean transportation infrastructure, clean water infrastructure, universal broadband infrastructure, clean power infrastructure, remediation of legacy pollution, and resilience to the changing climate. Cumulatively across these areas, the Framework invests two-thirds of the resources that the President proposed in his American Jobs Plan."[768]

The new framework[769] included nearly $580 in investments to

768 President Biden Announces Support for The Bipartisan Infrastructure Framework | The White House. (2021). Retrieved 5 July 2021, from https://www.whitehouse.gov/briefing-room/statements-releases/2021/06/24/fact-sheet-president-biden-announces-support-for-the-bipartisan-infrastructure-framework/

769 Thrush, G. (2021). Here's What Made It into The Bipartisan Infrastructure Plan. Retrieved 5 July 2021, from https://www.nytimes.com/2021/06/24/us/politics/what-is-in-the-infrastructure-plan.html

upgrade and expand transportation, broadband Internet, and electric grid infrastructure. When the agreement was announced, the President said he believed "physical and human infrastructure are inextricably intertwined, both make us better off and stronger."

"Economists left, right and center, independent Wall Street forecasters," the President explained, "they all say that these kinds of public investments mean more jobs, more workers participating in the labor force, higher productivity, and higher growth for our economy over the long run."[770]

The agreement mainly pertained to the physical infrastructure portion of the 'New Deal.'

Bipartisan Framework Basics

The bipartisan framework would address many of America's most pressing infrastructure needs[771], including:

- Modernizing public transport, providing sustainable transit options for Americans, expanding rail networks, and reducing CO2 emissions. "The Plan is the largest federal investment in public transit in history and is the largest federal investment in passenger rail since the creation of Amtrak," the White House said.
- Repairing and rebuilding bridges and roads, making them safe for users and more resilient in the face of extreme weather events.

770 Remarks by President Biden on The Bipartisan Infrastructure Deal | The White House. (2021). Retrieved 5 July 2021, from https://www.whitehouse.gov/briefing-room/speeches-remarks/2021/06/24/remarks-by-president-biden-on-the-bipartisan-infrastructure-deal/

771 Fact Sheet: Bipartisan Infrastructure Framework Will Address Barriers Communities of Color Face to Economic Opportunity | The White House. (2021). Retrieved 5 July 2021, from https://www.whitehouse.gov/briefing-room/statements-releases/2021/06/29/fact-sheet-bipartisan-infrastructure-framework-will-address-barriers-communities-of-color-face-to-economic-opportunity/

- Expanding electric vehicle infrastructure by building a nationwide network that will comprise over half a million chargers.
- Transitioning school and transit buses to electric power and incentivizing zero-emission vehicle manufacturing.
- Eliminating lead pipes and delivering clean drinking water to millions of families and over 400,000 schools, where it is currently unavailable. This has been touted as "the largest investment in clean drinking water and wastewater infrastructure in American history."
- Providing high-speed Internet access to every American, indirectly slashing Internet costs.
- Upgrading the nation's power infrastructure and building thousands of miles of transmission lines for renewable energy.
- Investing in cleanup efforts to address legacy pollution.
- Taking preventive actions and preparing our infrastructure for the potential impacts of climate change and cyber attacks. This aspect of the framework, the White House wrote, will become "the largest investment in the resilience of physical and natural systems in American history."
- Financing all of these projects through a mix of "closing the tax gap, redirecting unspent emergency relief funds, targeted corporate user fees, and the macroeconomic impact of infrastructure investment."

The bipartisan $579 billion infrastructure deal[772] comprised:

- Roads, bridges, large physical infrastructure projects — $109 billion
- Rail transportation — $66 billion

772 Wasson, E., Litvan, L., & Epstein, J. (2021). Biden, Senators Get $579 Billion Bipartisan Infrastructure Deal. Retrieved 5 July 2021, from https://www.bloomberg.com/news/articles/2021-06-24/biden-s-push-for-infrastructure-deal-closer-to-senate-goal-line

- Public transit investments — $49 billion
- Airport construction and upgrades — $25 billion
- Infrastructure financing — $20 billion
- Port and waterway infrastructure — $16 billion
- Investments in safety — $11 billion
- Electric Vehicle infrastructure — $7.5 billion
- Public Transit and electric buses — $7.5 billion
- Reconnecting communities — $1 billion

Aside from the funds allocated to infrastructure projects in the bipartisan agreement, the White House said it would spend another $266 billion[773] on:

- Power infrastructure — $73 billion
- Broadband Infrastructure — $65 billion
- Water infrastructure — $55 billion
- Overall infrastructure resilience — $47 billion
- Environmental cleanup and remediation projects — $21 billion
- Western Water Storage — $5 billion

The Future

The bipartisan agreement was excellent news for our country's ailing infrastructure, but we are not quite there yet. The President's endorsement of the reduced bipartisan budget for infrastructure upgrades does not mean he will forget about the rest of his proposals for the country's economic future.

---

773 Wasson, E., Litvan, L., & Epstein, J. (2021). Biden, Senators Get $579 Billion Bipartisan Infrastructure Deal. Retrieved 5 July 2021, from https://www.bloomberg.com/news/articles/2021-06-24/biden-s-push-for-infrastructure-deal-closer-to-senate-goal-line

Democrats said the infrastructure framework would not move forward if the opposition did not support other measures in the original infrastructure proposal. "If this is the only thing that comes to me, I'm not signing it," the President said.[774]

The bipartisan framework includes about 65 percent of funding proposed in the original AJP.[775] If it receives enough support in the Senate, it will be the first time that our country devotes substantial funds to restoring its crumbling infrastructure in more than a decade.

Democrats hoped to approve the rest of the President's economic proposals for childcare, education, and climate change relief in a new bill, without support from Republicans, using a procedure known as reconciliation.[776]

The President's remarks about his potential unwillingness to sign the bipartisan bill immediately backfired. To appease opponents and save the deal, he had to clarify that he didn't mean he wouldn't compromise. Meanwhile, liberals warned that if the bill was not accompanied by a second piece of legislation that fulfilled Democrats' campaign promises, it might never even make it to the President's desk.[777]

It took weeks of negotiations between Democratic and Republican senators, and the administration, to finalize the bipartisan framework. And the aftermath has revealed just how fragile the agreement is.

---

774 Biden: Remark on Infrastructure Measure Not Intended to Be Veto Threat. (2021). Retrieved 5 July 2021, from https://www.nbcnews.com/politics/congress/biden-remark-infrastructure-measure-was-not-intended-be-veto-threat-n1272458

775 Wasson, E., Litvan, L., & Epstein, J. (2021). Biden, Senators Get $579 Billion Bipartisan Infrastructure Deal. Retrieved 5 July 2021, from https://www.bloomberg.com/news/articles/2021-06-24/biden-s-push-for-infrastructure-deal-closer-to-senate-goal-line

776 What Is 'Reconciliation,' and Why Is It Holding Up The Infrastructure Package? (2021). Retrieved 5 July 2021, from https://www.usatoday.com/story/news/politics/2021/06/28/what-reconciliation-why-holding-up-infrastructure-deal/7787722002/

777 Lopez, G. (2021). Biden's Infrastructure Deal Proves Bipartisanship Can't Deliver. Retrieved 5 July 2021, from https://www.vox.com/22553888/joe-biden-infrastructure-deal-bipartisanship-democrats-republicans

While environmentalists and Democrats protested in front of the White House chanting "No climate, no deal," some Republicans who disagree with the infrastructure plan as a whole may seize the opportunity to kill the bipartisan agreement.[778] And Republicans who favored the deal may feel betrayed, assuming the White House was not really interested in reaching a bipartisan agreement.

Over the weekend following the announcement of the bipartisan deal, the President called senators on both sides of the aisle who had been involved in the negotiations, assuring them that he had simply misspoken and the administration would officially clarify his comment.[779]

The President fulfilled his promise, stating in a public letter, "At a press conference after announcing the bipartisan agreement, I indicated that I would refuse to sign the infrastructure bill if it was sent to me without my Families Plan and other priorities, including clean energy. . . That statement understandably upset some Republicans. . . My comments also created the impression that I was issuing a veto threat on the very plan I had just agreed to, which was certainly not my intent."[780]

With a 50-50 divide in the Senate, Republican support will be needed to pass the bipartisan framework. Whether the human infrastructure portion of the White House's original infrastructure plan is implemented or not, the worst-case scenario apparently involves an influx of at least $1 trillion into American infrastructure. It is as yet uncertain whether the projected

778 No Climate, No Deal: Congressional Tracker and Action Hub. (2021). Retrieved 5 July 2021, from https://www.evergreenaction.com/blog/no-climate-no-deal

779 Thomas, K., & Duehren, A. (2021). Biden Walks Back Threat on Bipartisan Infrastructure Deal. Retrieved 5 July 2021, from https://www.wsj.com/articles/biden-says-he-wasnt-threatening-to-veto-bipartisan-infrastructure-plan-11624740487

780 Statement by President Joe Biden on the Bipartisan Infrastructure Framework. (2021). Retrieved 5 July 2021, from https://www.whitehouse.gov/briefing-room/statements-releases/2021/06/26/statement-by-president-joe-biden-on-the-bipartisan-infrastructure-framework/

infrastructure upgrades will make us more competitive against China, but if the funds are spent wisely, Americans will undoubtedly benefit.

CHAPTER 28:

Build for the Ages | Balancing Infrastructure & Conservation

"Progress is impossible without change, and those who cannot change their minds cannot change anything."
—George Bernard Shaw

One of the biggest challenges the U.S. faces today is balancing infrastructure and conservation goals. At a time when America's failing infrastructure is in dire need of upgrades, environmental concerns are equally pressing. The question is, can we build everything that needs to be built without further harming the environment?

America The Beautiful

The current administration has made it clear that its massive infrastructure plan will not get in the way of conservation. In the first draft of the White House's "America the Beautiful" initiative, the authorities have laid out a plan to conserve nearly a third of the country's land and water by 2030. The scale of the conservation plan seems as ambitious as the projected infrastructure overhaul. Dubbed the "30x30" goal, the initiative projects saving 30 percent of land and water over the next decade; the biggest challenge will be to achieve that simultaneously with a switch to renewable energy.

According to an official press release, the initiative proposes "a decade-long effort to support locally led and voluntary conservation and restoration efforts across public, private, and Tribal lands and waters in order to create jobs and strengthen the economy's foundation; tackle the climate and nature crises; and address inequitable access to the outdoors."[781]

America The Beautiful Priority Areas[782]

- Supporting Tribally led conservation and restoration priorities.
- Increasing access for outdoor recreation.
- Incentivizing and rewarding the voluntary conservation efforts of fishers, ranchers, farmers, and forest owners.
- Expanding collaborative conservation of fish and wildlife habitats and corridors.
- Creating more parks and safe outdoor opportunities in nature-deprived communities.
- Creating jobs by investing in restoration and resilience projects and initiatives, including the Civilian Climate Corps.

The report, which has input from the Commerce, Interior, and Agriculture Departments, emphasizes local initiatives and creates jobs around the target communities. "It is our job to listen, learn, and provide support along the way to help strengthen economies and pass on healthy lands, waters, and wildlife to the generations to come," the administration said in a press release.

Renewing America's energy infrastructure matrix along the way won't be

781 Biden-Harris Administration Outlines "America The Beautiful" Initiative. (2021). Retrieved 18 June 2021, from https://www.doi.gov/pressreleases/biden-harris-administration-outlines-america-beautiful-initiative

782 Biden-Harris Administration Outlines "America The Beautiful" Initiative. (2021). Retrieved 18 June 2021, from https://www.doi.gov/pressreleases/biden-harris-administration-outlines-america-beautiful-initiative

easy. As the opposition characterizes the White House's conservation plans as a "land grab" and pressure increases to move to clean energy, so do the challenges our country faces.

The president's carbon emission goals are extremely ambitious. He has laid out a plan to bring emissions down to 50 percent of 2005 levels by 2030. Researchers project this will require dedicating about 230,000 square miles to wind and solar energy production.[783] In other words, producing the amount of clean energy needed will require an area equivalent to New Mexico and Arizona combined. It's hard to imagine that the impact of these large-scale renewable energy projects will be anything short of disastrous for wildlife and water conservation.

Renewable Energy and Conservation

In 2019, a group of NC State researchers published a very interesting book[784] about the environmental impact of clean energy developments. One of the conclusions they reached is that the amount of land required by clean energy projects implies that whole wildlife habitats could be destroyed in the name of sustainability. We rely on wind and solar energy to help us reduce carbon dioxide emissions. But despite its many advantages, a switch to renewable energy will pose many challenges.

According to Chris Moorman, one of the book's authors, "while renewable energy is one of the most effective ways to [reduce emissions and leave fossil fuels behind], it's not always free of environmental impacts."

After reviewing the documented impact of renewable energy

783 Net-Zero America. Retrieved 18 June 2021, from https://netzeroamerica.princeton.edu/?explorer=year&state=national&table=2020&limit=200

784 Moorman, C., Grodsky, S., & Rupp, S. (2019). *Renewable energy and wildlife conservation*. John Hopkins University Press.

projects on wildlife and evaluating current policies, the scientists offered recommendations about possible mitigation strategies. And after reading the book, the one thing that is clear is that balancing renewable energy development with wildlife conservation won't be easy, neither for this president, nor for the ones who will come after him.

The researchers are, however, not entirely pessimistic. "As renewable energy ecologists," Steven Grodsky explains, "we study novel challenges and synergistic benefits to conservation presented by renewable energy development. We have great opportunities to inform sustainable energy development to make for a bright energy future for people, wildlife, and the planet, which is very exciting."[785]

Moorman, Grodsky, and their co-author Susan P. Rupp believe it is possible to balance conservation with renewable energy expansion, and they have made some basic recommendations to achieve it.

Strategies to Balance Conservation with Clean Energy Goals

- Solar farms doubling as pollinator habitats.
- Placing solar panels on top of buildings and on landfills.
- Focusing on conservation when siting renewable projects.
- Carefully analyzing impacts and planning accordingly.

These strategies can help reduce the harmful effects of renewable energy developments, which include:

- Millions of birds killed every year after colliding with wind turbines

785 Moore, A. (2019). Renewable Energy Poses Challenge For Wildlife Conservation. Retrieved 18 June 2021, from https://cnr.ncsu.edu/news/2019/11/renewable-energy-poses-challenge-for-wildlife-conservation/

- Fish migration routes blocked by hydroelectric dams, fish unable to breed
- Intense sunlight from a high concentration of solar panels incinerating insects and birds

Greenhouse Gas Reduction Targets

In April 2021, the White House unveiled its greenhouse gas pollution reduction targets for 2030. These goals include:

- Reaching 100 percent carbon pollution-free electricity by 2035.
- Reducing emissions and energy costs by supporting efficiency upgrades in buildings by adopting modern energy codes and investments in new technology to construct high-performance/low-emission buildings.
- Reducing carbon pollution from the transportation sector by funding charging infrastructure for electric cars and investing in research to develop aircraft that can run on renewable fuels, investing in rail, transit, and biking upgrades.
- Reducing emissions from industry and agriculture.
- Reducing greenhouse gases other than CO2.
- Investing in innovation and clean technology infrastructure.

Politicians often overpromise and underdeliver. Sometimes, one president lays down the foundation of a project and the next one undermines it. The current greenhouse gas policies will have little effect if the next president disagrees with their guiding principles. The White House's plans could also fail miserably if the administration doesn't truly do what it takes to reach these very ambitious targets.

A Smart Balance

The problem of balancing conservation and infrastructure development has worried politicians and researchers alike for many years. Boosting the economy and the standard of living while ensuring environmental sustainability has often been a concern of environmental scientists and government officials worldwide. Progress is dependent on developing infrastructure, but this can create catastrophic habitat connectivity disruptions.

As each project is developed, the administration must assess its economic and social benefits against its ecological impact. The goal is to maximize socio-economic benefits while minimizing ecological costs. In a paper about the conservation/infrastructure dilemma, researchers concluded that "a detailed spatial analysis" can balance national objectives "while maintaining ecological integrity."[786]

In 2018, Heather Tallis, a lead scientist at The Nature Conservancy, and Stephen Polasky, an environmental economics professor from the University of Minnesota, published a paper addressing the issue on the World Economic Forum's website. "For too long," they wrote, "dire messages and gloomy assumptions about the fate of the planet have lent an air of hopelessness to one of the biggest challenges facing society. Conservationists feel stymied. Businesspeople feel villainized. We have come to accept the view that preserving the planet and growing the economy are mutually exclusive."[787]

The researchers propose we shouldn't view the conservation/human

786 Hopcraft, J., Bigurube, G., Lembeli, J., & Borner, M. (2015). Balancing Conservation with National Development: A Socio-Economic Case Study of the Alternatives to the Serengeti Road. *PLOS ONE*, *10*(7), e0130577. doi: 10.1371/journal.pone.0130577

787 Polasky, S., & Tallis, H. (2018). Here's How We Can Balance Conservation and Development. Retrieved 18 June 2021, from https://www.weforum.org/agenda/2018/10/can-we-balance-conservation-and-development-science-says-yes/

development dichotomy as an either-or proposition. The secret of success in both areas, they believe, is to act fast.

As the threat of low oxygen levels, melting ice caps, and water scarcity looms on the horizon, America needs to revise the concept of sustainability. The administration must not only pay attention to what sustainability researchers are saying, it must also allocate resources in the right areas. "Our view," Tallis and Polasky wrote, "calls for smart energy, water, air, health, and ecosystem initiatives that balance the needs of economic growth and resource conservation equally. Rather than a zero-sum game, these elements are balanced sides of an equation, revealing the path to a future where people and nature thrive together."[788]

The Nature Conservancy has proposed a number of strategies[789] to foster infrastructure development while contributing to the United Nations' Sustainable Development Goals, including:

- Switching to renewable zero-emission fuels.
- Decoupling aspects of economic growth from environmental impacts.
- Carefully siting crops and clean energy infrastructure, minimizing habitat conversion and negative impacts on protected areas.
- Better matching crops to growing conditions to consume less water and land for food production.

Prepared in collaboration with the University of Minnesota and over 10

788 The Science of Sustainability — Can A Unified Path for Development and Conservation Lead to A Better Future? (2018). Retrieved 18 June 2021, from https://www.nature.org/en-us/what-we-do/our-insights/perspectives/the-science-of-sustainability/

789 The Science of Sustainability — Can A Unified Path for Development and Conservation Lead to A Better Future? (2018). Retrieved 18 June 2021, from https://www.nature.org/en-us/what-we-do/our-insights/perspectives/the-science-of-sustainability/

other institutions, the Nature Conservancy's sustainability study says there is hope for those looking to balance infrastructure with environmental goals.

A careful reading of this and other relevant studies reveals that one of the keys to thriving over the next few decades is siting different projects and initiatives appropriately. To achieve that, the federal government will have to invest heavily in studies analyzing the potential impact of renewable energy farms, agricultural developments, industrial complexes, and other relevant projects.

Science is telling us that there is no contradiction between conservancy and development. But we must shift how and where we produce energy to meet growth projections while "achieving national habitat protection commitments, reducing greenhouse gas emissions. . . ending overfishing, reducing water stress and dramatically improving air quality."

Science does not advocate going back to the way things were done in the past to mitigate the impact of pollution. On the contrary, we must adopt modern technologies and upgrade our production systems to achieve a sustainable future.

With cooperation between the health, conservation, economics, and development sectors, quick action, and appropriate siting of different projects, we can rebuild America's infrastructure without further harming wildlife and the environment.

Researchers project that we can sufficiently reduce greenhouse gas emissions by adopting an energy matrix based on solar, wind, and nuclear power. While we transition, we must invest in "conservation and land management strategies that maximize the carbon storage potential of our landscapes and coasts."

Funding Issues

The Great American Outdoors Act is a piece of bipartisan legislation that was passed shortly before the last presidential election. The bill funnels royalties generated by the oil and gas industry towards the conservation of national parks, other public lands, and wildlife refuges.

The Act's annual $2.8 billion influx into conservation projects will be essential for achieving sustainable development over the next decade. The newly created Land and Restoration Fund will receive up to $1.9 billion per year to maintain long neglected national parks and public lands. Meanwhile, the Land and Water Conservation Fund will pour $900 million annually into environmental programs.

As the oil and gas industry directly funds these projects, the White House has imposed a temporary ban on new federal oil and natural gas leases.[790] Industry representatives have expressed outrage at this apparent contradiction. However, the government has vowed to resume leasing once a full environmental analysis is completed. This will, of course, take time. Opponents argue that the current president may be long gone by the time the studies are finalized.

While science supports the concept of carefully analyzing where to initiate development and exploration projects, we also need to act fast to balance conservation and economic goals. Bureaucracy may be getting in the way of the administration's best intentions. We all believed it took many years to develop a vaccine. It turns out it doesn't. So, it is reasonable to wonder, is the White House managing the environmental analyses efficiently? Should they really take more than four years?

790 Rott, N., Wise, A., & Detrow, S. (2021). Biden Hits 'Pause' on Oil and Gas Leasing on Public Lands and Waters. Retrieved 18 June 2021, from https://www.npr.org/sections/president-biden-takes-office/2021/01/27/960941799/biden-to-pause-oil-and-gas-leasing-on-public-lands-and-waters

The Western Energy Alliance, an industry group, argues that the ban on public land leases "would wipe out conservation and infrastructure funding for national parks," creating a "blind spot."[791] One thing is certain, whoever is in the White House over the next three decades will have to find creative solutions to these types of dilemmas. The economic and environmental future of our nation will depend on it.

How Nature Can Save Nature

Unsustainable growth has depleted resources, devastated ecosystems, and led to the extinction of many wildlife species. Today, the world is investing $133 billion annually in sustainable solutions. According to a United Nations report, that figure will have to rise to $536 billion by 2050, and the U.S. will need to keep up.

According to Inger Andersen, the Executive Director of the UN Environment Program, we must shift towards a nature-based economy. "Nature," Andersen explains, "holds solutions to many of society's challenges: the quality of life, the planet's temperature, our jobs, the water we drink, the food we eat, the clothes we wear and much more. Instead of pulling the rug from beneath our own feet, exploiting society and the economy by degrading nature, we need to be in harmony with nature's capital as it is essential for all life on Earth."[792]

Besides investing in infrastructure and conservancy projects, Andersen believes, policymakers must expand regulations and incentives to protect

791 Sgamma, K. (2021). Great American Outdoors Not Possible Without Oil and Natural Gas. Retrieved 18 June 2021, from https://thehill.com/blogs/congress-blog/energy-environment/555572-great-american-outdoors-not-possible-without-oil-and

792 Wood, J. (2021). This Is Why It's Good Business to Invest in Nature Conservation. Retrieved 18 June 2021, from https://www.weforum.org/agenda/2021/05/this-is-why-it-s-good-business-to-invest-in-nature-conservation-87370deb94/

natural habitats. The private sector, which currently contributes less than 10 percent of the global conservancy budget, must also play a crucial role.

Nature-Based Solutions

The Living Shorelines Act of 2019, the Climate Stewardship Act, and the American Transportation Act of 2019 are three initiatives designed to provide climate-resilient, nature-based solutions to our nation's infrastructure needs.

When combined with traditional 'grey' solutions, a nature-based approach can offer the best of both worlds. This strategy can provide a viable answer to both our crumbling infrastructure and the issues faced by local communities, which need to become more resilient as they confront climate impacts.

Nature-based solutions can offer pre-disaster mitigation while also addressing infrastructure needs. The Nature Conservancy defines nature-based solutions as "project solutions that are motivated and supported by nature and that may also offer environmental, economic, and social benefits, while increasing resilience." For this organization, nature-based solutions include "both green and natural infrastructure."

Mitigating Flood Risks

As coastal communities endure the devastating impact of climate change, infrastructure is needed to mitigate risks. Recent hurricanes have created hundreds of billions of dollars in damages, and the 'grey' infrastructure solutions of the past have failed miserably. Nature-based solutions for coastal storms and sea-level rise are a prime example of what can be achieved when conservancy and infrastructure development go hand in hand.

Nature-based solutions implemented by coastal states include the restoration of wetlands, oyster reefs, mangroves, and marshes. These green infrastructures can absorb very significant amounts of wave energy. The same can be achieved through the installation of living shorelines. One of the main advantages of marshes and other green coastal infrastructures is that, unlike seawalls, they can naturally adapt, accumulating sediments, and growing in height as sea levels increase.

Cost-efficiency analyses of these types of projects have shown that they end up reducing billions of dollars worth of damages. According to estimates, in the case of Hurricane Sandy, coastal wetlands helped prevent over $600 million in property damages. Nature-based solutions are also more affordable. One linear foot of living shoreline costs approximately $361 to install, compared to over $1000 for one linear foot of concrete structures serving the same purpose. Additional benefits of nature-based solutions include water quality improvement, habitat creation, carbon sequestration, erosion reduction, and indirect benefits for the tourism industry.

Green infrastructure solutions are also beneficial for communities at risk of inland flooding. Costing billions of dollars annually in the shape of FEMA grants to finance repairs, floods devastate crops, farms, infrastructure, and the livelihoods of local people.

Green storm drainage systems are more efficient and cheaper than gray projects to address similar issues. EPA estimates that green flood-mitigating infrastructure could save hundreds of millions of dollars over the next two decades. Whether rivers or storms cause flooding, there is an efficient green solution at hand to prevent damage and make communities more resilient to its effects.

Nature-based infrastructure to mitigate flooding impacts includes green roofs, rain gardens, bioswales (channels of plants along parking lots and roads), urban tree planting, and permeable pavements that allow water to filter through. Green roofs, for instance, can collect up to 80 percent of precipitation. Though steeper than that of traditional structures, the cost of installing green roofs is offset by their benefits in the long term. By absorbing and filtering rainwater, some of these flood-mitigating infrastructures, like bioswales and permeable pavements, can also help replenish groundwater reserves.

Green infrastructure installed around rivers can help prevent floods. Besides wetlands and marshes, it is possible to create forested buffers on the banks of rivers and lakes. These natural structures can absorb as much as 90 percent of precipitation. They have the added benefit of boosting water quality and reducing the cost of water treatment projects.

Nature-based solutions can also help mitigate the impact of extreme heat. They are applicable to many of our nation's infrastructure needs and provide indisputable proof that we don't need to destroy the planet to build the infrastructure we need.

What's Next?

While the destruction of ecosystems to obtain profits offers only short-term benefits for businesses, a nature-based approach can yield long-term gains. A welcome initiative in this direction is the creation of the Net-Zero Banking Alliance and the Net-Zero Asset Owner Alliance, two organizations that can contribute to shifting investor interest towards sustainability projects.

As the U.S. administration sets out to rebuild the country's infrastructure, it cannot do so, to paraphrase Andersen, in the same old destructive ways that will leave future generations with a huge debt burden and a broken nation.

Any large-scale infrastructure plan must take into consideration food system sustainability, clean energy, and clean transport. The administration must balance the needs of American nature and society. This will require massive investments and a profound cooperation between all relevant stakeholders, including many prominent private-sector players.

If we want to balance infrastructure and conservation, we will need innovation on a scale we have rarely seen before. America needs pioneering solutions to pressing environmental concerns and infrastructure failings, the kind that will be almost impossible to achieve without bipartisan support and a paradigm shift.

The good news is that scientists believe there is hope, and, in spite of some discrepancies, the private sector generally appears ready to cooperate.

A tremendous wealth of valuable research is readily available to policymakers and industry players today. Over the next critical decades, we must learn to read cost and impact analyses differently. The cost of an infrastructure project with long-term implications requires a new type of assessment. Spending one million less today to have to spend 100 million in 10 years because of an environmental impact we overlooked is no longer acceptable. At the same time, America's failing infrastructure costs billions; it costs lives. No matter how hard it may seem to find the equilibrium between preserving nature and developing neglected regions, our leadership has a duty to achieve it.

The solutions will not only require Republicans and Democrats to come together to pass important laws and kickstart key projects. Scientists, innovators, entrepreneurs, corporations, NGOs, government agencies, and community organizations will have to collaborate to rebuild America sustainably.

CHAPTER 29:

Green Infrastructure | Networks of Resilience

"Savvy states and communities are starting to think about green space in a more thoughtful and systematic way. They realize that green infrastructure is not a frill—it is smart conservation for the twenty-first century."[793]

Mark A. Benedict *and* ***Edward T. McMaho***

As defined by the Clean Water Act, green infrastructure is "the range of measures that use plant or soil systems, permeable pavement or other permeable surfaces or substrates, stormwater harvest and reuse, or landscaping to store, infiltrate, or evapotranspirate stormwater and reduce flows to sewer systems or to surface waters."[794]

This definition is sometimes loosely expanded to encompass the use of renewable energy and carbon-neutral materials. Broadly speaking, we can call infrastructure green when it is based on the use of green spaces and vegetation to harvest and filter water or when it is carbon neutral and contributes to the sustainability of cities and helps prevent the impact of climate change.

793 Benedict, M. A., Mark A. the Conservation Fund, & McMahon, E. T. (2006). *Green Infrastructure: Linking Landscapes and Communities.* Washington,DC: Island Press.

794 What is Green Infrastructure? | USEPA. (2021). Retrieved 27 July 2021, from https://www.epa.gov/green-infrastructure/what-green-infrastructure

Green vs. Grey

Green infrastructure used to prevent floods and other storm impacts is more resilient and cost-effective than traditional drainage and seawalls. Gray infrastructure merely moves stormwater away from the built environment, while green infrastructure can filter and reuse the water, providing enhanced protection for buildings and reducing water pollution.

When stormwater is collected through sewage, it is discharged into rivers and seas, polluting freshwater sources and harming natural habitats. Instead of building walls to contain stormwater and pipes to drain it, green infrastructure proposes using vegetation and soils to absorb and filter it.

Common Types of Green Infrastructure

Scientific research has shown that green infrastructure is cost-efficient, resilient, and capable of protecting beaches, cities, and water bodies from the impact of floods, hurricanes, and rising sea levels.

Downspout Disconnection

Installation of systems that filter water from rooftops. Instead of going into sewers, stormwater is redirected into cisterns or permeable soil. Local governments have incentivized this type of green infrastructure in places like Portland and Milwaukee.

Between 1993 and 2011, Portland's Downspout Disconnection Program offered incentives and free work to people who installed green stormwater management systems in their homes and businesses.[795] The result was the disconnection of more than 56,000 downspouts from the city's sewer system. Portlanders who manage stormwater on their property can receive up to a 100 percent discount on their on-site stormwater management charges as a reward for "[protecting] rivers, streams, and groundwater from the damaging effect of stormwater runoff."[796]

Rainwater Harvesting

Designing and installing rainwater harvesting systems adapted to a building's design and its environment. Slowing runoff, this type of system can be vital for providing access to water in low-precipitation regions.

Harvested rainwater can be channeled to irrigate trees and plants or stored in tanks, disinfected, and reused. Many jurisdictions offer incentives for every resident who harvests rainwater on their property. The City of Tucson offers commercial and residential property owners up to a $2,000 rebate for installing rain harvesting systems.[797]

Rain Gardens

Used for evaporating and transpiring stormwater runoff, these bioretention gardens can be installed almost anywhere. Rain gardens can absorb runoff from streets, rooftops, and sidewalks. In the Puget Sound region, Washington State University has initiated a campaign to install 12,000 rain gardens.

---

795 Downspout Disconnection Program | The City of Portland, Oregon. Retrieved 27 July 2021, from https://www.portlandoregon.gov/bes/54651

796 Stormwater Discount Program | The City of Portland, Oregon. Retrieved 27 July 2021, from https://www.portlandoregon.gov/bes/41976

797 Rainwater Harvesting Rebate. Retrieved 27 July 2021, from https://www.tucsonaz.gov/water/rainwater-harvesting-rebate

According to the program's leaders, rain gardens can "reduce water pollution, prevent flooding, increase home values," create "beautiful, low-maintenance landscapes," and help communities "save millions of dollars in pollution clean-up and expensive stormwater projects."

"Rain gardens work like a native forest by capturing and infiltrating polluted runoff from rooftops, driveways, and other hard surfaces," Washington University's researchers explain. "Twelve thousand rain gardens would soak up 160 million gallons of contaminated runoff "to protect [the region's] waterways."[798]

Planter Boxes

The EPA defines planter boxes as "urban rain gardens with vertical walls and either open or closed bottoms" that can "collect and absorb runoff from sidewalks, parking lots, and streets."[799]

Planter boxes have elevated sides and small openings that serve to catch runoff, which is then absorbed by vegetation. They can be an optimal solution for dense cities with few green spaces. Many U.S. cities have implemented them with excellent results.

Bioswales

Bioswales are linear rain gardens installed in long narrow spaces, for example, between a sidewalk and the curb. They filter stormwater, providing treatment and retention. They are typically placed along roadsides and in parking

798 12,000 Rain Gardens in Puget Sound. (2021). Retrieved 27 July 2021, from https://www.12000raingardens.org

799 What is Green Infrastructure? | US EPA. (2021). Retrieved 27 July 2021, from https://www.epa.gov/green-infrastructure/what-green-infrastructure

lots. These vegetated ditches slow down the flow of stormwater, allowing for infiltration and treatment. They are ideal for managing runoff in large parking lot systems.

Permeable Pavements

Permeable pavements are made of porous material, like pervious concrete or porous asphalt. They can be used to catch, infiltrate, and treat rainwater. The City of Sultan, Washington, reportedly saved over $250,000 in construction costs after installing porous pavements.[800] Located in the vicinity of Salem, the community of Pringle Creek has enjoyed the benefits of porous asphalt roads for years.

"It's pretty remarkable to see water disappear into the street," the eco-friendly development's VP has commented.[801] "We've been really impressed with how effective the streets have been." Dating back to 2007, Pringle Creek's green infrastructure development was the first full-scale permeable pavement project in the country.

Green Roofs

Green roof systems facilitate rainfall infiltration through strategically placed vegetation atop buildings. They can help reduce the ambient air temperature, mitigating the "urban heat island" effect in cities. Green roofs also help manage rainwater, decreasing the burden of runoff on sewer systems.

They provide bio-filtration, which prevents harmful pollutants from

800 Stiffler, L. (2021). The Porous Road Less Traveled. Retrieved 27 July 2021, from https://www.sightline.org/2012/01/03/the-porous-road-less-traveled/

801 Stiffler, L. (2021). The Porous Road Less Traveled. Retrieved 27 July 2021, from https://www.sightline.org/2012/01/03/the-porous-road-less-traveled/

reaching waterways. Studies have shown that the substrate retains 95 percent of rainwater's most dangerous contaminants.[802] Other benefits of green roofs include CO2 reduction, natural habitat formation, cleaner air, longer roof life, energy-consumption reduction (through their cooling effect in summer and heating effect in winter), and sound insulation.

Urban Tree Canopies

Tree canopies in urban areas provide shade and soak up stormwater. They offer countless benefits for built environments. Trees store rainfall in their canopies and later release it into the atmosphere.

Their roots promote rainwater infiltration and absorb contaminants, transforming them into less toxic substances. Cities like Chicago and Philadelphia have implemented successful urban forest initiatives.[803]

Green Wastewater Management

Urban wastewater infrastructure is largely outdated in America. This is also true for the rest of the world. As global freshwater reserves dwindle, treating and reusing wastewater becomes a necessity for numerous communities. As previously mentioned in the Wastewater chapter, sustainable wastewater management can also be beneficial for human health and economic development.

Centralized wastewater systems are largely inefficient, and decentralized green solutions appear to be our only hope.

---

802 Research on Phosphorus Removal in Artificial Wetlands by Plants and Their Photosynthesis. Retrieved 27 July 2021, from https://www.scielo.br/j/babt/a/QktFyXTgRpWrFhVRKQMMLmf/?lang=en&format=pdf

803 Vibrant Cities Lab — American Forests. Retrieved 27 July 2021, from https://www.americanforests.org/magazine/article/vibrant-cities-lab/

Detroit's Bioretention Gardens

In May 2021, the Detroit Water and Sewerage Department announced the completion of a project involving bioretention gardens installed in 10 boulevard medians.[804] Located in the Aviation neighborhood, the project was designed to prevent flooding by redirecting snow melt and rain into the newly planted gardens.

Consisting of a set of 10 restructured street medians on Oakman Boulevard, the gardens can reduce the burden on the city's centralized wastewater system by 37.3 million gallons of stormwater every year.[805]

The project was part of the city's response to a massive flood that took place in 2014, when heavy rains submerged highways and filled basements, causing approximately one billion dollars in damages.[806]

Green wastewater infrastructure is not uncommon in the Great Lakes Basin, and developments are likely to increase as climate change makes rainstorms more and more frequent.

Detroit's new rain gardens filter stormwater and collect some of it in underground tanks. The filtered water is then released slowly into the city's sewerage system. When the water reaches waterways, it is cleaner, boosting overall water quality in the region.

Similar projects are spreading rapidly over the Great Lakes Basin. The Milwaukee Metropolitan Sewerage District has plans to capture 740 million gallons of stormwater through green infrastructure by 2035.[807] Ohio's

804 City's Largest Stormwater Management Project Completed on Oakman Blvd; DWSD Demonstrates How It Will Reduce Flooding | City of Detroit. Retrieved 27 July 2021, from https://detroitmi.gov/news/citys-largest-stormwater-management-project-completed-oakman-blvd-dwsd-demonstrates-how-it-will

805 Stormwater Project: Oakman Boulevard | City of Detroit. Retrieved 27 July 2021, from https://detroitmi.gov/departments/water-and-sewerage-department/dwsd-projects/stormwater-project-oakman-boulevard

806 Story to Remember, 2014: August Flooding in Metro Detroit. Retrieved 27 July 2021, from https://www.crainsdetroit.com/article/20141222/NEWS/141229993/aftermath-of-august-flooding-10-billion-gallons-of-sewer-overflows

807 Green Infrastructure. Retrieved 27 July 2021, from https://city.milwaukee.gov/WCC/Principles/Fishable-

Northeast District has awarded multiple green infrastructure grants that resulted in a 26-million-gallon reduction of stormwater runoff.

Cleveland and Chicago have implemented large green wastewater projects to comply with the EPA's requirements. Green infrastructure has brought economic benefits for these cities. When grey infrastructure fails, and urban areas are plagued by floods, adding green infrastructure is more cost-efficient than replacing traditional wastewater infrastructure. Rainfall in the Great Lakes region is expected to increase by up to 20 percent over the coming years,[808] and the existing sewerage simply cannot handle the load. Besides preventing floods, bioretention gardens can boost air quality and improve quality of life.

EPA Recommendations

The EPA recommends exploring opportunities to "green the gray"[809] in every community. Integrating green infrastructure practices into the built environment can reduce costs and maximize benefits. In urban areas, parking lots, parks, and streets provide many opportunities to install green wastewater management features.

According to the federal agency, green wastewater infrastructure can:

- Reduce flooding
- Enhance neighborhood aesthetics

Swimmable-Water/Healthy-Drinking-Water/Green-Infrastructure

808 Great Lakes | U.S. Climate Resilience Toolkit. Retrieved 27 July 2021, from https://toolkit.climate.gov/regions/great-lakes

809 Why You Should Consider Green Stormwater Infrastructure for Your Community | US EPA. Retrieved 27 July 2021, from https://www.epa.gov/G3/why-you-should-consider-green-stormwater-infrastructure-your-community

- Encourage socialization
- Increase property values
- Create opportunities for local businesses[810]

Green infrastructure can help slow down traffic, increase the number of green spaces and walkable streets, offer shade in the summer, and boost commerce through increased foot traffic in shopping districts. The EPA expects communities to create grants and incentives to integrate decentralized green infrastructure solutions into their wastewater systems.

One way to optimize "green the grey" initiatives is to include green infrastructure features whenever communities are planning to repair roadways, parking lots, and sidewalks; upgrade water supply lines and sewer systems; or redevelop vacant properties.

The Environmental Protection Agency has published a document titled "Green Infrastructure Opportunities that Arise During Municipal Operations" to highlight how local governments can take advantage of infrastructure repairs to incorporate green wastewater solutions into their municipal operations.[811]

Sigma Research predicts that growth in green infrastructure will support recovery from the COVID-19 shock. Analysts estimate that infrastructure projects will offer the private sector "an estimated USD 1.4 trillion annual global opportunity to fill the funding gap, particularly for green and sustainable infrastructure."[812]

---

810 Why You Should Consider Green Stormwater Infrastructure for Your Community | US EPA. Retrieved 27 July 2021, from https://www.epa.gov/G3/why-you-should-consider-green-stormwater-infrastructure-your-community

811 Green Infrastructure Opportunities that Arise During Municipal Operations | US EPA. Retrieved 27 July 2021, from https://www.epa.gov/nep/green-infrastructure-opportunities-arise-during-municipal-operations

812 Growth In Green Infrastructure to Support Recovery from COVID-19. (2021). Retrieved 27 July 2021, from https://www.swissre.com/institute/research/sigma-research/Economic-Insights/green-infrastructure.html

Supporting the Grey to Green Transition

Green infrastructure requires advanced research, and its optimization requires data-driven design. Efficient bioretention projects demand stormwater models and detailed outflow calculations. As urban populations grow and the weather becomes more extreme, it will be impossible to build new homes without balancing grey infrastructure with green spaces and green stormwater infrastructure.

Thanks to modeled data, scientists have developed vegetated structures that can efficiently detain or delay the outflow of rainwater. As it becomes costlier for urban planners to ignore rising global temperatures, nature-based projects are spreading all over the U.S. and the world.

Examples of communities that implemented financially sound green infrastructure projects include Bangkok's Chulalongkorn University Centenary Park.[813] In fact, analysts believe the park literally saved the whole town from sinking. Its design was based on a resilience approach that took into account different climate change scenarios. Centenary Park helped mitigate the impact of the city's rapid growth, efficiently managing wastewater and reducing the urban heat island effect.

The park's environmental benefits encompassed adjacent roads, transit networks, and wastewater filtration for neighboring areas. Because the city is at sea level, it faces huge challenges as global temperatures increase, seas rise, and storms become more frequent. Fast-paced urban development burdens the city's stormwater systems and causes frequent flooding.

The 12-acre park sustainably collects and treats rainwater through

813 Holmes, D. (2019). Chulalongkorn University Centenary Park — green infrastructure for the city of Bangkok. Retrieved 27 July 2021, from https://worldlandscapearchitect.com/chulalongkorn-centenary-park-green-infrastructure-for-the-city-of-bangkok/

several features, including storage tanks, human-made wetlands, a retention pond, and Thailand's highest green roof. The park's vegetation belongs to native species, which are prepared to endure the local weather. Research has shown that Centenary Park has successfully prevented severe environmental damage, providing a valuable example for policymakers worldwide.

Science-based models have been instrumental in showing decision-makers how beneficial green infrastructure can be for our societies. By modeling climate scenarios, irrigation requirements, and plant stress, data-driven models can help designers build efficient green infrastructure. We now have access to data that can help us develop projects that can bring economic, societal, and ecological benefits.

CHAPTER 30

The Future of Healthy Buildings and the Health Impact of Built Environments

"A healthy building does more than conserve resources: it improves the health and productivity of the people inside."[814]

*—**Joseph G. Allen** and John D. Macomber*

Built environments can be vital for promoting well-being and preventing health risks. From air and water quality to energy consumption and daylight levels, numerous factors impact the health and well-being of building occupants.

The built environments of the future will support health by promoting physical activity, providing access to green spaces, and adjusting room temperature and ventilation based on multiple conditions. Since buildings account for up to 40 percent of energy consumption in developed countries and 45 percent of greenhouse gas emissions worldwide, energy efficiency is also a vital concern.[815]

"Buildings and the built environment stand to play an important role

814 Allen, J. & Macomber, J. (2020). *Healthy Buildings: How Indoor Spaces Drive Performance and Productivity.* Cambridge, MA and London, England: Harvard University Press. https://doi.org/10.4159/9780674246102

815 Buildings — Topics - IEA. (2021). Retrieved 26 July 2021, from https://www.iea.org/topics/buildings

in climate change mitigation, as well as adaptation to changing climatic conditions, creating opportunities for co-benefits for public health," researchers wrote in a paper titled "Integrating Health into Buildings of the Future."[816] Analysts believe climate change "can modify existing health threats that are relevant to the built environment, such as urban heat islands, air pollution, and flooding. In particular, extreme heat events are increasing in both magnitude and duration."[817] The heatwaves of summer 2021 in the Northern hemisphere exemplify the threat observed by climate researchers.

Associating climate change with how we build homes and offices is not the first idea that comes to mind, but the connections are apparent. If we want to promote human health and a healthy environment for the coming generations, we must change how we think about designing buildings and cities.

Built environment features like wastewater treatment and drinking water systems impact overall water quality. If we don't optimize wastewater treatment as we deplete our freshwater resources, what little freshwater is left will become heavily polluted.

Engineers, developers, and scientists are now designing the next generation of healthy buildings, which could have a tremendous impact on human health worldwide. This transformation will be a demanding one. If we see buildings as standalone units, we are not going to make progress. The built environments we inhabit are more than a group of buildings; they are complex systems encompassing buildings, transportation networks, infrastructure, and green spaces.

In the future, buildings will communicate with each other as well as with

---

816 Heidari, L., Younger, M., Chandler, G., Gooch, J., & Schramm, P. (2016). Integrating Health into Buildings of The Future. *Journal of Solar Energy Engineering, 139*(1), 010802. https://doi.org/10.1115/1.4035061

817 Heidari, L., Younger, M., Chandler, G., Gooch, J., & Schramm, P. (2016). Integrating Health into Buildings of The Future. *Journal of Solar Energy Engineering, 139*(1), 010802. https://doi.org/10.1115/1.4035061

their managers and residents, providing multiple data points to enhance conditions and contribute to environmental health and urban development.

Smart buildings won't be able to function without smart cities, and the transformation will be bigger than anything we have seen in our lifetime.

The Pandemic's Impact on Healthy Building Developments

The 2020-2021 pandemic has forced urban planners and building designers to think more deeply about sustainability and healthy living. It is now clear that the built environments of tomorrow will have to mitigate health risks and promote physical and emotional well-being.

In a recent survey of asset managers who control over $1 trillion in real estate assets, the majority of respondents said their portfolios would focus on wellness and health over the coming year. According to one of the organizations responsible for the study, the United Nations Environment Program Financial Initiative (UNEP FI); environmental, social, and governance criteria are vital for real estate investors today.[818]

The report, titled "A New Investor Consensus: The Rising Demand for Healthy Buildings," offers a global perspective on healthy building trends.

Analysts from UNEP FI, real estate investment advisor BentallGreenOak, and the healthy-design nonprofit Center for Active Design, identified the following trends:

- Demand for healthy buildings has surged. "Against the backdrop

818 New Global Study Finds COVID-19 Accelerating Investments in "Healthy Buildings". (2021). Retrieved 26 July 2021, from https://www.prnewswire.com/news-releases/new-global-study-finds-covid-19-accelerating-investments-in-healthy-buildings-301259614.html

of COVID-19, 100 percent of respondents in Asia, 90 percent of respondents in North America, and 85 percent of respondents in Europe expressed that current demand for healthy buildings is moderate or strong. Collectively, nearly 87 percent of respondents experienced increased demand over the past 12 to 24 months."

- Demand for healthy buildings will keep growing. "Ninety-two percent of respondents agree that demand for healthy buildings will grow in the next three years."
- Commercial and residential tenants drive demand. "Ninety-five percent of respondents identify tenants as the leading stakeholder group driving demand, with most of that strong or moderate demand coming from the office (87 percent) and residential sectors (61 percent), followed by retail (48 percent). This reinforces the conclusion that the pandemic has brought health and wellness to the fore in spaces where people primarily live and work. "
- Investments in healthy buildings respond to diverse factors. "While 89.5 percent of respondents plan to enhance their company's health and wellness strategies in the coming year, the motivations for doing so are diverse—respondents cite COVID-19 response (100 percent), human health (86 percent), tenant satisfaction (71 percent), market differentiation (71 percent), enhancing reputation (57 percent) and compliance concerns (43 percent) as core reasons for investing in these strategies."
- Building managers have an opportunity to align on best practices. "Nearly three-fourths of respondents (74 percent) agree that tracking data is a key priority for implementing healthy buildings into their ESG strategies. The availability of healthy building certification systems—which 61 percent of respondents report using in some form—can offer a pathway for the industry to more

> consistently accomplish this by establishing clear benchmarking and reporting standards."[819]

In 2021, the impact of social factors on asset value has increased. Without operational excellence and stellar tenant engagement, multi-home and commercial real estate investments can suffer.

Massachusetts Institute of Technology (MIT) researchers recently found that renting an apartment located in a building with a healthy building certification costs between 4.4 and 7 percent more, and certified rental spaces attract tenants much faster than non-certified units.[820]

Healthy Building Features and Technology

The World Health Organization has defined healthy built environments as spaces that support "the physical, psychological, and social health and well-being of people."[821]

Healthy buildings can achieve this goal through a variety of features and strategies, including:

- Adopting a no-smoking policy
- Boosting indoor air quality through efficient HVAC and filters
- Eliminating asbestos
- Facilitating safer, infection-free interactions between people through digital twins

---

819 Franklin, N. (2021). 'Healthy buildings' Enjoy A Surge in Demand Worldwide — Workplace Insight. Retrieved 26 July 2021, from https://workplaceinsight.net/healthy-buildings-enjoy-a-surge-in-demand-worldwide/

820 The Financial Impact of Healthy Buildings. (2021). Retrieved 26 July 2021, from https://realestateinnovationlab.mit.edu/wp-content/uploads/2020/12/201214_Healthy-Buildings_Paper_V2.pdf

821 José, C. (2020). How Technology Can Help Create Healthy Buildings — Work Design Magazine. Retrieved 26 July 2021, from https://www.workdesign.com/2020/07/how-technology-can-help-create-healthy-buildings/

- Implementing AI-informed design
- Implementing green purchasing policies
- Incorporating fitness rooms
- Installing IoT sensors
- Installing adjustable shading
- Maximizing natural daylight
- Offering views into nature
- Opting for ergonomic furniture
- Relying on Big Data to monitor health risks
- Using sanitizing robots
- Using wearables to track the health of workers and tenants and identify virus threats

Commercial buildings are driving healthy infrastructure development. Research has shown that employees are more productive in a healthy environment,[822] and big corporations have taken note.

Touchless Technology

Healthy building designers consider aspects like natural light, access to quality transit, access to healthy drinking water, ergonomics, and access to green spaces. The COVID pandemic has made the risks of coexisting in a closed environment much more palpable than before, and this has led healthy building designers to focus on touchless technology.

In a standard office, interactions with computer systems require touch, but with advanced touchless technology, people can communicate with

822 What Makes An Office Building "Healthy." (2020). Retrieved 26 July 2021, from https://hbr.org/2020/04/what-makes-an-office-building-healthy

different devices through voice commands, remote instructions, and hand gestures.

With touchless technology, biometrics can be used to grant access to building areas and control automatic doors. Voice recognition can be used to set up conference rooms, and touchless payment systems can facilitate risk-free financial transactions. By implementing these technologies, building managers and employers will be able to reduce the spreading of germs.

These systems and features are only the beginning. As mentioned in other chapters, there are many healthy and sustainable buildings currently in operation around the world. Buildings that clean their own wastewater and generate their own energy. Enhanced ventilation, ergonomics, and touchless technology are part of the first wave of a revolution that will soon dominate architectural design and urban planning.

Post-Pandemic Trends

The threat of COVID-19 has ushered in changes that are making workplaces safer. Investments in healthy building infrastructure have surged during the pandemic, with corporations spending hundreds of millions of dollars to upgrade built environments and contribute to global sustainability and the well-being of employees.

Modern companies are investing in infrastructure to improve air quality, reduce carbon emissions, and optimize energy consumption. Going all-electric is one of the trends that are gaining more traction. Gas is a much less sustainable choice for heating and cooking, considering it accounts for a tenth of our country's carbon emissions. Gas stoves and heaters release dangerous gases into our living environment, and as employers try to boost indoor air quality, they are increasingly opting for all-electric installations.

Commercial real estate managers are currently focusing on air cleaners and filters, which are often a necessity in large cities plagued by smog. The healthy-building trend also involves energy efficiency upgrades and solar panel installations.

Demand for healthy building certifications and audits has surged over the last year.[823] Tech companies are now offering air quality, emissions, and temperature monitoring software that allows managers to adjust ventilation, HVAC, and other systems to make built environments safer for their inhabitants.

The WELL Health-Safety Seal

One effort that brought healthy buildings into the mainstream was the International WELL Building Institute's ad campaign featuring Lady Gaga, Jennifer Lopez, and Robert DeNiro.[824]

WELL's Health-Safety Rating Seal guarantees that commercial spaces adhere to COVID-19 protocols and have implemented strict sanitary measures. Retailers and restaurant managers can apply for the seal, which reassures consumers and can boost sales as a result.

In WELL's TV commercial, Jennifer Lopez advises, "Look for the WELL Health-Safety Seal outside and feel more confident going inside." Spike Lee directed the ad.

"On the customer side, it is a consumer-awareness campaign. . . we want to spread awareness around the seal," WELL's CMO explains. "On the business side, this is also angled at owners and operators that can help them

---

823 Towards Healthier, More Efficient Buildings Post-Pandemic. (2021). Retrieved 26 July 2021, from https://www.weforum.org/agenda/2021/06/covi19-inspiring-healthy-efficient-buildings-transition/

824 Spike Lee Directs IWBI Spot Featuring Lady Gaga, Jennifer Lopez, Michael B. Jordan, Robert De Niro. (2021). Retrieved 26 July 2021, from https://www.shootonline.com/video/spike-lee-directs-iwbi-spot-featuring-lady-gaga-jennifer-lopez-michael-b-jordan-robert-de-niro

validate their procedures and guidelines."[825]

Barely a year after starting operations, WELL has already been appointed to certify high-profile facilities like Yankee Stadium and the Empire State Building. The company's seal typically costs between $2,500 and $100,000, depending on factors like building size and number of locations. On average, WELL has been hired to certify commercial surfaces amounting to one million square feet daily during the pandemic.[826]

LEED and Fitwel Certifications

WELL is not the only third-party certification program on the market. LEED (Leadership in Energy and Environmental Design) offers building efficiency and sustainability certification worldwide. Offered by the U.S. Green Building Council (USGBC), LEED is the global standard for green building ratings.

According to USGBC, a LEED certificate can boost market differentiation, attract more tenants, and help administrators manage building performance. The Green Business Certification Incorporation administers both the WELL and the LEED rating systems, which are complementary rather than competitive.

On the other hand, the Center for Active Design's Fitwel certificate is focused on building design that promotes human health. This reputable organization has partnered with the Centers for Disease Control and Prevention to research and evaluate health-promoting design. Self-described as "the world's leading certification system that optimizes buildings to

825 Spike Lee directs Celebrity Campaign for International WELL Building Institute. (2021). Retrieved 26 July 2021, from https://adage.com/article/cmo-strategy/spike-lee-directs-celebrity-campaign-international-well-building-institute/2308161

826 International WELL Building Institute. (2020). Retrieved 26 July 2021, from https://resources.wellcertified.com/press-releases/yankee-stadium-becomes-first-sports-venue-in-the-world-to-achieve-well-health-safety-rating/

support health," the Fitwel standard is the result of an analysis comprising over 5,600 scholarly studies. Fitwel is "implementing a vision for a healthier future where all buildings and communities are enhanced to strengthen health and well-being," according to the CfAD's website.[827]

The rising demand for healthy building technology and certifications has created new opportunities for innovators. As the administration pushes legislation to incentivize zero emissions and the use of renewable energy, we will see many new and exciting developments in the healthy building sector.

The NIBS Report

In July 2021, the National Institute of Building Sciences Consultative Council released a report containing several recommendations for the President and other policymakers.[828]

Titled "Moving Forward," the document makes a case for healthy buildings, analyzing how they can promote public health. It focuses on three vital aspects: indoor environmental quality, healthy building design, and knowledge transfer between health officials and building owners.

For NIBS CEO Lakisha A. Woods, the concept of healthy buildings "goes well beyond continual sanitation of a building's indoor environment to eliminate pathogens."

NIBS Recommendations

- Federal agencies must "increase investment into critical research on

827 The Center for Active Design. (2021). Retrieved 26 July 2021, from https://centerforactivedesign.org/about/

828 2020 Moving Forward: Findings and Recommendations from The Consultative Council | National Institute of Building Sciences. (2021). Retrieved 26 July 2021, from https://www.nibs.org/reports/2020-moving-forward-findings-and-recommendations-consultative-council

the impacts of indoor environmental quality (IEQ) and resilience on health and productivity." The report highlighted the importance of retrofitting existing buildings to improve IEQ.

- Federal agencies should work to upgrade building codes to foster better building performance.
- Federal agencies should collaborate with community organizations and the private sector to implement incentives for healthy building developments and support improvements in the case of communities affected by unsafe conditions and the use of toxic building materials.[829]

The administration has already expressed its interest in upgrading building infrastructure throughout the nation, and it will likely pay heed to some of NIB's key recommendations.

Conclusion

The future of healthy buildings is here. Thousands of startups all over the world are developing technologies to make buildings smarter and greener. With healthy buildings and healthier built environments, our cities, including the massive metropolises of tomorrow, will improve public health and prepare us for the impact of climate change.

The private sector has seen an opportunity in the healthy buildings revolution, and the U.S. government is developing various initiatives to accompany and incentivize the trend. Developers and designers are finding

829 2020 Moving Forward: Findings and Recommendations from The Consultative Council | National Institute of Building Sciences. (2021). Retrieved 26 July 2021, from https://www.nibs.org/reports/2020-moving-forward-findings-and-recommendations-consultative-council

ways to make healthy building developments financially sustainable as they simultaneously contribute to public health.

As building developers and managers embrace these health-centric strategies, they can attract more tenants and buyers while also contributing to the betterment of society and the prevention of disease.

CHAPTER 31:

Leadership | The Sturdy States of America

"The measure of intelligence is the ability to change."
—Albert Einstein

COVID-19 has put global leadership to the test, accelerating digitalization and broadening the range of decisions leaders need to make. From developing strategies to implementing technology roadmaps and engaging stakeholders, modern leaders now face unforeseen challenges.

Infrastructure leadership used to be based on basic cost-benefit analyses. Now, leaders must make decisions in environments they have never experienced before, involving technologies and scenarios that were unimaginable only a few years ago.

Today's leaders need new capabilities and new goals. Above all, they need a tremendous capacity for learning, and they must be aware of the new demands for transparency, sustainability, and inclusivity arising in civil society. They must be capable of collaborating with organizations and individuals from very different backgrounds, with extremely different agendas.

The Six Paradoxes of Leadership

In his book *Ten Years to Midnight*, Blair Sheppard outlines six paradoxes of leadership that apply to the challenges modern leaders face in the post-pandemic era.[830]

- Globally-minded localist — How can leaders balance the global objectives and local specificities?

  In Sheppard's vision, the globally-minded leader is "agnostic about belief systems and market structures" and remains perpetually "a student of the world." The localist, on the other hand, is entirely committed to the success of a specific locale.

  This paradox is very relevant for the infrastructure sector. As American politicians develop projects to compete with other world powers, they sometimes lose sight of the needs of local communities. On the other hand, focusing too much on solving local problems sometimes leads to overlooking negative impacts on a global scale.

- High-integrity politician — How can leaders navigate the politics of getting things done while retaining their character?

  High-integrity: Building trust and maintaining personal and institutional integrity. Politician: Adapting and negotiating to secure support, forming coalitions to overcome resistance from different sectors and keep moving forward.

  As American society remains polarized, how can leaders fulfill their electoral promises while reaching needed compromises with those whom their electorate considers mortal enemies?

830 Sheppard, B., 2020. *Ten Years to Midnight: Four Urgent Global Crises and Their Strategic Solutions*. Berrett-Koehler Publishers.

- Humble hero — How can our leaders combine high confidence with the humility to recognize their mistakes?

  In the information age, seeming is as important as being. Leaders need to be humble enough to ask for help when they need it and to change course when they have made a mistake, but they must also exude confidence to be able to secure and maintain support.

- Strategic executor — How can leaders get things done while also remaining open to adopting better strategies?

  Strategic leaders are constantly on the lookout for insights about potential futures that can inform decision-making. Executors are more focused on delivering on present challenges.

- Tech-savvy humanist — In the age of the IoT and AI, how can we leverage technology and automation without forgetting about the importance of people?

  Tech-savvy leaders focus on improving technology, while humanists prioritize the importance of human effectiveness.

- Traditioned innovator — How can we maintain our roots in past experiences while also creating a culture that fosters innovation, trial and error, and growth?

  Traditioned leaders focus on connecting with the purpose of a project's original idea, while innovators are more ready to try new things and are not afraid of failing and starting over.

Infrastructure leaders must navigate all these challenges to deliver value both to the present day and to the next generation of Americans. Our nation needs visionaries who can see the bigger picture and imagine the world many decades into the future.

As the world moves faster and faster, only the leaders who can understand the impact of technology on people and help them adapt will succeed. Additionally, leaders must be efficient communicators to facilitate the planetary shifts we are about to experience in how we move, work, and exercise our citizenship. We need innovators who are ready to reach compromises and capable of thinking globally and locally at the same time.

The leaders of tomorrow need to focus on good governance. They must consider at once the needs of a local farmer and those of the whole planet. Without inclusivity, we will not be able to build the sustainable infrastructure we need.

As the pandemic crippled the global economy, many leaders responded poorly to the new challenges, and millions of people died preventable deaths. In the future of infrastructure, leaders will constantly face difficult decisions. It wasn't easy to choose between saving the economy and saving lives, but some countries managed to do both. These are unequivocally nations with resilient and robust leadership.

Infrastructure leaders need to decide between satisfying current needs and preparing for the future. They must learn new skills, implement new policies, and aim for a level of accountability and inclusivity we haven't seen before. If we want to change our world, we must change the way we view leadership. We need leaders who are transparent, who can handle criticism, and who are always ready to change and adapt for the benefit of the people.

Leadership Goals 2021

Smart infrastructure developments require robust leadership. The ASCE's

2021 infrastructure report[831] has identified seven objectives for all levels of private and public sector leaders:

1. Encourage asset management and the use of infrastructure data sets.
2. Streamline development processes implement safeguards and protections.
3. Evaluate investments in terms of ROI based on economy, sustainability, and public safety.
4. Leverage new technologies to maximize results.
5. Implement life cycle cost analyses.
6. Incentivize research and development of new materials and technologies, including big data and IoT.
7. Foster long-term social, economic, and environmental sustainability.

Infrastructure leaders are tasked with optimizing investments and realizing a modern vision for our nation, enhancing resiliency, plasticity, sustainability, governance, and inclusivity.

Leadership Challenges

Abraham Maslow once said, "In any given moment, we have two choices: step forward into growth or step backward into safety." The choice has never been more explicit than it is today, as America struggles to rebuild its infrastructure and prepare for the challenges ahead.

The infrastructure sector currently faces many challenges, including:

831 *Infrastructure Report Card | Leadership*. (2021). Retrieved 16 August 2021, from https://infrastructurereportcard.org/solutions/leadership-action/.

- Shifting market conditions.
- Transition to new funding models.
- New regulatory frameworks.
- "An evolving leadership profile, requiring first-rate management of teams as well as projects, a focus on the consumer and a commercial, strategic, technology and media skill-set suitable to managing increased demands from new and existing stakeholders."[832]
- Need to train and retain talent to face new challenges.

The infrastructure business model is changing, and we need strong leadership to guide us through the technological revolution.

As technology drives change, infrastructure leaders must incorporate efficient design and new methodologies while navigating a constantly shifting financing landscape.

One of the critical points for leaders has to do with mastering digital trends. Implementing 5D planning and Building Information Modeling will be very demanding for leaders in the sector.

According to Karl-Heinz Strauss, CEO of mega-project service provider Porr, "The 'paperless building-site' is rapidly becoming real—from planning, calculation and project management to ongoing documentation: Nothing will be done without computers. But this needs a lot of equipment and training before all the advantages can be realized."[833]

On the other hand, as public funding declines or becomes inadequate, government leaders must facilitate public-private partnerships. Political and business leaders alike need to negotiate these agreements to spread out risk

832 *Building the Future*. Spencerstuart.com. Retrieved 16 August 2021, from https://www.spencerstuart.com/research-and-insight/building-the-future.

833 *Building the Future*. Spencerstuart.com. Retrieved 16 August 2021, from https://www.spencerstuart.com/research-and-insight/building-the-future.

and enhance project governance. According to Allard Nooy, CEO of InfraCo Asia, "There is no doubt [Public Private Partnerships] will be a key driver for infrastructure development and implementation for the next five to 10 years."[834]

A few years ago, a study identified 13 key strategic trends that continue to be relevant today in the infrastructure sector:

1. Growing size, complexity, and risk profile of projects
2. Budgetary constraints of governments
3. Advances in information technology
4. Changes in regulatory policies
5. Increased use of public-private partnerships
6. Increasingly demanding environmental standards
7. Talent shortage in the infrastructure sector
8. Sustained volatility of global economies
9. Transfer of risk from public to private companies
10. Consolidation of infrastructure businesses (M&A)
11. Globalization of markets
12. Rapid urbanization
13. Constraints on financing capacity[835]

As infrastructure projects become more complex, the way stakeholders measure return on investment needs to adapt. Living in rather unpredictable times, it will be impossible to navigate these potentially treacherous waters without outstanding leadership.

834 *Building the Future*. Spencerstuart.com. Retrieved 16 August 2021, from https://www.spencerstuart.com/research-and-insight/building-the-future.

835 *Building the Future*. Spencerstuart.com. Retrieved 16 August 2021, from https://www.spencerstuart.com/research-and-insight/building-the-future.

The infrastructure leaders of tomorrow need to be tech-savvy and consumer-oriented with outstanding financial and regulatory negotiation skills. We need leaders who can think strategically, drive results, and streamline change. Over the next decades, infrastructure leadership will require envisioning multiple scenarios and making seemingly prescient decisions. Investing too late can be as catastrophic as investing early, which can lead to high costs and underutilized assets.

We are living in an era of constant change. The shift towards more private financing has resulted in a more consumer-oriented mindset. Leadership must now balance public service ethics with agile consumer responses.

The ability to reach consensus and remain flexible will be essential to develop the infrastructure projects America requires today. We need agile teams capable of collaborating effectively to deliver projects that can catalyze the transition to the hyperconnected space age that awaits.

Without leaders who can simultaneously cater to the needs of various stakeholders with very different agendas, American infrastructure will suffer. The current political landscape is a testimony to the critical importance of balancing different interests. If each political faction, business group, or advocacy organization continues to focus on their own needs and desires, we will end up with projects that go over budget and are indefinitely under construction.

The leaders America needs will be able to articulate consensus to benefit the economy and the people. They will understand that binary oppositions are misleading and will be capable of reaching across the aisle and forging compromise. They will understand the language of the private sector if they are public sector leaders and will be fluent in the public sector's language if they work in the private sector. They will communicate effectively with all stakeholders and always find ways to deliver on their promises.

Within the public sector, additional challenges are created by the scope of federal legislation and budgets and the relative autonomy of states and smaller jurisdictions. According to Susan Story, CEO of American Water, "Our leaders have a lot of autonomy at the state level because being a successful utility in California can be very different than being a successful utility in Pennsylvania. It requires not only technical competence and leadership competence to be able to lead people and establish a vision but also a sharp focus on customers along with the political acumen to balance the needs of employees, customers, regulators, investors, and elected officials."[836]

In the past, it seemed enough for infrastructure leaders to know about identifying problems and designing projects to solve them. Now, they must negotiate with key players in both the private and the public sectors, identify trends, plan ahead many decades into the future, and manage complex financing matrixes.

The responsibility to appoint the right professionals to streamline project design and construction will also fall upon the shoulders of infrastructure sector leaders. The individuals in the highest hierarchies in the space will need technical and leadership skills to adapt to a rapid change environment. In the end, leadership is all about building teams.

A great leader with a team that is not up to the task cannot salvage a project, and we are already seeing talent shortages in the industry today. The project managers and financial leaders America needs to rebuild its infrastructure require new skills and training. It is not possible to manage 21st-century projects with a 20th-century mentality. The engineers and technical experts we need will not grow on trees. Our government must

836 *Great Water Cities Panelist Susan Story Discusses Need for Infrastructure and Water Supply - WEF Highlights*. WEF Highlights. Retrieved 16 August 2021, from https://news.wef.org/great-water-cities-panelist-susan-story-discusses-need-for-infrastructure-and-water-supply/.

certainly play a role in catalyzing the transformation we need, focusing on everything from university programs to specialized training opportunities.

Focus on Governance

The Global Infrastructure Hub defines governance as "structures, processes, and systems that define decision-making and interactions amongst various stakeholders. . . the exercise of functions and power through a country's economic, social, and political institutions. . . it is linked to how government institutions are structured and operate in infrastructure development and implementation, and how they interact with the various public and private sector stakeholders."[837]

Governance, in other words, impacts every aspect of decision-making and project implementation. Like leadership, governance determines how the infrastructure sector secures resources and develops assets.

To be a great leader in the infrastructure sector, good governance is vital, especially when it comes to building new projects. Only governance-focused leaders can transform a vision into reality, not their vision, but a vision shared throughout the target communities.

Infrastructure undoubtedly stimulates economic growth, catalyzes inclusion, and connects vulnerable populations to political processes. With effective private-public financing and responsive governance, leaders can help reduce structural discrimination of underprivileged communities.

When governance realizes the potential of improved inclusiveness, the infrastructure sector can thrive. Good governance requires accountability and transparency. The leadership must also remain open to new demands and

837 *Global Infrastructure Hub — A G20 INITIATIVE*. Gihub.org. Retrieved 16 August 2021, from https://www.gihub.org.

proposals. According to the Global Infrastructure Hub (GIH), "Improved governance, with an emphasis on capacity building, empowers citizens and fosters accountability and a shared sense of responsibility on the part of the government, provided there is consistent application of the strategy over time and a commitment to cultural change instead of one-off interventions."[838]

Instruments like open access to government data and participatory budgets involve taxpayers in the infrastructure development process, enabling them to have a say in how their needs are addressed and how public funds are spent. Expenditure controls and external audit systems facilitate financial accountability, while transparency in procurement processes and budget allocations reduce the risk of corruption and waste.

The participation of affected communities from the earliest stages of infrastructure development is critical to good governance. It is very hard to garner the support and commitment needed to complete projects efficiently without listening to what a project's target communities have to say.

The inclusive infrastructure of tomorrow will require openness about the potential positive or negative impact of a project on different target groups. We need clear communications about risk-mitigating efforts as opposed to secrecy and insufficient impact analyses.

Inclusivity should be embedded into leadership and governance. Administrative and regulatory frameworks need to change to accommodate this transition. Complex projects also require coordination and alignment across different government bodies, industries, and community organizations.

The transparency needed to support governance can be enhanced through new technologies, using new platforms to allow affected communities to

838 *Governance and Capacity Building*. Inclusiveinfra.gihub.org. Retrieved 16 August 2021, from https://inclusiveinfra.gihub.org/action-areas/governance-and-capacity-building/.

express their opinions and propose solutions throughout all the stages of infrastructure development, including post-implementation evaluation.

GIH's Guidance for Governance recommends:

- Creating a governance structure that fosters inter-agency collaboration as policies and projects are implemented.
- Improving transparency and accountability, allowing free access to information, enhancing pre- and post-procurement disclosures, and implementing anti-corruption policies.
- Holding public officials and management accountable through policy inquiry commissions, social partnerships with community advocacy groups, and citizen engagement programs.
- Mapping governance levels and outlining the organizational structures and responsibilities of all government entities involved in each project across its lifecycle.
- Implementing governance assessments, adequate data collection, and monitoring processes.
- Encouraging decentralization to foster inclusion of traditionally excluded groups.[839]

Tools for Transparency and Inclusivity

There are many ways to encourage co-creation between the government and the people. Community engagement and empowerment are key to successful infrastructure projects. From sharing information to facilitating

839 Hub, G. *Governance and Capacity Building*. Inclusiveinfra.gihub.org. Retrieved 16 August 2021, from https://inclusiveinfra.gihub.org/action-areas/governance-and-capacity-building/.

collaboration with all stakeholders, there are many ways to enhance transparency, including:

- Designating a dedicated oversight authority in charge of publishing data.
- Incorporating public perspectives into policy design.
- Implementing open data systems.
- Allocating sufficient funding for the implementation of open data policies and ensuring the quality of the data to be shared.
- Implementing periodical assessment of open government data policies.

To assess the success of transparency and inclusive governance, it is important to regularly evaluate government commitment, the quality of institutional structures, regulatory frameworks, developed capabilities, civic demand for open data, and the funding and technological infrastructure available to support governance goals.

Infrastructure leaders will find their own ways to face the challenges ahead. It is imperative that they build resilience to adapt projects and policies to shifting industry trends. We rely on our leaders to prioritize the right projects, create jobs, provide training, rebuild America's crumbling physical assets, and fund the development of cyber-, automation, and space infrastructure. Refining leadership will be instrumental in building an infrastructure vision that can support America's growth over the next decades.

CHAPTER 32:

Infrastronger | Why Act Now?

"For an economy built to last we must invest in what will fuel us for generations to come. This is our history—from the Transcontinental Railroad to the Hoover Dam, to the dredging of our ports and building of our most historic bridges—our American ancestors prioritized growth and investment in our nation's infrastructure."
*—**Cory Booker**, U.S. Senator for New Jersey*

America cannot thrive and stay competitive with a crumbling and outmoded infrastructure. The world is changing faster than ever before, and we must act now. As we rebuild our infrastructure, we can create jobs and make the nation safer and more efficient.

Improving infrastructure also means improving the quality of life. Our infrastructure is in such a state of disrepair that there are many opportunities for improvement. As I have described throughout this book, our transit, levees, and bridges need urgent upgrades. So do schools and hospitals across the nation.

When infrastructure is working, we hardly notice it. But when levees erode and we inch through congested highways, when we turn on a faucet and blackened water comes out, we realize how vital infrastructure is for our daily lives. We are surrounded by bridges that are still in use decades after the end of their useful lives, decaying sewage systems, and structurally deficient buildings.

Rural populations need good roads, people living in urban areas need clean air and efficient transit networks. Every community in America could benefit from a new and upgraded infrastructure. The task of bringing our country up to date in terms of transportation, cybersecurity, and energy seems nearly insurmountable. And yet we must get it done now, not tomorrow, not in five years, because the potential benefits of doing it are as massive as the disasters that await if we don't. It's not just about driving on better roads or building nicer airports. We must rebuild our infrastructure to protect the health and well-being of Americans.

Infrastructure to Power The U.S. Economy

In the wake of the pandemic, our country needs an influx of capital and employment. Infrastructure projects can bring new life to neglected communities, driving new investments and generating wealth. Texas is one of the few states that have done it right, offering numerous examples of how to boost a region's economy through transit projects and other vital developments.

Austin's Cap Metro, Dallas's DART, and the Dallas-Houston high-speed rail corridor are prime examples of how infrastructure can power the economy. DART is the largest light rail network in the country, and it has had a phenomenal impact on the 700-square-mile area it services.

DART's Economic Impact 2016-2018

- $10.27 billion for the regional economy.
- 61,017 new construction jobs.
- $286.4 million in tax revenue.
- Real estate developments surrounding the Downtown Dallas to Bishop Arts streetcar route had an economic impact of $454.7 million.

- Over 80 development projects were completed in the vicinity of DART stations with a combined property value of more than $5 billion.
- The rent for residential properties located near DART stations is 17.9 percent higher than in other areas. The rent premium for commercial properties is 23 percent.[840]

The benefits of DART don't end there. By enabling Texans to commute via efficient public transit, the system reduces traffic congestion and air pollution and improves quality of life. There are many lessons that other U.S. cities could learn from Dallas and Austin. Investing in transit does work. It creates jobs, drives developments, and generates tax revenue.

DART, CAP, and other successful projects were once visionary ideas. Many people and organizations came together to turn them into realities. We need to embrace new visions that can support a future with a thriving economy, easier commutes that help protect the environment and lower unemployment rates.

Disasters Waiting to Happen

Thinking about the future can help us move forward, but before we focus on building the infrastructure we will need in 2050, we must pay urgent attention to the projects the ASCE has described as "disasters waiting to happen."[841]

In its Failure to Act section, the ASCE Infrastructure Report Card analyzes the gradual decline of infrastructure systems based on the current investment

840 DART Economic Impact. Retrieved 4 August 2021, from https://www.dart.org/about/economicimpact.asp
841 Disasters Waiting to Happen: 5 Major Infrastructure Projects in Need Of Repair. (2021). Retrieved 4 August 2021, from https://infrastructurereportcard.org/external-news-item/disasters-waiting-to-happen-5-major-infrastructure-projects-in-need-of-repair/

trends. The report predicts that we should prepare for disaster if we don't invest enough. It also reveals that when our country invests in infrastructure, the positive impact spreads through every sector of the U.S. economy. Infrastructure decline is progressive. If we fail to remedy documented issues, the consequences will be devastating. The math is very simple: if we don't invest $5.6 trillion by 2039, we will lose over $10 trillion in GDP.[842]

Major Infrastructure Projects in Need of Repair

Millions of Americans have no access to clean drinking water; lead and PFAS contamination are rampant. We have bridges and tunnels that could collapse any minute. This is not what one would expect from the infrastructure of a global superpower.

The next disaster is around the corner. The threat of massive public health concerns connected to contaminated water is as real as that of floods and catastrophic dam failures.

After disaster strikes, the cost of fixing infrastructure can grow exponentially. The sooner we fix deficient roads, bridges, and dams, the lower the costs. There are many infrastructure projects in a state of disrepair in the U.S. today, but a few of them stand out for the serious risks they pose to public health and safety.

The Hudson River Tunnel

Dating back to 1910, the Hudson River Tunnel stretches along ten miles of

842 Deteriorating Infrastructure and Growing Investment Gap Will Reduce U.S. GDP by $10 Trillion in 20 Years: Economic Study. (2021). Retrieved 4 August 2021, from https://www.asce.org/templates/press-release-detail.aspx?id=39801

the Northeast Corridor, linking New York with New Jersey. Approximately 200,000 riders pass through it each day. The tunnel was already in a state of advanced deterioration when it was flooded during Superstorm Sandy. Leftover saltwater inflicted damage on both the structure and signaling systems. The cost of repairing the dual tunnel was once estimated at $11.6 billion.[843]

As of July 2021, the federal government has confirmed it will partially fund the repair project. New Jersey and the Port Authority have agreed to invest a combined $4.6 billion, but New York is hesitating and may not be ready to shell out its share. Governor Cuomo has proposed reducing the scale of the planned repairs and limiting service disruption.[844]

According to an engineering report, however, "Based on the specific engineering requirements for rehabilitating the North River Tunnel, the tunnel's heavy train volumes throughout the day, and the lack of alternative rail access from west of the Hudson River, these in-service approaches to rehabilitation cannot be reliably conducted without material delays to commuter and intercity rail service."[845]

While politicians try to reach a compromise, the deteriorating tunnel poses a significant risk to transit passengers and local residents in general.

Highway 1, Florida

A section of U.S. Highway 1 that runs along the east coast of Florida has been

843 Shepardson, D. (2021). U.S. Says $11.6 Billion NYC-Area Tunnel Project Reaches Milestones. Retrieved 4 August 2021, from https://www.reuters.com/business/autos-transportation/us-says-116-billion-nyc-area-tunnel-project-reaches-key-milestones-2021-05-28/

844 As Cuomo Waffles, Schumer Says Hudson River Gateway Tunnel Expansion Is A Go. (2021). Retrieved 4 August 2021, from https://gothamist.com/news/cuomo-waffles-schumer-claims-hudson-river-gateway-tunnel-expansion-go

845 New York's Commitment to Gateway Project Unclear as Urgency Grows. (2021). Retrieved 4 August 2021, from https://gothamist.com/news/new-yorks-commitment-to-gateway-project-unclear-as-urgency-grows

ranked as one of the deadliest roads in the country. An analysis published in 2017 found that this particular stretch of road saw an average of 1,079 deaths per year from fatal crashes over a 10-year period.[846] Even for someone who has no idea about the statistics elsewhere, the number seems quite shocking.

In a three-day stretch in March 2017, the portion of Highway 1 between Miami and the Keys witnessed: six people being airlifted to hospitals after serious accidents, a head-on collision that left one woman in critical condition, and a crocodile wandering onto the highway and causing a crash.[847]

Many of those accidents could have been prevented by lowering speed limits, improving transit to reduce traffic, improving signaling, and repairing the highway. In this case, the cost of failing infrastructure can be measured in lives lost, and this is something our country cannot allow.

The Mojave River Dam in San Bernardino

According to the ASCE, almost one in six U.S. dams have high-hazard potential. High-hazard translates to dangerous conditions that could potentially cause fatalities.[848]

Dating back to 1971, the 200-foot-high Mojave River dam poses a threat to a region inhabited by a total of 300,000 people. By 2025, over two-thirds of U.S. dams will be past their useful life. The Mojave River dam already is. It would cost $64 billion to repair all U.S. dams,[849] and the damage they could cause if they fail would cost much more to fix.

---

846 Roustan, W. (2021). Advertisement Transportation Florida's U.S. 1 Tops List of Deadliest Roads in The Nation Study Says. Retrieved 4 August 2021, from https://www.sun-sentinel.com/news/transportation/fl-reg-most-dangerous-roads-20170424-story.html

847 Elfrink, T. (2021). Florida's U.S. 1 the Deadliest Highway in America, Study Shows. Retrieved 4 August 2021, from https://www.miaminewtimes.com/news/floridas-us-1-ranked-deadliest-highway-in-america-9286083

848 Overview of Dams. (2021). Retrieved 4 August 2021, from https://infrastructurereportcard.org/cat-item/dams/

849 Dam Facts and Stats. Retrieved 4 August 2021, from https://damsafety.org/media/statistics

In 2019, the U.S. Army Corps of Engineers raised the Mojave River Dam's risk factor from "low" to "high urgency action."[850] Climate change mixed with a severely stressed dam is a recipe for disaster. According to the Army Corps' safety engineer Gary Lee, "This dam was built in 1971, when climate change was still an unknown phenomenon. Climate change creates more uncertainty, which, going forward, will be taken into account."[851]

If the dam fails, 16,000 people and $1.5 billion in property could be inundated. Dams that were built before the notion of climate change came to be, are ill-prepared to withstand the climate events of the future. "The risks of catastrophic flooding are not as rare as they once were, and they will be less rare in the future," UCLA climate researcher Daniel Swain explains.[852]

There are many well-documented examples of old dams failing under new conditions. In 2017, heavy rains caused a concrete spillway to disintegrate at the Oroville Dam in the Sierra Nevada foothills, triggering the evacuation of over 180,000 people.[853]

The Mojave River Dam is not the only one in urgent need of upgrades. Based on 2020 inspections, the Army Corps of Engineers listed the following dams[854] among the riskiest in America:

---

850 Army Corps Reclassifies Mojave River Dam Risk Characterization. (2019). Retrieved 4 August 2021, from https://www.spl.usace.army.mil/Media/News-Releases/Article/2006597/army-corps-reclassifies-mojave-river-dam-risk-characterization/

851 Sahagun, L. (2019). Extreme Storm Could Overwhelm Southern California Dam and Flood Thousands. Retrieved 4 August 2021, from https://www.latimes.com/environment/story/2019-11-06/mojave-river-dam-flood-climate-change

852 Sahagun, L. (2019). Extreme Storm Could Overwhelm Southern California Dam and Flood Thousands. Retrieved 4 August 2021, from https://www.latimes.com/environment/story/2019-11-06/mojave-river-dam-flood-climate-change

853 Oroville Dam (California, 2017) | Case Study. Retrieved 4 August 2021, from https://damfailures.org/case-study/oroville-dam-california-2017/

854 Dam Safety Facts and Figures. (2021). Retrieved 4 August 2021, from https://www.usace.army.mil/Media/Fact-Sheets/Fact-Sheet-Article-View/Article/2523036/dam-safety-facts-and-figures/

- Magnolia Levee, OH
- Jennings Randolph Dam, PA/MD
- Kinzua Dam, PA
- Canyon Lake Dam, TX
- O.C. Fisher Dam, TX
- Thomaston Dam, CT
- Oahe Dam, SD
- Garrison Dam, ND
- Carbon Canyon Dam, CA

The Brooklyn Bridge

An American Road & Transportation Builders Association (ARTBA) analysis found that there are 231,000 bridges in need of major repairs nationwide.[855] New York's iconic Brooklyn Bridge is one of them.

Connecting Manhattan and Brooklyn, the bridge is one of the 46,000 in America that are structurally deficient. Stories of blocks of concrete falling from old bridges and killing motorists are unfortunately not uncommon in the U.S. The Brooklyn Bridge's original structure dates back to the 19th century. Structural repairs initiated in 2010 are still ongoing.

Contaminated Drinking Water in Chicago

About 20 million Americans have water delivered to their homes via lead piping systems.[856] In Chicago, 80 percent of homes rely on lead service lines.

---

855 ARTBA Reports 231,000 Bridges Need Repairs. (2021). Retrieved 4 August 2021, from https://www.ttnews.com/articles/artba-reports-231000-bridges-need-repairs

856 Chow, L. (2021). Safe Drinking Water in America: Not Everyone Has It. Retrieved 5 August 2021, from https://www.downtoearth.org.in/blog/water/safe-drinking-water-in-america-not-everyone-has-it-75518

A 2018 study found that two-thirds of local homes received water with lead content.[857]

There is currently a plan to replace lead piping in the city, but lawmakers have pointed out that the replacement rate is unacceptable. One policymaker estimated the project would only be completed by 2553 unless the city moves faster.[858] The American Water Works Association reports that it would cost $1 trillion to ensure every American has access to clean drinking water.[859]

Brent Spence Bridge

Brent Spence Bridge is one of the worst bridges in the country. Dating back to the 1960s, it was first described as "functionally obsolete" in the 1990s. Both President Obama and President Trump promised to fix it, but neither one delivered.[860]

Carrying I-71 and I-75 traffic over the Ohio River, Brent Spence Bridge is visibly rusty and has been the site of numerous crashes and bottlenecks.

In late July 2021, President Biden spoke at a town hall event in Cincinnati. "We gotta fix that damn bridge of yours going into Kentucky," he said.[861] Though some repair work is underway, we are still far from fixing the problem.

Connecting Kentucky and Ohio, the bridge is not only one of the worst in

857 Caine, P. (2021). Chicago Has More Lead Service Pipes Than Any Other U.S. City, Illinois The Most of Any State. Retrieved 5 August 2021, from https://news.wttw.com/2021/03/24/chicago-has-more-lead-service-pipes-any-other-us-city-illinois-most-any-state

858 Lightfoot Tackles Lead Water Line Replacement by Starting Small. (2021). Retrieved 5 August 2021, from https://chicago.suntimes.com/city-hall/2020/9/10/21430706/lead-pipes-chicago-water-main-service-lines-replacement-program-lightfoot

859 Infrastructure Report Card | Drinking Water. (2021). Retrieved 5 August 2021, from https://infrastructurereportcard.org/cat-item/drinking-water/

860 Gomez, H. (2021). Presidents Have Been Promising to Fix This Bridge for Years. Now It's Biden's Turn. Retrieved 5 August 2021, from https://www.nbcnews.com/politics/joe-biden/presidents-have-been-promising-fix-bridge-years-now-it-s-n1263684

861 Pitts, J. (2021). Biden Mentions Brent Spence Bridge at Cincinnati Town Hall Wednesday | The Bottom Line. Retrieved 5 August 2021, from https://kychamberbottomline.com/2021/07/22/biden-mentions-brent-spence-bridge-at-cincinnati-town-hall-wednesday/

America; it is also one of the busiest. It carries freight equivalent to 3 percent of our national GDP every year.[862] The problem is that it was designed to hold about half the volume of vehicles it currently carries.

There appears to be bipartisan agreement as far as Brent Spence is concerned. "If there is any project eligible, this would be it," Republican Senator Mitch McConnell has commented. "Hopefully somewhere in the bowels of this multitrillion [infrastructure] bill, there's a solution."[863]

Though there is a plan to fix the bridge, the $2.5 billion project has been characterized by local authorities in Kentucky as "an existential threat."[864] The controversial plan involves building a new bridge alongside Brent Spence Bridge yet keeping the old structure operational.

Schools at Risk of Earthquake Damage

The January 2020 earthquake completely destroyed a school in Puerto Rico, calling attention to hundreds of schools on the island which are not designed to withstand tremors. Following risk assessment, many vulnerable schools have remained closed.[865] Sixty of the inspected schools also showed severe structural deficiencies, and 25 among them had problems that were not caused by the earthquake. During the pandemic, schools were closed, and repairs could be carried out safely, but no work was done on any of the vulnerable facilities.

---

862 Project Overview | Brent Spence Bridge Corridor. (2021). Retrieved 5 August 2021, from https://www.brentspencebridgecorridor.com/project-overview/

863 New York Times: Brent Spence Among 7 U.S. Problems in "Urgent Need of Fixing". (2021). Retrieved 5 August 2021, from https://www.rcnky.com/articles/2021/04/02/new-york-times-brent-spence-among-7-us-problems-urgent-need-fixing/

864 Clark, R. (2021). Covington Mayor Tells Commission Brent Spence Project an 'Existential Threat' to City Revitalization | NKyTribune. Retrieved 5 August 2021, from https://www.nkytribune.com/2021/03/covington-mayor-tells-commission-brent-spence-project-an-existential-threat-to-city-revitalization/

865 Jimenez, L. (2020). *Puerto Rico's Earthquakes Have Put Thousands of Schoolchildren at Risk — Center for American Progress*. Center for American Progress. Retrieved 5 August 2021, from https://www.americanprogress.org/issues/education-k-12/news/2020/02/10/480206/puerto-ricos-earthquakes-put-thousands-schoolchildren-risk/

Mississippi Water Crisis

What happened in Mississippi in early 2021 is a testimony to the whole country's crumbling water systems. Residents of Jackson had no access to clean running water for a whole month following an ice storm.[866] Images of people washing their hands with bottled water and city officials distributing water bottles on street corners spread fast over the Internet.

For years, locals have known about Jackson's crumbling water system, Mississippi Free Press founder Donna Ladd explains. "It's coming in one way or another. There was a big 2013 study that warned about all of these things. So we know the conditions of them. But there's a systemic breakdown in the willingness to actually do something about it."[867]

Years of disinvestment and systemic breakdown have left Jackson to rely on outdated pipes, ready to collapse at any minute. According to Aaron Packman, a civil and environmental engineering professor at Northwestern University, "Most of the infrastructure we have in the eastern half of the United States is quite old. . . I live in Chicago. We're still using the water intakes from Lake Michigan that were built in the 1960s. And in places like Philadelphia, the water infrastructure goes back 300 years. So clearly, infrastructure that age needs a lot of maintenance to work properly. And it's very hard to do because most of the pipes are underground and inaccessible. So we definitely have an issue with its aging, deteriorating water infrastructure in a lot of the country."[868]

---

866 Tatter, G., & Chakrabarti, M. (2021). *The Jackson, Mississippi Water Crisis and America's Crumbling Water System.* Wbur.org. Retrieved 5 August 2021, from https://www.wbur.org/onpoint/2021/03/26/the-jackson-mississippi-water-crisis-and-americas-crumbling-water-system

867 Tatter, G., & Chakrabarti, M. (2021). *The Jackson, Mississippi Water Crisis and America's Crumbling Water System.* Wbur.org. Retrieved 5 August 2021, from https://www.wbur.org/onpoint/2021/03/26/the-jackson-mississippi-water-crisis-and-americas-crumbling-water-system

868 Egan, D. (2021). *A Battle Between A Great City and A Great Lake.* Nytimes.com. Retrieved 5 August 2021, from https://www.nytimes.com/interactive/2021/07/07/climate/chicago-river-lake-michigan.html

The Projected Economic Impacts of America's Failure to Act

If we don't fill the investment gap for urgent infrastructure developments, the next generation of Americans will greatly suffer. Failing infrastructure drives up costs to consumers, threatens public health, and negatively impacts business production.

The ASCE concluded that available funding will only cover 57 percent of the infrastructure projects America needs through 2029. Underinvesting in infrastructure will result in costly infrastructure services, lower incomes, longer travel times, expensive energy, and unreliable waterways and ports.[869] The costs of manufacturing and transporting goods will rise, making American products less competitive in the international market. By 2039, underinvestment in infrastructure will lead to the loss of three million jobs. About 47 percent of the jobs lost will be high-wage positions. If we don't act fast, we will lose 220,000 jobs in manufacturing, over 580,000 jobs in health care, and 436,000 jobs in professional services.[870]

For The Benefit of Future Generations

We must recycle our infrastructure for future generations. We must be willing to fund improvements without seeing a benefit for years to come.

America needs to invest in maintaining existing infrastructure and building projects that can help us keep pace with technological advances.

869 *Failure to Act: Economic Impacts of Status Quo Investment Across Infrastructure Systems.* (2021). Retrieved 5 August 2021, from https://infrastructurereportcard.org/wp-content/uploads/2021/03/FTA_Econ_Impacts_Status_Quo.pdf

870 *Failure to Act: Economic Impacts of Status Quo Investment Across Infrastructure Systems.* (2021). Retrieved 5 August 2021, from https://infrastructurereportcard.org/wp-content/uploads/2021/03/FTA_Econ_Impacts_Status_Quo.pdf

One of the biggest problems our government faces has to do with funding and investments. We need projects that can attract investors. While investing in innovative projects can be risky, investing in asset recycling can be more predictable.

The government has invested billions of dollars into infrastructure that is now crumbling. Making recycling and rehabilitation projects attractive to private investors can help our country tap into the value of existing assets. This is a way to free up capital to invest in new infrastructure projects. Recycling proven assets that generate stable returns is thus essential for ensuring the next generations will have the infrastructure they need to increase our nation's productivity and compete globally.

The recycling of physical infrastructure creates new opportunities for investors and can help boost the economy. We need to create solutions to public needs that are also feasible and profitable for investors. America must learn to finance infrastructure with cost of capital efficiency. At the rate the world around us is changing, we need to access sustainable financing sources that can help our country realize both our social and economic objectives.

Infrastructure is a vital enabler of economic development. In the context of climate change and population growth, funding infrastructure has become increasingly challenging. If we want to rebuild our infrastructure for future generations, we need to develop a new framework to regulate public-private partnerships.

Deteriorating infrastructure results in inefficient businesses and excessive costs of goods and services. If we don't find a way to invest in America's infrastructure, the new generations will have less disposable income, their businesses will suffer, there will be fewer jobs, and the national GDP will decrease.

The stages of design and construction imply high costs for infrastructure projects. The decision to invest and lure private investors cannot be made thinking of short-term impacts and costs. When infrastructure fails, the negative impacts reverberate and spread through many areas of the economy.

Infrastructure systems depend on each other to function efficiently. Energy powers every industry, transportation facilitates commerce and the delivery of parts for infrastructure projects, efficient roads and bridges facilitate transit. If one area fails, others are affected. This is one of the reasons infrastructure recycling and new developments must be planned very carefully.

If we address documented deficiencies over the next decade, we can prevent major infrastructure crises, boost the economy, and pave the way for future Americans to thrive in the Space Age.

Act Now, Act Fast

We don't only need to get started fixing our crumbling infrastructure right away; we must also do it fast. While we may have become accustomed to waiting decades for infrastructure projects to come to fruition, that was not always the case.

Efficient infrastructure doesn't have to take a long time to build. History offers numerous examples of great projects that were completed at amazing speeds.

Fast Infrastructure Projects of The Past

- Eiffel Tower — 793 days
- Empire State Building — 410 days
- Boeing 747 — 930 days
- Alaska Highway — 234 days
- Disneyland — 366 days

- Pentagon — 491 days
- Apollo 8 — 168 days[871]

Some of these important projects were completed more than a hundred years ago. Yet today projects much smaller in scale are taking longer. A new bus lane in San Francisco takes 7,000 days to build.[872] We can blame bureaucracy for the shift. But there is hope; when the world needed it, we were able to go from identifying a virus to phase-3 testing of a vaccine in only 300 days.

We need a new mindset to build the infrastructure our children and grandchildren will need. Diversifying public-private partnerships, increasing transparency, and funding new projects through asset recycling can be part of the solution.

If America will truly thrive in the Space Age, we need to recover the capacity to come together to build monumental things in record time. We cannot lag behind China; we must pioneer modern infrastructure because it will be instrumental to the survival of America and humanity as a whole.

---

871 *Examples of People Quickly Accomplishing Ambitious Things Together*. Patrickcollison.com. Retrieved 5 August 2021, from https://patrickcollison.com/fast

872 *Van Ness Improvement Project*. SFMTA. (2021). Retrieved 5 August 2021, from https://www.sfmta.com/projects/van-ness-improvement-project

CHAPTER 33:

Infrastructure for the Next Era

"Life can only be understood backwards; but it must be lived forwards."
—Søren Kierkegaard

Infrastructure is about creating opportunities. In times of COVID-19, the world is hungry for a shift towards more resilient systems and structures. The expansion of remote work and other trends driven by technology will lead to permanent changes. As countries struggle to leave the pandemic crisis behind, infrastructure investments are becoming essential for creating jobs and developing vital technologies.

Policymakers must focus on aligning public initiatives with private ones and diversifying infrastructure funding strategies. Incentivizing technological developments led by private companies is key. The private sector has access to innovators and expertise and enjoys lighter, more fluid structures and leaner bureaucracy, while the public sector can focus on investments that are not always profitable in the short term but can be of great benefit to society.

Sustainability is already a major concern for the U.S. and the rest of the world, and it will continue to be one. Under the Paris Agreement, there is a consensus to reduce carbon emissions to zero by 2050.[873] The target is ambitious, but the technology to get there is already available.

873 Paris Agreement — Climate Action — European Commission. Retrieved 30 July 2021, from https://ec.europa.eu/clima/policies/international/negotiations/paris_en

In the next era, mega projects will require policymakers and designers who can think forward. In today's fast-paced environment, planning for the future has become extremely challenging. The transformations the world needs will demand a periodic adjustment of our expectations about the future. Even if we can't imagine what the world will look like in 2100, we must pave the way for the technological developments and societal changes humanity will demand in 20, 50, or 80 years.

3D Design

Building Information Modeling (BIM) and 3D modeling have revolutionized construction, and they can also revolutionize transportation. Different infrastructure projects could benefit from BIM technology, but we are still relying on outdated design technology in the case of most industries.

America's aging transportation infrastructure could greatly benefit from 3D design implementation. This technology can help us build the resilient and cost-efficient structures that the growing urban populations of tomorrow will demand.

With advanced digital models, designers can minimize risks and reduce costs. Three- and four-dimensional models allow developers to test their designs before spending millions of dollars on building them. When designers and planners use 4D and 5D models, they gain cost predictability. The fourth dimension is schedule and the fifth is cost, two aspects that cannot be possibly included in 2D planning.

Designing a bridge in 2D does not compare to seeing the structure in real life. Digital modeling enables designers, contractors, and financiers to see exactly what they are creating, building, and paying for. There are fewer surprises. They know exactly how much concrete they will need, how long each stage of building will take, and what features they will need to implement. Rail expansions gone awry are a testimony to the fact that America hasn't been budgeting or scheduling infrastructure right. How can a project that was supposed to cost X and take 10 years suddenly cost 10X and take 30 years?

When scheduling is integrated into the blueprint of a project, plans become much more realistic. When budgeting is also integrated, the parties involved know exactly when materials must be delivered and when invoices must be paid. There is little room for budget drains.

An exhaustive 3D model makes it much easier to detect errors before it is too late. With 2D models, things can easily go wrong; pipes can be laid at the wrong angle, and structures can become unstable. In a 3D model, there are hundreds of cross-sections that show exactly where each feature is located. There is nothing left to the contractor's imagination; they can see everything they must build and where each item should be placed.

With the help of virtual reality, stakeholders can actually walk through a 3D model of the structure under construction. Only engineers understand certain calculations, but investors with no engineering training can virtually experience a space and see if everything appears to be in the right place. For ICC Group designer Emily Wetherell, "It gives us a very real and, more importantly, accurate image of the space we're designing in. We can see potential obstacles to our design, and we can draw designs that we know will fit the space without having to go back out to the site for more measurements."[874]

While it costs more to design in 3D, the extra spending is a sound investment that can often lead to significant cost cuts. According to Wetherell, cost reductions in some projects can surpass 15 percent. Typically, 3D design costs 10 percent more than 2D design, but it consistently results in savings of

874 Precision That Saves Time and Money: Smart 3D Design. Retrieved 30 July 2021, from https://icc-nw.net/2019/02/28/precision-that-saves-time-and-money-smart-3d-design/

5 percent or more. If a whole project costs one billion dollars, these savings would translate to a significant $50 million.

The future will require 3D modeling on a regular basis. It will not be possible to embed all the sensors we will need in pavements, bridges, and other structures without accurate 3D designs. There is simply no end to the opportunities this technology will bring. No matter what type of physical infrastructure we are building, we can derive tremendous benefits from the integration of 3D, 4D, and 5D design.

5G Infrastructure

In the hyperconnected world that awaits us, 5G will be vital for America to thrive. With 5G, data will travel up to 20 times faster than with 4G networks.[875] As 5G becomes the global standard, our wireless connections will be more reliable, and virtually every device we use will be connected to the network. Researchers estimate that there will be more than one million connected devices per square km.[876]

Over time, 5G will modernize government operations and public infrastructure. It will propel artificial intelligence and edge computing into the next era.

From 1G's local coverage to 4G's speedy global data transfers, we have seen it all. But the completion of the transition to 5G will truly change the world. Users may be excited about jumping from 1 Gigabyte per second to 20 Gigabytes, but 5G is much more than a jump in speed; it is a whole new concept of connectivity.

---

875 What is 5G | Everything You Need to Know about 5G | 5G FAQ | Qualcomm. Retrieved 30 July 2021, from https://www.qualcomm.com/5g/what-is-5g

876 5G in Government. Retrieved 30 July 2021, from https://www2.deloitte.com/us/en/insights/industry/public-sector/future-of-5g-government.html/#endnote-4

In the next era, we are going to enjoy ubiquitous connectivity no matter where we go, and we will be able to access complex business applications remotely in real-time. Entertainment will also change as our connected devices expand further into virtual reality.

Hyperconnectivity will also catalyze the transformation of cities. Without it, the IoT wouldn't be able to handle the load of millions of sensors transferring information in real-time, and it will be instrumental for the shift towards autonomous cars and smart roads.

Likewise, the implications of 5G for the healthcare industry will be wide-ranging. For instance, remote surgery could be risky with the broadband available today, but it may become a common occurrence with the reliability of 5G connectivity.

Meanwhile, urban safety monitoring will never be the same. Thanks to 5G, smoke detectors and other sensors will transfer data about pressure in pipes, room temperature, air quality, and other conditions, enabling managers to detect fire and explosion threats. The amount of information that needs to be exchanged in real-time to protect every building in a city could cause a 4G network to collapse, but 5G can handle it.

A recent report by Deloitte[877] advised government leaders to consider the implications of 5G across seven important categories:

- *"Modifications to existing network infrastructure, systems, and applications."* — Integrating 5G into existing systems and infrastructure to maximize its potential and upgrading communication infrastructure as needed.
- *"Cloud integration."* — For example, selecting the appropriate cloud adoption models, for example, deciding whether to buy cloud

877 5G in Government — The future of hyperconnected public services. Retrieved 30 July 2021, from https://www2.deloitte.com/us/en/insights/industry/public-sector/future-of-5g-government.html/

services or build clouds in-house.

- *"Network security and supply chain vulnerabilities."* — Understanding the supply chain and network security risks involved in 5G adoption and taking action to mitigate risks and eliminate threats.
- *"Data ethics and privacy."* — Finding the right balance between ubiquitous surveillance through millions of cameras and sensors and privacy protection.
- *"Long-term spectrum policy."* — Making informed decisions about electromagnetic band spectrums to balance coverage and capacity.
- *"Urban-rural connectivity divide."* — Implementing technological solutions to bridge the gap between rural and urban connectivity.
- *"Workforce implications."*— The advent of 5G will impact how we work, even on a psychological level. Policymakers should be aware of this to facilitate the transition and protect the workforce's health and well-being.

Hyperconnectivity will enable governments to become more efficient and broaden their cybersecurity strategies. Information will travel faster more safely. "Over a 5G network," analysts explain, "data is sent separately from its routing instructions; devices communicate with numerous points on the network and on numerous frequencies (unlicensed and licensed); and data is only reassembled at the device. This is a shift as transformational as the move from traditional IT architecture to cloud computing, and to have at least a basic understanding of the underlying technology is important for those who are designing, building, operating, and securing the network as well as those communicating over the network."[878]

878 5G in Government — The future of hyperconnected public services. Retrieved 30 July 2021, from https://www2.deloitte.com/us/en/insights/industry/public-sector/future-of-5g-government.html/

Our government is already preparing for the shift, and how prepared we are when 5G reaches global scale will have a big impact on our country's geopolitical position over the next decades.

Crypto Infrastructure

Digital tokens are experiencing meteoric spikes. Governments are starting to adopt them, banks have agreed to custody cryptocurrency for their customers, and crypto exchanges are chartering banks. In other words, cryptocurrency has effectively entered the mainstream. However, our government remains reluctant to categorize blockchain and cryptocurrency as critical infrastructure.

When our country designates a type of infrastructure as critical, it devotes more resources to keep it safe from attacks and minimize vulnerabilities. The Cybersecurity and Infrastructure Security Agency (CISA) defines critical infrastructure sectors as those "whose assets, systems, and networks, whether physical or virtual, are considered so vital to the United States that their incapacitation or destruction would have a debilitating effect on security, national economic security, national public health or safety, or any combination thereof."[879]

There are currently 16 critical infrastructure sectors:

- Chemical
- Commercial facilities
- Communications
- Critical manufacturing

879 Critical Infrastructure Sectors | CISA. Retrieved 30 July 2021, from https://www.cisa.gov/critical-infrastructure-sectors

- Dams
- Defense industrial base
- Emergency services
- Energy
- Financial services
- Food and agriculture
- Government facilities
- Healthcare and public health
- Information technology
- Nuclear reactors, materials, and waste
- Transportation systems
- Water and wastewater systems

To protect critical infrastructure, the government establishes best practices and collaborates with private companies to develop policies that can help mitigate risks and secure the sector. While financial services and communications are included in CISA's list, cryptocurrency isn't, and this is a major vulnerability.

The financial sector is considered critical because of its potential vulnerabilities. The cryptocurrency sector provides a similar mix of services and handles billions of dollars worth of assets, but it is not protected.

With a $1.5 trillion[880] market cap, the crypto sector is still significantly smaller than the global banking sector, which boasts a market capitalization of over $8.2 trillion.[881] Foreign hackers pose a huge threat to the U.S. crypto sector, which warrants special government protection.

880 June 2021 data. There was a $2 trillion high in April 2021.

881 Banking Sector 2021 — Promising First Half | BankingHub. Retrieved 30 July 2021, from https://www.bankinghub.eu/banking/research-markets/banking-sector-2021-first-half#banking-industry

Legacy finance decision-makers agree that cryptocurrency will keep growing. As foreign governments integrate and adopt crypto, streamlining international transactions, America cannot lag behind.

The changes we are about to experience require a resilient financial infrastructure, and that already has a name; it's called cryptocurrency. The U.S. Treasury should not continue to discuss finance without considering the challenges faced by the cryptocurrency market. Our government must allocate the necessary resources to protect the sector because if this emerging sector suffers, so will our national security.

If it integrates cryptocurrency into critical infrastructure discussions, our government will have the opportunity to learn from crypto innovators what the sector needs in terms of risk management and security. Traditional finance could also learn from the crypto world's experiences, and these information exchanges would be vital for our national security and economic development.

Rethinking Infrastructure

As we strive to decouple economic growth from greenhouse gas emissions, we must think about infrastructure in new ways. In the next era, the connection between hard and soft infrastructures and inclusive infrastructure will dominate the global conversation.

As we develop smart cities and focus on green infrastructures, we must rethink the governance of urban infrastructures. We must ask ourselves what policies benefit whom. Are we fostering developments to favor certain companies, or are we doing it in a way that can truly benefit society? The synergy we need will be complex. When we deploy 5G and secure the crypto industry, we will have to ask this type of question repeatedly.

As we develop smart cities, how will we ensure inclusive territorial development? What can we do today to bridge the inequality gap and boost economic growth in the metropolises of tomorrow? Investments in large-scale infrastructure can drive social benefits and reduce spatial inequalities in our cities. Urban growth is happening and will continue to happen, but the pandemic has shown us that it requires better planning. Reducing biodiversity and altering ecosystems could ignite many more zoonotic epidemics. And this is perhaps one of the most important lessons we must learn from the COVID-19 pandemic.

We need to revise our approach to infrastructure development in light of our sustainability goals. According to a document prepared by the G20 meeting in Japan, "Harmonized regional and global scale analysis to measure the co-benefits between biodiversity and the sustainable design and management of infrastructures is missing."[882] We must make use of big data analysis "to anticipate the impacts of ecosystems degradation and biodiversity losses, to build urban environment plans at local and global levels, including biodiversity tradeoffs, to limit the risks of infrastructure failures."[883]

If our species is to thrive, we must change the paradigm. How can we develop infrastructure that benefits biodiversity instead of destroying it? Technology is on our side. In the earlier stages of humanity, we created technology to conquer and dominate nature. Now, we must approach progress the other way around. How can we build with nature and for nature, and at the same time for humans, with humans? This is the challenge for the next era of infrastructure.

882 The Infrastructure Nexus: From the Future of Infrastructures to the Infrastructures of the Future - G20 Insights. Retrieved 30 July 2021, from https://www.g20-insights.org/policy_briefs/the-infrastructure-nexus-from-the-future-of-infrastructures-to-the-infrastructures-of-the-future/

883 The Infrastructure Nexus: From the Future of Infrastructures to the Infrastructures of the Future - G20 Insights. Retrieved 30 July 2021, from https://www.g20-insights.org/policy_briefs/the-infrastructure-nexus-from-the-future-of-infrastructures-to-the-infrastructures-of-the-future/

We have recently witnessed large-scale deforestation in countries like Brazil. We need efficient metrics to measure how these problematic events affect our planet and what it will take to remedy some of the damage.

We can no longer think about digital, physical, and social infrastructure separately. Digital infrastructure needs physical infrastructure, and they are both deeply connected with communities and organizations in our societies. When one of the three elements fails, everyone loses.

Any decision local governments make in one of these three dimensions (social, physical, and digital) will impact the other two. We need to view infrastructure through an integrated lens, and the sooner we start planning accordingly, the faster—and better—we will transition to the next era of infrastructure.

CHAPTER 34:

Visionaries | New Foundations

"We must develop a comprehensive and globally shared view of how technology is affecting our lives and reshaping our economic, social, cultural, and human environments. There has never been a time of greater promise, or greater peril."

—Klaus Schwab[884]

Victorian visionaries catalyzed the creation of modern cities through imagining and building ambitious infrastructure projects. The disruption created by railroads, the light bulb, and radio technology owes much to the vision of a group of men and women who contributed original innovations to enhance human life.

In 2021, change is equally radical, and visionaries play a key role in imagining the infrastructure of the future. Over the next decade, cheaper and cleaner energy, better Internet connectivity, digital solutions, and AI will make the difference between global leaders and nations that lag behind.

In the past, the most impactful infrastructure projects were the ones that one could see and admire, like massive bridges and lengthy railroads. Today, cyber infrastructure and competitive industrial sustainability are taking the lead. Building America's future heritage requires a unique brand of visionaries.

Future infrastructure analysts let us envision a world of energy efficiency

---

884 Founder and Executive Chairman, World Economic Forum.

and high demand for innovation. Sustainability will be at the center and not on the fringes of both public and private sector strategies and investments.

Digitalization has provided us with a spectacular opportunity to achieve sustainability. As innovators push the regulatory transformation humanity needs, visionaries take us by the hand and help us imagine what our world could be.

Lessons From the Past

When Sir Joseph Bazalgette was commissioned to design London's sewage system, he calculated how big the pipes needed to be to meet the demands of the Victorian era, and he doubled their diameter.[885] Thanks to this long-term vision, the infrastructure Bazalgette created is still in use over 150 years later.

Fortunately, America has many visionaries capable of Bazalgette's foresight, engineers, and entrepreneurs who have exciting ideas about balancing our ecological footprint and Earth's finite biocapacity while fostering economic growth.

We need to listen to these visionaries because we will not solve modern problems with the solutions of the past.

From carbon neutrality and sustainable business models to blockchain security and smart cities, these original thinkers are paving the way for a better future for America and all of humanity.

Jeffrey Decoux

Texas-based Jeffrey Decoux is Chairman of the Autonomy Institute, a research

---

885 Collinson, A. (2019). How Bazalgette Built London's First Super Sewer. Retrieved 24 June 2021, from https://www.museumoflondon.org.uk/discover/how-bazalgette-built-londons-first-super-sewer

consortium dedicated to advancing autonomy and artificial intelligence at the edge. Aligning government, academia, and industry, the Institute focuses on maximizing the community benefits of autonomous infrastructure. The pioneering organization recently launched an intelligent infrastructure pilot with the Texas Military Department to "enable autonomous vehicles, smart cities, and connected things."[886]

Decoux is also CEO of Atrius Industries, a company created to leverage innovations and facilitate the evolution of industrial infrastructure. He has raised more than $100 million in venture capital[887] and is committed to the development and implementation of Intelligent and Autonomous Infrastructure. At the center of his vision is the deployment of Public Infrastructure Network Nodes (PINNs), the beating heart of the smart cities of the future. Deployed as a pilot program in Austin, Texas, PINN networks will expand from there to other major U.S. cities and the world.[888]

PINNs Explained

PINNs constitute a single unified system that incorporates 5G wireless, Edge Computing, Radar, Lidar, Enhanced GPS, and Intelligent Transportation Systems. They are designed to deliver real-time edge sensor and computing capabilities to support the IoT and advanced autonomy. "PINN is a breakthrough in digital infrastructure, solving the current challenge of delivering low-latency computing and sensors at the edge while avoiding

---

886 Autonomy Institute Launches Intelligent Infrastructure Pilot with Texas Military Department to Enable Autonomous Vehicles, Smart Cities, and Connected Things. (2021). Retrieved 24 June 2021, from https://www.prnewswire.com/news-releases/autonomy-institute-launches-intelligent-infrastructure-pilot-with-texas-military-department-to-enable-autonomous-vehicles-smart-cities-and-connected-things-301244224.html

887 Jeffrey DeCoux, Chairman, Autonomy Fellow, Autonomy Institute. Retrieved 24 June 2021, from https://www.topionetworks.com/people/jeffrey-decoux-58125f3018732bb18f000000

888 Intelligent Infrastructure Pilot Launched in Texas. (2021). Retrieved 24 June 2021, from https://www.smartcitiesworld.net/news/news/intelligent-infrastructure-pilot-launched-in-texas-6179

unsightly urban infrastructure sprawl,"[889] the pilot program's creators explain.

PINNs deliver valuable information and computing to enable Connected and Autonomous Vehicles to operate efficiently and safely. Similar to a light post in appearance, these sensor-packed nodes are placed throughout cities, 1,000 feet away from each other.[890]

Decoux believes organizations like the Autonomy Institute cannot be focused on simply developing and testing technologies. "It's not about creating new standards," he says. "It's not about doing some really nice tests. It's about how we can accelerate the path to commerce for these enabling technologies and bring autonomous or semi-autonomous systems into our cities and into our states." The Autonomy Institute is "a non-profit organization but it is going to be focused on heavy investment into creating and developing labs and corridors to allow this new infrastructure to be deployed."[891]

Investment in smart cities and autonomous Infrastructure can power our economy and create jobs. Delivery drones, autonomous vehicles, air taxis, and 5G connectivity need to be part of a powerful infrastructure network. Decoux believes in a single open and intelligent infrastructure. "The integration process is ready for a jump start," he wrote. "The country that does this well first will likely capture the preponderance of the economic benefit."[892]

---

889 Autonomy Institute Launches Intelligent Infrastructure Pilot with Texas Military Department to Enable Autonomous Vehicles, Smart Cities, and Connected Things. (2021). Retrieved 24 June 2021, from https://www.prnewswire.com/news-releases/autonomy-institute-launches-intelligent-infrastructure-pilot-with-texas-military-department-to-enable-autonomous-vehicles-smart-cities-and-connected-things-301244224.html

890 One of The Most Important Infrastructure Projects for Smart Cities Is Raleigh's EDJX, Its Edge Computing Platform | North Carolina Chronicle. (2021). Retrieved 24 June 2021, from https://nocarolinachronicle.com/one-of-the-most-important-infrastructure-projects-for-smart-cities-is-raleighs-edjx-its-edge-computing-platform/

891 *The Edge episode #7 with Jeff DeCoux 145 vues 19 juin 2020.* (2020). [Video]. Retrieved from https://www.youtube.com/watch?v=SKNow5ZM0mE

892 *The Edge episode #7 with Jeff DeCoux 145 vues 19 juin 2020.* (2020). [Video]. Retrieved from https://www.youtube.com/watch?v=SKNow5ZM0mE

Ed Curtis – YTexas

A native of New York, Ed Curtis has lived in Texas most of his life. Once a banking executive, he formed YTexas in 2013 to cater to an increasing number of businesses looking to operate in the Lone Star State. YTexas is an elite business network dedicated to supporting and connecting companies interested in relocating or expanding into Texas.[893]

As some of the top tech companies in the world begin operations in Texas, Curtis has become an influential voice. He is the author of *Why Texas: How Business Discovered the Lone Star State*, a book that celebrates and explains the phenomenon. The book contains exclusive interviews with 18 Texas-based Fortune 500 CEOs and business gurus.[894]

Curtis is known for promoting San Antonio as a biotech center and Austin's metro area as the new Silicon Valley,[895] and for helping businesses navigate the complexities of a move or expansion. As Texas becomes a hub of innovation and the site of pilot programs to develop smart cities, Curtis is one of the leaders in a trend that brought Samsung, Fotowatio Renewable Ventures Solar Farm, Apple, Tesla, SpaceX, and Charles Swab to the Lone Star State.[896]

By facilitating the formation of a cluster of cutting-edge tech companies in a booming region, Curtis is undoubtedly bringing us one step closer to the future. With Elon Musk building Tesla's gigafactory in Austin and launching rockets into space from Boca Chica, and Google opening a $50 million

---

893 YTexas - Elite Business Network. Retrieved 24 June 2021, from https://ytexas.com/about/

894 Curtis, E. (2019). *Why Texas: How Business Discovered The Lone Star State*. [Place of publication not identified]: BROWN Books PUB Group.

895 Curtis, E. (2019). *Why Texas: How Business Discovered The Lone Star State*. [Place of publication not identified]: BROWN Books PUB Group.

896 Boomtown or Bust? The Big Companies Getting Big Incentives to Move to Austin. (2021). Retrieved 24 June 2021, from https://www.kvue.com/article/money/economy/boomtown-2040/austin-travis-county-businesses-incentives-samsung-tesla-apple/269-f83ff2f3-56a3-439f-8194-bdb4f7ad1ad3

office in Houston,[897] we can safely say that if the new industrial revolution is happening anywhere, it is happening in Texas, and Ed Curtis's vision is already a reality.

Albert Han Ph.D.

Albert Tonghoon Han is a prestigious scholar in the fields of urban planning and environmental design. His research explores how policies impact the environment in fast-growing urban centers in North America and worldwide. Han's work also focuses on energy efficiency in cities and how to mitigate the effects of climate change. He has lectured and led multiple environmental projects at the University of Pennsylvania, the University of Calgary, and the Korea Environment Institute.[898]

Han's main research topics center on a vision of sustainability for the future of our country and our planet. They include:

- "Evaluating regional growth management and local land use policies for urban sprawl mitigation and land preservation."
- "Analyzing the effectiveness of environmental policies (e.g., building energy disclosure policies, waste management policies) for air pollution and climate change mitigation."
- "Enhancing public participation in decision-making process with data mining and online platforms."[899]

---

897 Taylor, B. (2021). Is Google Coming to Houston? What You Can Expect to See in May. Retrieved 24 June 2021, from https://www.click2houston.com/news/local/2021/03/30/is-google-coming-to-houston-what-you-can-expect-to-see-in-may/

898 Albert T. Han, Ph.D., Curriculum Vitae. (2021). Retrieved 24 June 2021, from http://cacp.utsa.edu/images/faculty/Albert_Han_CV_2019.pdf

899 Albert Han, Ph.D., Assistant Professor Urban and Regional Planning. Retrieved 24 June 2021, from http://cacp.utsa.edu/faculty-and-staff/albert-han-phd/

Currently an Assistant Professor at UTSA in San Antonio, Texas, Dr. Han is one of the leading thinkers on smart growth, land planning, and urban development.[900] His vision has a significant influence on decision-makers, especially in the fields of energy efficiency and urban planning.

Nikos A. Salingaros, Ph.D.

Nikos Salingaros is a mathematician and urbanist who develops modern architectural theories incorporating "adaptive design, biophilia, design complexity, neuro-design, and patterns."[901] He has taught urban design at universities in Italy, the Netherlands, and Mexico, and currently lectures at the University of Texas at San Antonio.

A mathematician who applies mathematical thinking to urban theory, Salingaros has often discussed the "artificial complexity"[902] of contemporary architecture, which leads to buildings that pollute the environment and deplete resources. His vision for modern buildings and modern cities is much more harmonious.

The Future of Built Environments

At the forefront of built environment analysis, Salingaros once wrote, "Simple yet powerful rules that govern complex systems shed light on human environments. Built environments that evolve freely over time develop a

900 Han, A. T., Graham, R., & Tsenkova, S. (2020). The Inside and Outside Game of Growth Management: Tracking Sprawl of Canada's Largest Metropolitan Areas. Journal of Planning Education and Research. https://doi.org/10.1177/0739456X20937335

901 Nikos A. Salingaros, Ph.D, Professor (Math and Architecture). Retrieved 24 June 2021, from http://cacp.utsa.edu/faculty-and-staff/rogelio-palomera-arias/

902 Houston, M. (2021). Architecture and The Environmental Impact of Artificial Complexity. Retrieved 24 June 2021, from https://www.archdaily.com/957549/architecture-and-the-environmental-impact-of-artificial-complexity

working complexity that is characteristic of both nature and traditional urban fabric. A city or portion of a city without sufficient variety is a sign of either decay or totalitarian control. This can be judged by how responsive a governing entity is to the complexity of human needs. By forcefully imposing design monotony, post-war governments and building regulations deprive human habitats of the requisite complexity needed to create livable environments."[903]

Salingaros has advocated the development of a new interactive urbanism in the megacities that dominate the global landscape today. As human ingenuity, "guided by an innate biological sense of connectivity and organized complexity" naturally creates living urban fabric, he believes that growth must be supported and guided, rather than suffocated by top-down control. "Nor should the built environment be sacrificed to twisted and useless trophies of a new global elite," he wrote in an influential paper.[904]

An Alfred P. Sloan Foundation Grant recipient, Salingaros was appointed by the previous U.S. administration to the President's Council on Improving Federal Civic Architecture, which later became the non-partisan American Committee on Federal Architecture. He is a faculty member at the University of Texas at San Antonio's Department of Mathematics.

One of the most respected visionary urbanists in the world, Salingaros has been ranked 11th among "The top 100 urban thinkers of all time"[905] and 26th among "The 100 most influential urbanists of all time."[906] He has also been listed among the top "50 visionaries who are changing your world."[907]

903 Salingaros, N. (2016). The "Law of Requisite Variety" and The Built Environment. *Journal Of Biourbanism*, *4*(1), 47-52.

904 Salingaros, N. (2016). The "Law of Requisite Variety" and The Built Environment. *Journal Of Biourbanism*, *4*(1), 47-52.

905 Fish, C. (2009). Nikos Salingaros Ranks 11th in Planetizen's Top 100 Urban Thinkers. Retrieved 24 June 2021, from https://www.utsa.edu/today/2009/11/salingaros.html

906 The 100 Most Influential Urbanists. (2017). Retrieved 24 June 2021, from https://www.planetizen.com/features/95189-100-most-influential-urbanists

907 50 Visionaries Who Are Changing Your World. (2009). Retrieved 24 June 2021, from https://content.utne.com/politics/50-visionaries-changing-your-world-hope-2009/

Michael Larranaga

A risk and process safety analyst and lecturer, Michael Larranaga has honed his expertise working in various sectors, including energy, healthcare, and semiconductor technology. He is the president of Dallas-based REM Risk Consultants. A reputable safety advisor, he has served on the Board of Scientific Counselors for the National Institute for Occupational Safety and Health, and as a member of the Department of Homeland Security First Responders Advisory Group.[908]

Perpetually on the cutting edge of technological developments, he has led a global risk management plan for semiconductor sites. Investigating everything from fire risks at propellant manufacturing plants to fire in nuclear power plants, he notoriously led a probe into the human factors that contributed to the BP/Macondo blowout.[909]

Larranaga was responsible for the first risk-based analysis of America's oil pipeline infrastructure, which identified several pressing issues.[910] He is one of the nation's leading specialists in risk factors related to climate change. In his vision, there is no greater risk facing humanity today.

"Climate change is a viable threat to U.S. homeland security," he wrote in an influential paper. "The nation is ill-prepared for risks presented by climate change. . . we have a duty to prepare for and securitize climate change a priori rather than a posteriori, as is typically the case for focusing events such as the nation's reactive response to the 9/11 terrorist attacks. Acting to prevent and mitigate future global warming now will result in lower societal costs and

908 Michael Larrañaga - R·E·M Risk Consultants. Retrieved 24 June 2021, from https://remrisk.com/about/michael-larranaga/

909 Smith, P., Kincannon, H., Lehnert, R., Wang, Q., & D. Larrañaga, M. (2013). Human Error Analysis of The Macondo Well Blowout. *Process Safety Progress*, *32*(2), 217-221. doi: 10.1002/prs.11604

910 Smith, P., Bennett, J., Darken, R., Lewis, T., & Larrañaga, M. (2014). Network-based Risk Assessment of The US Crude Pipeline Infrastructure. *International Journal of Critical Infrastructures*, *10*(1), 67. doi: 10.1504/ijcis.2014.059550

other benefits such as improvements in quality of life in the near term while providing for the prosperity of future generations and the preservation of America's legacy as a leader among nations in the long term."[911]

In the 2019 paper, co-authored with John Comiskey, the scientists applied game theory to climate change to evaluate the potential of preventive action plans. They concluded that whatever the outcome, whether climate change actually occurs or not, the safest bet is to assume it is going to happen, an attitude that might eventually help us avoid catastrophe. In other words, the risk of doing nothing about climate change is just too high. "Prudent risk management suggests that we should work to avoid the catastrophic outcome and prepare for and mitigate climate change,"[912] Larranaga and Comiskey wrote.

His background in industrial sectors and his government experience make Larranaga one of the most knowledgeable risk management experts in the country today. Because he has worked both in the public and private sectors, his vision encompasses corporate and societal benefits.

Dylan Ratigan

Dylan Ratigan is a *New York Times* best-selling author and a former *CNBC* and *MSNBC* show host. After commenting on global finance on cable news and running Corporate Finance at *Bloomberg*, he made a radical move and began focusing on financing and implementing the 'shift' in global infrastructure and resources.[913] To realize his vision of a sustainable

911 Larrañaga, M., & Comiskey, J. (2019). Climate Security: A Pre-Mortem Approach to A Sustainable Global Future. *Homeland Security Affairs Journal, 15.*

912 Larrañaga, M., & Comiskey, J. (2019). Climate Security: A Pre-Mortem Approach to A Sustainable Global Future. *Homeland Security Affairs Journal, 15.*

913 About Dylan Ratigan. Retrieved 24 June 2021, from https://dylanratigan.com/about-dylan-ratigan/

future, he founded Helical Holdings. The company is dedicated to creating a sun/water-powered portable unit that integrates water, food, energy, and communication systems.[914] He is also a partner at The SOIL Fund and Golden Triangle Industrial Hemp Company, among other innovative businesses.[915]

Ratigan believes humanity must adapt to avert disaster, but he also sees this moment of transformation as a tremendous opportunity to render local infrastructure more sustainable.

In June 2021, Ratigan's company U.S. Medical Glove closed a $63.6 million deal to provide nitrile gloves to the U.S. Department of Defense.[916]

After running for the House of Representatives in 2018,[917] Ratigan has continued to express his views on public policy, cryptocurrency, and climate change in his popular podcast "Truth or Skepticism."[918]

Steve Case

AOL's prescient founder has a track record that extends far beyond creating a corporation that went on to become the world's most valuable Internet company. Over the years, Steve Case has managed to stay on top of rising trends and futuristic investment opportunities. Over the last 15 years, he has been busy building and scaling Revolution, an investment firm that backs some of the world's most promising innovators. A frequent speaker on disruption, Case has invested in wildly successful startups, growth-stage, and

914 Helical Holdings' Sustainable Solutions — Saving The World, One Outpost at A Time. (2017). Retrieved 24 June 2021, from https://amhydro.com/helical-holdings/

915 About Dylan Ratigan. Retrieved 24 June 2021, from https://dylanratigan.com/about-dylan-ratigan/

916 U.S. Medical Glove Signs $63.6 Million Deal with Pentagon to Secure Domestic PPE. (2021). Retrieved 24 June 2021, from https://www.wfmz.com/news/pr_newswire/pr_newswire_health/u-s-medical-glove-signs-63-6-million-deal-with-pentagon-to-secure-domestic-ppe/article_eda47393-5698-5ee9-8c45-8540d60bf5f0.html

917 Dylan Ratigan — Ballotpedia. Retrieved 24 June 2021, from https://ballotpedia.org/Dylan_Ratigan

918 Truth or Skepticism. [Podcast]. Retrieved 24 June 2021, from https://podcasts.apple.com/us/podcast/sosnoff-ratigan-truth-or-skepticism-from-tastytrade/id1495112303

venture-stage companies, including Sweetgreen, Tempus, and DraftKings, through his company's various funds.[919]

In particular, Revolution's Rise of the Rest Seed Fund has given impulse to over 100 startups run by pioneering entrepreneurs across more than 50 American cities.[920] Having once delivered over 11,000 percent returns to stakeholders (during his time as AOL CEO), Case has never lost his passion for catalyzing innovation and helping visionary entrepreneurs. He has chaired the White House's Startup America Partnership and co-chaired the National Advisory Council on Innovation & Entrepreneurship.[921]

An influential voice in shaping policies to encourage entrepreneurship and innovation, he played a key role in passing the JOBS (Jumpstart Our Business Startups) Act and the Investing in Opportunities Act. Revolution's CEO is currently advocating immigration reform to facilitate access to top global talent and local policies that can favor the emergence of tech hubs and startup ecosystems beyond America's coastal areas.[922]

He was elected as Chair of the Smithsonian Institution's Board of Regents in 2019. Upon his nomination, he vowed to increase the powerful research organization's impact. "The Smithsonian is one of America's most treasured institutions," he said. "I look forward to working with Secretary Bunch and the Regents to implement the bold Smithsonian 2022 strategic plan, leaning into the future as a more innovative and agile organization that effectively deploys a digital-first strategy to showcase America at its very best."

Steve has written one of the golden age of entrepreneurship's most

---

919 Steve Case. Retrieved 24 June 2021, from http://technet.org/executive-council/steve-case

920 Revolution's Rise of The Rest (ROTR) Seed Fund. Retrieved 24 June 2021, from https://www.revolution.com/entity/rotr/

921 Steve Case — Chairman & CEO of Revolution. Retrieved 24 June 2021, from https://www.revolution.com/team-member/steve-case/

922 Clifford, C. (2014). Steve Case: JOBS Act Is Working, But D.C. Still Needs to Do More for Entrepreneurs. Retrieved 24 June 2021, from https://www.entrepreneur.com/article/232834

celebrated books, the *New York Times* bestseller, *The Third Wave: An Entrepreneur's Vision of the Future.*

The tech investor envisions a nation where venture capital can flow through different regions. When he implemented Revolution's Rise of the Rest in 2014, 75 percent of venture capital was sucked up by startups in Boston, New York, and Silicon Valley. The initiative was a spectacular success and helped companies in the heartland develop valuable innovations and products.

Case has lately focused on catalyzing the synergy between the digital world and the healthcare industry. Analysts have called Revolution "prophetic" for its remarkable ability to stay ahead and invest in the next big thing.[923]

Over the last few years, Revolution has attracted affluent and visionary investors like Jeff Bezos, hedge fund guru Ray Dalio, and Howard Schultz.[924]

Rise of The Rest's recent success stories include Des Moines-based Pear Deck, a remote learning company, and Kentucky-based AppHarvest, a vertical-farming company. Following ROTR's impulse, Pear Deck merged with GoGuardian, while AppHarvest went public and was valued at $1 billion.[925] The fund has been extremely successful in Texas, investing in blockbusters like BigCommerce, SpareFoot, and ZenBusiness.[926]

In line with his vision about decentralization across America, Steve Case's interests also include the potential for developing smart cities. In a recent interview, he discussed the future of America's urban centers. "It

923 Saporito, B. (2021). Steve Case Has Bet on Rust Belt Startups for Years. In the Pandemic, More VCs Have Joined Him. Retrieved 24 June 2021, from https://www.inc.com/magazine/202104/bill-saporito/steve-case-rise-of-the-rest-midwest-cities-startup-hub-ecosystem.html

924 Shafer, D. Jeff Bezos and Howard Schultz Join $150M Rise of The Rest Fund. Retrieved 24 June 2021, from https://seattlebusinessmag.com/economy/jeff-bezos-and-howard-schultz-join-150m-rise-rest-fund

925 Saporito, B. (2021). Steve Case Has Bet on Rust Belt Startups for Years. In the Pandemic, More VCs Have Joined Him. Retrieved 24 June 2021, from https://www.inc.com/magazine/202104/bill-saporito/steve-case-rise-of-the-rest-midwest-cities-startup-hub-ecosystem.html

926 Revolution's Rise of The Rest (ROTR) Seed Fund & Road Trip. Retrieved 24 June 2021, from https://www.revolution.com/entity/rotr/

really depends on what these cities do in the next 10 or 20 years. If they really embrace the idea that they have a shot at emerging as a thriving startup community and they rally together in a collaborative way, working with the mayors, governors, university presidents, CEOs of big local companies, and they all embrace startups, seeding and championing these companies, those are the cities that are gonna rise the most. . . [who] the leaders in the Third Wave [will be] has less to do with what I think, and more to do with what they do."[927]

Dan Doctoroff

The concept of smart cities is making headlines these days, but that was not the case when Dan Doctoroff, CEO of Sidewalk Labs, presciently wrote, "Advances in autonomous vehicles, ubiquitous connectivity, construction, and clean energy have the potential to make cities more affordable and sustainable. To accelerate these innovations, we should create an urban district as a living laboratory to improve quality of life. The district would offer a vision for other cities to follow, and a foundation for people to build on."[928]

Often ahead of his time, Doctoroff once shared his vision of integrated technologies capable of enhancing the quality of life in urban environments. "We've surveyed innovations across a range of domains—mobility, infrastructure, buildings, public space, social and community programs, even governance—that are available today or will be soon," he said in 2017. "We're convinced that by implementing a set of technologies—autonomous

927 *AOL Co-Founder Steve Case Predicts The Cities That Could Create The Next Silicon Valley | Inc.*. (2020). [Video]. Retrieved from Revolution's Rise of the Rest (ROTR) Seed Fund & Road Trip. Retrieved 24 June 2021, from https://www.revolution.com/entity/rotr/

928 Big Ideas for America's Infrastructure from Visionary Thinkers. (2017). Retrieved 24 June 2021, from https://time.com/4717811/american-infrastructure-big-ideas-from-visionary-thinkers/

vehicles, modular building construction, or new infrastructure systems—we can, for example, reduce cost of living by 15 percent. With new mobility services and radical mixed-use development that brings homes near work, we can give people back an hour in their day. With new materials and weather-mitigation technology, we can improve the usability of outdoor space in a cold climate. With adaptable loft structures and outcome-based codes, we can make buildings dramatically more flexible."[929]

Focused on improving built environments and urban life, Doctoroff's Sidewalk Labs is owned by Alphabet Inc. As some environmentalist movements advocate moving to rural areas, the entrepreneur firmly believes in people's desire to congregate and be together. "There are enormous benefits to being in dense places," he said in 2020.[930]

Doctoroff is a world leader in infrastructure planning and development. In 2020, Sidewalk Infrastructure Partners LLC, a Sidewalk Labs spinoff, won a contract[931] with the State of Michigan to develop a pioneering autonomous vehicle lane linking Detroit with Ann Arbor.[932]

An authoritative voice on autonomous vehicle developments, Doctoroff believes it is a big mistake to pour billions of dollars into developing autonomous vehicles while neglecting the infrastructure they require to operate safely in our cities.[933] In his view, the Michigan corridor has the potential to turn the State into a leading mobility innovator.

---

929 Dan Doctoroff on How We'll Realize The Promise of Urban Innovation. (2017). Retrieved 24 June 2021, from https://www.globalinfrastructureinitiative.com/article/dan-doctoroff-how-well-realize-promise-urban-innovation

930 Livengood, C. (2020). NYC's Doctoroff Bullish on Cities Bouncing Back from COVID-19. Retrieved 24 June 2021, from https://www.crainsdetroit.com/detroit-homecoming/nycs-doctoroff-bullish-cities-bouncing-back-covid-19

931 Frank, A. (2020). State Plans Detroit-to-Ann Arbor Mobility Corridor. Retrieved 24 June 2021, from https://www.crainsdetroit.com/mobility/state-plans-detroit-ann-arbor-mobility-corridor

932 Frank, A. (2020). Hopes Ride on Futuristic Connected Detroit-Ann Arbor Corridor. Retrieved 24 June 2021, from https://www.crainsdetroit.com/transportation/hopes-ride-futuristic-connected-detroit-ann-arbor-corridor

933 Irwin, J. (2019). No Light Rail, Then No Interest in Quayside AV Showcase, Says Sidewalk Labs. Retrieved 24 June 2021, from https://canada.autonews.com/technology/no-light-rail-then-no-interest-quayside-av-showcase-says-sidewalk-labs

Sidewalk Labs once partnered with Waterfront Toronto to develop the Canadian city's Eastern Waterfront. The projected district was touted as "the most innovative district in the world."[934] The ambitious project didn't come to fruition; the company cited economic uncertainty attributable to the COVID-19 pandemic. Torontonians were not entirely happy with the plans, likely due to rumors that the company would install sensors in the pavement and mine data for Google, Alphabet's parent company.[935]

Toronto's loss is Miami's win. In June 2021, Mana Common announced a partnership with Sidewalk Labs to design the infrastructure of a 24-acre development in Wynwood.[936] The endeavor promises to minimize carbon emissions and landfill waste, while modernizing transportation and parking through digital tools.

According to Mana Common's CEO, Moishe Mana, the partnership will boost "sustainability, innovation, and equity in Miami."[937]

The Sidewalk Labs CEO believes the implementation of smart cities will require visionary leadership. "Political leaders need the courage to overcome the natural resistance that comes with any changes," he said in an interview. "You need leaders who are capable of analyzing the problem, understanding the technology, and communicating the benefits and the costs in an honest way—and who are willing to take the political heat from some percentage of the population. That courage is unfortunately not as common as we'd like."[938]

---

934 Irwin, J. (2019). No light rail, Then No Interest in Quayside AV showcase, says Sidewalk Labs. Retrieved 24 June 2021, from https://canada.autonews.com/technology/no-light-rail-then-no-interest-quayside-av-showcase-says-sidewalk-labs

935 Shastri, A. (2020). Why The Sensor-Laden Rethink of Toronto's Waterfront Is in Trouble. Retrieved 24 June 2021, from https://www.forbes.com/sites/arunshastri/2020/03/19/why-the-sensor-laden-rethink-of-torontos-waterfront-is-in-trouble/?sh=51d9f9961970

936 Echikson, J. (2021). Moishe Mana, Sidewalk Labs Partner for Mana Wynwood Project in Miami. Retrieved 24 June 2021, from https://commercialobserver.com/2021/06/moishe-mana-sidewalk-labs-google-alphabet-wynwood/

937 Billionaire Teaming Up with Sidewalk Labs on Miami Development. (2021). Retrieved 24 June 2021, from https://www.bisnow.com/south-florida/news/commercial-real-estate/wynwood-mana-common-sidewalk-labs-109312

938 Doctoroff, D. (2017). Dan Doctoroff on How We'll Realize The Promise of Urban Innovation. Retrieved 24 June 2021, from https://www.mckinsey.com/business-functions/operations/our-insights/dan-doctoroff-on-how-well-realize-the-promise-of-urban-innovation

Dan Doctoroff's vision of infrastructure resembles a flexible platform capable of adopting many efficient applications. Cities should be a platform where traditional infrastructure combines with modular, replaceable, and upgradeable infrastructure to make up efficient and resilient urban systems. "Today, if you want to change or update a utility," he explains, "you have to dig up the streets, which is very disruptive to pedestrians and traffic and very expensive. But if you designed a city with accessible utility channels, you could make it easier and cheaper to upgrade utility networks and reserve space for new types of connections we haven't yet imagined."[939] Sounds a bit like Bazalgette's double-diameter pipelines. Undoubtedly, Doctoroff and his company will remain key players in the smart city sector over the next few years.

Maya Lin

Known for her massive environmental artworks, Maya Lin has often moved between art, architecture, design, and environmental innovation in a manner that defies categorization. Her artistic vision combines green urban solutions with aesthetic aspirations. She proposes reimagining landfills to create "beautiful landscaped earthworks" capable of recouping billions of dollars in resources.

Born in 1959, she is the author of Boundaries,[940] a visual and verbal sketchbook that also functions as a manifesto of her philosophy, based on a desire to constantly make people aware of their surroundings.

Lin has a Master of Architecture degree from Yale. Before graduating,

---

939 Doctoroff, D. (2017). Dan Doctoroff on How We'll Realize The Promise of Urban Innovation. Retrieved 24 June 2021, from https://www.mckinsey.com/business-functions/operations/our-insights/dan-doctoroff-on-how-well-realize-the-promise-of-urban-innovation

940 Lin, M. (2000). *Boundaries*. New York: Simon & Schuster.

she won a competition to design the Memorial for Vietnam Veterans in the nation's capital.[941] She has come a long way since this early success.

Lin's work exists at the intersection between landscape, history, memory, and language. Her artwork is part of prestigious collections at the National Gallery of Art; The Metropolitan Museum of Art; The Museum of Modern Art; and The Smithsonian Institution. As an architect, she was behind the Neilson Library renovation at Smith College in 2021 and the Novartis Institutes for Biomedical Research in 2015.[942]

Establishing a close dialogue between landscape and built environment, her designs emphasize sustainability and the integration of old and new construction. Her memorial piece "What is Missing" was a multimedia installation designed to raise awareness about biodiversity loss and climate change.

Featured in top media outlets like *The New Yorker* and *The New York Times*, she has also been the subject of an Academy Award-winning documentary.[943] She has received the National Medal of Arts and the Presidential Medal of Freedom.

In May 2021, Maya Lin completed an installation in Madison Square Park. Titled "Ghost Forest," the work will be on view until November. Part of her ongoing project, "What is Missing," the installation documents habitat loss caused by climate change, focusing on the dead forests that line the East Coast of the U.S.[944]

Featuring nearly 50 cedar trees ranging between 40 and 45 feet in height, the work explores the devastating effects of recent droughts on these imposing trees. All of the trees in the installation were set up in the park after dying of salt-water intrusion in New Jersey.

---

941 Blakemore, E. (2017). This 21-Year-Old College Student Designed The Vietnam Veterans Memorial. Retrieved 24 June 2021, from https://www.history.com/news/the-21-year-old-college-student-who-designed-the-vietnam-memorial

942 Maya Lin. Retrieved 24 June 2021, from https://www.mayalinstudio.com/about

943 Maya Lin: A Strong Clear Vision — IMDb. Retrieved 24 June 2021, from https://www.imdb.com/title/tt0110480/

944 Maya Lin: Ghost Forest — Madison Square Park Conservancy. (2021). Retrieved 24 June 2021, from https://madisonsquarepark.org/art/exhibitions/maya-lin-ghost-forest/

The work is a powerful way of communicating, in a poetic way, the unrelenting impact of sea level rise, storm surge, and reduced CO2 absorption on natural habitats. By raising awareness about climate change and designing sustainable built environments, Maya Lin has placed herself at the forefront of architectural planning and environmentalist thinking.

Sarah Rosen Wartell

Sarah Rosen Wartell has presided over the Urban Institute since 2012. Under her leadership, the Institute has vowed to "leverage cutting-edge technology and data science, understand and confront structural racism, and deliver timely, relevant, and actionable research to communities, capitals, boardrooms, and wherever innovators are pursuing bold ideas."[945]

A former deputy director of the National Economic Council and founding COO of the Center for American Progress, she has focused on housing markets, community development, and urban innovation throughout her career. An influential figure in both the private and public sectors, she serves on the board of Bank of America's National Community Advisory Council, Enterprise Community Partners, and The Sadie Collective.[946]

A long-time affordable housing advocate, in early 2021, Rosen Wartell celebrated Amazon's announcement that it would invest $2.1 billion in the construction of more than 20,000 housing units for moderate- to low-income families in the Puget Sound region; Arlington, Virginia; and Nashville, Tennessee.[947]

---

945 Sarah Rosen Wartell. Retrieved 24 June 2021, from https://www.urban.org/author/sarah-rosen-wartell

946 Sarah Rosen Wartell | Enterprise Community Partners. Retrieved 24 June 2021, from https://www.enterprisecommunity.org/about/our-people/sarah-rosen-wartell

947 Amazon Creates $2 Billion Fund for Affordable Housing in Wash. State, Tenn., Virginia. (2021). Retrieved 24 June 2021, from https://komonews.com/news/local/amazon-creates-2-billion-fund-to-preserve-affordable-housing

As other visionaries imagine the smart homes of tomorrow, the Urban Institute's President is intent on making them affordable and creating benefits for urban communities.

"In booming cities across the U.S., many apartment buildings affordable for teachers, healthcare providers, transit workers, and others with modest incomes are increasingly being redeveloped into luxury apartments, causing displacement and reducing housing options for working families," she told reporters. "Investments like those announced today by Amazon help preserve these existing buildings and maintain moderate rent levels [for] moderate- and low-income families."[948]

During her tenure at the Urban Institute, the policymaker has launched the Regional Housing Framework in Washington's metropolitan region. Her work has focused on how cities can manage rapid growth and capitalize on the opportunities it brings.

"Cities are where local decision-making happens," she said in a 2019 interview. "Cities are places where progress can be made, where we don't fall into our normal ideological sides of the equation as quickly and where we truly see innovation."[949]

Antonio Grasso

Italian innovator Antonio Grasso is the CEO of Digital Business Innovation and the Internet of things (IoT) software innovator at semiconductor giant Intel. He has been involved in catapulting startups and scaling up established

948 Amazon creates $2 billion Fund for Affordable Housing in Wash. state, Tenn., Virginia. (2021). Retrieved 24 June 2021, from https://komonews.com/news/local/amazon-creates-2-billion-fund-to-preserve-affordable-housing

949 Haynie, D. (2019). Urban Institute President on How Cities Can Manage Rapid Growth. Retrieved 24 June 2021, from https://www.usnews.com/news/cities/articles/2019-04-19/urban-institute-president-on-how-rapid-growth-poses-risks-for-cities

companies' emerging technology operations. He has collaborated with Huawei, Oracle, IBM, Automation Anywhere, and Ericsson, among others.[950]

Boasting 200,000 Twitter followers, Grasso is a voice that resonates across the global emerging-technology landscape. A digital transformation guru, he contributes to the global discussion about the role of Artificial Intelligence, cybersecurity, the Internet of Things, and blockchain in the 21st century.[951]

As coveted startup mentor and UN Global Entreps Award juror, he believes the digital revolution requires a cultural change. He has written about the potential of the synergistic relationship between automation infrastructure and 5G connectivity.

His vision for the cities of the future features driverless cars and buses that communicate with each other in real time, fuel-efficient vehicles, widespread car-sharing, and safer roadways. "Sharing the car," Grasso explains, "does not mean giving up comforts; it means sharing one's passion and commitment for a sustainable future and contributing to greater liveability of urban spaces."[952]

The Digital Business Innovation CEO has a lengthy track record in the integration of innovative technologies and healthcare. Having developed pioneering medical history software in the 1980s, he is now a passionate advocate of telehealth. "Bridging the divide between patients and clinicians," he wrote, "modern technology has enabled whole-person care by helping physicians to look beyond mere symptomatology."[953]

Grasso believes augmented medicine infrastructure holds tremendous potential to improve human life. "Imagine using a machine capable of

950 Antonio Grasso Entrepreneur, Technologist, Sustainability Passionate. Retrieved 24 June 2021, from https://it.linkedin.com/in/antonio-grasso-0544007

951 Antonio Grasso on Twitter. Retrieved 24 June 2021, from https://twitter.com/antgrasso

952 Lunden, C. (2021). 5G and A World without Traffic Jams. Retrieved 24 June 2021, from https://www.ericsson.com/en/blog/2021/1/5g-a-world-without-traffic-jams

953 Grasso, A. (2020). Telehealth: The New Normal for Patient Care. Retrieved 24 June 2021, from https://www.insight.tech/5g/telehealth-the-new-normal-for-patient-care?utm_source=twitter&utm_medium=influencer-twitter&utm_campaign=Q2-antonio-grasso

capturing, storing, and transmitting clinical data, diagnostic images, and audio, and then integrating everything into a single digital platform," he proposes. "Now imagine that this same platform can be used to facilitate consultations and deliver rapid results to you anytime, anywhere." This is the basic concept of augmented medicine.[954]

At Intel, he has explored the potential of Medpod Inc.,[955] a company that develops a variety of cloud-based services that enable providers to deliver medicine remotely.

Grasso's research also encompasses the sustainability space. A self-proclaimed environmental advocate and sustainability enthusiast, he has spoken in favor of using digital fire-monitoring systems to prevent forest fires and protect the environment from some of the impacts of climate change.[956] He is a frequent speaker and advisor on various AI-related issues.

His vision for the coming decades involves humans and artificial intelligence working together "to build a better future for us and our planet."[957]

Brian Dillard

San Antonio's Chief Innovation Officer, Brian Dillard, dropped out of the University of Texas at San Antonio and enlisted in the Air Force in 2002. He went on to work in the cybersecurity sector, which put him on track to

954 Grasso, A. (2020). Telehealth: The New Normal for Patient Care. Retrieved 24 June 2021, from https://www.insight.tech/5g/telehealth-the-new-normal-for-patient-care?utm_source=twitter&utm_medium=influencer-twitter&utm_campaign=Q2-antonio-grasso

955 Medpod Health (Home) — Medpod. Retrieved 24 June 2021, from https://medpodhealth.com/

956 Grasso, A. (2021). AI Fire Detection: Computer Vision Guards The Forest. Retrieved 24 June 2021, from https://www.insight.tech/content/ai-fire-detection-computer-vision-guards-the-forest

957 Grasso, A. (2021). AI Fire Detection: Computer Vision Guards The Forest. Retrieved 24 June 2021, from https://www.insight.tech/content/ai-fire-detection-computer-vision-guards-the-forest

become the man charged with turning San Antonio into a "smart city."[958]

Known as SmartSA, the city's effort involves collaborations with CPS Energy, San Antonio Water System, and other relevant agencies. Dillard's first posting at the city was that of Smart City Administrator. His vision is centered on what communities need and what technology can do for them.[959]

San Antonio has designated three pilot areas to test out smart city initiatives, including collaborating with CPS Energy to implement air quality, temperature, and flood risk detection through smart streetlight installation. If some of these initiatives succeed, they will soon spread to the rest of San Antonio.

"We're constantly trying to avoid the smart-city buzzword because we don't want to be bucketed into that," Dillard explains. "Our projects, our initiatives are really people-driven. That's why our smart-city program is a challenge-driven model; it's not tech-driven. We're trying to solve issues that affect our communities here in San Antonio."[960]

For Dillard, innovation must be community-driven rather than technology-driven. His office's projects aim to make the city more efficient with solar panel installations, the addition of sensors to solid-waste vehicles, and AI on traffic cameras. During the pandemic, San Antonio Innovation has also worked to bridge the digital divide that exists in the community. "We didn't want to go down this path of calling ourselves a smart city," Dillard

---

958 *TechTonics: Brian Dillard on Making San Antonio 'Smart,' One Conversation at a Time.* San Antonio Report. Retrieved 2 September 2021, from https://sanantonioreport.org/techtonics-brian-dillard-on-making-san-antonio-smart-one-conversation-at-a-time/.

959 TechTonics: Brian Dillard on Making San Antonio 'Smart,' One Conversation at a Time. (2019). Retrieved 24 June 2021, from https://sanantonioreport.org/techtonics-brian-dillard-on-making-san-antonio-smart-one-conversation-at-a-time/

960 TechTonics: Brian Dillard on Making San Antonio 'Smart,' One Conversation at a Time. (2019). Retrieved 24 June 2021, from https://sanantonioreport.org/techtonics-brian-dillard-on-making-san-antonio-smart-one-conversation-at-a-time/

explains. "When a quarter of our residents don't have access to the internet in 2020." Through an initiative called Connected Beyond the Classroom, San Antonio enabled 20,000 low-income area students to access the Internet from their homes.[961]

Other pioneering initiatives projected by Dillard's office include plans to update the city's aging energy infrastructure and diversify transportation by installing sensors in scooters and other micromobility devices, and improving the biking infrastructure. One of the fastest to materialize among many projects has been the installation of interactive digital kiosks that offer directions and WiFi connectivity. Through the SmartSA Sandbox program, the City of San Antonio holds events that showcase smart technology, giving the public the opportunity to test it out.[962]

Sally Eaves

Dr Sally Eaves is a blockchain specialist dedicated to the implementation of emergent technology solutions for the betterment of society. She is a senior policy advisor for the Global Foundation for Cyber Studies and Research and a member of the Forbes Technology Council.

A global influencer on smart tech, she focuses on new thinking about disruptive technologies and innovations.

Imagining 2050, Eaves anticipates that smart cities will be front and center when the number of people who live in cities surpasses six billion, corresponding to over 65 percent of the global population. She envisages an "increasingly urban, data-driven, and hybrid world" that seamlessly

961 *City of the Future: Interview with Brian Dillard, Chief Innovation Officer, City of San Antonio.* (2021). [Video]. Retrieved from https://www.youtube.com/watch?v=grSoagxZJ0Q

962 Smart SA — Office of Innovation. Retrieved 24 June 2021, from https://www.sanantonio.gov/smartsa

integrates the physical and the virtual. For the blockchain consultant, the concept of smart cities will be instrumental in reaching the UN's 2030 sustainable development targets.[963]

In her vision of a smart city, "sensor-rich, fully automated buildings, intuitive parking, and traffic-management systems, and utilities" come together to "make our everyday easier to navigate and to optimize, while reducing frictions such as ageing or legacy IT."[964]

In a smart city, as Sally Eaves conceives it, there are systems in place that anticipate what we want to buy, monitor our health, prescribe needed maintenance for our devices, and keep us perpetually informed and entertained. Autonomous taxis and minibuses help reduce traffic and pollution, and there is autonomy-ready infrastructure all around us to prevent accidents and optimize transportation.[965]

Over the next couple of decades, Eaves believes urban populations will greatly benefit from integrating the Internet of Things, 5G wireless, AI, cloud infrastructure, big data analytics, blockchain, autonomous mobility, robotics, biometrics, voice activation, and delivery drones. In her vision, the ultimate goal of these technological developments should always be community, inclusion, universal access, and diversity.[966]

Privacy issues pertaining to the use of sensed data have long preoccupied Eaves, who believes communities must be involved in the transformation process, and views trust and transparency as key elements for the successful implementation of smart city infrastructure.

---

963 Eaves, S. (2020). Forecasting A Decade Where Smart Tech Becomes The Norm. Retrieved 24 June 2021, from https://www.irishexaminer.com/opinion/commentanalysis/arid-30974095.html

964 Technology as Empowerment 5G for Good. (2020). Retrieved 24 June 2021, from https://www.linkedin.com/pulse/technology-empowerment-5g-good-sally-eaves

965 Eaves, S. (2020). From Smart City to Smart Society. Retrieved 24 June 2021, from https://www.citiesabc.com/smart-city-smart-society/

966 Harwood, S., & Eaves, S. (2020). Conceptualising Technology, Its Development and Future: The six genres of technology. *Technological Forecasting And Social Change*, *160*, 120174. doi: 10.1016/j.techfore.2020.120174

Sally Eaves envisages the implementation of smartness as a means to enhance "equality of digital, economic, and educational opportunities, alongside mobility and sustainability." In this visionary thinker's view, "Smart is also about enabling informed choice, such as the cheapest, fastest, or most eco-friendly solution."[967]

---

967 Eaves, S. (2020). Forecasting a Decade Where Smart Tech Becomes The Norm. Retrieved 24 June 2021, from https://www.irishexaminer.com/opinion/commentanalysis/arid-30974095.html

CHAPTER 35:

Texas Leading the Nation

"I love Texas because Texas is future-oriented, because Texans think anything is possible. Texans think big"
—Senator Phil Gramm

Texas has consistently ranked as the top U.S. state to do business over the better part of the last two decades. In 2021, it topped Chief Executive's Best and Worst States for Business list for the 17th year in a row.[968] The ranking is the result of a nationwide poll of CEOs, who reportedly chose Texas for its tax policy, regulatory climate, and talent availability. Meanwhile, affluent states like New York and California are lagging.

The pandemic has made CEOs "more open than before to examining new locations," and a surprising amount of them are looking at Texas.[969]

With abundant sunshine and scarce taxes, Florida was chosen as the second-best state to do business. But no jurisdiction can beat Texas. The Lone Star State is thinking ahead, and business owners know it. With a friendly regulatory framework and several pilot programs to implement cutting-edge technology, Texas has become a magnet for innovative tech companies and top talent.

---

968 2021 Best & Worst States for Business. (2021). Retrieved 21 July 2021, from https://chiefexecutive.net/2021-best-worst-for-states-business/

969 Blankley, B. (2021). CEO Magazine: Texas, Florida Best States For Business; California, New York, Illinois The Worst. Retrieved 21 July 2021, from https://www.thecentersquare.com/national/ceo-magazine-texas-florida-best-states-for-business-california-new-york-illinois-the-worst/article_209d1b6a-a8ef-11eb-b9b8-772dec4e3f44.html

Solar Power Boom

As solar power begins to dominate the energy sector, Texas is taking steps to get in on the trend. While the state's installed capacity is still relatively low, it is growing rapidly. Over a short period of time, solar went from nothing to becoming the fifth contributor to the power mix for Texas.[970] Today, only California surpasses Texas, which has become a leader in solar developments.

For the summer of 2021, the Electric Reliability Council of Texas (ERCOT)[971] expects to generate a staggering 3.3 gigawatts through solar plants. ERCOT has plans to connect solar farms with 92 gigawatts capacity to the state's power grid.

According to Husch Blackwell's Chris Reeder, "There's been a huge uptick. . . the ERCOT figures will show that as recently as a few years ago solar was such a very tiny sliver of our overall resource mix that they didn't even bother to break it out separately from the 'other' category."[972]

ERCOT manages a grid that provides 90 percent of Texas' electric load. In 2020, natural gas contributed about 50 percent of power generation, followed by wind with 23 percent, coal with 18 percent, nuclear with 11 percent, and solar with 2.3 percent.[973]

Ten years ago, solar was not even mentioned in the mix but lumped together with other negligible energy sources. Between 2015 and 2020, solar

970 State of Texas Energy Sector Risk Profile. (2021). Retrieved 21 July 2021, from https://www.energy.gov/sites/prod/files/2016/09/f33/TX_Energy%20Sector%20Risk%20Profile.pdf

971 Saul, J., & Eckhouse, B. (2021). Texas Renewables Defy GOP Backlash with $20 Billion in Projects. Retrieved 21 July 2021, from https://www.bloomberg.com/news/features/2021-06-09/texas-renewables-defy-gop-backlash-with-20-billion-in-projects

972 Solar Poised to Shine in Texas After Steady Growth. (2021). Retrieved 21 July 2021, from https://www.law360.com/articles/1371897/solar-poised-to-shine-in-texas-after-steady-growth

973 State of Texas Energy Sector Risk Profile. (2021). Retrieved 21 July 2021, from https://www.energy.gov/sites/prod/files/2016/09/f33/TX_Energy%20Sector%20Risk%20Profile.pdf

installed capacity experienced a 20-fold increase. Meanwhile, wind capacity barely doubled over the same period.[974]

According to the Solar Energy Industry Association, in 2020, solar energy powered over one million homes in Texas.[975] Solar energy's meteoric rise in Texas has a lot to do with the state's newly acquired standing as a tech hub. As more businesses and people move to Texas, the electricity demand grows, and solar has helped the state bridge the gap.

Solar is profiting from the distribution infrastructure originally built for wind energy. The reason solar power plants have multiplied faster than wind farms is no mystery. They take up less space and can be built virtually anywhere, unlike wind farms, which require certain atmospheric conditions. Homeowners often place solar panels on their rooftops, but more and more small solar farms are being built in the vicinity of cities.

When talking about energy, cost always plays a key role. In the case of solar, the reduction of generation costs over the last few years has dramatically favored developments in Texas. According to Lazard's most recent Levelized Cost of Energy Analysis, "the cost of renewable energy continues to decline," and solar remains very cost-competitive in the current market.[976]

Energy Price Comparison

- Utility-scale solar: $31/MWh
- Utility-scale wind: $26/MWh
- Utility-scale coal: $41/MWh

974 Solar Poised to Shine in Texas After Steady Growth. (2021). Retrieved 21 July 2021, from https://www.law360.com/articles/1371897/solar-poised-to-shine-in-texas-after-steady-growth

975 Texas Solar. (2021). Retrieved 21 July 2021, from https://www.seia.org/state-solar-policy/texas-solar

976 Levelized Cost of Energy and of Storage. (2020). Retrieved 21 July 2021, from https://www.lazard.com/perspective/levelized-cost-of-energy-and-levelized-cost-of-storage-2020/

- Utility-scale nuclear: $29/MWh
- Combined-cycle gas: $28/MWh[977]

In 2009, it cost $394 to generate 1 MWh with unsubsidized solar. By 2020, the cost had decreased by 90 percent.[978] Texas has been well-positioned to take advantage of solar power's potential, and it will continue to do so.

Another reason solar has outpaced wind in Texas is that the cost of wind power generation has declined more slowly. While the cost of solar went down about 11 percent annually over the last five years, the cost of wind energy has only decreased by 5 percent. The reduction of storage costs has also played an essential role in Texas' solar boom.[979] In fact, storage technology development has become a business opportunity that Texas has eagerly seized.

According to energy investments specialist George Humphrey, "Texas historically was kind of behind in solar development, but as solar panel costs have plummeted over the last decade, now that the costs have come down so much, they're basically competitive with fossil fuel generation. The cost now to install solar is so cheap that it's cost-competitive or maybe cheaper than gas generation."[980]

Houston as A Tech Hub

As the Internet of Things, AI, and automation transform the world, Texas wants to stay on the cutting edge, and so does Houston. In the state's

977 Levelized Cost of Energy and of Storage. (2020). Retrieved 21 July 2021, from https://www.lazard.com/perspective/levelized-cost-of-energy-and-levelized-cost-of-storage-2020/

978 Renewable Electricity. (2021). Retrieved 21 July 2021, from https://www.usitc.gov/publications/332/pub5154.pdf

979 Renewable Power Generation Costs in 2019. (2020). Retrieved 21 July 2021, from https://www.irena.org/publications/2020/Jun/Renewable-Power-Costs-in-2019

980 Solar Poised to Shine in Texas after Steady Growth. (2021). Retrieved 21 July 2021, from https://www.law360.com/articles/1371897/solar-poised-to-shine-in-texas-after-steady-growth

former capital, old department stores are being converted into startup incubators. For instance, a 300,000-square-foot complex that used to house Nabisco houses innovators working for companies like Johnson & Johnson and AT&T.[981] The phenomenon has been described as an "industrial resurrection" that is reinventing past industrial glories as hubs of futuristic tech development.

Once at the heart of the oil boom, Houston is flourishing thanks to technology projects. In 2022, Hewlett Packard Enterprise (HPE) will open its new headquarters there, a 439,000-square-foot building that will house 3,000 employees.[982] This will make HPE the biggest employer in the fourth largest city in the country.

Houston's strategy to attract successful tech companies involves great technology programs at major local universities, investments in medical research, and a favorable regulatory climate for startups to blossom.

The oil town of years ago is no more. As Austin's booming tech companies focus on software and app development and San Antonio attracts data centers, Houston has tried to position itself as a provider of hardware solutions.

High-profile relocations and expansions to Texas include Oracle and Tesla.[983] While other states lost some of their strategic positions due to the pandemic, the relocation of savvy tech professionals from California to Texas accelerated a trend that was already in motion.

According to Greater Houston Partnership's Bob Harvey, Houston's tech sector traditionally lagged behind other regions of Texas. "Houston

---

981 Swartz, J. (2021). Houston Is Winning The Competition to Establish Tech Hubs in Texas. Retrieved 21 July 2021, from https://www.marketwatch.com/story/in-the-oil-boomtown-of-houston-tech-is-building-a-new-home-in-the-shell-of-an-older-economy-11625782190

982 In 2022, Hewlett Packard Enterprise (HPE) Will Open Its New Headquarters There, A 439,000-Square-Foot Building That Will House 3,000 Employees.

983 Oracle Joins HPE, Tesla in Moving HQ to Texas. (2020). Retrieved 21 July 2021, from https://www.crn.com/news/cloud/oracle-joins-hpe-tesla-in-moving-hq-to-texas

was always an industrial, major organization city," Harvey explains. "What we didn't do well was startups. Houston is now showing up in lists of tech talent."[984]

Fostering Talent

The Houston area is home to three major higher education institutions: Rice University, the University of Houston, and Texas A&M University. As major companies relocate to the region, they bring in top tech talent, creating a synergy with the people graduating from the universities' tech-related programs. In fact, there are more tech workers in non-tech companies in Houston than anywhere else in America.[985] Amazon, Alphabet's Google Cloud, and Microsoft's Azure are among the many top corporations flooding Texas with tech talent.

Today, Houston has everything to attract startups and established tech companies alike. The cost of living is low, there are plenty of engineers available, and the health industry is thriving. Many companies have jumped at the opportunity of relocating to Houston, including Italian robotics company Roboze, which services the aerospace industry; Nuro, an autonomous driving unicorn; Bill.com, a fintech company; and Solugen, which cleans water for the petrochemical industry.[986]

Houston's success can also be observed in the amount of venture capital local companies are attracting. In 2016, the city attracted only $284 million.

---

984 Swartz, J. (2021). Houston Is Winning The Competition to Establish Tech Hubs in Texas. Retrieved 21 July 2021, from https://www.marketwatch.com/story/in-the-oil-boomtown-of-houston-tech-is-building-a-new-home-in-the-shell-of-an-older-economy-11625782190

985 Swartz, J. (2021). Houston Is Winning The Competition to Establish Tech Hubs in Texas. Retrieved 21 July 2021, from https://www.marketwatch.com/story/in-the-oil-boomtown-of-houston-tech-is-building-a-new-home-in-the-shell-of-an-older-economy-11625782190

986 It Was Houston, Not Austin, Who Won The Competition to Set Up A Tech Hub in Texas. (2021). Retrieved 21 July 2021, from https://exbulletin.com/tech/1049133/

By 2020, it was already attracting $753 million, and the number will likely increase in 2021.[987]

While Austin competes with Houston in attracting business relocations and expansions, there is a silver lining; Austin's boom has made it increasingly expensive, and Houston offers many of the same benefits at a lower cost.

In San Francisco, the average apartment costs over $3,035 per month. In Austin, the average rental is $1,539, but in Houston, it's only $1,172.[988] In the future, if Texas keeps developing, the gap will become smaller. Today, however, with similar salaries across many locations, it makes total sense for tech professionals to move to Houston.

Salary Comparison: San Francisco/Austin/Houston

While rentals and real estate are significantly cheaper in Texas than in California, the variation for salaries is typically smaller. The most shocking difference is perhaps the median price of homes: $1,355,200 in San Francisco[989] and $371,900 in Austin.[990] Looking at the hard data is very revealing when trying to understand why Texas has become so popular among tech professionals.

Average Salaries in San Francisco[991]

- Senior Software Engineer: $153,000

987 It Was Houston, Not Austin, Who Won The Competition to Set Up A Tech Hub in Texas. (2021). Retrieved 21 July 2021, from https://exbulletin.com/tech/1049133/

988 Rentcafe US Market. (2021). Retrieved 21 July 2021, from https://www.rentcafe.com/

989 Richardson, B. (2019). From Condos to Mansions, What $1 Million Gets You in Today's Housing Market. Retrieved 21 July 2021, from https://www.forbes.com/sites/brendarichardson/2019/10/17/from-condos-to-mansions-what-1-million-gets-you-in-todays-housing-market/?sh=7ef17d5856af

990 4 Reasons Austin Is Poised to Become Tech's Hottest New Hub. (2021). Retrieved 21 July 2021, from https://builtin.com/company-culture/austin-tech-hub

991 Average Salary in San Francisco, California. (2021). Retrieved 21 July 2021, from https://www.payscale.com/research/US/Location=San-Francisco-CA/Salary

- Senior Product Manager: $153,000
- Product Manager, Software: $125,000
- Data Scientist: $124,000
- Software Engineer: $123,000
- Project Manager (General). $93,000
- Operations Manager. $81,000

Average Salaries in Austin[992]

- Senior Software Engineer: $118,000
- Software Engineer: $88,000
- Project Manager, (General): $76,000
- Software Developer: $77,000
- Marketing Manager: $64,000
- Operations Manager: $62,000
- Account Manager: $53,000

Average Salaries in Houston[993]

- Project Manager (General): $83,000
- Software Engineer: $83,000
- Mechanical Engineer: $79,000
- Project Engineer: $79,000
- HR Manager: $76,000
- Operations Manager: $73,000

---

992 Houston, Texas Salary. (2021). Retrieved 21 July 2021, from https://www.payscale.com/research/US/Location=Houston-TX/Salary

993 Houston, Texas Salary. (2021). Retrieved 21 July 2021, from https://www.payscale.com/research/US/Location=Houston-TX/Salary

- Office Manager: $52,000

Houston at the Edge

Since Houston's startup incubators often focused on climate change and medicine research, the city's ambitions as a tech hub focus on a global scale. Innovation centers like Greentown Labs and Texas Medical Center, home to some of the most advanced cancer research on the planet, are dedicated to solving some of humanity's most pressing problems.

It is hard to predict where the next planet-saving, disruptive technology will come from, but I wouldn't be surprised if it came from Houston.

Fortune 1000 Companies Headquartered in Texas

These are the 95 FORTUNE 1000 companies that have their headquarters in Texas in 2021.[994] The list includes some of the nation's largest employers.

Company	Number of Employees
Yum China Holdings	271,000
AT&T	230,760
Dell Technologies	158,000
Oracle	135,000
American Airlines Group	102,700
CBRE Group	100,000
Tenet Healthcare	97,900
Exxon Mobil	72,000

994 Texas Facts & Faqs: Fortune 1000 Companies Based in Texas. (2021). Retrieved 21 July 2021, from https://ytexas.com/facts-faqs/texas-facts-faqs-fortune-1000-companies-based-in-texas-2021/

McKesson	70,000
Brinker International	62,200
Hewlett Packard Enterprise	59,400
Sysco	57,000
Southwest Airlines	56,537
Baker Hughes	55,000
Jacobs Engineering Group	53,500
Waste Management	48,250
Kimberly-Clark	46,000
Fluor	43,717
Halliburton	40,000
USAA	35,935
Quanta Services	35,800
Charles Schwab	32,000
Texas Instruments	30,000
Sally Beauty Holdings	30,000
KBR	29,000
Michaels	28,000
NOV	27,631
Builders FirstSource	26,000
GameStop	22,000
Service Corp. International	20,319
Academy Sports and Outdoors	16,500
Flowserve	16,000
Resideo Technologies	14,700
Rent-A-Center	14,320
Phillips 66	14,300
Group 1 Automotive	12,337
Occidental Petroleum	11,800

Nexstar Media Group 11,749
Energy Transfer 11,421
Commercial Metals 11,297
Comfort Systems USA 11,100
Kinder Morgan 10,524
Primoris Services 10,414
Lennox International 10,300
Valero Energy 9,964
Mr. Cooper Group 9,800
D.R. Horton 9,716
ConocoPhillips 9,700
iHeartMedia 9,588
CenterPoint Energy 9,541
Trinity Industries 9,375
Westlake Chemical 9,220
Huntsman 9,000
Comerica 7,681
Celanese 7,658
Copart 7,600
Core-Mark Holding 7,534
Rackspace Technology 7,200
Enterprise Products Partners 7,130
ChampionX 6,600
Arcosa 6,410
Rush Enterprises 6,307
Stewart Information Services 5,800
Kirby 5,400
Vistra 5,365
Hilltop Holdings 4,925

Crown Castle International	4,900
Clear Channel Outdoor Holdings.	4,800
Atmos Energy	4,694
American National Group	4,600
Plains GP Holdings	4,400
HollyFrontier	3,891
Insperity	3,600
Globe Life	3,261
AMN Healthcare Services	3,000
EOG Resources	2,900
Digital Realty Trust	2,878
Valhi	2,784
MRC Global	2,600
Targa Resources	2,372
APA	2,272
Match Group	1,890
Pioneer Natural Resources	1,853
Marathon Oil	1,672
Cheniere Energy	1,519
Par Pacific Holdings	1,403
EnLink Midstream	1,069
Western Midstream Partners	1,045
Darling Ingredients	1,000
LGI Homes	938
Southwestern Energy	900
Diamondback Energy	732
Crestwood Equity Partners	731
Murphy Oil	675
Range Resources	533

The list keeps growing, and the pandemic has contributed to this. Now, analysts are saying that as the global health crisis subsides, corporations are unlikely to stop flocking to Texas and other attractive U.S. markets, and tech workers who moved there while working remotely are unlikely to return to Silicon Valley.

Whether they moved to Texas to work for the Fortune 1000 companies above or not, workers have now gotten used to the lower costs and hassle-free lifestyle the Lone Star State has to offer.

According to a spokesperson for Workato, "Living costs have always been a huge issue in Silicon Valley. . . That is probably the most common reason people left, but there are many other factors that draw people away from the area: pace of life, family, lifestyle, and more."[995]

In a way, Silicon Valley lost some of its allure, now that Texas is offering the same opportunities combined with lower taxation and many other benefits. The fact that Texas has no income tax has played a crucial role in attracting Silicon Valley exiles. Today, it is up to tech employers to create great working and living environments in the vicinity of their offices and facilities, wherever they are located.

San Jose's Planning Commissioner believes the people who left Silicon Valley during the pandemic will not return. "They enjoy a great quality of life in rural areas and low housing costs," he said in an interview. "Some will come back since they pursue leadership positions. However, since most employees are not executive management, it is not necessary."[996]

Considering you can get double the space for half the price when you

995 Nicastro, D. (2021). In A Post-COVID World Will Silicon Valley Remain The Top US Tech Hub. Retrieved 21 July 2021, from https://www.reworked.co/customer-experience/can-silicon-valley-remain-the-top-us-tech-center-in-a-post-covid-world/

996 Nicastro, D. (2021). In A Post-COVID World Will Silicon Valley Remain The Top US Tech Hub. Retrieved 21 July 2021, from https://www.reworked.co/customer-experience/can-silicon-valley-remain-the-top-us-tech-center-in-a-post-covid-world/

buy a home in Austin as opposed to San Jose, it is clear that many engineers and developers are going to opt for first-rate cities like Austin and Houston, and they will not even miss the California weather.

Austin's Race to Space

Elon Musk's Tesla and SpaceX are running multiple operations in Texas, not to mention that Musk himself has relocated to the Lone Star State. Now, SpaceX is planning to open a factory in Austin. The facility will produce satellite dishes, Wi-Fi routers, and mounting hardware for the company's Starlink project.[997]

As usual, SpaceX has been very secretive about where or when the factory will be built, but it recently started advertising jobs at the projected facility.[998] There is some speculation that the facility will probably be located not too far from the Tesla Gigafactory.

Starlink is a fundamental piece in the SpaceX machinery. In fact, the satellite project is crucial to the company's valuation. The fact that Musk chose Austin to manufacture hardware for Starlink says a lot about the city's position as a tech hub, and its operations will certainly drive more space-related innovation in the region. According to the director of the University of Texas at Austin's Technology and Information Policy Institute, "As Austin grows... anything that suggests technology probably enhances its standing."[999]

Currently in the beta testing phase, Starlink is a high-speed, low latency

997 Boyle, A. (2021). SpaceX Aims to Expand Its Starlink Satellite Operation to Texas and Set Up Starbase City. Retrieved 21 July 2021, from https://www.geekwire.com/2021/spacex-will-expand-starlink-satellite-operation-texas-create-starbase-city/

998 SpaceX jobs in Austin. (2021). Retrieved 21 July 2021, from https://www.glassdoor.com/Jobs/SpaceX-Austin-Jobs-EI_IE40371.0,6_IL.7,13_IM60.htm?filter.countryId=1

999 With A New Spacex Starlink Factory, Austin Could Reach New Heights in Tech. (2021). Retrieved 21 July 2021, from https://austonia.com/spacex-starlink-austin

broadband internet service that will "continue expansion to near-global coverage of the populated world in 2021."[1000]

Offering between 50Mb/s and 150Mb/s Internet worldwide, Starlink relies on a network of dedicated satellites and ground stations. Users can purchase a Starlink Kit featuring a satellite dish, a Wi-Fi router, and accessories. Starlink's price tag is a steep $500 for the equipment and $100 per month for the service.[1001] The Starlink App informs users as to which is the best install location within their property.

There are more than 1,700 Starlink satellites.[1002] Because they are closer to Earth than standard ones, they offer lower latency, which results in fast and reliable Internet service, even for users located in remote and rural areas.

Starlink's webpage features the following comment by a user in Wisconsin: "Fantastic system/service. Finally able to use the Internet like a regular person. [They] won't update 50-year-old copper lines in my state. This is a lifesaver." A user from England reportedly wrote, "11 years waiting for a connection which is better than 900kbps :) thank you."[1003]

"Starlink is ideally suited for areas of the globe where connectivity has typically been a challenge," SpaceX claims. "Unbounded by traditional ground infrastructure, Starlink can deliver high-speed broadband internet to locations where access has been unreliable or completely unavailable."[1004]

Being the home of "the world's most advanced broadband internet system" can help boost Austin's standing as a prime tech hub. Though the

1000Starlink. (2021). Retrieved 21 July 2021, from https://www.starlink.com

1001SpaceX Prices Starlink Satellite Internet Service at $99 Per Month, According to E-Mail. (2020). Retrieved 21 July 2021, from https://www.cnbc.com/2020/10/27/spacex-starlink-service-priced-at-99-a-month-public-beta-test-begins.html

1002Elon Musk Counts on 500,000 Starlink Users Within The Next Year. (2021). Retrieved 21 July 2021, from https://www.theverge.com/2021/6/29/22556031/elon-musk-spacex-starlink-users-next-year-telecom-5g

1003Starlink. (2021). Retrieved 21 July 2021, from https://www.starlink.com

1004Starlink. (2021). Retrieved 21 July 2021, from https://www.starlink.com

city's residents already enjoy efficient broadband connectivity, rural Texans could greatly benefit from enhanced Internet access.

Starlink has the potential to do much more than merely improving broadband access; its satellites could guide automated cars and other connected devices. The company is only one piece in the grand scheme of Musk's plans for Texas. SpaceX has also announced it will build another plant in McGregor, which will support the company's Mars program. The McGregor facility will build up to 1,000 rocket engines per year. According to Musk, at that rate, it would take 10 years to have a fleet capable of building and sustaining a city on Mars.[1005]

Meanwhile, Starlink's operations keep growing, and Austin will soon reap the benefits. The company has nearly 70,000 active users in a dozen countries and could eventually service half a million homes globally. The project won't be profitable for a while, but Musk is not worried.

"Before we go to positive cash flow, it'll be at least $5 billion, and maybe as much as $10 (billion)," he commented. "So it's quite a lot."[1006]

As the Internet of Things grows and expands, Starlink will likely become more and more valuable, and it could eventually fund SpaceX's space exploration and Mars colonization projects.

Elon Musk Brings Hyperloop to Texas

Musk's multiple initiatives are spreading across Texas like wildfire. In July 2021, the Austin American-Stateman reported that his tunneling company

1005Area Leaders: Spacex Rockets Could Be Built in Mcgregor by Year's End. (2021). Retrieved 21 July 2021, from https://wacotrib.com/business/local/area-leaders-spacex-rockets-could-be-built-in-mcgregor-by-years-end/article_9c61f99a-e329-11eb-ad07-335e12f919b0.html

1006Elon Musk Counts on 500,000 Starlink Users Within The Next Year. (2021). Retrieved 21 July 2021, from https://www.theverge.com/2021/6/29/22556031/elon-musk-spacex-starlink-users-next-year-telecom-5g

was buying land locally. The Boring Company's affiliate, Gapped Bass LLC, recently acquired 73 acres in Bastrop County, a suburb of Austin.[1007] The company is now hiring people to work at its R&D site, precisely in that area.

Musk created The Boring Company to implement intercity Hyperloop transit. So far, the technology has only been tested in California and Nevada.

In 2020, The Boring Company acquired property in Austin's metropolitan area, which indicates its operations will expand in the region. A Hyperloop development in Texas would transform the state into an intercity transportation pioneer. Over time, in Elon Musk's vision, Hyperloop could also become a solution for long-distance, intracity transit.[1008]

Starbase, Texas

SpaceX wants to go beyond buying office space, building manufacturing facilities, and launching rockets from Texas. Elon Musk is not happy enough with having a location in Boca Chica; he wants to buy the whole town.

In a journalistic report published in May 2021, residents confirmed Musk's attempts to buy several houses in the vicinity of SpaceX's rocket launch facility in Boca Chica. There is some speculation that Musk wants to avoid the safety concern of having people living nearby in case rocket launches go awry, which is not uncommon.[1009]

The State of Texas has done a lot to incentivize SpaceX's investments.

1007Merano, M. (2021). Elon Musk's Boring Company Linked to 73-Acre Purchase in Texas. Retrieved 21 July 2021, from https://www.teslarati.com/elon-musk-boring-company-buys-73-acres-east-tx/

1008Elon Musk's Boring Company Concept Is Now Even More Hopelessly Complicated. (2021). Retrieved 21 July 2021, from https://gizmodo.com/elon-musks-hyperloop-concept-is-now-even-more-hopelessl-1823675120

1009Keates, N., & Maremont, M. (2021). Elon Musk's SpaceX Is Buying Up A Texas Village. Homeowners Cry Foul. Retrieved 21 July 2021, from https://www.wsj.com/articles/elon-musk-spacex-rocket-boca-chica-texas-starbase-11620353687

In 2013, state legislators passed a bill that permits the temporary closure of beaches for spaceflight activity in Boca Chica's jurisdiction, Cameron County. Musk's Boca Chica operations have also received at least $30 million in incentives.[1010]

In March 2021, the SpaceX CEO announced in a tweet that he was "creating the city of Starbase, Texas."[1011] His strategy to achieve it would be to incorporate the town, just like mining companies used to do, officially creating a 'company town.'

Since only 14 people without links to SpaceX live in Boca Chica, it would be enough for the company to prove that 200 people live in the area and to garner their votes to create the city of Starbase. This could give SpaceX the authority to close roads, force residents to sell their homes to the company, and issue municipal bonds.

Whether Musk succeeds in incorporating the town or not, Boca Chica will become a center for Mars exploration. The minuscule border town is the site of SpaceX's Super Heavy rocket development, which will take humans to Mars and the moon.[1012]

So far, SpaceX has acquired over 110 plots of land in the area.[1013] In Musk's vision, Starbase, Texas, will be a bustling city offering many recreational activities for SpaceX employees. Recently, the company listed a job opening for a resort manager who would be tasked with turning Boca Chica into an "epic place" to live and work. The job description mentioned some of the

---

1010Elon Musk Is Turning Boca Chica into A Space-Travel Hub. Not Everyone Is Starstruck. (2021). Retrieved 21 July 2021, from https://www.texasmonthly.com/news-politics/elon-musk-boca-chica-starbase-texas/

1011Elon Musk Is Creating A City in Texas. It Will Be Called Starbase and It Will Be Ruled by 'The Doge'. (2021). Retrieved 21 July 2021, from https://www.entrepreneur.com/article/366488

1012After Just 6 Weeks of Construction, Super Heavy Is Built and Ready to Move. (2021). Retrieved 21 July 2021, from https://www.universetoday.com/151731/after-just-6-weeks-of-construction-super-heavy-is-built-and-ready-to-move/

1013Is Elon Musk Seeking a Return to The Days of the Company Town?. (2021). Retrieved 21 July 2021, from https://www.insidehook.com/daily_brief/architecture-real-estate/elon-musk-company-town-starbase-texas

activities the selected candidate would have to organize, including volleyball tournaments and kayaking excursions.[1014]

When SpaceX first talked to local authorities about setting up operations in Boca Chica, the company promised to create 200 jobs. So far, it has created more than 1,400, far surpassing its original promise. Property values have multiplied by four or more since Elon Musk set his sights on the unassuming border town.[1015]

Earlier this year, Musk published a photo of him with his wife and son, marking its location as 'Starbase, Texas.' The tech billionaire later tweeted, "Please consider moving to Starbase or greater Brownsville/South Padre area in Texas & encourage friends to do so!"[1016] The Musk Foundation also announced a $30 million donation for town revitalization and local schools. Schools in the Brownsville area have already received $5 million.[1017]

Everything indicates Musk has a fair chance of making his dream come true. If he can prove the SpaceX employees living in makeshift homes are local residents, he will have enough votes to incorporate the town.

As of the writing of this book, SpaceX was planning to launch its Starship rocket for the first time. The fully reusable spacecraft has been designed to transport people and cargo to the moon and Mars.

Some of the most advanced technology in the world is being developed in Texas. We have smart city pilot programs, automated vehicle lanes, and

---

1014Keates, N., & Maremont, M. (2021). Elon Musk's SpaceX Is Buying Up A Texas Village. Homeowners Cry Foul. Retrieved 21 July 2021, from https://www.wsj.com/articles/elon-musk-spacex-rocket-boca-chica-texas-starbase-11620353687

1015Leinfelder, A. (2021). Elon Musk Brings Exploding Rockets and Real Estate to South Texas. Not Everyone Is Happy. Retrieved 21 July 2021, from https://www.houstonchronicle.com/news/houston-texas/space/article/Musk-has-brought-exploding-spacecraft-exploding-16317115.php

1016Touting SpaceX Jobs, Elon Musk Encourages Move to South Texas. (2021). Retrieved 21 July 2021, from https://spectrumlocalnews.com/tx/austin/news/2021/03/30/touting-spacex-jobs--elon-musk-encourages-move-to-south-texas-

1017Elon Musk Needs A Futuristic Workforce for SpaceX. Will His $20M Pledge to Schools Help? - EdSurge News. (2021). Retrieved 21 July 2021, from https://www.edsurge.com/news/2021-05-11-elon-musk-needs-a-futuristic-workforce-for-spacex-will-his-20-million-pledge-to-schools-help

rockets aiming for the stars. Texas may well be on the verge of an age of affluence that will surpass the glory of its oil boom days.

CONCLUSION

We are at a pivotal point, the hour of decision. We can build a strong future for America and set the standard for the world, build systems to last another hundred years, systems that are safer, more efficient, use less energy, and lower our carbon footprint.

But for each decision we make moving forward, it's critical to step back and view the overarching picture—why infrastructure matters, where it could take us. From local projects to politics, our decisions must honor the grand scheme. We must prioritize thoughtfully and invest our time and money in efforts to secure America's future and advance the world at large.

Financing is a primary challenge. Overcoming our infrastructure deficit will require significant spending and financing strategies utilizing federal funding and private sector development. For large-scale projects, federal funding may offer the best solution. State and local governments can benefit from public funding, shielding them from red tape and preventing wasteful spending.

New models of private sector involvement are proving efficient and cost effective. P3s are a promising alternative for local project funding. Private companies share project responsibilities and risks with public-sector partners. By working together, the private sector and state and local leaders can raise capital, share expertise, and brainstorm ideas for growing infrastructure needs.

But P3 and private sector financing tactics must emphasize long-term maintenance plans and other less immediate components of infrastructure projects, components that aren't going to generate rapid profits. Private financing of major infrastructure should also work to tackle potential conflicts involving public accessibility, for example, with transportation systems and public utilities.

No matter the financing source, approaches to reframing American infrastructure must recognize that the most important decisions on all infrastructure projects, large and small alike, are made at the local level. All change is local. While federal standards apply in any scenario, the decisions holding the most power for change are in the hands of local school districts, city councils, committees, boards, and commissions. Even federal interstate projects like highways are under the control of local decision-makers, not the federal government. Local decisions drive what happens next.

The new American infrastructure will dictate our 21st-century economy. Many of our most essential resources have reached the end of their operable life and need significant maintenance or renovation. Structures are failing without warning. Technology has skyrocketed since our last major investment in infrastructure, urging adaptation. Expansion is another immediate demand as current systems struggle to support our growing population.

Investment in American infrastructure builds opportunity, linking people, communities, and the world. From national leaders to local decision-makers, voters to visionaries, we are all responsible for fulfilling our duty to future generations. The state of American infrastructure directly reflects our values, our historical tradition of fighting to make life better for our children than it was for us. Thoughtful strategies based on perspective will generate dividends for decades to come.

ABOUT AUTHOR MARC GRAVELY

Marc Gravely founded and leads Gravely Attorneys and Counselors, a prominent Texas based national construction defect law firm focused on helping private and governmental property owners address contractors and their insurers when things go awry.

For his innovative work in construction law Marc was named Texas Trailblazer by Texas Lawyer Magazine and Plaintiffs Law Trailblazer by the National Law Journal. He has served as amicus counsel before the Texas Supreme Court more than a dozen times on behalf of property owners and trade groups.

A regular on the lecture circuit, Marc is a highly rated speaker including a recent appearance at the MENSA World Conference on the topic of infrastructure.

For more information: www.MarcGravely.com

Mr. Gravely is represented by Elite Lawyer Management, managing agents for extraordinary American attorneys.